ANDREW TRAVER

THE OPUSCULA OF WILLIAM OF SAINT-AMOUR

THE MINOR WORKS OF 1255–1256

ASCHENDORFF MÜNSTER

BEITRÄGE ZUR GESCHICHTE DER PHILOSOPHIE
UND THEOLOGIE DES MITTELALTERS

Texte und Untersuchungen

Begründet von Clemens Baeumker
Fortgeführt von Martin Grabmann und Michael Schmaus

Im Auftrag der Görres-Gesellschaft
herausgegeben von Ludwig Hödl und Wolfgang Kluxen

Neue Folge
Band 63

Gedruckt mit Unterstützung
der Görres-Gesellschaft zur Pflege der Wissenschaft

Druck: Druckhaus Aschendorff, Münster, 2003
Gedruckt auf säurefreiem, alterungsbeständigem Papier ∞

ISBN 3-402-04014-X

PREFACE

The name William of Saint-Amour has long remained a historical footnote. Although scholars often cite him as the chief opponent of the mendicant orders, he is rarely read, due in part to the unavailability of his works. The publication of Michel-Marie Dufeil's *Guillaume de Saint-Amour et la polémique universitaire parisienne* helped to draw attention to the life and works of the Parisian secular theologian, in particular, to the pivotal role William played during the secular/mendicant conflict at the University of Paris in the 1250s. The present work adds to that of Dufeil by analyzing William's minor works of 1255-6 and offering editions of his responses to Bonaventure's disputed question *De mendicitate* and his three extant sermons *Qui amat periculum, Si quis diligit me,* and *De pharisaeo et publicano.*

I would like to thank Professor Joseph Goering, Father James Farge, and Father Gideon Gàl(†) for their interest in this project.

ABBREVIATED REFERENCES

DP	William of Saint-Amour. *De periculis novissimorum temporum.* In *Opera omnia quae reperiri poterunt.* Ed. Alithophilius. Constance [Paris], 1632, 17-72.
Dephar.	William of Saint-Amour. *Sermo de pharisaeo et publicano, infra,* 191-205.
DQE	William of Saint-Amour. *De quantitate eleemosynae.* Ed. A. G. Traver. "William of Saint-Amour's Two Disputed Questions *De quantitate eleemosynae* and *De valido mendicante,*" *AHDL* 62 (1995):323-32.
DVM	William of Saint-Amour. *De valido mendicante.* Ed. A.G. Traver. "William of Saint-Amour's Two Disputed Questions *De quantitate eleemosynae* and *De valido mendicante,*" *AHDL* 62 (1995):333-42.
Ed. pr.	*Biblia latina cum glossa ordinaria.* Ed. Adolph Rusch. Strassburg, 1480-1. 4 voll. [rpt Turnhout: Brepols, 1992].
int.	*Glossa interlinearis*
ord.	*Glossa ordinaria*
QAP	William of Saint-Amour. *Qui amat periculum, infra,* 155-78.
QDM	Bonaventure. *Quaestio de mendicitate, infra,* 123-54.
Resp.	William of Saint-Amour. *Responsiones.* Ed. Edmond Faral. "Les *Responsiones* de Guillaume de Saint-Amour," *AHDL* 18 (1950-1):359-60.
SQD	William of Saint-Amour. *Si quis diligit me, infra,* 179-89.

TABLE OF CONTENTS

INTRODUCTION

William of Saint-Amour was born in Saint-Amour (Jura) sometime around 1200. He completed his masters in arts and most probably a degree in canon law at the University of Paris by 1238. He entered the Faculty of Theology at Paris and received a degree in that discipline c. 1250. For the next six years, he was a regent theologian at Paris.

From 1252-6, William was intensely involved in the University's conflict with the mendicant orders. Between the years 1252-5, William helped draft much of the University's statutory legislation against the friars and even represented the University in its legal suit at Rome against the mendicants. But during the years 1255-6, William began to expand the academic quarrel by challenging the mendicant form of religious life directly. In these years, in a series of disputed questions, sermons, and his magnum opus, *De periculis novissimorum temporum*, William questioned different aspects of the friars' ministry, concluding each time that the mendicant interpretation of the religious life had no scriptural basis, was dangerous, and could very easily lead to the destruction of the Church.

Due to his literary activities against the friars, he soon fell afoul of Pope Alexander IV. By December 1255, Alexander requested an enquiry into William's activities;[1] six months later, he recommended to the king of France, Louis IX, that he expel William from his kingdom.[2] Alexander received a copy of William's *De periculis* in fall 1256 and commissioned a committee of cardinals to investigate it. On 5 October 1256 Alexander condemned it, characterizing it as "evil, wicked, and accursed" and demanded that copies of it, wherever they were found, be burned.[3] William presented a defense of himself and his activities before the cardinals at Anagni, but offered no submission.[4] Pope Alexander therefore condemned him *in perpetuo*, excommunicated him, deprived him of his benefices and offices, and at King Louis' request, notified him that he

1 *Chartularium universitatis parisiensis* edd. Heinrich Denifle O.P. et Émile Chatelain (Paris: Delalain, 1889-1897), I, No. 262, 300. Hereafter cited as *Chart.*

2 *Chart.* I, No. 282, 323-4.

3 *Chart.* I, No. 288, 331-3.

4 A critical edition of William's self defense can be found in E. Faral, "Les *Responsiones* de Guillaume de Saint-Amour," *AHDL* 18 (1950-1):340-61.

would thereafter need a papal license to enter France.[5] Alexander then informed King Louis that William had lost the faculty to teach and preach by apostolic authority.[6] Thus ended the magisterial career of the University of Paris' most stalwart critic of the friars.

Throughout the years 1255-6, the secular theologian William of Saint-Amour emerged as the ringleader of the anti-mendicant faction at Paris. In these years, William transformed what had been essentially an academic conflict over the friars' refusal to obey university statutes into a polemical campaign against the actual legality of the mendicant orders, focusing on their rights to beg, preach, hear confession, and pursue an itinerant ministry. William broadened the scope of the controversy by incorporating the criticisms of the friars made by the clergy outside of the university milieu into his own writings. In so doing, he became the first critic of the friars to synthesize the hitherto disparate anti-mendicant sentiment into a coherent focus.

The mendicants, in the form of the Franciscan and Dominican Orders, received provisional approval from Pope Innocent III in 1215.[7] Both orders represented a newer conception of the religious life, modeled directly on the life of Christ, consisting of itinerant preaching, poverty both communal and individual, and mendicancy. The papacy zealously promoted both orders as diocesan coadjutors in accordance with canon ten of the Council of Lateran IV *Inter cetera*[8] to assist in preaching, hearing confession, and enjoining penance.[9] As both orders required preachers,

[5] *Chart.* I, No. 314, 362.

[6] *Chart.* I, No. 315, 363.

[7] Innocent had given oral permission to Francis for his rule c. 1210. In 1223, Pope Honorius III confirmed the third version of the Rule, the *regula bullata,* in his bull *Solet annuere.* In 1215 Dominic had received provincial authorization to create a new religious order yet when he approached Pope Innocent about this matter, canon thirteen of the Council of Lateran IV banning new religious orders had already went into effect. After consultation with Innocent, Dominic selected a previously approved rule, the Rule of St. Augustine, to which his followers appended customs and supplemented with constitutions. In 1216, Honorius confirmed the rule as adapted by Dominic in his bull *Religiosam vitam.* For the sources, see J. Moorman, *A History of the Franciscan Order* (Oxford: Clarendon Press, 1968), 18-19, 29-30, 57-8; W. Hinnebusch, *A History of the Dominican Order* (New York: Alba House, 1965), 42-8; M. Mulchahey, "*First the Bow is Bent in Study*": *Dominican Education before 1350* (Toronto: Pontifical Institute of Mediaeval Studies, 1998), 6-20.

[8] *Extra.* I, t. 31, c. 15 *Inter cetera*; *Conciliorum oecumenicorum decreta* edd. J. Alberigo et al. 3rd ed. (Bologna: Istituto per le scienze religiose, 1973), 215-6.

[9] Honorius first began to promote the Dominicans as coadjutor preachers. Mulchahey, *Dominican Education*, 25; L. Boyle, "Notes on the Education of the *Fratres* communes in the Dominican Order in the Thirteenth Centry," *Xenia medii aevi historiam illustrantia oblata Thomae Kaeppeli O.P.* (Rome: Edizione di storia e letteratura, 1978), I:251. Gregory IX (1227-41) was the first pontiff to promote the Franciscans as episcopal helpers. Landini has shown that that papacy was originally reluctant to associate the Minors as diocesan coadjutors because of the Order's large number of lay brothers. But during Gregory's

which assumed some degree of theological training, both were present at Paris at a very early date.

By the mid-1220s, both the Dominican and Franciscan Orders had become incorporated within the University of Paris. Despite their short tenure there, the mendicants' relationship with their secular colleagues within the theological faculty can best be described as a tenuous peace.[10] The secular theologians complained that the mendicants refused to observe academic decrees, most notably the university strike measure (*cessatio*) during the Great Dispersion of 1229-31, simply in order to gain teaching masters for their orders. Such actions, they complained, could very easily threaten all non-mendicant theologians with academic extinction as the theological faculty at Paris would become increasingly dominated by the friars.[11] The issue of teaching chairs in theology remained a bitter point of contention for the seculars, as the number of teaching positions in theology was strictly controlled and it could not exceed a set number. As chairs passed from the seculars to the mendicants, they thereafter remained in the possession of the mendicant masters and effectively closed to all aspiring secular graduates in theology.[12]

The secular masters also argued that the mendicants' refusal to abide by university regulations made them an institution within an institution, outside of the scope of official university supervision. By refusing to observe academic privileges at Paris, the friars helped to invalidate the efficacy of the time-honored tactic of calling for a suspension of lectures to protest violations made against the university community. The friars, for their part, claimed that university training was simply a means to an end: the instruction of new preachers and the improvement in the quality of

pontificate, legislation was secured to make the Franciscans principally clerical. L. Landini, *The Causes of the Clericalization of the Orders of Friars Minor* (Chicago: Pontificia universitas Gregoriana, 1968), 62-7.

10 On the origins of this conflict, see M.-M. Dufeil, *Guillaume de Saint-Amour et la polémique universitaire parisienne* (Paris: A. Picard, 1972); D L. Douie, *The Conflict between the Seculars and Mendicants at the University of Paris in the Thirteenth Century* Aquinas Paper 23 (London: Blackfriars, 1954); V. Mäkinen, *Property Rights in the Medieval Discussion on Franciscan Poverty* (Helsinki: Limes ry, 1998), 26-38; A.G. Traver, "Rewriting History? The Parisian Secular Masters' *Apologia* of 1254," *History of Universities* 15 (1997-9):9-45.

11 This was in fact the claim of the University of Paris' *Apologia* of 1254. *Chart.* I, No. 230, 230-8; Traver, "Rewriting History?," 27-9.

12 The chairs remained set at twelve in 1218 and remained at this number until 1256. *Chart.*, I, No. 27, 85. See Dufeil, *Guillaume de Saint Amour*, 50; G. Leff, *Paris and Oxford Universities in the Thirteenth and Fourteenth Centuries* (New York: John Wiley and Sons, 1968), 84; Traver, "Rewriting History?," 18-22.

pastoral care.[13] For these purposes, theological instruction took precedence over the academic prerogatives of the University.

Pope Innocent IV indirectly exacerbated this situation in 1250, when he enjoined the chancellor of the University of Paris to license all qualified students, especially those belonging to religious orders, even if they failed to ask for it.[14] Faced with a potential increase of mendicant masters and thus a very real possibility that theological studies at Paris would be monopolized by the friars, the secular masters took the offensive.

In 1252, in a general assembly of the Faculty of Theology, the secular theologians attempted to restrict the number of theological chairs available to the friars by limiting the Franciscans to their one teaching position and by trying to deprive the Dominicans of one of their two magisterial chairs.[15] The Dominicans successfully resisted these restrictive measures and their two masters continued to teach and preach. But in the early spring of 1253 an event would soon bring all parties at Paris into direct conflict. At this time, in a recurrent "town and gown" encounter, four students and their lay servants were attacked by the Parisian night watchmen. Of these, one was killed and four were arbitrarily incarcerated.[16] On the basis of this recent violation of scholarly liberty, the University called for a suspension of classes until appropriate compensation from civil authorities had been secured.

The mendicant masters and students refused to participate in the subsequent seven-week cessation. When the University returned, it retaliated by excommunicating the friars, subsequently expelling them from the University.[17] The friars appealed to Pope Innocent IV, launching in the process a round of litigation that would last the next three years.

The University likewise responded by recourse to the papacy. Innocent attempted to placate the University by rescinding the sentence of excommunication and ordering the reintegration of the friars until he could hear the case himself.[18] The University then promulgated a statute which described recent events *in toto* during the past few months and placed the friars under more rigid academic control.[19] The University next, in February 1254, published a dramatic *apologia* hoping to garner extra-university aid in its struggle with the friars, warning of the possibility that the friars could soon dominate the theological faculty.[20]

13 This was the view articulated by the Master General of the Dominicans, Humbert of Romans. *Opera de vita regulari* ed. Fr. J. Berthier (Rome, 1888-9), [rpt. Turin, 1956], II:41.

14 *Chart.* I, No. 191, 219.

15 *Chart.* I, No. 200, 226-7.

16 The events are retold in *Chart.* I, No. 219, 242 and *Chronica Normanniae* in *Recueil*, 23:215.

17 *Chart.* I, No. 219, 242-3.

18 *Chart.* I, No. 222, 247.

19 *Chart.* I, No. 219, 242-4.

20 *Chart.* I, No. 230, 252-8.

The University's case at Rome must have had some effect on Pope Innocent and his relationship with the friars as on 10 May 1254, he published his first restrictive decrees on the mendicants' activities.[21] On 4 July 1254, Innocent renewed the University's right to require complete obedience from all of its members, thus forcing the mendicants to observe all future suspensions of classes.[22] Later that year, Innocent promulgated *Etsi animarum*, a bull which emphasized the role of the parish priest within his jurisdiction with respect to sacramental matters and severely curtailed the friars' rights to preach, to hear confessions, and to bury the laity by placing their ministry under tighter parochial and diocesan control. Throughout 1254, Pope Innocent had made the connection between the criticisms of the friars voiced by the secular clergy both within and outside of the university structure.

Innocent's change of heart towards the friars might be due to the compelling arguments used by the University's proctor, William of Saint-Amour.[23] Alternately, it could be credited to the list of thirty-one errors which the University had culled from the Franciscan Gerard of Borgo San Donnino's *Liber introductorius evangelii aeternii* and sent to the curia in 1254.[24] Gerard's work had been heavily influenced by Joachim of Fiore's Trinitarian construct as the basis of a philosophy of history. But whereas Joachim's historical approach was always allegorical, Gerard gave it a literal interpretation. He had pushed Joachim's doctrines to a dangerous conclusion; he proclaimed the advent of a third age, in which Joachim's works would form a third or Eternal Gospel that would supersede both the Old and the New Testaments. Furthermore, Gerard prophesied the collapse of the traditional Church structure; sometime around 1260, he predicted that a new church dominated by barefoot spiritual men would supplant the existing Church. The mendicants' opponents capitalized on the scandal caused by the *Introductorius*, treating it as a blueprint which detailed the friars' intended goals for the Church.

Innocent did not take any action against the *Introductorius* before his death. However, an ecclesiastical tribunal commissioned to investigate the work, the Anagni Commission, reported its findings to Innocent's successor, Alexander IV, in 1255.[25] Alexander then requested that the

21 *Chart.* I, No. 236, 263-4.

22 *Chart.* I, No. 237, 265.

23 He is first listed as proctor in *Chart.* I, No. 238, 265.

24 *Chart.* I, No. 243, 272-5. A critical edition can be found in E. Benz, "Die Exzerptsätze der Pariser Professoren aus dem Evangelium Aeternum," *Zeitschrift für Kirchengeschichte* 51 (1932):415-55.

25 The minutes are contained in H. Denifle, "Das Evangelium aeternum und die Commission zu Anagni," *Archiv für Litteratur- und Kirchengeschichte des Mittelalters* 1 (1885): 49-142.

bishop of Paris destroy the work and excommunicate all who possessed a copy of it.[26]

Soon after the promulgation of *Etsi animarum*, Pope Innocent died and was replaced by Alexander IV, the former cardinal protector of the Franciscans. He immediately revealed his predisposition to the mendicant orders by issuing the bull *Nec insolitum.*[27] This bull, to the detriment of the secular clergy, nullified all of the prescriptions enumerated in *Etsi animarum.* Alexander followed *Nec insolitum* in April 1255 with the bull *Quasi lignum vite.*[28] This new bull required that the mendicants be reinstated in the Parisian Faculty of Theology and that any limit on the number of chairs that religious orders could hold in the theological faculty be made illegal. The University protested in its reply *Radix amaritudinis,*[29] it threatened to dissolve itself, and circulated a list of seven reasons why the theological faculty could not readmit the friars.[30]

William and his circle of secular theologians at Paris had hitherto limited their grievances to the mendicants' failure to conform to academic statutes. After the publication of *Quasi lignum vite,* one can witness a dramatic transformation in the nature and the scope of argumentation employed by the theologians against the friars. Instead of focusing narrowly on the mendicants' role within the academic consortium, the seculars began to contest the legitimacy of the friars' mission openly. William's extant works for this period bear witness to this change in strategy.

From the years 1255-6, William wrote five types of works against the friars: his disputed questions *De quantitate eleemosynae* and *De valido mendicante,* his objections to Bonaventure's disputed question *De mendicitate,* his treatise *De periculis,* his sermons *Qui amat periculum, Si quis diligit me,* and *De pharisaeo et publicano,* and his *Responsiones,* his defense before the papal commission delegated to investigate his writings. This present work offers an analysis of these works and editions of his responses to *De mendicitate* and his three extant sermons.

[26] *Chart.* I, No. 257, 297. He later entreated that this task be accomplished tacitly, lest the Franciscans be tainted by scandal. *Chart.* I, No. 258, 298.

[27] *Chart.* I, No. 244, 276-7.

[28] *Chart.* I, No. 247, 279-85.

[29] *Chart.* I, No. 256, 292-7.

[30] César-Égasse Du Boulay, *Historia universitatis parisiensis* (Paris, 1665-73), [rpt. Frankurt: Minerva, 1966], III:287-8; Wolfenbüttel, ms. Guelf 367, Helmst., f. 77va.

WILLIAM'S DISPUTED QUESTIONS

DE QUANTITATE ELEEMOSYNAE AND *DE VALIDO MENDICANTE*

William's first polemical assault on the mendicants in fall 1255 comes in the form of his disputed questions. William determined his first question, *De quantitate eleemosynae,* in October 1255 as a direct response to a disputed question of the chief apologist of the Franciscan Order, Bonaventure. Bonaventure had recently completed the requirements for the doctorate in theology at Paris but could not incept and be recognized as the Franciscan regent master due to the academic discord there.[1] He thus functioned as an internal master within the Franciscan convent at Paris, carrying on normal teaching duties such as preaching and presiding over disputed questions, until the mendicant/secular conflict there had subsided.[2] In this capacity, in late September or early October 1255 he determined the question *De paupertate quoad abrenuntiationem* (*De abrenuntiatione*), concluding that the renunciation of all temporal possessions both private and communal pertained to Christian perfection.[3] William responded in *De quantitate eleemosynae* by linking the the mendicant conception of voluntary poverty to sin, homicide, and flattery. William furthermore cast doubt on the spiritual benefits of the complete

1 D. Douie, "Saint Bonaventure's Part in the Conflict between Seculars and Mendicants at Paris," *S. Bonaventura: 1274-1974* (Grottaferrata: Collegium S. Bonaventurae, 1973), II: 589-90; J.F. Quinn, "Chronology of St. Bonaventure," *Franciscan Studies* 32 (1972):180-1.

2 In October 1256, Pope Alexander IV demanded that William's colleagues Odo of Douai and Chrétien of Beauvais admit Bonaventure and his Dominican confrère Thomas Aquinas to academic gatherings and accept them as regent theologians. *Chart.* I, No. 292, 339. In 1257, the University recognized both of them as regent theologians. Leff, *Paris and Oxford Universities,* 45.

3 The Quaracchi editors of Bonaventure have listed *Quoad abrenuntiationem* as the first article of the second question of Bonaventure's *De perfectione evangelica.* Bonaventure, *Opera omnia* (Quaracchi: Collegium S. Bonaventurae, 1882-1902), V:124-8; J. Bougerol, "De la *reportatio* à la *redactio,*" *Les genres littéraires dans les sources théologiques et philosophiques médiévales: définition, critique et exploitation* (Louvain: Institut d'études médiévales, 1982), 57; I. Brady, "The Edition of the *Opera omnia* of Saint Bonaventure (1882-1902)," *AFH* 70 (1977):370.

renunciation of temporal possessions by addressing the religious life in terms of the common ownership of Church property.

William's second question, *De valido mendicante*, represents an attempt on the part of William to gain the initiative in the Parisian mendicant/secular debates. He delivered this question in November 1255; Bonaventure replied to it in his disputed question *De paupertate quoad mendicitatem* (*De mendicitate*), determined the following month.[4] In this second question, William considers the mendicants' claim to the alms of the faithful.

In *De quantitate eleemosynae*, William argues that relinquishing all temporal possessions without reserving future provisions is a mortal sin. William has reversed an earlier argument of Bonaventure, who had professed that cupidity, which arises from temporal goods rather than poverty, gives occasion for sin.[5] William, however, asserts that the complete renunciation of private and communal belongings exposes one to the threat of sin since one is thenceforth required to beg for sustenance. Begging subjects one to the dangers of flattery, lying, stealing, perjury, homicide, and suicide–all of which can easily be avoided if one safeguards some temporal possessions.[6]

One who selects a life of voluntary poverty risks suicide by relinquishing one's means of support. By citing the Exodus pericope "Thou shall not kill,"[7] William identifies complete renunciation with intentional self-destruction. Since one who purposefully jeopardizes one's life acts contrary to the precepts of the Decalogue, voluntary poverty is therefore synonymous with death.

Homicide is another potential consequence of voluntary poverty; by dispensing all of our possessions to the poor, we can only alleviate their misery for a brief period and can no longer give charity.[8] Since the survival of the poor depends on alms, by granting all of our goods to them at once we can no longer continue to give alms, and thus potentially contribute to the death of those whom we originally wanted to assist.

Flattery also arises from voluntary poverty. Citing Saint Ambrose, William writes that some, prone to indolence, frequent other tables in order to eat;[9] one in such a situation must use flattery to obtain sustenance. No one, claims William, ought to place himself in such a state

4 *Opera*, V:134-149; Bougerol, "Reportatio," 57; Brady, "Edition," 370.

5 *De abrenuntiatione* in *Opera* V:129. On these two questions, see Traver, "William of Saint-Amour's Two Disputed Questions *De quantitate eleemosynae* and *De valido mendicante*," *AHDL* 62 (1995): 296-307.

6 *DQE*, 328.

7 Ex. 20:13.

8 D.86 c.21 *Pasce*; C.14 q.5 c.2 *Immolans*; *DQE*, 324.

9 Amb., *Comm. in Epist. ad Thess.* in *PL* 17:485C. *DQE*, 327; *DVM*, 339.

that he needs to depend on adulation to eat. Therefore, to avoid flattery, one should not forego all temporal possessions.[10]

William concedes that voluntary poverty is acceptable in only two instances. First, if one renounces all possessions with the intention of entering a monastery, in which all the necessities of life are held communally. Second, if one surrenders all temporal goods and continues to live by manual labor in order to provide future sustenance. William has qualified the New Testament counsels to relinquish all possessions and give to the poor. To give all to the poor and follow Christ means to emulate him in doing good, and either to enter a monastery or to perform manual labor.[11] And while voluntary poverty was an ideal, it was to be accompanied by manual labor.

Having attempted to connect complete renunciation with sin, William next examines the mendicant conception of the religious life. Basing his argument upon the practice of the primitive Church in Acts, William addresses the religious life in terms of the common ownership of property and depicts institutional monasticism as the inheritor of the apostolic life.[12] William finds further scriptural justification for the common ownership of property through the interlinear gloss on John 12:6, which considers Christ's purse.[13] The *loculos*, or apostolic purse, represents the communal property of the Church. William then juxtaposes the purse to the commonality of possessions in monasteries. Monasteries, following the common life of Christ and the Apostles, hold all goods communally. William thus treats Bonaventure's conclusion that poverty individual and common pertains to Christian perfection as an innovation without basis in scripture or tradition.

William questions whether the absolute renunciation of all temporal property could actually work in practice. He notes that those who undertake a transient ministry would have to carry some possessions in order to complete their mission. It would thus be better for them to be seculars rather than regulars to evade the risk of hypocrisy.[14] Against those who assert that it is better to beg than to hold communal possessions, William raises the example of Saint Paulinus of Nola who had relinquished all his possessions and later became a bishop.[15] As a bishop, he had

10 William provides a proper example of almsgiving by citing Zaccheus, the superintendent of taxes from Luke 19:8. Zaccheus gave half of his possessions to the poor, retaining enough for his own sustenance. *DQE*, 326.

11 *DQE*, 328.

12 "Immo retinet omnia sibi necessaria quia inter communi vita degentes nullus indigens debet esse. Act. 4: Erant illis omnia communia, nec quisquam erat egens inter illos." *DQE*, 328.

13 *DQE*, 330.

14 "Et ideo melius esset eos esse seculares quam regulares." *DQE*, 329.

15 C.12 q.1 c.13 *Expedit*; *DQE*, 329-30.

administered the Church's temporal wealth, yet this was not seen as an impediment to his perfection.

One of the principal arguments advanced by William in his disputed questions concerns the obligation of religious to perform manual labor. In support of the view that religious should maintain themselves by working with their hands, William relies heavily upon Augustine's *De opere monachorum* and Paul's epistles to the Thessalonians. In I Thessalonians 5:12, Paul advises the Thessalonians to recognize those among them who have labored with their hands[16] and in I Thessalonians 4:11, he orders us to work with our hands so we will desire nothing.[17]

William also cites the pericope II Thessalonians 3:14, in which Paul exhorts us not to keep company with those who do not follow apostolic warrant.[18] This citation is interpreted to have been directed against those who beg for sustenance while capable of manual labor.[19] Those who do not live by their hands, as did the Apostles, have deviated from the apostolic model and are therefore not true religious.

William's final attack on the friars in his disputed questions concerns their systematic begging. In *De valido mendicante*, William makes a careful distinction between the different types of beggars: those who beg of necessity, and those who order their life by begging. Those who beg of necessity, such as students, the poor, the infirm, and pilgrims, are to be given alms.[20] The poor and the infirm are incapable of manual labor, while students and pilgrims are only in a state of poverty for a limited time. However, those who beg when they are capable of labor are not to receive alms; rather, they transgress apostolic decree and ought to incur excommunication.[21]

William emphatically denies that mendicancy is living by the Gospel; in fact, he flatly denies that Christ had ever begged for bread.[22] His disputed questions conclude that poverty is not efficacious in furthering salvation unless one performs manual labor. Administrators of spiritual goods should not beg, lest it become an occasion for greed or a potential source of personal gain.[23] The claim to live by the Gospel by receiving offerings

[16] *DQE*, 326.
[17] *DQE*, 327; *DVM*, 337.
[18] *DQE*, 327; *DVM*, 336.
[19] *DQE*, 327; *DVM*, 336.
[20] *DVM*, 340-1.
[21] *DVM*, 333.
[22] "Sed quod <Christus> mendicaverit panem, non lego." *DQE*, 330. This is probably William's earliest articulation of this sentiment. It appears again in his responses to Bonaventure; *QDM*, *infra*, n. 32, *DP*, 51, and in his massive *Collectiones catholicae* of 1266. *Opera omnia quae reperiri poterunt* ed. Alithophilius (Constance [Paris], 1632), 255, 258, 261, and 284.
[23] *DVM*, 342.

from the faithful is simply a thinly-disguised attempt to profit from the word of God. *De quantitate eleemosynae* and *De valido mendicante* allege that the mendicant conception of the religious life as one of begging and itinerant preaching is not only devoid of scriptural authority, it is inherently opposed to the tradition of the Church.

WILLIAM'S RESPONSES TO BONAVENTURE'S *DE MENDICITATE*

William replied to Bonaventure's disputed question *De paupertate quoad mendicitatem* (*De mendicitate*) in December 1255 or January 1256;[24] this response survives in three manuscripts.[25] In two of the manuscripts, one each from Cambridge (*C*) and Paris (*P*),[26] William's objections immediately follow Bonaventure's arguments in the text. In the third manuscript (*L*), William's remarks are marginal glosses.[27]

Nature of the text

Michel-Marie Dufeil had suggested, on the basis of certain readings in *P*, that William had actually gone to the Franciscan convent at Paris and performed the role of opponent (*opponens*) at the disputation of *De mendicitate*.[28] The nature of the disputed question, however, makes this a

[24] He probably inserted his objections into the text before he left for a preaching tour in Mâcon in January. Dufeil, *Guillaume de Saint-Amour*, 180; idem, "Un universitaire parisien réactionnaire vers 1250: Guillaume de Saint-Amour," *Enseignement et vie intellectuelle (IXe-XVIe siècle)* (Paris: Bibliothèque nationale, 1975), 248. P. Glorieux simply places them between October and January. "Le Conflit de 1252-1257 à la lumière du mémoire de Guillaume de Saint-Amour," *RTAM* 24 (1957):368.

[25] On William's objections, see Bougerol, "Reportatio," 55-65; Dufeil, "Universitaire," 239-274; R. Lambertini, *Apologia e crescita dell' identità francescana (1255-1279)* (Rome: Nella sede dell'Istituto Palazzo Borromini, 1990), 16-20; Traver, "The Reportatio of St. Bonaventure's Disputed Question *De mendicitate*," *AFH* 92 (1999):287-298.

[26] *C* = Cambridge, Corpus Christi College, ms. 103, ff. 95a-105a; *P* = Paris, Bibliothèque Nationale, ms. lat. 15850, ff. 2-4. A transcription of *P* is contained in Dufeil, "Universitaire parisien réactionnaire," 248-274.

[27] Florence, Medicea Laurenziana, ms. Plt. 36 dextr., 12, ff. 124r-129v. This text of *L*, including both Bonaventure's arguments and William's marginal critiques has been transcribed by Delorme in "Quaestio reportata de mendicitate cum annotationibus Gulielmi de S. Amore," in *S. Bonaventurae Collationes in Hexaëmeron et Bonaventuriana quaedam selecta* (Quaracchi, 1934), 328-56. Only the marginal notes are edited in Bonaventure, *Opera*, V:viii-xii.

[28] *Guillaume de Saint-Amour*, 181-4 and "Universitaire parisien réactionnaire," 248. *P* includes the following addition before William's responses begin on f. 2rb: "Respondet Magister Guillelmus de Sancto Amore sustinens partem oppositam non sui auctoritate, sed per sacram

very unlikely hypothesis. Disputed questions were pedagogical exercises that followed a set format; a master presented a proposition and then appointed two students, an *opponens* and a *respondens* to proffer *pro* and *contra* arguments to the original statement. The master then determined the proposition, basing his conclusion on the positions raised by his student assistants.[29] The disputation and determination of these questions were scholarly exercises performed within a school for the benefit of its own master and students. They were private and internal and would therefore not have attracted an inter-university audience.

As William had already been a regent master in theology for at least five years when Bonaventure held this disputation, it is doubtful that he would have been permitted to assume a role specifically designed for the training of students. And as Bonaventure had not as yet attained magisterial status within the University in December 1255, his magisterial activities would not have been recorded on the Faculty's calender of academic events or announced publicly at Paris by the Faculty beadle.[30] William probably would even not have had knowledge of the question's disputation until well after it had been determined.

Bougerol has provided sufficient internal evidence from the reading of the manuscript *P* to prove that William's arguments against Bonaventure were made after the actual academic dispute had taken place. The explicit of *P* on f. 4va reads:

> Hanc questionem ita *determinavit* magister Bonaventura... *Respondet* magister Guillelmus de Sancto Amore ad omnia supradicta.[31]

If William had presented objections to Bonaventure's positions contemporaneously, then surely the verbs *determinare* and *respondere* would agree in their tenses.

The Quaracchi editors of Bonaventure had realized that manuscript *L* contained many readings which did not correspond to those of other

paginam etc., tota universitate magistrorum parisiensium contra Praedicatores et Minores et ordines consimiles..."

29 On the structure of the *quaestio disputata*, see B.C. Bazàn, "Les questions disputées, principalement dans les facultés de théologie," in *Les Questions disputées et les questions quodlibétiques dans les facultés de théologie, de droit et de médecine* (Turnhout: Brepols, 1985), 21-149; J. Verger, "*Nova et vetera* dans le vocabulaire des premiers statuts et privilèges universitaires français," *Vocabulaire des écoles et des méthodes d'enseignement au Moyen Age* ed. O. Weijers (Turnhout: Brepols, 1992), 198-9; O. Weijers, *Terminologie des universités au XIIIe siècle* (Rome: Edizioni dell'Ateneo, 1987), 335-43.

30 As noted by Bougerol, "Reportatio," 60.

31 Bougerol, "Reportatio," 60; Dufeil, "Universitaire parisien réactionnaire," 274; *QDM, infra,* n. 151.

manuscripts of *De mendicitate.* It is for this reason that they did not include it as a witness in their edition. However, *L* contains almost the same readings as both *C* and *P*; although the location of William's objections may differ in these manuscripts, they present substantially the same text and share a common ancestor. The text which these manuscripts contain is an early, unpolished version of *De mendicitate* recognized by Delorme to be a *reportatio* of the question's determination.[32]

What seems to have happened is that William obtained a manuscript of the question's deliberations before Bonaventure had time to proofread and circulate it publicly as an authorized *redactio.* The text to which William responded was therefore not a copy approved by Bonaventure; but it was also not simply a transcript of the question's proceedings. The relationship between the *reportatio* and the *redactio* is very close. They are so similar that the *reportatio* must represent a late-stage in the preparation of the final *redactio.* The proposition remained the same–whether to beg for Christ pertains to Christian perfection–but the *redactio* contains textual embellishments and clarifications which one would expect to find in a text made ready for publication. The *contra* statements have been slightly modified in the *redactio* but remain basically the same. There are twenty *contra* statements both in the *reportatio* and the *redactio*: ten from Scripture, three from canon and civil law, and seven *rationes* based on biblical interpretation. Proof that the *reportatio* was emended under Bonaventure's editorial eye can be seen by the fact that the order of the ten scriptural pericopes has been altered, but for no discernable reason.[33] A comparison of the readings of *contra* statement twenty will demonstrate how significantly Bonaventure revised some of the readings of the *reportatio* to prepare it for publication.

reportatio

Item persona praedicatoris debet esse discreta et nobilis sive honorabilis, non vilis. Sed nulla vilior persona quam persona mendicantis; ergo persona praedicantis vel praedicatoris non debet esse mendicans. Et sic mendicare praedicantibus non est opus perfectionis christianae.[34]

redactio

Item, tutius et perfectius est sequi viros probatiores et sapientiores; sed viri probatissimi et sapientissimi in religionibus fuerunt Basilius, Benedictus, Augustinus, Hieronymus, Gregorius, Hilarius et Paulinus; sed tales sic sua

[32] "Quaestio reportata," 328.

[33] In the *redactio* their order is: 1, 2, 3, 4, 5, 9, 10, 7, 8, 6.

[34] *Cf. QDM, infra,* n. 20.

> relinquerunt, quod communia possiderunt, nec mendicasse leguntur; ergo modus iste mendicandi de novo introductus per Dominicum et Franciscum videtur esse superstitiosus et vanus, cum stultum videatur sensum et spiritum duorum pauperum hominum praeponere tantae sapientiae et sublimitati Sanctorum praecedentium et doctorum.[35]

In the *reportatio*, Bonaventure speaks of the qualities of a preacher and then contrasts them with those of a beggar. Since the latter does not possess the same features as the former, he proposes that preachers should not beg. The *redactio*, however, defers to the judgment of wise and approved *auctoritates* in religious matters. Having relinquished their private possessions, they maintained communal ownership of goods. While Bonaventure does not distinguish these men as preachers, he does note that they never begged.[36] And although the *redactio* does not make a clear connection between mendicancy and the office of preaching, a relationship between the two is nevertheless implied in the reference to the founders of the two most renowned mendicant orders.

Contra twenty of the *redactio* also makes a criticism of the friars not included in the *reportatio*; it asserts that the "new way of begging" which Francis and Dominic invented is both superstitious and devoid of merit. While these charges are not contained verbatim in either of William's disputed questions, they could have been made by any of the mendicants' opponents and were certainly in the air at Paris in December 1255. Bonaventure undoubtedly chose to include this example in the *readactio* to address a current criticism of the friars.

Bonaventure cites twenty-eight *pro* statements in the *reportatio*; these have been expanded to thirty-seven in the *redactio*.[37] Bonaventure's conclusion in the *redactio* is considerably longer than the one in the *reportatio*; but the responses to the *contra* statements are almost the same in each.

[35] *Opera*, V:136.

[36] William had earlier cited one of these authorities, Paulinus of Nola, in *DQE*, 329-30. Bonaventure's usage of this example may reflect possible knowledge of William's question. Bonaventure's expanded repertoire of authorities who renounced all possessions and continued to distribute Church property is probably an attempt to address all such similar authorities at once. *Cf. ad oppositum* 20 in *Opera*, V:147-9.

[37] In the *redactio*, *pro* statements 3, 5, 7, 10, 14, 24, 26, 33, 36, and 37 all produce citations not contained in the *reportatio*. *Pro* argument 28 of the *reportatio* does not appear in the *redactio*. The order of the remaining *pro* citations is: 1, 2, 4, 6, 8, 9, 12, 11, 13, 15, 16, 17, 18, 19, 20, 21, 22, 23, 25, 27, 28, 29, 30, 31, 34, 35, 32.

The *reportatio*

The *reportatio* of *De mendicitate* begins with a question–whether begging pertains to Christian perfection. Bonaventure first replies in the negative, relying heavily upon the stock objections to the mendicant life popularized by William in *De valido mendicante.*[38] His goal is two-fold: 1) to enumerate the myriad authorities which have either eschewed or outlawed voluntary begging, and 2) to demonstrate that the dangers of mendicancy far outweigh its possible merits.

Citing II Thessalonians 3:10, Bonaventure notes that Paul has prescribed that those who do not work, should not eat. Augustine's gloss claims the one must work with one's hands specifically to avoid mendicancy.[39] Bonaventure therefore concludes that failure to perform manual labor will inevitably lead to begging–an act which cannot pertain to Christian perfection as it violates the express command of the Apostle.

Bonaventure next quotes several of Ambrose's glosses on Thessalonians,[40] highlighting the possible sins which could arise from not working. Failure to labor will undoubtedly cause us to flatter to obtain the necessities of life, to covet, to steal, to forget our own salvation, and to cause the death of the true poor by depriving them of their rightful alms. Paul's claim that he had labored amongst the Thessalonians to set an example for them is to be interpreted literally; abstaining from labor merely induces sin, and thwarts us in the quest for Christian perfection.

Bonaventure proposes a proper model for Christian living as Christ's injunction in Luke 12:33 to sell your possessions and give in charity.[41] Bede has clarified this command and explained that after one has relinquished all possessions for Christ, one should still continue to work and dispense alms.[42] While Christian perfection may consist in part in the abandonment of temporal goods for the sake of Christ, it cannot be meritorious unless one continues to distribute charity, and provides a legal livelihood for oneself.

In the *pro* section of the *reportatio,* Bonaventure attempts to counter the prohibition against mendicancy by proving that begging played an integral role both in the life of Christ and the Apostles. This portion reveals the polemical tactics of both Bonaventure and William, as it contains the latter's objections. William's strategy, not unexpectedly, is to disprove all

[38] Eleven of Bonaventure's objections to mendicancy can be found in either *De quantitate eleemosynae* or *De valido mendicante.*

[39] Aug., *De op. mon.* in *CSEL* 41.5.3, 535-6; *ord.* in II Thess. 3:10 in *Ed. pr.* 4:403B; *QDM, infra,* n. 6.

[40] *QDM, infra,* nn. 7, 9.

[41] *QDM, infra,* n. 10.

[42] Beda, *Expo. in Luc.* in *CCSL* 77:68; *int.* in Matt. 10:9 in *Ed. pr.* 4:187a; *QDM, infra,* n. 10.

of Bonaventure's citations which would seem to suggest a mendicant Christ. But it is the manner which William accomplishes this task that merits attention. William rarely relies upon the same material as Bonaventure within each *pro* statement. Rather, William frequently interjects new material from Scripture and the biblical *Glossa ordinaria* into the discussion; this matter usually stems from the Pauline epistles and Augustine's *De opere monachorum.* Moreover, William will often ignore the scriptural citation at hand and turn instead to disparate authorities, such as canon and civil law to refute Bonaventure's assertions.

Bonaventure first argues that Christ's instructions to the Apostles on their preaching mission prescribed that they should take nothing on their journey. Jerome's gloss emphasizes that the Apostles should take nothing except the clothes on their back.[43] William, however, mitigates Christ's advice with Augustine's gloss on II Timothy 2:6. Augustine had observed that the Apostles received both authority to take no possessions and permission to live off the goodwill of others directly from Christ.[44] Such authority cannot be called begging as it constitutes an apostolic power (*potestas*) and a privilege. And as the farmer who toils must be the first to partake of the fruit, so too may the Apostle who preaches the Gospel live from the Gospel and accept offerings from the faithful for his ministry.

Bonaventure continues by repeating Christ's request in Galilee that anyone who should receive a child in his name will receive him.[45] The interlinear gloss identifies the child as a poor man.[46] Bonaventure then remarks that as no one is poorer than a beggar, Christ's request must especially hold true for the poor beggar. And as Christ would not have intended that the faithful receive beggars if mendicancy were evil, begging must therefore be an act of Christian perfection.

William responds by deferring to Ambrose who details the varieties of people who can lawfully beg:[47] the infirm, those who do not know how to work, those who have no way to support themselves, and those who have become poor not by their own doing. But if any other type of mendicant seeks assistance, he is to be repelled and corrected.[48]

William qualifies the Psalms citation universally understood to be spoken in the person of Christ: *Ego mendicus sum et pauper.*[49] William

43 Hier., *Comm. in Matt.* in *CCSL* 77:66; *int.* in Matt. 10:9 in *Ed. pr.* 4:38a,b; *QDM, infra*, n. 21.

44 Aug., *De op. mon.*, in *CSEL* 41.5.3, 558; *QDM, infra*, n. 22.

45 Luc. 9:42; *QDM, infra*, n. 25.

46 *int.* in Luc. 9:48 in *Ed. pr.* 4:178a; *QDM, infra*, n. 25.

47 D. 86 c. 17 *Consideranda*; *QDM, infra*, n. 26.

48 *QDM, infra*, n. 26.

49 Ps. 39:18. This identification can be traced back to Augustine. It also appears in Cassiodorus and eventually found its way into the biblical ordinary gloss. Aug., *Enarr. in Ps.* in *CCSL* 38:446; Cassiodorus, *Expo. Psalm.* in *CCSL* 97:371; *int.* in Ps. 39:18 in *Ed. pr.* 2:503b; *QDM, infra*, n. 32.

explains that Christ can rightly be referred to as a beggar, but not because he begged for bread. Christ had assumed all aspects of humanity, including human misery, and for this reason he sought God's assistance. He asked for God's help not for himself, but for all his members;[50] Christ had deliberately not begged for sustenance lest his followers try to imitate him in this respect.[51]

Bonaventure and William both follow Ambrose's gloss when expounding Christ's request to Zaccheus for a place to stay.[52] While Bonaventure sees this request as an example of Christ's mendicancy, William claims that although Zaccheus had not yet asked Christ for accommodation, he already knew his intention.[53] Christ merely prevented Zaccheus from asking him first out of love.

Bonaventure cites Jerome through the *Glossa ordinaria* and employs Christ's departure from Bethany because he had no place to stay as yet another instance of his begging. William, however, also quotes Jerome and states that Christ left because he did not want to flatter anyone in order to obtain lodgings.[54]

Bonaventure follows Augustine and claims that Christ's request to the Samaritan woman to give him something to drink once again illustrates his mendicancy.[55] William calls this argument *ridiculosa* as there was already common use of the water;[56] and although Bonaventure cites Jerome to the contrary,[57] William nevertheless repeats the interlinear gloss and insists that the water Christ really sought from her was spiritual water or faith.[58]

Bonaventure recounts the travails of the early martyrs in Hebrews 11:37-8 to commemorate those who endured suffering and great need in the name of God.[59] Identifying mendicancy as a form of personal hardship, he then concludes that no one is needier than one who begs in Christ's name. To beg in Christ's name is therefore an act of perfection.

William reduces this syllogism to absurdity with the statement that "no one is needier than one who eats her own son on account of excessive

[50] "...ET PETEBAT AUXILIUM DEI NON TANTUM PRO SE QUANTUM PRO MEMBRIS SUIS." *QDM, infra*, n. 32.

[51] *QDM, infra*, n. 38.

[52] Luc. 19:5; *QDM, infra*, nn. 33, 34

[53] "QUIA ETIAMSI NONDUM AUDIERAT VOCEM INVITANTIS, AUDIERAT AFFECTUM." Amb., *Expo. in Luc.* in *CCSL* 14:331; *int.* in Luc. 19:5 in *Ed. pr.* 4:205A; *QDM, infra*, n. 34.

[54] Hier., *Comm. in Matt.* in *CCSL* 77:190; *ord.* in Marc. 11:11 in *Ed. pr.* 4:119A; *QDM, infra*, n. 35, 36. Jerome's passage is reproduced in Bede's, *Expo. in Marc.* in *CCSL* 120:576.

[55] Ioan. 4:7; Aug., *Tract. in Ioan.* in *CCSL* 36:155; *QDM, infra*, n. 39.

[56] *Cf. QDM, infra*, n. 41.

[57] Hier., *Epist. 125* in *CSEL* 56.1.3, 119; *QDM, infra*, n. 40.

[58] *int.* in Ioan. 4:7 in *Ed. pr.* 4:232B; *QDM, infra*, n. 41.

[59] *QDM, infra*, n. 44.

need."[60] Therefore, William concludes, that if one follows Bonaventure's line of reasoning, to eat one's son is an act of perfection.

While this extreme example could lead one to presume that William had simply constructed his arguments against Bonaventure fallaciously, William has in fact raised a very important objection. Excessive need compels us to perform many deeds which would not normally be recognized as meritorious *per se.* Indigence can induce theft. Should thievery therefore be commended if it were provoked by need and performed in the name of Christ?

While Bonaventure stresses the connection between begging and contempt for the world, William views mendicancy as a weakness which encourages avarice. He further notes that not every self-degradation is commendable; indeed, some are even sinful. As an example, he cites the prostitute who ought to be treated as *stercus* on the road.[61]

William abruptly dismisses Bonaventure's examples of the meritorious mendicancy of Saints Benedict and Alexius with the explanation that not everything a saint does is in itself perfect. While Benedict accepted alms in the name of Christ, he also ate and was needy, yet these two acts are not particularly exemplary. In the case of Alexius, who relinquished his patrimony and wandered begging throughout the world, William points out that the example of one man does not establish a new law. He then insinuates that Alexius might have become an itinerant mendicant because he was deprived of God's counsel, rather than inspired by it.[62]

Saint Francis performed miracles, but these do not by themselves make him a saint. Augustine had noted that many wicked men have possessed the power to perform miracles;[63] the Evangelist Matthew had warned that the Pseudo-Prophets of the Last Days will announce their arrival by means of signs and miracles.[64] And although Francis himself begged, one should not draw too many conclusions from this action, since his brethren, from the Order's earliest days, performed manual labor.[65]

William is even able to counter Bonaventure with the Gloss when the latter cites Aristotle. Although the Philosopher may claim that what is difficult and not prohibited to me pertains to perfection,[66] William notes

60 "NULLA EST MAGIS EGENS QUAM QUAE MANDUCANT FILIUM SUUM PRAE NIMIA EGESTATE..." *QDM, infra,* n. 45; *Cf.* Reg. 6:29; Bar. 2:3.

61 *QDM, infra,* n. 67; Eccli. 9:10.

62 *QDM, infra,* n. 55.

63 Aug., *Tract. in Ioan.* in *CCSL* 36:140; C.56 q.1 c.1 *Teneamus*; *QDM, infra,* n. 59.

64 Matt. 24:24; *QDM, infra,* n. 59.

65 William's source for this statement was probably Francis' *Testament. Cf. QDM, infra,* n. 59.

66 "Circa difficilia semper est ars et virtus." in *Les Auctoritates aristotelis. Un Florilège médiévale: étude historique et édition critique* in Philosophes médiévales XVII ed. J. Hamesse (Louvain: Publications universitaires, 1974), 235; Aristotle, *Ethica Nicomachea* ed. R.A. Gauthier in *Aristoteles latinus* (Leiden: E.J. Brill, 1973), XXVI^3 B2 1105a 9; *QDM, infra,* n. 62.

that this dictum certainly does not hold true for begging as it has been prohibited by the Apostle, the Gloss, and civil law.[67]

In the response, Bonaventure creates a tripartite division of begging based on 1) the necessity of nature; 2) vice or defect; and 3) the supererogation of justice. Bonaventure uses the story of Lazarus in Luke to illustrate the first type of mendicancy.[68] Lazarus' begging was licit as he was covered with sores;[69] he was therefore unable to procure a means of livelihood for himself.

The second manner of begging is shameful, and can been seen by those who beg out of laziness, or for a desire for temporal gain, or perhaps for both reasons. Bonaventure then asserts, in a clever tactical ploy, that Augustine has spent the majority of *De opere monachorum* dismissing the legitimacy of these mendicants. In one fell swoop, Bonaventure simply dismisses all the *Glossa* extracts which William had previously cited in his disputed questions from *De opere monachorum* by claiming that Augustine had written the work against one specific type of monk:[70] idle monks who refuse to labor yet expect the faithful to support them and not those who occupy themselves in spiritual activities.

The third manner of begging is to follow in the imitation of Christ's life. Christ was the true despiser of himself, as was displayed by his utter nakedness at the Passion; Christ was a true worshiper of God, as can be seen in how he commended himself to God at his death; Christ was also a true lover of his neighbors, as can be seen in his Passion, as he subjected himself to a vile death on our account.[71]

In the response to the *contra* section, Bonaventure has a two-fold strategy: first, in scriptural citations which disprove religious mendicancy, Bonaventure will rely on material from the interlinear or ordinary glosses to explain how these citations could be understood to include begging. Second, in citations which he had relied upon glossed matter to counter the proposition, Bonaventure will qualify, reinterpret, or occasionally subject to a lengthy division, to explain that although at first appearance the Gloss may seem to refute a mendicant Christ, it either does not apply or really suggests the opposite.

Bonaventure expounds Psalms 36:25 "I was young, and am now grown old, but I have never seen a righteous man forsaken or his children

[67] *QDM, infra*, n. 63.

[68] Luc. 16:20-22; *QDM, infra*, n. 80.

[69] Bonaventure may well have culled this example from William's *De quantitate eleemosynae. Cf. DQE*, 331.

[70] "Qui illis modis volunt mendicare, reprehensibiles sunt; quos Augustinus reprehendit in libro *De opere monachorum*, et solum ibi contra tales loquitur in toto libro." *QDM, infra*, n. 81.

[71] *QDM, infra*, n. 83.

seeking bread," through recourse to the interlinear gloss; it interprets the bread in question as spiritual–that is, the word of God.[72] Bonaventure thus concludes that there is therefore no need for the righteous man or his children to be seeking the word of God, as it is always with them.

In his reply to Ecclesiasticus 40:29, "it is better to die than to want," Bonaventure again quotes the interlinear gloss explaining that death would be preferable than to lack virtue or good morals.[73] The passage is therefore inconclusive as it does not apply to temporal want.

Bonaventure responds to Acts 20:35, "it is better to give than to receive," by quoting the ordinary gloss from Bede. He repeats Bede's claim that while it is certainly better to give than to receive, it is even more blessed to bestow your possessions upon the poor and continue both to work and distribute alms.[74] He then notes that if labor detracts from our devotion to spiritual pursuits, then one should not be held to it, as the spiritual ought not be forgotten on account of the temporal.[75]

In his rejoinder to Paul's command that "those who do not work, should not eat," Bonaventure carefully divides Augustine's gloss into two parts.[76] Augustine had written that the Apostle wanted God's servants to work lest they be compelled to beg for necessities. But as Augustine expressly mentions those who are compelled to beg, this gloss naturally cannot include those who beg *pro Christo* voluntarily.[77]

Next, as Augustine observes, the Apostle wanted God's servants to work. Since he only wanted them to work, and did not command it, this request must be a counsel rather than a precept, and therefore whoever does not follow it, does not necessarily act contrary to the Apostle's wishes.[78]

Finally, Bonaventure states that the only ones who should be held to observe manual labor as a precept are those poor beggars who are lazy busy-bodies. But those who spend their days in spiritual pursuits should be supported by alms.[79] William, however, insists that manual labor is a precept, and that the glosses in question refer only to those legally sent to preach directly by Christ.[80]

72 *int.* in Ps. 36:25 in *Ed. pr.* 2.498B; *QDM, infra*, n. 94.

73 *int.* in Eccli. 40:29 in *Ed. pr.* 2:786B; *QDM, infra*, n. 97.

74 Beda, *Expo. Act. Apost.* in *CCSL* 121:84; Beda, *Expo. in Luc.* in *CCSL* 120:254-5; *ord.* in Act. 20:35 in *Ed. pr.* 4:498A; *QDM, infra*, n. 98.

75 *QDM, infra*, n. 98.

76 Aug., *De op. mon.* in *CSEL* 41.5.3, 535-6; *ord.* in II Thess. 3:10 in *Ed. pr.* 4:403B; *Cf. QDM, infra*, nn. 6, 103, 105.

77 *QDM, infra*, n. 103.

78 *QDM, infra*, n. 105.

79 *QDM, infra*, n. 107.

80 *QDM, infra*, nn. 106, 108.

Bonaventure then addresses Ambrose's concern that begging can lead to flattery.[81] After inquiring whether one can relinquish one's possessions for Christ and survive without adulation, Bonaventure concludes that those who labor for Christ by evangelizing in imitation of him will not succumb to flattery.[82] William, however, warns that although one may relinquish all possessions for Christ, as one is human, one will still be tempted to steal, flatter, and sin in order to obtain food.[83]

Bonaventure again treats the Apostle's command to labor with one's hands, lest anything else be desired.[84] To seek, Bonaventure explains, can be understood in two ways. One may seek out of desire or cupidity, which the Apostle prohibited, or one may seek for the salvation of souls. Those who give charity to those who evangelize for Christ are to be commended, not chastized, as they will receive heavenly rewards. Those religious who administer spiritual goods and accept the offerings of the faithful are thus providing those same faithful with an opportunity to merit eternal salvation.

William responds by accusing Bonaventure of flagrantly contradicting the Gloss.[85] Begging, William argues, cannot bring salvation; rather, it helps damn both the one begging and the one giving.[86]

Bonaventure writes that Ambrose's gloss on I Thessalonians 5:4 warning that "excessive want will led us to seek to be satiated" certainly does not apply to those who preach and evangelize for Christ.[87] They seek not to have their bellies filled but rather to spread the word of God. William nevertheless replies that they will eventually become hungry and will then seek sustenance.[88]

In his reply to Bede's gloss on Luke 12:33, that "all should spurn worldly possessions for God, and then work with one's hands in order to give charity," Bonaventure once again subdivides the gloss.[89] First, he notes that it contains a counsel to spurn all temporal goods; meritorious advice, which pertains to all men. However, Bede's suggestion that one ought to work with one's hands is not a counsel, but rather a work of supererogation because not even Paul and the other Apostles followed it.

81 Amb., *Comm. in Epist. ad Thess.* in *PL* 17:485C; *ord.* in II Thess. 3:9 in *Ed. pr.* 4:403B; *QDM, infra,* nn. 7, 109.

82 *QDM, infra,* nn. 109, 111.

83 *QDM, infra,* n. 111.

84 *QDM, infra,* n. 113.

85 "HIC VIDE QUALITER DICIT APPERTISSIME CONTRA GLOSSAM!" *QDM, infra,* n. 115.

86 "ITEM, QUOD DICIT: 'MENDICARE LICET PROPTER SALVATIONEM ANIMARUM' NIHIL EST, QUIA MENDICARE NON SALVAT MENDICANTEM, IMMO POTIUS DAMNAT..." *QDM, infra,* n. 115.

87 Amb., *Comm. in Epist. ad Thess.* in *PL* 17:477B; *ord.* in I Thess. 5:12 in *Ed. pr.* 4:399B; *QDM, infra,* nn. 9, 116.

88 *QDM, infra,* n. 117.

89 *QDM, infra,* nn. 10, 118.

Sometimes Paul worked with his hands, while other times he accepted offerings from the faithful. As the Apostles followed all of the Lord's counsels, manual labor was clearly not among them.

In his rebuttal, William presents his particular understanding of the Gloss. He claims that Bonaventure's argument is sophistical and that individual glosses cannot be divided. Furthermore, he notes that "every Gloss is one text and both its construction and its meaning remains valid until the end,"[90] thus treating the Gloss as an *auctoritas* in itself. William also concedes that Paul did not have to live by manual labor as he had permission not to do so, but as for the other Apostles, although they were legally sent, they were also fishermen.

Discrepancies between the *reportatio* and the *redactio*

A significant discrepancy between the *reportatio* and the *redactio* of *De mendicitate* is the claim in the former that the mendicant manner of life, as espoused by St. Francis, had received approbation from a general council. This assertion appears twice in the report; first in *pro* statement seventeen[91] and later in the response to *contra* eleven.[92] In the *redactio*, however, Bonaventure omits any reference to a general council.

But other sources attest that the Order of Friars Minor had received conciliar approval. Two thirteenth-century sources, the *Intentio Regulae* (*IntReg*),[93] written by Francis' companion Brother Leo, and the *Scripta Leonis*,[94] both mention that the Rule had received conciliar approbation. Moreover, several early fourteenth-century sources, including the *Legenda antiqua* (*LegDelorme*) of St. Francis,[95] Angelo of Clareno's *Expositio regulae Fratrum Minorum*,[96] and an epistle of Brother Angelo,[97] all attest that Pope Innocent III had announced his endorsement of the Franciscan Order before a council; the obvious conclusion is that the general council in

90 "...ET TOTA GLOSSA UNIUS EST TEXTUS ET PENDET ETIAM CONSTRUCTIO ET SENTENTIA ILLIUS USQUE IN FINEM." *QDM*, *infra*, n. 119.

91 *QDM*, *infra*, n. 56.

92 *QDM*, *infra*, n. 126.

93 Edited by Fr. L. Lemmens in *Documenta antiqua franciscana* (Quaracchi: Collegium S. Bonaventurae, 1901), 83-99.

94 R.B. Brooke, *Scripta Leonis, Rufini et Angeli sociorum S. Francisci* (Oxford: Clarendon Press, 1970), 204-5.

95 *La legenda antiqua S. Francisci: texte du ms. 1046 (M.69) de Pérousse* ed. P. F.-M. Delorme (Paris: Éditions de la France Franciscaine, 1926), No. 67, 39.

96 *Expositio Regulae fratrum minorum* ed. P.L. Oliger (Quaracchi: Collegium S. Bonaventurae, 1912), 6, 16.

97 See F. Ehrle in "Die Spiritualen, ihr Verhältniss zum Franciscanerorden und zu den Fraticellen," *Archiv für Litteratur- und Kirchengeschichte des Mittel Alters* 1 (1885): 559.

question is none other than the Council of Lateran IV in 1215.[98] Indeed, in the prologue of his *Expositio regulae*, Angelo explicitly relates that the council in question took place in 1215.[99] Similarly, the *Chronicle of the Twenty-four Generals* (*C24G*) places Francis in Rome at 1215, but does not state whether the Rule received conciliar approval at that time.[100]

Although Brother Leo and his companions report that Innocent approved Francis' Rule and then afterwards informed everyone in attendance at the Lateran Council, the records of the Council preserve no such mention of it.[101] Nevertheless, it appears that within the Franciscan sources, there was a long-standing tradition that the Order had been approved by the assembly of prelates gathered at Lateran IV. This claim does not appear in the lives of Francis written by Thomas of Celano and Bonaventure.

As we have seen, the earliest sources it appears in are the *Intentio Regulae* and the *Scripta Leonis* both written c. 1246.[102] Leo begins his narrative by announcing that Francis had written three rules; one which was approved by Innocent *sine bulla*, a shorter one which was subsequently lost, and a third one which was confirmed by Pope Honorius.[103] But shortly thereafter, Leo makes a further claim for the Minors. In the *Intentio Regulae* Leo writes:

> ...sicut revelatum fuit beato Francisco, ut deberet vocari religio Fratrum Minorum; et ita scribi fecit in ipsa regula et portavit eam domino Papae Innocentio; et ipse approbavit et concessit et postea *in concilio* omnibus annuntiavit...[104]

The same passage appears almost verbatim in *Scripta Leonis*.

> Unde sicut revelatum fuit beato Francisco ut deberet vocari religio Minorum Fratrem, ita scribi fecit in prima Regula, cum portavit eam coram domino papa Innocentio tertio et ipse

98 However at *QDM, infra*, n. 56, Bonaventure states that the council took place after Francis' death.

99 "Postea vero in generali concilio Rome per eum celebrato anno Domini MCCXV prelatis omnibus annuntiavit se vitam et evangelicam regulam sancto Francisco et eum sequi volentibus concessisse." *Expositio*, 6.

100 *Chronica XXIV generalium ordinis minorum* in *Analecta Franciscana* 3 (1897):9.

101 M. Robson, *St. Francis of Assisi: The Legend and the Life* (London: Geoffrey Chapman, 1997), 76; Brooke, *Scripta Leonis*, 204-5.

102 Edited by Fr. L. Lemmens in *Documenta antiqua franciscana* (Quaracchi: Collegium S. Bonaventurae, 1901), 83-99.

103 *IntReg*, prol., 83.

104 *IntReg*, c. 3, 85.

approbavit et concessit sibi et postea *in consilio* omnibus annuntiavit.[105]

This same passage is repeated, with very little modification, in the three fourteenth-century sources: Angelo's *Expositio regulae*, the *LegDelorme*, and the *Speculum perfectionis*. A comparison of these three sources will serve to prove that either the *IntReg* or the *Scripta Leonis* was the common source for this assertion.

> *Expositio regulae* (1317/8)
> Unde sicut hoc revelatum fuit beato Francisco, ut deberet vocari religio Fratrum Minorum, ita scribi fecit in prima regula, cum portavit eam domino papae Innocentio, et ipse approbavit et sibi concessit, et postea *in concilio* omnibus annuntiavit.[106]
>
> *LegDelorme* (c. 1311)
> Unde sicut revelat[um] fuit B. Francisco ut deberet vocari religio Minorum fratrum, ita scribi fecit in prima Regula, cum portavit eam coram domino papa Innocentio III° et ipse approbavit et concessit sibi et postea *in consilio* omnibus annuntavit.[107]
>
> *Speculum perfectionis* (1318)
> Unde, sicut revelatum fuit beato Francisco ut deberet vocari religio fratrum Minorum, sicut fecit scribi in prima regula quam portavit coram domino papa Innocentio III, qui eam approbavit et concessit, et postea *in consistorio* omnibus annuntiavit.[108]

The *Speculum perfectionis* departs from the others by substituting the word *consistorio* for *concilio*. Likewise, the relevant passage in the *Legenda trium sociorum* (c. 1246) reads:

> Et sic amplexatus est eum et regulam quam scripserat approbavit. Dedit etiam sibi licentiam praedicandi ubique poenitentiam ac fratribus suis, ita tamen quod qui praedicaturi erant a beato Francisco licentiam obtinerent. Et hoc idem postea *in consistorio* approbavit.[109]

105 Brooke, *Scripta Leonis,* 204.
106 *Expositio,* 16. Angelo notes Brother Leo as the source for this passage.
107 *LegDelorme,* No. 67, 39.
108 *Speculum perfectionis ou Mémoires de Frère Léon* ed. P. Sabatier. 2nd ed. British Society of Franciscan Studies vol. 13 (Manchester: University Press, 1928), c. 26, No. 7, 74.
109 *Legenda trium sociorum: édition critique* ed. T. Desbonnets in *AFH* 67 (1974): c. 12, No. 51, 128.

But even here, the phrase is rendered *in concilio* or *in consilio* in one family of manuscripts.

The thirteenth-century sources were divided over whether Francis' Rule received conciliar approval; this confusion can be witnessed in the conflation of the readings for *consistorio* and *concilio*. The fact that it does not appear in the *redactio* and was not repeated in either of Bonaventure's lives of Francis, would indicate that Bonaventure himself was not willing to support such a claim in a text prepared for publication.

Yet another significant modification Bonaventure made in the *redactio* was to strengthen the connection between the mendicants' mission and papal authority. In the *reportatio*, Bonaventure makes three references to the papal approbation which the Franciscan order has received; he twice notes that Francis has commanded his brethren to beg and this injunction has received papal endorsement.[110] He later identifies Gregory and Innocent as the pontiffs who had endorsed the mendicant form of religious life.[111]

But in the *redactio*, Bonaventure qualifies the papal sanction of Francis' command to beg. In an attempt to avoid turning papal confirmation of Francis' directive into a *carte blanche* authorization of begging, Bonaventure shifted the focus of the argument to the papal approval of Francis' Rule.[112] By this editorial emendation, Bonaventure emphasized that mendicancy, although an important part of Francis' concept of the religious life, was merely one aspect of the Rule.

Bonaventure also added a new section to the conclusion of the *redactio* intended to stress the intimate connection between the Friars Minors and papal prerogative. Bonaventure writes,

> But if one wants to oppose or to disprove every type of begging followed by those serving Christ, it would seem that he opposes not only the order of poor men, but even the pope himself who approved this way of life.[113]

Bonaventure's effort to turn any attack on systematic begging into an assault on papal authority to create new orders was one of the strongest

110 *Cf. QDM, infra*, nn. 56, 126.

111 "Unde Gregorius papa et Innocentius, qui istos Ordines confirmavit..." *QDM, infra*, n. 130. This roster was lengthened in the *redactio* to include Honorius. *Opera*, V:141. On Bonaventure's usage of papal precedents, see R. Lambertini, *Apologia e crescita*, 21-2.

112 "...et per regulam a summo pontifice approbatam confirmari fecit..." *Opera*, V:138.

113 "Nam si quis impugnare et improbare velit omnem mendicandi modum in servis Christi, impugnare videbitur non tantum ordinem pauperum, verum ipsum summum pontificem, qui approbavit hunc vivendi modum..." *Opera*, V:141. Bonaventure had earlier cited papal confirmation of Francis' rule for justification of complete renunciation in *De abrenuntiatione. Opera*, V:130.

arguments made by any of the mendicant apologists. As the pope had given the friars permission to observe a life of mendicancy, any further attempt to question its legitimacy could quickly be constructed as a *de facto* challenge to papal plenitude of power.

Another manner in which Bonaventure tried to strengthen the connection between papal authority and the mendicants' mission can be seen in his usage of the concept of *subauctoritas.* In the *reportatio* he mentions subauthority four times, but never explains it in very definite terms.[114] Bonaventure claims that those who have authority to preach could rightfully live by the Gospel on the basis of that same authority.[115] He also adds that those who have received permission to preach can beg for alms in Christ's name without sin.[116] He then explains that while the mendicant orders do not have a principal power to preach, they still have a delegated power, or a *subauctoritatem* to do so.[117]

In citing subauthority, Bonaventure was responding to the ancient, ideologically conservative Church construct favored by William of Saint-Amour. William had revived and championed an ecclesiological model based on the model of the two *ordines*–the episcopacy and the priesthood. These two orders stemmed from the missions of the twelve Apostles and the seventy-two disciples commissioned by Christ in Luke 9 and 10 respectively. Within the Church there are only two orders empowered to administer pastoral functions: the episcopacy, or the successors of the twelve Apostles, and the parochial clergy, who have succeeded the seventy-two disciples.[118] As Christ had established the parochial and diocesan framework of the Church, William argued that there could no other orders possessing the *cura animarum* in their own right.[119] The implication for the mendicants was that as their rights to preach, to beg, and to administer the care of souls must completely be dependant upon episcopal and parochial approval.

In the *reportatio,* William had attacked the notion of subauthority on the basis that it lacked scriptural justification. He labelled Bonaventure's

114 *Cf. QDM, infra,* nn. 78, 144.

115 I Cor. 9:14; *QDM, infra,* n. 78.

116 *Cf. QDM, infra,* n. 144.

117 "Dico ergo quod praedicatores mendicantes dictorum Ordinum auctoritatem habent non principalem, sed delegatam sive subauctoritatem, sicut Ordo Minorum et Praedicatorum ..." *QDM, infra,* n. 144.

118 This position is elaborated in *De periculis,* his sermons *Qui amat periculum* and *Si quis diligit me,* and later in his *Collectiones catholicae.* See *DP* in *Opera,* 24; *QAP, infra,* n. 17; *SQD, infra,* n. 9; *Collectiones catholicae* in *Opera,* 145, 179, 183. William's exegesis on the two *ordines* relies heavily on Bede's *Expositio in Lucam* in *CCSL* 120:213-4 as it was transmitted to the ordinary gloss.

119 *DP* in *Opera,* 24. On this point, see J.D. Dawson, "William of Saint-Amour and the Apostolic Tradition," *Mediaeval Studies* 40 (1978):333-6.

definition of *subauctoritas* a notion "created to pursue evil courses."[120] His position was that power to live by the Gospel had only been conferred upon prelates. One either had this power or not: there was no intermediate stage. If one does not have this power, he sins when accepting offerings for spiritual services.[121]

Bonaventure further clarified his position of subauthority in the *redactio* of *De mendicitate*. In his reply to the objections, he states that the power necessary to preach the Gospel can be acquired in two manners. First, one can attain this power by authority held *ex prima institutione* or *ex iniuncto officio.*[122] Prelates and curates receive this power upon consecration as the rightful descendants of the twelve and the seventy-two. But a similar, although a less principal power to preach can also be obtained by means of commission or by privilege. Bonaventure found scriptural backing for authority held by commission in Paul's dispersal of his preachers. For additional support, Bonaventure cited the pope, who not only holds the place of the chief apostle, Peter, but also represents Christ within the Church and can therefore rightfully be said to have a fullness of power.[123]

And Bonaventure continues, as prelates may accept offerings for performing spiritual services as a power, so too may those commissioned by the pope seek sustenance as a demonstration of apostolic subauthority. Indeed, Bonaventure argues, such preachers licensed by the pope are to be praised since the Holy Spirit wanted the Church to be strengthened not only by preaching, but also by the example of humility. And Bonaventure argues that those who presume to contest the right of such preachers to live from the alms of the faithful would do well to heed Christ's advice to be gentle and humble of heart.[124]

One interesting point which Bonaventure had initially raised in his response to *contra* eleven,[125] but moved in the *redactio* to his reply to *contra* twenty, was the comparison of the *primitiva ecclesia* with the current church practice. In the *redactio* Bonaventure writes,

> Nevertheless because poverty is the foundation of evangelical perfection and, so to speak, its complement, it therefore flourished in the beginning of the Church and it is fitting that it should flourish in the final state of the Church ... Jerome says

[120] "...AD EXCUSANDUM EXCUSATIONES IN PECCATIS..." *QDM, infra*, n. 79.

[121] *Cf. QDM, infra*, n. 79.

[122] *Opera*, V:147.

[123] *Opera*, V:147. On Bonaventure's connection between papal plenitude and the mendicants' mission, see M. Peuchmard, "Mission canonique et prédication: Le prêtre ministre de la parole dans la querelle entre mendiants et séculiers au XIIIe siècle," *RTAM* 30 (1963):261-8.

[124] *Opera*, V:147.

[125] *Cf. QDM, infra*, n. 128.

> that "omega revolved to alpha," that is, the final state agreed with the first.[126]

Bonaventure himself conceived of his Order as a recent institution; but he also maintained that it corresponded to a way of life which Christ had established at the very foundation of the Church. The creation of the mendicant orders was therefore a reinstitution of apostolic discipline.

But for William, this claim smacked of heresy. He argued that to assert that the Church would return to its original state of poverty through certain new religious orders merely repeated the errors of Joachim of Fiore.[127] William refuted Bonaventure's position by citing the communal practice of the early Church at Jerusalem described in Acts and the decretal *Videntes* attributed to Pope Urban I.[128] Bonaventure had erred by treating the *primitiva ecclesia* in terms of poverty, when it had maintained from the beginning, as William argued, communal possessions. And William added that as Urban had instructed in *Videntes*, anyone who attempted to change this arrangement, either in the present or future, would be struck with the sentence of excommunication.[129]

Conclusion

Bonaventure does not seem to have been aware of William's objections to *De mendicitate* when he prepared the *redactio* for circulation. Although he expanded and rearranged much of the material within his own question, he made no attempt to address any of William's arguments. Bonaventure eventually did respond to William's objections in the former's treatise entitled *Replicatio adversus objectiones postea factas* (*Replicatio*).[130] While he does not cite William by name in the work, he refutes his objections by dividing them into five categories: irrelevant, false, illogical, dubious, and

126 "Nihilominus tamen, quia paupertas fundamentum est evangelicae perfectionis, et ipsa est quasi complementum eiusdem; ideo viguit in Ecclesiae primordio, et congruum est, ut vigeat circa Ecclesiae statum finalem...Hieronymus...dicit ibidem, quod 'omega revolvit ad alpha', id est, finalis status concordavit cum primo." *Opera*, V:148; Trans. in B. Tierney, *The Origins of Papal Infallibility 1150-1350* (Leiden: E.J. Brill, 1972), 74.

127 "HOC ENIM SAPIT SENTENTIAM IOACHIM..." *QDM, infra*, n. 129.

128 C.12 q.1 c.16 *Videntes*; *QDM, infra*, n. 129.

129 *QDM, infra*, n. 129. Bonaventure attempted to balance adeptly the decrees of Popes Urban, Gregory, and Innocent in the *reportatio*. But in the *redactio*, he remarked simply that "an equal has no power over an equal". *Opera*, V:145; Cited in Tierney, *Origins of Papal Infallibility*, 89-90.

130 In Bonaventure, *Opera*, V:149-65 and discussed in Bougerol, "Reportatio," 62-3.

inimical to apostolic teaching.[131] The *Replicatio* need not concern us here as it in effect forms a separate *determinatio* written after William's objections. But as Bougerol has noted, the *Replicatio* simply would not exist if Bonaventure had known of William's responses before publishing his own *redactio*.[132]

In his objections, William repeats many of the points raised in *De valido mendicante*. He enumerates the types of people who can licitly beg: those who do not know how to work, those who cannot perform manual labor and those who are reduced to extreme poverty by unfortunate circumstances. Those who are bodily able sin when they beg. If they dare solicit offerings in the name of Christ, they are to be corrected and repelled.[133]

131 "...quedam ex eis refellere volens tanquam impertinencia, quedam ut falsa, quedam ut inconsequentia, quedam ut dubia, plurima autem ex eis tanquam doctrine apostolice inimica." Bougerol, "Reportatio," 62; *Opera*, V:149.

132 Bougerol, "Reportatio," 63.

133 *DVM*, 340-1; *QDM*, *infra*, n. 26.

DE PERICULIS NOVISSIMORUM TEMPORUM

The most influential and unquestionably the most controversial of all of William's literary productions was *De periculis novissimorum temporum.* Written at the request of the French episcopacy,[1] the work assembled a vast array of pericopes to demonstrate that the Last Times, as predicted in Scripture, were presently at hand. However, he not only enumerated the biblical signs of the Last Age, he also connected them all with the ministerial activities of the friars. The mendicants' mission, William argued, had been foretold in Scripture as a prelude to the advent of the Antichrist. The work itself was an immediate success; William revised it four times throughout 1256,[2] and despite its condemnation, it survives today in over sixty known manuscripts.[3]

MANUSCRIPTS AND PRINTINGS

While this work still awaits a critical edition, Michel-Marie Dufeil has done much of the preparatory groundwork for such an endeavor. He has identified the five different versions and has linked fifty-one of the manuscripts with their respective groupings.[4] He has found that very little difference exists between these five versions; indeed, the discrepancies between them consist of little more than the addition of stylistic phrases.[5]

1 *Resp.*, 359-60.

2 As he himself admitted to his judges at Anagni: "Sed volumen illud immutatum fuit quinquies successive magis ac magis corrigendo, quaedam addendo, quaedam subtrahendo, quaedam vero declarando." *Resp.*, 360.

3 In 1962, Dufeil had discovered sixty-two mss. of *De periculis.* "Correction au «Répertoire des maîtres en théologie de Paris au XIIIe siècle» de P. Glorieux," *Bulletin de la Société internationale pour l'étude de la philosophie médiévale* 4 (1962):135.

4 For a discussion of the manuscript tradition, the differences between the five versions of *De periculis*, and a list of the manuscripts Dufeil associated with each version, see *Guillaume de Saint Amour*, 215-6, 221-2, 241, 252, 269-70, n. 75, 271-2, nn. 91-3, 276, nn. 157, 159, 278 n. 182.

5 *Guillaume de Saint-Amour*, 214-5. In 1962 Dufeil had discovered two recensions of *De periculis*: a Roman and a Parisian one. "Correction au Répertoire," 135. In a private communication with H.F. Dondaine in 1968, Dufeil explained that he found evidence for five versions of *De periculis* but that the differences between them were minimal. As he related, the differences were: "caractérisées par des longueurs et surtout des prudences

He explains that the first version differs from the second in the length of its prologue and its word choice; the second diverges from the others in the length of its *explicit*; the third version has slightly reordered materials and different phrasings; the fourth contains a more developed conclusion than the third; while the fifth varies from the others in twenty-three variant readings.[6] The third version of *De periculis* represents the "Roman version" or the version that the committee of cardinals at Anagni investigated and Pope Alexander condemned.[7] The fourth version, in Dufeil's estimation, forms the most complete manuscript grouping of the "Parisian family."[8]

While Dufeil had envisioned a critical edition of the work, his death left this undertaking unfulfilled. In his magisterial *Guillaume de Saint-Amour et la polémique universitaire parisienne*, he listed the manuscripts of *De periculis* that he examined, thereby laying a foundation for a future edition of the work. However, he did not identify the types of texts that circulated with it and he made only sporadic attempts at dating the manuscripts. Moreover, he did not account for the extra eleven manuscripts of *De periculis* which he had earlier heralded[9] nor did he make any effort to provide invaluable manuscript descriptions of the copies of *De periculis* he studied.

But what Dufeil has discovered is a very complicated and highly contaminated pattern of manuscript dissemination. Although there are five versions, some are so highly contaminated that they form subsets within the version's lines of transmission. As examples, the third and fourth versions have contaminated one set of manuscripts of the second version; both the first and fourth versions have contaminated another group of the second version.[10] Dufeil has also noted a group of manuscripts from the fourth version which show the influence of the second version. He detected further contamination in some manuscripts of the fifth version which contain readings of the third version.[11]

Until a critical edition does appear, one must make use one of the various printings of the text. The text has been printed five times:

grandissantes; mais ces prudences ne sont que trois ou quatre formules de quelques mots, et il n'y a pas lieu de mettre en garde contre l'édition de 1632." Cited in the Dondaine's introduction to Aquinas' *Contra impugnantes* in *Opera omnia* (Rome: S. Sabina, 1970), 41A:10, n. 6.

6 *Guillaume de Saint Amour*, 215, 221-2, 241-2, 252.

7 "Secundum quod perpendere potui inspiciendo volumen illud quod vos mihi, domini mei Cardinales, respiciendum dedistis, volumen illud, secundum quod possum recolere, fuit tertiae compilationis, quae postmodum bis mutata fuit et correcta addendo, subtrahendo, et declarando." *Resp.*, 360.

8 *Guillaume de Saint Amour*, 241-2. Dufeil notes the popularity of the fourth version at Paris from the years 1257-1280 and shows how in one of these manuscripts, a scribe has inserted additional apocalyptic material.

9 "Correction au Répertoire," 135.

10 Dufeil, *Guillaume de Saint-Amour*, 221, 271, n. 93, n. 94.

11 Dufeil, *Guillaume de Saint-Amour*, 276, n. 157, 278, n. 182.

Guilielmus de Sancto Amore, *Opera omnia quae reperiri poterunt.* Ed. Alithophilius. Constance [Paris], 1632, 17-72.

M. Bierbaum, *Bettelorden und Weltgeistlichkeit an der Universität Paris.* Münster, 1920, 1-36.

Matěje z Janova Mistra Pařižského, Regulu veteris et novi testamenti. Ed. V. Kybal. Innsbruck, 1911, III:256-314.

Flaccius Illyricus, *Antilogia papae, hoc est de corrupto ecclesiae statu et totius cleri papistici perversitate, scripta aliquot veterum auctorum, ante annos plus minus CCC et interea.* Basel, 1555.
Reprinted in:

Appendix ad fasciculum rerum expetendarum et fugiendarum. Ed. E. Brown. London, 1690, II:18-41 [reprint Tucson, AZ: Audax Press, 1967].

Bierbaum has reproduced an incomplete copy of the text of Alithophilius' *Opera.*[12] Brown's printing in *Appendix ad fasciculum rerum* is a reprint of Flaccius Illyricus' text in *Antilogia papae,*[13] and Kybal's printing in *Regula veteris et novi testamenti* is based on a late contaminated manuscript tradition. The printed text in *Antilogia papae,* and reprinted in *Appendix ad fasciculum rerum,* is, according to Dufeil, based on a manuscript of the fourth version of *De periculis.*[14] Kybal's *Regula veteris et novi testamenti* was printed from a contaminated member of the third version.[15] Alithophilius' *Opera* and Bierbaum's reprint of it appear to be based on a manuscript from the fourth version.[16] Alithophilius' printing is to be preferred and hereafter citations from *De periculis* will direct the reader to the appropriate pages of his *Opera.*

[12] Bierbaum has reproduced chapters 1-3, 5, 8, and 11-12 of Alithophilius' *Opera. Bettelorden und Weltgeistlichkeit,* 1-36.

[13] Dufeil, *Guillaume de Saint-Amour,* 242, 276, n. 158.

[14] *Guillaume de Saint-Amour,* 242, 276, n. 158.

[15] *Guillaume de Saint-Amour,* 222, 271, n. 95. It is extremely close to the version contained in Munich, Bayerische Staatsbibliothek, ms. Clm. 14635 ff. 146r-167r.

[16] *Guillaume de Saint-Amour,* 242.

Dating of the work

While the importance of *De periculis* has been demonstrably proven, its dating still remains a source of contention. Glorieux has dated it to 1256;[17] Congar,[18] Dufeil,[19] and McKeon all follow his position.[20] Alternately, other scholars have placed its publication to sometime in 1255.[21] Marrone, in particular, favors a 1255 dating, possibly even before the publication of *Quasi lignum vite* on 15 April.[22] Marrone has based his argument both on internal evidence within *De periculis* as well as on references to this work in the University's dissolution threat *Radix amaritudinis* of October 1255.

In chapter eight of *De periculis*, in which William expounds the errors of the *Introductorius*, he makes several allusions to the year 1255. At the beginning of the chapter, William forewarns of the impending end of the world. He writes;

> We are therefore in the last age of this world and this age has already lasted longer than the others ages, since others have lasted one thousand years, but this one has lasted 1255.[23]

Later in the chapter's introduction, he adds;

17 In *Répertoire des maîtres en théologie de Paris au XIIIe siècle* (Paris: Librarie philosophique J. Vrin, 1933-4), I:344; "Le «*Contra impugnantes*» de S. Thomas: ses sources-son plan," *Mélanges Mandonnet* (Paris: Librairie philosophique J. Vrin, 1930), I:73; "Le Conflit de 1252-1257," 369-70. H.F. Dondaine follows him in the introduction to *Contra impugnantes* in *Opera*, 41A:10.

18 "Aspects ecclésiologiques de la querelle entre mendiants et séculiers dans la seconde moitié du XIIIe siècle et le début du XIV," *AHDL* 28 (1961):45-6.

19 "Gulielmus de Sancto Amore, opera omnia 1252-1270," *Miscellanea Mediaevalia* 10 *Die Auseinandersetzungen an der Pariser Universität im XIII. Jahrhundert* (1976):215 and *Guillaume de Saint-Amour*, 221-7, 229, 238, 241, 252-5, and 260-4.

20 P. McKeon, "The Status of the University of Paris as *Parens Scientiarum*: An Episode in the Development of its Autonomy," *Speculum* 39 (1964):651-675.

21 M. Bierbaum, *Bettelorden und Weltgeistlichkeit*, 379, simply dates the work to 1255 without further comment. P. Féret, *La Faculté de théologie de Paris et ses docteurs les plus célèbres.* Moyen Age (Paris: A. Picard, 1894), II:68, argues unpersuasively that its contents were made public in 1252, yet it was not published until 1255. Thouzellier, "La Place du *De periculis* de Guillaume de Saint-Amour dans les polémiques universitaires du XIIIe siècle," *Revue Historique* 46 (1927):69, dates it somewhere between the promulgation of *Nec insolitum* and *Radix amaritudinis*.

22 His argument is that *De periculis* was intended to dissuade Alexander IV from pursuing the pro-mendicant policy as revealed in *Nec insolitum*. "The Ecclesiology of the Parisian Secular Masters, 1250-1320," unpublished Ph.D. thesis Cornell University, 1972, 53.

23 "Ergo nos sumus in ultima aetate huius mundi; et ista aetas iam plus duravit quam aliae quae currunt per millenarium annorum; quia ista duravit per 1255 annos." *DP*, 37; Marrone, "Ecclesiology," 53. The printing in Brown's *Appendix ad fasciculum rerum*, II:27 reads "...per 1264 annos."

> Item, Matt. 20. And as the eleventh hour has arrived; and since the Gloss notes that this hour lasts from the Lord's arrival until the end of the world, it is certain that this hour has lasted 1255 years.[24]

Elsewhere in this chapter, William lists eight signs which attest to the arrival of the Last Age. The first portent is an attempt to subvert the teachings of Christ. He warns;

> ...for fifty-five years now, there are those who strive to turn the Gospel of Christ into another Gospel which they say is more perfect, better and more worthy. They call this the Gospel of the Holy Spirit, or the Eternal Gospel. By its arrival, as they profess, Christ's Gospel will be emptied, as we are prepared to show in that accursed Gospel.[25]

The fifty-five years in question refers to the date, according to the minutes of the Anagni Commission, that the Holy Spirit had left the Church.[26] It also signifies the year in which Joachim's followers had begun to compose the *Eternal Gospel.*[27] In the following paragraph William writes;

> The second sign is that that doctrine, which will be preached in the time of the Antichrist, namely the Eternal Gospel, has already been published for explanation at Paris in the year of the Lord 1254.[28]

This second sign obviously alludes to the publication of the *Introductorius* in 1254.

The most probable explanation for the 1255 dating of *De periculis* is that it reflected the date of its Parisian publication, since Easter (16 April 1256) marked the beginning of the New Year according to the Gallican calendar.

24 "Item Matt. 20. Circa horam undecimam exiit, Glos. quae hora est ab adventu Domini usque ad finem mundi; et certum est, quod huius undecimae horae iam transacti sunt 1255 anni." *DP*, 38; *int.* in Matt. 20:6 in *Ed. pr.* 4:63B. Again, the printing in Brown's *Appendix ad fasciculum rerum,* II:27 reads "...transacti sunt 1264 anni."

25 "...quoniam iam sunt 55 anni, quod aliqui laborant ad mutandum Evangelium Christi in aliud Evangelium, quod dicunt fore perfectius, melius, et dignius; quod appellant Evangelium Spiritus Sancti, sive Evangelium Aeternum; quo adveniente evacuabitur, ut dicunt, Evangelium Christi, ut parati sumus ostendere in illo Evangelio maledicto." *DP*, 38.

26 Denifle, "Evangelium aeternum," 99.

27 *DP*, 18, 38, 39.

28 "Secundum signum est, quod illa doctrina, quae praedicabitur tempore Antichristi, videlicet, Evangelium Aeternum, Parisius...iam publice posita fuit ad explicandum anno Domini 1254." *DP*, 38. Brown's *Appendix ad fasciculum rerum,* II:27 contains the date 1255.

Glorieux posits its publication in March;[29] Dufeil places it somewhere between 1 March and Palm Sunday (9 April).[30] As William had prepared the text throughout 1255 and early 1256 but published it before the New Year actually began in Paris, one would expect to find a date of 1255.

However, William often refers to the year 1255 in his works–even in ones which can be demonstrated to have been written in 1256. In his sermon for Saints James and Philip (*Qui amat periculum*) he claims that the dangers of the Last Times had begun to manifest themselves fifty-five years ago.[31] In his Pentecost sermon *Si quis diligit me*, he states that the followers of Joachim has spent the last fifty-five years composing the *Eternal Gospel*[32] Furthermore, when discussing the *Eternal Gospel*, William repeatedly states that its adherents presume that their gospel will supersede that of Christ in five years; this assertion occurs in his sermons *Qui amat periculum* and *Si quis diligit me.*[33] These references would naturally lead one to believe that William was writing in 1255; but both external and internal evidence, as well as William's own admission, serve to prove that these sermons were in fact preached in 1256.

The ecclesiastical tribunal delegated to investigate the *Introductorius*, the Anagni Commission, published its condemnation of it in 1255; Pope Alexander IV notified the bishop of Paris of its censure in October of the same year.[34] Although Alexander's letter does not mention any of the specific errors of the work, the report of the cardinals at Anagni is quite detailed in its description of Gerard's heterodox statements. Amongst other errors, the Commission denounced as heretical Gerard's claims that the spirit of life had left the two testaments in 1200 so that the Eternal Gospel could be written,[35] that Christ's Gospel will come to an end in five years,[36] and that the sacraments will only remain valid until 1260.[37]

29 *Répertoire des maîtres en théologie*, I:344; "Le «*Contra impugnantes*» de S. Thomas," I:73; "Le Conflit de 1252-1257," 369.

30 *Guillaume de Saint-Amour*, 214.

31 "Nec sunt ista pericula huius libri penitus nova, immo sunt quinquaginta quinque anni, quod primo fuerant incohata." *QAP*, *infra*, n. 20.

32 "Quinto modo non servatur sermo Domini ab illo, qui totaliter legem Dei destruit et annihilat, sicut destruitur per illum maledictum librum Ioachim, in quo faciendo multi laboraverunt. Unde quinquaginta quinque anni elapsi sunt quod inceptus fuit." *SQD*, *infra*, n. 18.

33 "...quod tantum per quinque annos adhuc evangelium Christi praedicabitur." *QAP*, *infra*, n. 20; "...quod regnum Dei adhuc non durabit nisi usque ad quinque annos..." *SQD*, *infra*, n. 18; "...quod deficient sacramenta ecclesiae infra quinquennium" *SQD*, *infra*, n. 18; "...quod evangelium Christi deficiet infra quinquennium..." *SQD*, *infra*, n. 18.

34 *Chart.* I, No. 257, 297.

35 Denifle, "Evangelium aeternum," 99.

36 Denifle, "Evangelium aeternum," 112.

37 Denifle, "Evangelium aeternum," 136.

William's frequent references to the year 1255 and his usage of the motif that the New Testament will end in five years were more than likely direct references to the Anagni Commission's conclusions. Without regard to the year in which he was actually writing, William could have deliberately used the year 1255 and the "five-year" phrase to link his opponents with the purported arrival of a third age in 1260. As this belief had been condemned by a papal committee, William would therefore be identifying his adversaries with a doctrine that had been censured at the highest ecclesiastical level. Indeed, like many of his contemporaries, William intentionally associated the *Eternal Gospel* with not only the Franciscans, but also the Dominicans.[38] Thus, the five-year *topos* cited throughout William's sermons probably is not in fact a valid criterion for dating, but rather a conscious attempt by William to recycle the phraseology of a papally sponsored commission to cast further suspicion upon both mendicant orders.

Marrone's external evidence for a 1255 dating of *De periculis* comes from the University's letter of protest *Radix amaritudinis* (2 October 1255). In this letter, the University objected to Pope Alexander's bull *Quasi lignum vite* and related the consequences it had had on the University. In so doing, the masters reiterated the events of the late summer and early fall at Paris. In particular, they explain how the Dominicans had sought to stir up trouble by convincing a papal chaplain named Gregory of their cause. Gregory, while present in Paris, was persuaded by the Dominicans that it was the activities of William that had caused the academic conflict at Paris. Gregory then accused him, in front of the bishop and the king, of having composed a *libellum* which maligned the pope; Gregory further claimed that William had recited passages from this work before university congregations frequently. Bishop Reginald next summoned William to appear before him; William then absolved himself from all suspicion in the presence of four thousand students and thus restored his honor.[39]

If the *libellus* in question did indeed refer to *De periculis*, then the work, or at least portions of it, can be assured of a date before October 1255.[40]

38 As McKeon has noted, this effort can be seen especially in *QAP*, which continually emphasizes the word *praedicator*. "Status of the University," 661, n. 51. Similar statements can be found throughout his sermons, in chapters 9, 10, 12 and 14 of *DP*, and *Resp.*, 340, 350.

39 *Chart.* I, No. 256, 294.

40 This *libellus* has never been identified. Leff, following the editors of the *Chartularium*, suspects that it may be *De periculis*. *Chart.*, I, No. 256, 296, n. 6; *Paris and Oxford Universities*, 43. McKeon, in "Status of the University," 660, n. 51, argues that it was the *Liber de antichristo*, a work which William did not write until after 1260. On the dating of the *Liber de antichristo*, see A.G. Traver, "The *Liber de antichristo* and the Failure of Joachite Expectations," *Florensia* 15 (2001): 87-98. The *libellus* was most likely an early draft of *De periculis*.

But as the point of the letter was to describe the effects of *Quasi lignum vite* upon the University throughout the summer and the fall of that year, there seems to be no reason to push its dating back to spring 1255.[41]

William himself later confessed to his judges at Anagni that he had not begun to publicize the dangers of the Last Times until after King Louis IX had intervened into the academic quarrel and obtained a peace agreement that reincorporated the friars into the University.[42] On 1 March 1256, a committee of French prelates selected by Louis IX established a temporary solution to the university problem in the agreement *Noverit universitas vestra.*[43] Although William's admission referred specifically to his preaching activities, it may provide a *terminus post quem* for the public circulation of *De periculis.* Other contemporary sources, the *Chronicon Normanniae* in particular, place the discussion of the 1 March accord before the public appearance of *De periculis.*[44]

It is therefore probably the case that William had been circulating sections of *De periculis* throughout late 1255 and early 1256 before the entire work was completed and published in March, before the beginning of the Gallican New Year. This would both account for how university assemblies were familiar with its material as early as fall 1255 and how William could claim to his tribunal that the dangers of the Last Times were not actually announced publicly until after the promulgation of *Noverit universitas vestra.*

De periculis novissimorum temporum

De periculis consists of a prologue and fourteen chapters of varying lengths; chapters one, three, four, five, six, seven, nine, ten, eleven, and thirteen are extremely brief. The bulk of William's arguments against the friars is found in chapters two, eight, and twelve; the final chapter contains a list of forty-one signs by which one can distinguish true preachers from false ones. The framework of the text consists almost entirely of biblical citations. When attempting to emphasize a point, William occasionally draws upon canon and civil law, a Church father or Pseudo-Dionysius, and even more rarely upon Boethius or Seneca; but the setting itself is primarily scriptural and almost exclusively apocalyptical.

41 Glorieux places the Gregory affair in August or September 1255. "Le Conflit de 1252-1257," 367. Dufeil places between July and September 1255. *Guillaume de Saint-Amour,* 168.

42 *Resp.,* 358-9.

43 *Chart.* I, No. 268, 304-5.

44 In *Recueil des historieens des Gaules et de la France* ed. M. Bouquet et al. (Paris: Imprimerie nationale, 1876), 23:215; also noted by Faral, *Resp.,* 362.

William begins the prologue of *De periculis* with a citation from the exilic liturgy of the prophet Isaiah. Hark, he quotes, how the valiant cry aloud for help and the angels of peace weep bitterly.[45] He then connects the Isaiah citation to the ordinary gloss on Ephesians 4:11 which identifies prophets as expositors of Scripture.[46] William laments that although an abundance of dangers currently threaten the Church, there is a dearth of prophets to forewarn the faithful.

Those who govern the Church need to be notified of the imminent perils. Even though ecclesiastical prelates have sufficient knowledge of Scripture, William fears that they have not as yet noticed the risk. If the parochial clergy are aware of the danger, why have they not announced it? And if the episcopacy, with whom William associates the angels of peace,[47] knew of the threat, they surely would have reported it.

William's suggestion as to who should warn the prelates provides the framework for the remainder of the work. He writes;

> Therefore we professors of the Christian faith studying at Paris have assumed the teaching of holy Scripture and have paid much attention to these matters. And we have noticed the dangers of the Last Times in Scripture now seem to threaten the entire Church. We want these dangers to be recalled to the minds of everyone.[48]

William has made a claim to prophecy for the *Sacra Facultas* based on the masters' capacity as exegetes; as modern-day prophets, the Parisian theologians should shoulder the burden of revealing these dangers. The idea that Parisian theological *magisterium* would provide an adequate body to inform Christendom that the biblical perils had arrived may in fact be evidence that *De periculis* was a collaborative effort of several theologians and not solely a product of William.[49] Following the recommendation that the Parisian theologians recount the perils threatening the Church, William strings together a list of citations from the Pauline epistles to

45 Is. 33:7.

46 *ord.* in Eph. 4:11 in *Ed pr.* 4:375A. The source of the gloss is Amb., *Comm. in Epist. ad Ephes.* in *PL* 17:409.

47 *DP*, 17.

48 "Nos igitur Christianae fidei professores...Parisius studentes, qui ex assumpto gymnasio Scripturas sacras...etiam frequentius intuemur, attendentes in illis literis pericula novissimorum temporum...toti Ecclesiae quasi iam de prope imminere, ad cunctorum memoriam illa duximus revocanda." *DP*, 18.

49 Further proof that it may have been a group enterprise can be found in William's *Responsiones*. He writes: "...ego, una cum aliis magistris et baccalariis theologiae et magistris decretorum, collegi auctoritates praedictas et per multas collationes ego et alii praedicti in volumen unum sub certis rubricis illas redegimus." *Resp.*, 359-60.

Timothy as scriptural support for the dangers of the Last Times.[50] These dangers to which William constantly alludes portend the time of troubles which will foreshadow the Antichrist's arrival.

After the pericopes from Timothy, William describes the ways in which he will explain these dangers; these correspond to the chapter divisions of the text. Following this explanation, he exhorts those who read the work and do not agree with his argumentation not to dismiss it by means of subtle philosophical disputation. William is prepared both to refute all objections to the work and to demonstrate the veracity of these dangers. But he refuses to defend these imminent dangers through disputations or philosophical argumentation. Instead, he states that a Church council ought to be the appropriate forum in which these perils are addressed.[51]

After his recommendation for a council, William commences the first chapter by arguing that many great dangers will soon threaten the Church. Chapter one employs three New Testament citations to prove that there is a genuine threat looming within the Church. William quotes the pericope II Timothy 3 at length to show that the Apostle had warned of dissension within the Church while I John 2:18 and II Thessalonians 2:7 foretell the appearance of the Antichrist.[52]

In chapter two, William explains the theological principles which underlie *De periculis*; this chapter can be divided into roughly three sections. In the first part, William glosses the pericope II Tim. 3:2-4 *in extenso* to describe the types of men through whom these dangers will appear. His exegesis reveals a detailed word by word analysis of the eighteen sins mentioned by Paul to describe the heralds of the Antichrist.[53] They will be lovers both of themselves (*seipsos amantes*) and of money, arrogant, boastful, and blasphemous; they will have no respect for their parents, no gratitude, no piety, and no natural affection. They will be implacable in their hatreds, scandal-mongers, intemperate and fierce, strangers to all goodness, traitors, adventurers, blind and swollen with self-importance. They are *penetrantes domos*; they creep into private homes and probe the consciences of the faithful to expose their secrets.[54]

The second section of chapter two concerns the authority to administer pastoral duties within a set ecclesiastical jurisdiction. In it, he sets forth the ecclesiological construct of two *ordines*. William notes that the Apostle Matthew had predicted the appearance of false prophets.[55] These prophets

[50] II Tim. 3:1, I Tim. 4:1 and II Tim. 4:1; *DP*, 18.

[51] *DP*, 19-20.

[52] *DP*, 21-2.

[53] II Tim. 3:2-4; *DP*, 22. In fact, William relies so heavily upon II Tim. 3, that Thouzellier has called *De periculis* merely a commentary on it. "La Place du *De periculis*," 75.

[54] II Tim 3:6; *DP*, 22.

[55] Matt. 24:11; *DP*, 24.

will spread their message by preaching. But these *Pseudo-Praedicatores*, William explains, are those who preach although they have not been sent (*missi*). Conjoined to this phrase is a citation from Paul's epistle to the Romans "How can they preach unless they have been sent?"[56] William then elaborates upon the implications of the term *missi.* He explains;

> But they are not sent unless they have been rightly chosen by the Church. Similarly, they are not called to God unless they have been rightly chosen.[57]

William quotes extensively from the two canons *In Novo Testamento* and *Corepiscopi*, as well as Bede's gloss on Luke 10, all of which provide the exegetical and canonical support for his two ecclesiological orders.[58]

However, William remarks that one could object to this model by claiming that it does not include archdeacons or vicars or anyone who exercises the care of souls in the place of another. To this criticism, William cites the example of the *opitulationes* mentioned in I Corinthians 12:28.[59] Titus, as an *opitulator*, could perform the *cura animarum* since he had been commissioned by an Apostle. Anyone appointed by a bishop or a parish priest, as a successor of the twelve or the seventy-two, can licitly act as a *opitulator* throughout a specific ecclesiastical district. But no one is permitted to administer the care of souls unless he is a bishop, a parish priest, an *opitulator*, or anyone else legitimately instituted by one of the two *ordines.*[60]

William then inserts a brief excursus on whether those who have either papal or episcopal authority to preach can licitly embark on their mission. In perhaps his strongest statement of papal authority, William writes that in one Church there can be only one rector; otherwise the Church would not be a bride, but rather a harlot.[61] Similarly, in one Church there can be only one head, lest the Church become a monster.[62] But even if the pope, as the rector of the Church, confers the power of preaching everywhere to

56 Rom. 10:15; *DP*, 24.

57 "Missi autem non sunt, nisi qui ab Ecclesia recte eliguntur; sicut nec a Deo vocantur, nisi qui recte eliguntur." *DP*, 24.

58 Beda, *Expo. in Luc.* in *CCSL* 120:313-4; D.21 c.2 *In novo*; D.68 c.5 *Corepiscopi.* Both of these canons stem from the False Decretals attributed to the anonymous ninth-century French canonist known as Pseudo-Isidore. *Decretales* ed. P. Hinschius (Leipzig, 1863), 79, 509-15. K. Schleyer, *Anfänge des Gallikanismus im 13. Jahrhundert* Historische Sudien 314 (Berlin, 1937) [rpt. Vaduz: Kraus, 1965], 5-6, first pointed out that many of the canons cited by William in Gratian's *Decretum* actually originated from the Pseudo-Isidorian Collection.

59 Bonaventure had cited the *opitulationes* to strengthen his position of *subauctoritas* in the *Replicatio.* William may well be responding to him here. *Opera,* V:149.

60 *DP*, 24.

61 C.21 q.2 c.4 *Sicut in unaquaque*; *DP*, 25.

62 *Extra.* 1.31.14 *Quoniam in plerisque*; *DP*, 25.

anyone, the preacher in question first ought to be invited. He notes that even bishops do not have the power to preach outside their diocese, unless they have been requested to do so.[63] After having cited an assortment of civil and ecclesiastical canons which concern proper areas of jurisdiction,[64] William quotes the scriptural passage II Corinthians 10:13;

> We will not attempt to boast beyond our proper sphere; and our sphere is determined by the limit God has laid down for us, which permitted us to come to you.[65]

Even the Apostle Paul, as an instrument of God, acknowledged that he had a prescribed area in which he could evangelize. A pope, by granting the right to preach outside of a set boundary, would therefore necessarily act contrary to the Apostle. William concludes this brief digression by quoting the canon *Sunt quidam* attributed to Urban I, which states what procedure should be followed if a pope attempted to contradict Apostles and Prophets by proposing pernicious laws.[66]

William then explains that the right of preaching *ubique* simply cannot be licitly bestowed upon anyone, since it would in effect create a universal bishop who could preach anywhere in any diocese even if not invited. Pope Gregory I had objected to the designation "universal";[67] moreover, canon law does not permit any patriarch to usurp the title "universal".[68] This universal bishop would exhaust the resources of the established diocesan and parochial clergy, since he would require unlimited maintenance. Furthermore, he would burden the laity by increasing their proportion of alms and offerings.[69] Since the creation of a universal episcopacy has neither canonical nor scriptural basis, William maligns it as a dangerous innovation which would certainly undermine the structure of the Church. There is therefore no precedent and thus no basis for a pope to bestow a license to preach everywhere.

63 C.9 q.2 c.9 *Non invitati*; *DP*, 25.

64 *Extra.* 1.8.5 *Ex tuarum tenore* states that an archbishop cannot use his pallium outside of his province; *Digest* 43.8.2(16) *Si quis a principe* notes that even when a prince has given permission for someone to construct an edifice, it is not to be understood as a *fiat*, lest the edifice is found to be an inconvenience for anyone (and by extension, the same holds true for a papal *licentia praedicandi ubique*); *Codex* 8.4.6 *Meminerint cuncti*; *Extra.* 5.1.24 *Qualiter et quando* support the Digest citation by forbidding that injustices be created out of new laws and C.25 q.2 c.10 *Quod vero dicitis* prohibits the implementation of canonical laws which will infringe upon ecclesiastical rights. *DP*, 25.

65 "Nos autem non in immensum gloriabimur, sed secundum mensuram regulae, qua mensus est nobis Deus, mensuram pertinendi usque ad vos." II Cor. 10:13; *DP*, 26.

66 C.25 q.1 c.6 *Sunt quidam*; *QDM*, *infra*, n. 129; *DP*, 25-6.

67 D.99 c.5 *Ecce*; *DP*, 26.

68 D.99 c.4 *Nullus*; *DP*, 26.

69 *Extra.* 1.21.15; *DP*, 26.

In the third section of chapter two, William analyzes the types of men who can canonically perform the *cura animarum*. He inaugurates this section with a lengthy commentary on Pseudo-Dionysius' *Ecclesiastical Hierarchy*. The Church structure, as Pseudo-Dionysius has described, is a terrestrial imitation of the established order in Heaven. Within the ecclesiastical hierarchy, there exist two tripartite orders: the order of the perfect (*ordo perficientium*), and its corresponding three grades of bishops, priests, and deacons, and the order of those becoming perfect (*ordo perficiendorum*), consisting of monks, the laity, and catechumens. Pseudo-Dionysius has assigned each grade a specific function. In the *ordo perficientium*, deacons purify, priests illuminate and purify, and bishops consecrate.[70] In the *ordo perficiendorum*, catechumens are brought to purification by deacons, the laity are further purified and begin illumination by priests, and monks are completely purified and commence sacred contemplative activities with the assistance of bishops.[71]

As an earthly reproduction of an immutable and sacred order, no lower order can exercise a higher function. Therefore monks, as members of the lower order, cannot assume the duties of the *cura animarum*. This prohibition has been condoned and reiterated repeatedly in canon law.[72] But what should happen, William wonders, if someone should try to alter this arrangement? He then warns of the dire consequences such an action would have upon the Church, asserting that it is not permitted for any mortal to transform a divinely inspired structure. To emphasize this point, William concludes this section by quoting once again Pope Urban's canon, *Sunt quidam*.[73]

William thus concludes that there are only two orders mentioned in Scripture empowered to administer the care of souls: priests and bishops. In Pseudo-Dionysius' description of the ecclesiastical hierarchy, these two orders are subsumed, along with deacons, in the *ordo perficientium*. If a member of a lower order attempted to fulfill a role entrusted to the *ordo perficientium*, he would overturn this structure. He would therefore be an intruder, devoid of scriptural mandate and *non missus*. In William's words, such a usurper would be *pseudo* and should necessarily be extirpated. And it is through these *Pseudo-Praedicatores* that the dangers of the Last Times will appear.

Chapters three and four of *De periculis* describe both how people will be persuaded by the arguments of the *Pseudo-Praedicatores* and how they will

70 Pseudo-Dionysius, *The Ecclesiastical Hierarchy* in *Pseudo-Dionysius: The Complete Works The Classics of Western Spirituality* trans. C. Luibheid (Mahwah, N.J: Paulist Press, 1987), 5.3, 235-6.

71 *Ecc. Hier.*, 6.1-3, 243-5.

72 C.16 q.1 c.19 *Adicimus*; C.25 q.1 c.3, *Que ad perpetuam*. *DP*, 27.

73 C.25 q.1 c.6 *Sunt quidam*; *DP*, 27.

unquestionably accept them as new apostles. Through their appearance of piety and their simulated religion, they will win many adherents. But William adds that even as Gregory the Great had warned, no one can cause more harm in the Church of God than those who perversely wear the name and the order of sanctity.[74] And as the Egyptian magicians Jannes and Mambres had resisted Moses, so too will these false preachers resist the truth.[75] They will subvert the faithful from obeying the advice of prelates and will lead them into errors against the faith. The laity risks eternal damnation simply by listening to them. Once these preachers have started to evangelize, brothers will betray brothers, fathers will forsake their children, children will turn against their parents, and send them to their death.[76]

In chapter five, William notes that although these false preachers do not have the care of souls licitly committed to them, they still hear the confessions of the faithful. However, he argues, that a pastor can only know the souls and acts of his parishioners if they confess to him at least once a year. In a reaffirmation of canon twenty-one of the Council of Lateran IV, William states that the laity must confess annually to their parish priest or to someone entrusted to the *cura animarum* by him.[77] Those who have not received this permission and continue to hear confessions are *penetrantes domos*, seducers, and thieves. And like the serpent in the Garden, these seducers will lead women into sin and through them their husbands.[78] Chapter six adds that whoever does not see the manifestation of these dangers and thus does nothing to resist them, will undoubtedly perish in them—the future theme of his sermon *Qui amat periculum.*[79]

Chapter seven identifies four ways in which these false preachers can be detected. Since they are thieves and robbers,[80] they will attempt to enter the congregations of the faithful by preaching and teaching and expropriate the powers of prelates for themselves. Although they are not sent, they will infiltrate the homes of the laity and counsel them to damnation with their lethal doctrine.[81] They will appear dressed as sheep while underneath they are savage wolves. They will profess a desire to teach spiritual things by means of good example when interiorly they crave only the carnal. Moreover, these Preachers will be corrupted in their

74 Greg., *Reg. Past.* in *SC* 381, I.234; *DP*, 29. This passage was also cited in the University's letter of protest *Radix amaritudinis. Chart.* I, No. 256, 295.

75 *cf.* Ex. 7:11, 9:11; II Tim. 3:8; *int.* in II Tim. 3:8 in *Ed. pr.* 4:416A; *DP*, 30.

76 Matt. 10:21; *DP*, 31.

77 *Extra.* 5.38.12. *Omnis*; *DP*, 33.

78 *ord.* in II Tim. 3:6 in *Ed. pr.* 4:416A; Amb., *Comm. in Epist. ad Thess. PL* 17:521A; *DP*, 32-3.

79 Eccli. 3:27 *DP*, 35.

80 Ioan. 10:1; *DP*, 35.

81 Rom. 10:15; Matt. 7:15; Ier. 23:15; *DP*, 36.

faith; they have deserted Christ and are to be counted amongst the ranks of the reprobate.[82]

William reveals his historiographical methodology in chapter eight. His approach is extremely conservative, based largely on the Augustinian conception of the world-week as set forth in book twenty-two of *De civitate Dei* and transmitted to the Middle Ages through the standard reference manuals of Isidore of Seville and Bede.[83] Following Augustine, Christ became incarnate during the sixth age, corresponding to the sixth day of creation when God made man. But even as Augustine had noted, this age cannot, as were four of the previous five ages, be measured by the passing of generations.[84] After the passing of the last earthly age before the Last Judgment, the seventh age will appear, *quae est quiescentium*, and God will rest as he did on the seventh day. This age will be brought to a close by the second coming of Christ.

However, William adds, as we are already in the Last Age, and as this age has lasted longer than any of the other ones, it seems that we must therefore be approaching the end of the world. William proposes that it is currently the eleventh hour of the last age;[85] the advent of the Antichrist must be rapidly advancing. Following this introduction, William proffers a list of eight signs which confirm that the perils of the Last Age are at hand.

First, there are those who have attempted to transform the Gospel of Christ into a new gospel which they claim is more perfect. To this end, they have labored for the past fifty-five years, and have succeeded with the coming of the second sign, the publication of the *Introductorius* in Paris.

The writing on the wall of *Mane*, *Tekel*, and *Phares* at the royal palace in Babylon during Belshazzar's banquet bear witness to the arrival of the third sign. As these three words are written in Scripture, so too are they recorded in the *Eternal Gospel*.[86] *Mane*, as Daniel had translated it, indicated that God had numbered the years of Belshazzar's kingdom and had brought them to an end. William extends this conclusion to the *Eternal Gospel*; the days of Christ's Gospel have been numbered and will end, as Gerard had believed, in 1260.[87]

Daniel interpreted the second word, *Tekel*, to explain that Belshazzar had been weighed in the scales and found to be wanting. So too this

82 *int.* in II Tim. 3:8 in *Ed. pr.* 4:416A; *DP*, 37.

83 Aug., *De civitate Dei* in *CCSL* 48:865; Isidore, *Etymologiarum* edd. J.O. Reta et M.-A. M. Casquero (Madrid: Biblioteca de autores cristianos, 1982), V:550-64; Beda, *De temp. rat.* in *CCSL* 123B:310-2.

84 *De civ. Dei*, in *CCSL* 48:865

85 Matt. 20:6; *DP*, 38.

86 These words do not appear in the University's excerpts of the *Introductorius*; but they can be found in the Anagni Commission's examination and condemnation of it. Denifle, "Evangelium aeternum," 100.

87 Dan. 5:6; *DP*, 39.

message applies to the New Testament; Christ's message has been found to have less perfection and honor than the *Eternal Gospel*.[88]

Finally, the third word, *Phares*, denoted that Belshazzar's kingdom had been divided and handed over to the Medes and Persians. This prophecy holds particularly true for the Church, which is now divided between adherents of Christ's message and proponents of the *Eternal Gospel*.[89] Although William never resolves to which group the Church would eventually be given, using the Daniel citation as a guide to the future, the proponents of the *Eternal Gospel* would presumably emerge victorious.

As the end of the world approaches, there will appear in the Church some who are holier than others; yet they insult Christ by their actions. Although some will attempt to correct these *sanctiores*, their excessive sanctity will win them so many disciples that their adversaries will face persecution and death simply because of their fraternal correction. But these *sanctiores* will still be chastized for their presumption and false sanctity; nevertheless, many will fall from their faith and will turn to hate and betray each another.[90]

The sixth sign proclaims that preachers will arise in the Church who will commend themselves to many contrary to the Apostle's admonition.[91] They seek glory through their sermons and, with their appearance of sanctity, they will seduce many and lead them away from the counsel of prelates. The connection between false preachers who commend themselves and the numerous letters of papal recommendations which the mendicants had received would undoubtedly not have been lost on contemporaries.[92]

The seventh sign again warns of the *zelatores* who will appear in the Church who profess great love for Christ. Yet these *zelatores* have denounced Christ's Gospel and replaced it with the one they call eternal. Christian faith, as they profess, is absorbed into this new Gospel; but through it the charity of many will grow cold.[93]

The eighth sign must have been particularly relevant for William and his followers. In his analysis of it, he claims that some in the Church will publicize the appearance of the preceding signs. Since ecclesiastical prelates have not as yet noticed them and have instead lain asleep,[94] it is the duty of expositors of Scripture to announce these dangers to the

88 Dan. 5:27; *DP*, 39.

89 Dan. 5:28; *DP*, 39.

90 Matt. 24:9-10; *DP*, 40.

91 II Cor. 10:12; *DP*, 40.

92 Between 1215 and 1250, the papacy directed 580 bulls to the friars; 347 of these were from Innocent IV alone. M.-M. Dufeil, "Le roi Louis dans la querelle des mendiants et séculiers," *Septième centenaire de la mort de Saint Louis* (Paris: Les Belles Letters, 1976), 282.

93 Matt. 24:12; *int.* in Matt. 24:12 in *Ed. pr.* 4:73B; *DP*, 40.

94 Contrary to Paul's warnings in I Thess. 5:6 and I Cor. 15:34; *DP*, 41.

Church hierarchy. William and his associates thus represent the eighth sign.

As the eighth sign has already appeared, it is therefore not surprising that he argues that the previous seven signs have also started to manifest themselves. One can no longer remain at ease; we must begin to speculate and inquire into the manner in which these dangers will unfold. Once this process has begun, we can then determine how these perils can best be repelled.

The following two chapters explain how prelates should announce and counter the mentioned dangers. Following established canonical procedure, bishops ought to search out their dioceses to investigate, to capture, and to extirpate these false preachers.[95] In case of necessity, they may even request the assistance of the secular arm.[96] All bishops must preach these dangers publicly and vigorously purge their dioceses of all error. If prelates are negligent in this respect they will incur punishment both for themselves and their flocks.[97] Chapter eleven further notes that although these dangers had been prophesied, they can still be defeated. William again cites Moses' victory over the Egyptian magicians for justification.

Chapter twelve begins by recounting six ways in which prelates can ward off the dangers of the Last Times. But the remainder of the chapter consists of a conglomeration of theological arguments which William had previously raised in his disputed questions of fall 1255. Although William mentions the same issues and the same *auctoritates* in both his disputed questions and *De periculis*, the latter work provides evidence of a later dating because of the maturer development of his specific positions on certain points.

In the first part of chapter twelve, William asserts that prelates are to determine who have been prophesied as *penetrantes domos*. Once this has been established, they can transmit this information to the laity so that they may avoid them. He then entreats prelates to avoid these harbingers of evil, to prohibit them from teaching and from preaching, to convince their followers to desert them, and to dissuade potential adherents from joining them.[98]

This second section is arranged as a series of theological *quaestiones* which are loosely joined to specific objections (*sed dicet quis*) and responses (*respondemus*). William first discusses *Pseudo-Praedicatores* in general and

95 In *Extra.* 5.7.15 *Excommunicamus itaque* § 2 *Adicimus*, bishops are urged to purge their dioceses of heretics; if they fail to comply, they risk deposition and removal. *DP*, 43.

96 *Extra.* 1.31.1 *Perniciosa* notes that bishops are to try and to punish crimes committed in their dioceses. If there is a need, they can invoke the secular arm. *DP*, 43.

97 *DP*, 44.

98 *DP*, 46.

explains why they should be avoided. He claims that they are dissenters who foment schism and live contrary to apostolic warrant. But if prelates want them to preach in their dioceses, they must be prepared to accept the two most suspect aspects of their ministry: their desire to live from the Gospel and their excessive curiosity about the affairs of others.[99]

These Preachers have expressed their desire to live from the Gospel by sustaining themselves off the alms and offerings of the laity. But, as William notes, as a pseudo order lacking all biblical validity, these Preachers simply cannot licitly live from the Gospel, since they have no claim to apostolic power. And even as Paul had written, the Apostles refrained from begging for sustenance during their ministry lest they burden their converts.[100]

These Preachers' curiosity about the affairs of others has inextricably bound them to secular affairs. As gossiping busy-bodies, they wander to and fro paying too much attention to worldly concerns.[101]

William then raises a criticism based on Bonaventure's two disputed questions of fall 1255: if one were to renounce all of one's possessions for Christ and accept voluntary mendicancy, would this not be a work of Christian perfection?[102] He responds to this argument by explaining that to relinquish all for Christ and then to follow him means to imitate him by performing good works, but not by begging.

The renunciation of all possessions for Christ to attain a perfect life can be achieved either by performing manual labor[103] or by entering a monastery.[104] In both of these ways one may still obtain the necessities of life without incurring the risks associated with begging. Furthermore, canon law has extolled the life of prelates who have relinquished all of their possessions and yet administered the Church's temporal wealth.[105] They are, in fact, following a manner of life which the Lord prescribed, since he himself carried a purse. The apostolic purse symbolizes the temporal goods of the Church, from which the Apostles could support the needy and sustain themselves during their ministry.

After a lengthy recitation of scriptural citations to demonstrate that the Apostles had eschewed begging, William argues that they had never

[99] I Cor. 9:14; II Thess. 3:7; *DP*, 47.

[100] I Thess. 2:5-7; *DP*, 48.

[101] William cites the example of II Tim. 2:4; "Nemo militans Deo implicat se saecularibus negotiis." *DP*, 48.

[102] *DP*, 49.

[103] *ord.* in *Ed. pr.* 4:187A; Beda, *Expo. in Luc.* in *CCSL* 120:254-5; *DP*, 50.

[104] Act. 4:32-4. C.12 q.1 c.16 *Videntes*; *DQE*, 328; *DP*, 50. However, in *DQE*, William acknowledges his debt to an earlier secular theologian, William of Auxerre, for this response. *Summa aurea* lib. 3, tract. 24, c.4, 447-8.

[105] C.12 q.1 c.16 *Videntes*.

actively solicited offerings.[106] His next line of attack attempts to prove that Christ had never begged. He repeats many of the examples which Bonaventure had used in *De mendicitate* concerning his supplication to the Samaritan woman for water and his request to Zaccheus for a place to sleep.[107] He had furthermore not begged for bread himself, but had sent the Apostles into town to buy food.

Christ was a good shepherd sent to feed and to protect his sheep, not to take away from them.[108] However, Paul wrote to Timothy that the farmer who gives his labor has first claim on the crop.[109] The ordinary gloss qualifies this statement by asserting that Timothy could have received offerings for his ministry, but he would have taken only what was necessary and then distributed the rest amongst the faithful.[110] Such an action cannot be construed as begging. Similarly, although Christ could have begged for assistance in his ministry, he chose not to lest he both oppress the faithful and convey the impression that he was accepting money for spiritual services. Therefore whoever asserts that Christ begged, claims by extension that he was not a pastor that he was not sent by the Father, nor was he the Messiah promised in the Law nor the son of God. Such an affirmation, as William notes, would certainly destroy the foundation of the Christian faith. Thus one who upholds Christ's mendicancy is not only a heretic, but also a heresiarch.[111]

Mendicancy for the able-bodied has been prohibited in Scripture[112] and in both canon[113] and civil law.[114] In his harshest denunciation of voluntary mendicancy, William professes that if an able-bodied person begs for alms he has committed a sacrilege.[115]

But should this prohibition hold true for religious orders, especially for those whom the Church has lawfully permitted to beg? The ban must stay in force for everyone, especially those religious orders who have received canonical sanction to beg, since it contradicts the Apostles and papal decree.[116] To uphold the reverse would simply mean to state that the Church had erred. And even if the Church had granted this privilege,

[106] *DP*, 50-1.

[107] *DP*, 52; *QDM, infra*, nn. 33, 39.

[108] Ioan. 10:11; *DP*, 51.

[109] II Tim. 2:6; *DP*, 51; *DQE*, 331k; *QDM, infra*, n. 22.

[110] *ord.* in II Tim. 2:6 in *Ed. pr.* 4:414A; Amb., *Comm. in Epist. ad Tim.* in *PL* 17:816C.

[111] "...non tantum haereticus, sed etiam haeresiarcha." *DP*, 52.

[112] I Tim. 5:9; I Thess 4:11; Matt. 5:42.

[113] C.31 q.1 c.10 *Quomodo virginibus*; D.82 c.1 *Episcopus pauperibus*; C.16 q.1 c.68 *Quoniam quicquid.*

[114] *Codex* 11.26(25).1 *De mendicantibus validis.*

[115] *DP*, 52.

[116] William cites *Extra.* 5.3.8 *Non satis* for justification. This canon notes that anyone who receives money for a sacrament has committed simony.

once its error had been revealed, it would be revoked.[117] One cannot profess that the complete renunciation of possessions, both individual and communal, is a higher state of perfection than simple individual renunciation. The Church itself maintains the communal use of wealth and this is in no way a diminution of its perfection. Those who renounce all possessions and subsequently beg for sustenance are imposters and ought to be expelled from the Church.[118]

In chapter thirteen, William uses the biblical interlinear gloss as his guide to determine how and where these *Pseudo-Praedicatores* can be found. Through the process of elimination, he first establishes that these Preachers are neither Barbarians, Gentiles, nor Jews. Since, according to Timothy, they will appear with the pretense of piety, they must therefore be Christians.[119] But amongst Christians, there are those who are covertly evil and openly malevolent. To which group do these Preachers belong? The interlinear glosses on Matt. 7:15 and II Cor. 6:6 answer his question. They walk in humility with false religion and feign love in order to deceive.[120] Therefore they must appear as good Christians, while concealing their true objectives.

Both amongst the openly good and the covertly evil one can find those who devote all their time to studies. As Paul had forewarned, the Antichrist's heralds will appear amongst those who are always learning. However, Paul adds that these *semper discentes* will never attain the knowledge of truth.[121] These seducers are therefore those who always study yet never learn the truth.

Amongst the learned, there are those who are renowned for their good counsel. William then employs the example of the counselor Achitophel, who once adhered to David, but later advised his rebellious son Absalom.[122] Similarly, those who once followed Christ will soon depart from him.

Amongst those who study, there are some who are obliged to follow only the Lord's precepts; others follow both precepts and counsels. This latter group includes those who profess the highest degrees of humility, poverty, and chastity; they will seem to all to be members of the elect. But as Gregory had recognized, perils within the Church will come from those who appear to be the elect.[123] Those who have claimed to have mastered

[117] C.35 q.9 c.6 *Sententiam* states that a decision by the Holy See can be commuted; C.35 q.9 c.8(9) *Grave* records that the Apostolic See can retract previously made judgements.

[118] *DP*, 53.

[119] II Tim 3:5; *DP*, 54.

[120] *int.* in Matt. 7:15 in *Ed. pr.* 4:30B; *int.* in II Cor. 6:6 in *Ed. pr.* 4:345A; *DP*, 54.

[121] II Tim. 3:7; *ord.* in *Ed. pr.* in 4:416A; Aug., *Tract. in Ioan.* in *CCSL* 36:486; *DP*, 54.

[122] II Reg. 16-7; *DP*, 55.

[123] Gregory, *Mor.* in *CCSL* 143A:1038; *DP*, 55.

both the Lord's precepts and counsels will thus attempt to usurp the power of the Church for themselves and send the faithful into error.

The final chapter of *De periculis* contains a list of forty-one signs by which true Apostles can be identified from false ones.[124] All of these signs have scriptural backing; but William bolsters some of them with canonical citations. Most of them repeat positions raised earlier in the text; true Apostles are not *penetrantes domos,* they do not commend themselves and they do not preach unless they are sent.[125] Many of these signs raise specific objections to the mendicants' *modus vivendi*–true Apostles did not beg[126] but they labored with their hands[127]–while others focus on their teaching activities at Paris.[128] William proceeds to make a contrast between the original apostles and these new *Pseudo-Praedicatores.* He claims that the former were poorly received at the first coming, and even when they had attained great progress in the Church, they did not boast. This differs markedly from the imposters who are always well-received by recommendations, some of which they have actively sought,[129] and who exult in their converts.[130]

Three signs identify what William has in mind for the future of the mendicant orders. In sign twenty-three he writes that true Apostles did not evangelize those who already had Apostles.[131] He repeats this theme in sign thirty-six; true Apostles did not preach to those who had already been converted.[132] In sign thirty-seven, he claims that true Apostles, when they were sent, did not embark as ambassadors to their own country, but to other ones.[133] Yet the pseudo-prophets preach in areas which have already been converted and have their own apostles in the form of bishops and priests. They are, William recommends, to be directed to the Jews, heretics, and to infidel countries such as Egypt, Babylonia, and other countries which observe the law of Mohammed.[134] But they are in no way to be sent to Christian lands since they have no apostolic authority.

[124] But William himself qualified the accuracy of some of the signs; "Signa plurima, quaedam infallibilia, quaedam vero probabilia, per quae poterunt praedicti homines cognosci." *DP,* 57.

[125] Signs 1, 4, 6, *DP,* 57-9.

[126] Signs 14, 15, 26, *DP,* 62, 66-7.

[127] Sign 9, *DP,* 60.

[128] Such as sign 39, "Veri Apostoli non intendunt, nec innituntur rationibus logicis, aut philosophicis." *DP,* 71.

[129] Sign 5, *DP,* 58.

[130] Sign 24, *DP,* 62.

[131] *DP,* 65.

[132] *DP,* 69-70.

[133] *DP,* 70.

[134] "Id est, ad Iudeos, Hereticos et illos Gentiles, qui aliquando fuerunt Christiani, sicut Aegyptii, Babylonii, et omnes, qui tenent legem Mahometi." *DP,* 70.

He concludes *De periculis* by remarking that since sacred Scripture is infallible, and the Holy Spirit does not lie, these perils have already begun to manifest themselves. He once more exhorts prelates to investigate these dangers, but perhaps more importantly, he advises them to exercise their spiritual functions themselves.

WILLIAM'S SERMONS AND THE *RESPONSIONES*

WILLIAM'S SERMONS

William is traditionally credited with having delivered at least nine sermons, one at Mâcon and eight at Paris. The Mâcon sermon is no longer extant and only three from the Parisian cycle survive. Our knowledge of the material contained in William's lost sermons derives entirely from the *Responsiones.* The eight sermons William preached at Paris were for Palm Sunday,[1] Holy Thursday,[2] Saints James and Philip,[3] the fifth Sunday after Easter,[4] Ascension,[5] Pentecost,[6] the eighth Sunday after Pentecost,[7] and the tenth Sunday after Pentecost.[8] Of the Parisian sermons, only those for Saints James and Philip (*Qui amat periculum*), Pentecost (*Si quis diligit me*), and the tenth Sunday after Pentecost (*De pharisaeo et publicano*) survive.

Dating of the sermons

As with most of William's works, scholars have disputed the dates of his sermons. Dondaine, Dufeil, Faral, and Glorieux place all of the Parisian ones in 1256.[9] But McKeon has proposed a different system of dating; he claims that at least the sermon *Qui amat periculum* (Saints James and Philip), and probably all of William's extant sermons, were delivered in

1 *Resp.,* 347-8.

2 *Resp.,* 347, 351-2.

3 *Appendix ad fasciculum rerum,* II:48-54; *Matěje z Janova Mistra Pařížského,* III:315-32; *Opera,* 491-504; *Resp.,* 349-50.

4 *Resp.,* 350.

5 *Resp.,* 349-50.

6 S. Clasen "Die Kampfpredigten des Wilhelms von Saint-Amour gegen die Mendikanten Orden," *Kirchengeschichtliche Studien* (1941): 80-95; *Resp.,* 347-8.

7 *Resp.,* 353-4.

8 *Appendix ad fasciculum rerum,* II:43-7; *Opera,* 7-15.

9 Dondaine, int. to Thomas Aquinas, *Contra impugnantes* in *Opera,* 41A:9; M.-M. Dufeil, "Gulielmus de Sancto Amore, opera omnia 1252-1270," *Miscellanea Mediaevalia* 10 (1976):218-9; *Resp.,* 364, 371; Glorieux, "Le Conflit de 1252-1257," 368-70.

1255.[10] His argument is based primarily on William's knowledge of Gerard of Borgo San Donnino's *Introductorius* in *Qui amat periculum.* In this sermon, William states the following;

> We now have at Paris certain things concerning these errors, namely, that book which is called the Eternal Gospel; And we have seen *a good portion* of that book, and I have heard that, wherever it is, it contains as much or more than the whole Bible.[11]

McKeon inquires why William would claim to have seen *non modicam partem* of the *Introductorius* if he had actually seen more than a part of the work.[12] McKeon quoted the sermon as contained in Brown's *Appendix ad fasciculum rerum* which contains the reading "non modicam partem". As the appended edition illustrates, the text's original reading would have been "Et nos vidimus non nisi modicam partem illius libri" and probably indicates that William only had scant knowledge of the *Introductorius.*

McKeon constructs his new chronology for this sermon on the assumption that William's knowledge of Gerard's *Introductorius* increased and played a larger role in the secular theologian's polemic as time progressed. Thus *De periculis,* which according to McKeon was written later than *Qui amat periculum,* should reveal a greater familiarity with of the Franciscan's teachings.

McKeon also argues that *De periculis* relies upon the teachings of Joachim of Fiore much more frequently than *Qui amat periculum*; the latter only reveals a passing familiarity with Joachim's doctrines. Since *De periculis* devotes more attention to Joachim's teaching, it witnesses a more mature development in William's polemical thought and must, according to McKeon, follow *Qui amat periculum* in time. The sermon must therefore be placed in 1255 before the publication of *De periculis.*

However, it seems that William only ever had a very limited knowledge of the *Introductorius.* If one compares the extracts from Gerard's *Introductorius* quoted in *Qui amat periculum* and *De periculis,* it becomes readily apparent that not only are they very similar, but they also almost identical to the ones which appear in the list of errors the University

[10] McKeon, "Status of the University," 660, n. 51. Marrone, "Ecclesiology," 44, n. 30, follows McKeon's argument.

[11] "De istis novis periculis iam habemus quaedam Parisiis, scilicet librum illum qui vocatur Evangelium sempiternum. Et nos vidimus non modicam partem illius libri et audivi quod ubicumque sit, tantum vel plus contineat ille liber quam tota Biblia." *Appendix ad fasciculum,* II:51-2.

[12] "Et nos vidimus non nisi modicam partem illius libri, et audivi quod ubicumque ille liber sit, tantum vel plus continet quam tota Biblia!" *Cf. QAP, infra,* n. 20.

originally sent to Innocent IV.[13] In fact, there are only two references to Gerard's work contained in *De periculis* which are not found in *Qui amat periculum*–and both of them are also contained in the report of the Anagni Commission.[14] The fact that *Qui amat periculum* makes fewer references to the errors of the Eternal Gospel than *De periculis* rather indicates that the sermon was an abridged copy of certain portions of *De periculis* and thus written later than it.

McKeon's argument that Joachim's thought played a larger role in William's writings of 1256 than those of 1255 would certainly be difficult to prove since neither *Qui amat periculum* nor *De periculis* make any specific references to the abbot.[15] Furthermore, neither of these works reveals any dependence upon Joachim's particular style of exegesis. In *Qui amat periculum,* William quotes three passages from Revelations; but his analysis of these citations remains indebted to the standard tradition of Apocalypse commentaries. Through the interlinear and ordinary glosses, William cites Augustine, Primasius, and Bede directly, and Richard of St. Victor indirectly, but never Joachim.[16] *De periculis* cites Revelations more

[13] "...quod sacramentum ecclesiae nihil est..." *Chart.* I, No. 243, 275, Benz,"Exzerptsätze," 425, *QAP, infra,* n. 20; This phrase is not stated in *DP*, but it is certainly implied that the sacraments of the Church will be meaningless in new dispensation, *DP*, 38-9; "...quod evangelium Christi non verum evangelium," *Chart.* I, No. 243, 272-3, Benz, "Exzerptsätze," 417, *DP*, 38-9, *QAP, infra,* n. 20; "...quod ille liber sit evangelium Spiritus Sancti et dicitur esse evangelium eternum," *Chart.* I, No. 243, 273, Benz, "Exzerptsätze," 419, *DP*, 38-9, *QAP, infra,* n. 20; "...quod tantum per quinque (sex *Chart.*, Benz) annos adhuc evangelium Christi praedicabitur," *Chart.* I, No. 243, 272-3, Benz, "Exzerptsätze," 419, *DP*, 39, *QAP, infra,* n. 20; "...quod illi, per quos haec pericula venient, dabunt aliam legem vivendi et aliter disponent ecclesiam," *Chart.* I, No. 243, 275, Benz, "Exzerptsätze," 424, *DP*, 38-9, *QAP, infra,* n. 20.

[14] In *DP*, 39 he makes mention both of the writing on the wall at Babylon and of the sun/moon comparison between the Eternal Gospel and the New Testament. Denifle, "Evangelium aeternum," 100.

[15] In fact, he very rarely even mentions Joachim at all in any of his works of 1255-6. The statement "iuxta haeresiarche Ioachimi prophetias " in reference to the *Introductorius* appears in the University's dissolution decree, which is permeated with William's influence. *Chart.* I, No. 256, 296. In his responses to *QDM*, he accuses Bonaventure of following Joachim by suggesting that the Church would be renewed through new religious orders. *infra*, n. 129. In *SQD, infra*, n. 18, he refers to "illum maledictum librum Ioachim" and at his trial, he was accused of having preached the following statement in his Ascension sermon: "...quod liber Ioachim, qui continet multas haereses, non potest condemnari Romae, quia sunt ibi plures defensores qui defendunt eum." *Resp.*, 346-7.

[16] *QAP, infra*, n. 15 cites Apoc. 6:6 examining the first four seals. In this section, William follows Augustine, Ambrosius Autpertus, Primasius, and Richard of St. Victor closely. The red horse signifies the persecution of tyrants; the black horse represents heretics within the early Church, and the pale horse heralds the imminent persecution of hypocrites. In fact, William completely ignores Joachim's treatment of the fourth seal; the abbot treated it as the persecution of Saracens. Joachim of Fiore, *Expo. in Apoc.* (Venice, 1527),[rpt. Frankfurt: Minerva, 1964] 116r-v; Ambrosius Aut., *In Apoc.* in *CCCM* 27:277-82; Aug., *Enarr. in Ps.* in *CCSL* 38:70; Beda, *Expl. Apoc.* in *PL* 93:146-8; Prim., *Comm. in Apoc.* in *CCSL*

frequently than *Qui amat periculum*;[17] but none of the exegesis is indebted to Joachim.

McKeon also employs a secondary argument to place William's sermons in 1255. He asserts that the accusations brought against William in the *libellum* affair mentioned in *Radix amaritudinis* were in fact related to his preaching material.[18] This hypothesis would be impossible to substantiate, since William's role as an anti-mendicant polemicist would have already been recognized by contemporaries in the University's decrees against the friars from 1253-5 and in his role as the University's proctor in the legal proceedings against the friars at Rome. By summer 1255, William was already well known as the ringleader of the mendicants' opponents within the Faculty of Theology. Thus the Parisian friars' antipathy towards him would have existed whether his sermons were delivered in 1255 or 1256. Furthermore, the denunciation against William was based on the contents of a *libellum*, not William's sermons.[19]

McKeon also states that a later denunciation of William, made by the archbishop of Tours, Peter of Lamballe, to King Louis IX in 1256, was ultimately based on sermons William had preached.[20] This assertion can be supported in the *Responsiones*, where Peter is reported to have accused William of having preached many falsehoods.[21] The archbishop delivered his accusation before King Louis and Bishop Reginald in July 1256.[22] But following the standard chronology as established by Dondaine, Dufeil, Glorieux, and Faral, William would have already preached at least six and possibly seven sermons between January and July 1256, before the

92:94-7; Rich., *In Apoc.* in *PL* 196:765-8. William's closest model in this passage is Augustine who incidentally mentions only the persecutions and not the seals or the horses.

William once more repeats Bede and Primasius at *QAP*, *infra*, nn. 25 and 26 when he cites Apoc. 13:1 and 9:5. Prim., *CCSL* 92:147, 193-5; Beda, *PL* 93:158, 169. On the exegetical background on the opening of the seals, see R.K. Emmerson, *Antichrist in the Middle Ages* (Seattle: University of Washington Press, 1981), 64-6; R. Lerner, "Refreshment of the Saints: The Time After Antichrist as a Station for Earthly Progress in Medieval Thought," *Traditio* 32 (1976):116.

17 Apoc. 1:20 in *DP*, 17 follows Bede's *Explanatio* in *PL* 96:137B and Richard's *In Apocalypsin Ioannis* in *PL* 196:701C; Apoc. 2-3 in *DP*, 40, 42-3, 69 follows Prim., *CCSL* 92:24, Beda, *PL* 96:137-8, and Rich., *PL* 196:712-3; Apoc. 4:6 in *DP*, 64 follows Prim., *CCSL* 92:51, Beda, *PL* 96:144A, and Rich., *PL* 196:749-50; Apoc. 6:7-8 in *DP*, 29 follows Aug., *Enarr. in Ps.* in *CCSL* 38:70, Prim., in *CCSL* 92:94-7, Beda, *PL* 96:147C,D, and Rich., *PL* 196:765-8; Apoc. 20:7 *DP*, 23, 33 cites the interlinear gloss from Bede's *Explanatio*. *PL* 96:193C, *Ed. pr.* 4:575A.

18 *Chart.* I, No. 256, 294-5; McKeon, "Status of the University," 660, n. 51.

19 *Chart.* I, No. 256, 254.

20 McKeon, "Status of the University," 660, n. 51.

21 *Resp.*, 353-4.

22 Dufeil, *Guillaume de Saint-Amour*, 290-1; Glorieux, "Le Conflit de 1252-1257," 370. Faral in *Resp.*, 372-3, suggests early July.

archbishop's tirade against him. These are his Mâcon sermon[23] and those for Palm Sunday,[24] Holy Thursday,[25] the feast of Saints Philip and James,[26] the fifth Sunday after Easter,[27] Ascension,[28] and Pentecost.[29] The preaching material to which Peter reacted negatively is not specified, thus it cannot be attributed to one certain sermon. However, Peter could have known the contents of at least six of William's sermons of 1256. It seems more plausible that the archbishop's denunciation was based on his knowledge of one or several of William's sermons which were preached earlier in 1256, rather than this knowledge of any possible sermon of 1255.

Moreover, the *Responsiones* presents William's activities of 1256 in a roughly chronological order. The cardinals examine William first on his preaching activities and denunciation at Mâcon in early 1256; they then discuss his role at the 1 March University assembly sponsored by Louis IX to restore order to the studium. Next, the committee examines William on extracts from his Parisian sermons which it had deemed erroneous.[30] The discussion of William's sermons occurs before the committee considers his censure in July 1256 by the archbishop of Tours. The location of these sermons in the *Responsiones* is further evidence against McKeon's argument of a 1255 dating, as they lie between the discussion of the 1 March accord and the July denunciation. Therefore, there seems to be no definite reason to place the dating of *Qui amat periculum*, or of any of William's sermons, in 1255.

23 Placed in February 1256 by Dondaine in the introduction to *Contra impugnantes* in *Opera*, 41A:8-9 and by Dufeil both in "Gulielmus de Sancto Amore," 218 and more convincingly in *Guillaume de Saint-Amour*, 201, n. 18. Faral places it between October 1255 and February 1256 in *Resp.*, 370, while Glorieux, "Le Conflit de 1252-1257," 368, places it in July-August 1255. Dufeil's dating seems the most plausible.

24 9 April 1256, Dondaine, int. to *Contra impugnantes* in *Opera*, 41A:9; Dufeil, "Gulielmus de Sancto Amore," 219; Faral, *Resp.*, 371; Glorieux, "Le Conflit de 1252-1257," 369.

25 13 April 1256, Dondaine, int. to *Contra impugnantes* in *Opera*, 41A:9; Dufeil, "Gulielmus de Sancto Amore," 219; Faral, *Resp.*, 371; Glorieux, "Le Conflit de 1252-1257," 369.

26 1 May 1256, Dondaine, int. to *Contra impugnantes* in *Opera*, 41A:9; Dufeil, *Guillaume de Saint-Amour*, 228; idem, "Gulielmus de Sancto Amore," 219; Faral, *Resp.*, 371; Glorieux, "Le Conflit de 1252-1257," 369.

27 21 May 1256, Dondaine, int. to *Contra impugnantes* in *Opera*, 41A:9; Dufeil, *Guillaume de Saint-Amour*, 228; Faral, *Resp.*, 372; Glorieux, "Le Conflit de 1252-1257," 369.

28 24 May 1256, Dondaine, int. to *Contra impugnantes* in *Opera*, 41A:9; Dufeil, *Guillaume de Saint-Amour*, 228; idem, "Gulielmus de Sancto Amore," 219; Faral, *Resp.*, 372; Glorieux, "Le Conflit de 1252-1257," 369.

29 4 June 1256, Dondaine, int. to *Contra impugnantes* in *Opera*, 41A:9; Dufeil, *Guillaume de Saint-Amour*, 228-9; idem, "Gulielmus de Sancto Amore," 219; Faral, *Resp.*, 372; Glorieux, "Le Conflit de 1252-1257," 369. William's sermon for the eighth Sunday after Pentecost was presumably preached on 30 July. In *Resp.*, 354, William admits to having delivered a sermon before the archbishop of Tours. Glorieux suspects that it was this one. "Le Conflit de 1252-1257," 370.

30 *Resp.*, 346-53.

Qui amat periculum

Of the three extant sermons, the sermon for the Feast of Saints James and Philip is the earliest and, judging by the surviving witnesses, the most popular. It survives today in three printings[31] and eight manuscripts.[32] Out of all his sermons, *Qui amat periculum* best exemplifies how William monopolized on the scandal caused by Gerard's *Introductorius.*

William first announces the theme, a pericope from Ecclesiasticus: He who loves danger will perish in it.[33] William then confesses that he knows many dangers threaten the Church, and as he can no longer remain silent, he must expose them. Although some may deride and scorn him, he knows that these dangers are authentic and can all be validated scripturally.[34]

His opening prayer repeats the Ecclesiasticus pericope; he next reiterates that one must have knowledge to ward off the imminent dangers, and strengthens this assertion by quoting Isaiah 5:13 and Proverbs 5:23, both warning of impending doom.[35] A sinner, he continues, who does not have learning or does not know how to avoid dangers will necessarily die in them. But all mortal sins can be defined as dangers–not any dangers, but dangers to eternal life. And although a great number of dangers exist, the one to which William devotes this sermon threatens the Church and the faithful immediately. It is the greatest danger, is common to everyone and ought especially to be avoided.[36]

William claims that some wonder why he does not preach about luxury, pride, greed or gluttony instead of harping on hypocrisy. For this reason, his opponents have cited him to appear before magnates and even the papal curia.[37] Using a clever analogy, William writes:

> If some doctor had the whole world in his care, and he saw that almost everyone was in a state of advanced illness, and only two or three people had a less threatening sickness, he would not be considered a good doctor unless he devoted greater care

[31] *Appendix ad fasciculum rerum,* II:48-54; *Matěje z Janova Mistra Pařižského,* III:315-332; *Opera,* 491-506.

[32] Erfurt, Amplon. Q 170, ff. 174v-175v; Munich, BS, Clm. 14635, ff. 168ra-174ra; Naples, BN, VII.D.9, ff. 189r-196v; Nurenburg, Cent. I, 80, ff. 98r-101r; Stuttgart, Württemberg, LB, HB I 91, ff. 325v-333r; Vat. lat. 1160, ff. 47v-60r; Vienna, NB, 4941, ff. 194v-203v; Wolfenbüttel, Guelf 367, Helmst., ff. 81r-86v.

[33] Eccli. 3:27; *QAP, infra,* n. 1.

[34] *QAP, infra,* n. 3.

[35] *QAP, infra,* n. 4.

[36] *QAP, infra,* n. 4.

[37] "Et etiam detrahunt mihi apud magnates et in curia Domini Papae." *QAP, infra,* n. 5.

> and attention to the suffering of the many, rather than to those two or three.[38]

William notes that some sins are particular to the religious state, while others predominate amongst the active. However, the sin of hypocrisy is common to both groups. Moreover, it has permeated the entire Church.[39] Therefore, as a good doctor, William prescribes that a sermon against hypocrisy would be a fitting remedy to the threatening dangers. William next states the five divisions of *Qui amat periculum*: 1) how these dangers will appear; 2) what the dangers are; 3) through which men these dangers will come; 4) in which ways they will spread these dangers throughout the world, and 5) how those through whom the dangers will be known can be identified.

Section one is merely a *précis* of chapter one of *De periculis.* William again cites Paul's second letter to Timothy to prove that the Last Days are at hand. Men have appeared who love nothing but money and themselves; they are arrogant and abusive with no respect for their parents, no piety, or natural affection; they are *pentrantes domos.* Yet in this sermon, William emphasizes that fact that not only had the Apostle predicted these dangers, Christ had foreseen them as well and warned of the tribulations.[40]

Section two is an abridged version of chapter four of *De periculis.* It merely reiterates that once these dangers appear, brother will betray brother, father will betray son, sons will arise against their parents, and a man's enemies will be in his own household.[41]

Section three begins by repeating in a new format much of chapter thirteen of *De periculis.* Through the process of elimination, William tries to determine through what types of men these dangers will manifest themselves. After having established that these dangers will appear not through princes, barons, well-armed knights or well-dressed burgers, he concludes that they will come from those laden with sin who feign an appearance of sanctity.

William then offers a series of propositions and objections, many of which contain material not found in *De periculis.* William first asks who would desire more honor than God–he responds by stating those who love themselves more than the truth.[42] His authoritative support for this

38 "...quia si medicus aliquis esset, qui totum mundum haberet in cura sua, et videret quod fere omnes essent in una magna infirmitate, et duo vel tres ex omnibus haberent unam modicam infirmitatem, non reputaretur ille bonus medicus, nisi maiorem curam et sollicitudinem adhiberet illi gravi infirmitati omnium, quam modicae infirmitati istorum duorum vel trium." *QAP, infra,* n. 5.

39 *QAP, infra,* n. 5.

40 *QAP, infra,* n. 7.

41 Matt. 10:21; *QAP, infra,* n. 8.

42 *QAP, infra,* n. 11.

statement consists in two excerpts from the Pauline epistles and a citation each from Gregory and Augustine.[43] However, William notes that some would prefer the testimony of Christ to that of the Saints and thus subsequently cites an appropriate passage from Matthew, warning of the ministry of Pseudo-Prophets.[44]

William concedes that some of the works which those who simulate false sanctity perform may in fact be good. But William warns, be cautious of those who are known by the fasts and alms, for those may be acts of false sanctity and be performed only to deceive.[45]

William then responds to yet another objection. When asked if all of these Pseudo-Preachers' teachings about sin are to be believed, he answers in the negative, citing Matthew 7:22. As the Lord had predicted, when Judgment Day arrives, some will claim to have prophesied, to have driven out demons, and to have performed mighty deeds in his name. But he will respond:

> I never knew you: Get away from me, you who do wrong.[46]

If their teachings about sin are not to be believed, should one have confidence in their miracles and virtuous acts? Certainly not, William retorts, since all miracles are performed by the Lord for the conversion and utility of everyone. Wearing their appearance of sanctity, these deceivers will perform miracles in the name of Christ only to deceive the faithful and gain adherents.[47]

The remainder of section three consists of a long apocalyptic narrative explaining how these *Pseudo-Praedicatores* enter into Salvation history. The three horses of the Apocalypse represent the three persecutions of the Church: the red horse signifies the persecution of the tyrants against the Apostles and martyrs of the early Church; the black horse symbolizes the persecution of the Church by heretics in the time of Saints Hilary and Augustine, but the pale horse represents the impending persecution of the Church by hypocrites.

The devil, employing the agency of tyrants, attempted to destroy what the Apostles and other saints had handed themselves over to death in order to construct. But the Church remained triumphant; William provides two instances in the case of France. First, following the martyrdom of Saint Dionysius, the Church of St. Denis was constructed.

[43] II Cor. 6:6; Col. 2:18; Aug., *De serm. Dom.* in *CCSL* 35:132; *int.* in 2 Cor. 6:6 in *Ed. pr.* 4:345B; Greg., *Reg. Past.* in *SC* 381, I.234; *QAP, infra,* n. 11.

[44] "Multi Pseudo-Prophete surgent et seducent multos." Matt. 24:24; *QAP, infra,* n. 12.

[45] *QAP, infra,* n. 12.

[46] "*Discedite a me qui operamini iniquitatem.*" Matt. 7:23; *QAP, infra,* n. 14.

[47] *ord.* in Matt. 7:22 in *Ed. pr.* 4:31A; *QAP, infra,* n. 15.

Later, the same king who had ordered Dionysius' death was, along with his people, converted to Christianity. This example is paralleled in the martyrdom of St. Nicasius and the cathedral of Reims.[48]

After the devil saw that the Church multiplied and was strengthened by the tyrants, he availed himself of heretics. But Augustine and Hilary so vigorously defended the Church that heresy was soon vanquished.[49]

However, the devil's next assault on the Church, in the form of the pale horse, will come in the form of hypocrites and false brothers. This new persecution is prophesied to be greater than the previous two. Therefore the prayers, miracles, and fasts of these Pseudo-Preachers are not to be believed. They merely represent an unfortunate but necessary episode in salvation history.

In his exegesis, William omitted the traditional interpretations of the white horse as the sacraments,[50] the early Church, or alternately as a period in which the primitive Church was attacked by the Jews.[51] Moreover, although William follows Augustine's exposition through the ordinary gloss on Psalm 7:2, Augustine was not attempting to connect these three persecutions with the seals. William also departs from Augustine by positing the false brothers in the third, rather than the second persecution.[52]

William's fourth section is an abbreviated portion of chapter two of *De periculis,* in which he sets forth his ecclesiological construct of two *ordines.* William asserts that these hypocrites will attempt to preach, although they are not bishops, parish priests or *opitulationes.* William notes that these preachers are not *idoneos* and rather presumptuous, wicked, and completely separated from Christ.[53]

William next inserts a long digression on the preaching style of these hypocrites. He claims that they labor in their sermons to make their speech particularly eloquent–and they do this only in order to make their sermons more pleasing to the laity than those of prelates. These Preachers delight in ornate and polished words, while the Apostles themselves used simple unembellished speech. And while the Apostles only preached the truth, these Preachers' primary concern is decorated speech.[54] William laments that many would in fact rather listen to those who preach well than those who announce God's message. He further warns that the

48 *QAP, infra,* n. 15.

49 *QAP, infra,* n. 15.

50 Ambrosius Aut., *In Apoc.* in *CCCM* 27:274-6; Beda, *Expl. Apoc.* in *PL* 93:146.

51 Prim., *In Apoc.* in *CCSL* 92:94; Rich., *In Apoc.* in *PL* 196:760-2.

52 *ord.* in Ps. 9:2 in *Ed. pr.* 2:467A; Aug., *Enarr. in Ps.* in *CCSL* 38:70. *QAP, infra,* n. 15.

53 The word *idoneos* recalls canon ten of Lateran IV which requested that bishops find *viros idoneos* to serve as diocesan coadjutors. *Extra.* I, t. 31, c. 15 *Inter cetera*; *QAP, infra,* n. 17.

54 *QAP, infra,* n. 17.

Apostle Paul had condemned the preaching style of the Pseudo-Apostles;[55] however, William's main fear is that through mellifluous words, these hypocrites will attract the support of nobles, lay and even clerical magnates. When this occurs, superiors will cease to love their inferiors and inferiors will forsake their superiors.

The remainder of this section consists in William's speculations of what other perils these hypocrites will cause in the Church. The laity will confess to those hypocrites who have canonical permission neither to hear nor to absolve their sins.[56] But these hypocrites are actually the agents of the Antichrist; he has employed them to disseminate pernicious laws throughout Christendom. And their evil laws can be confirmed in the *Introductorius*: the sacraments and Christ's Gospel will be replaced in five years by a new dispensation.[57] William concludes this section by again citing Pseudo-Dionysius to prove that these hypocrites have no place in the ecclesiastical hierarchy and therefore no authority for the care of souls.[58]

William's final section of *Qui amat periculum* is a brief reiteration of chapter thirteen of *De periculis*. He offers a list of possible choices of groups from which these hypocrites are likely to originate and then whittles down the register with *pro* and *contra* biblical citations. His conclusion is the same as in *De periculis*; these hypocrites are Christian, they are false religious, and they will always study, though never attain the truth.[59]

The remainder of section five consists of seven ways in which false preachers can be distinguished from true ones. These signs reveal this sermon's debt to *De periculis*; many in fact are repetitions or combinations of signs previously used in *De periculis*. Before introducing his signs, William states:

> I shall now present seven signs by which these men may be known. Although I can show many other signs, due to the lack of time, these will suffice.[60]

The many other signs refer to the forty-one signs enumerated in chapter fourteen of *De periculis* and provide further evidence that William wrote the sermon after *De periculis*.

False Preachers want to live from the Gospel and hear confessions;[61] they are impatient and cannot endure the truth when it is revealed to

55 I Cor. 2:4.

56 *QAP*, *infra*, n. 17-19.

57 *QAP*, *infra*, n. 20.

58 *QAP*, *infra*, n. 20.

59 *QAP*, *infra*, n. 21-8.

60 "Signa septem ad praesens ponam, quibus possint cognosci; licet multa possim ostendere, tamen causa brevitatis temporis haec sufficiant." *QAP*, *infra*, n. 29.

them;[62] they use embellished speech;[63] they want to preach in areas which already have a sufficient number of preachers;[64] they cannot bear insults;[65] they desire to be well received,[66] and they seek their own honor rather than that of Christ.[67]

William concludes *Qui amat periculum* by repeating a short story he had heard about a "certain religious" who claimed that before his Order was created, the world had been in darkness.[68] But the Virgin Mary had lain prostrate before the Lord for three days; when the Lord asked her what she wanted, she requested that a new religious order be created to illuminate the world. The Lord granted her petition, and the religious claimed that the order in question was his own. William finds it reprehensible that a preacher would dare lie in this manner in the presence of the laity and adds that a bishop had compelled the religious to retract his story publicly.

The source for this story is the *Vita Sancti Dominici* of Theodore of Apolda (Theodoricus de Appoldia).[69] As the story immediately follows the seven signs to identify false preachers from true ones, William may have intended it to designate the Dominicans more specifically as the Pseudo-Preachers in question.

Qui amat periculum largely represents a continued re-emphasis of the apocalyptic themes as presented in *De periculis.* The friars symbolize the persecution of the Church in the pale horse and are the hypocrites and false brothers who will inaugurate what will be the greatest period of tribulation for the Church. William's goal is to recall Gerard's *Eternal Gospel* to mind and treat it as detailed description of how the mendicants will destroy the Church. The friars' stated purpose, following William's line of reasoning, is to appropriate the office of preaching to themselves, to deceive the laity, and to set the stage for the Antichrist's arrival.

61 *QAP, infra,* n. 30-1; signs 11, 20, *DP,* 60-1, 64.

62 *QAP, infra,* n. 32; sign 3, *DP,* 58.

63 *QAP, infra,* n. 33; signs 2, 13, *DP,* 57, 61-2.

64 *QAP, infra,* n. 34; signs 23, 36, *DP,* 65-6, 69-70.

65 *QAP, infra,* n. 35; sign 21, *DP,* 65.

66 *QAP, infra,* n. 36; signs 22, 24, *DP,* 65-6.

67 *QAP, infra,* n. 37; sign 25, *DP,* 66.

68 *QAP, infra,* n. 38.

69 *Vita S. Dominici* of Theodore of Apolda in *Acta sanctorum* edd. J. Bollandus et al. (Paris: Victor Palmé, 1863), 4 August, I:570-1; first noted by McKeon, "Status of the University," 661, n. 51.

Si quis diligit me

William's Pentecost sermon, *Si quis diligit me* is unique of all his extant sermons. Unlike the other two, it never received an early modern printing and survives today in only one manuscript.[70] This sermon, however, is an important polemical piece as it both bears witness to William's recurring attempts to attack the mendicants' pastoral activities and provides ample testimony to the controversy of Gerard's *Eternal Gospel* within the university milieu. This sermon also discloses the principal reasons why the Parisian theologians and William of Saint-Amour in particular, lost the support of the king of France, Louis IX.

Either exasperated by the pro-mendicant policies of Alexander IV, or perhaps swelled by his role as the chief spokesperson of the Parisian theologians, William started leveling charges against the friars' secular partisans; in so doing, William gained an irrevocable enemy in the form of the king of France.

When the conflict between the friars and the seculars first erupted in the Parisian Faculty of Theology in 1253, the regent Alphonse of Poitiers, according to university sources, openly expressed his sympathy for the mendicant masters.[71] After the failure of his crusade and his return from the debacle at Mansourah (1250), Louis switched strategies and attempted to reconcile the two parties. Such a policy might seem surprising, given Louis' predilection for the friars, as witnessed by his tendency to support mendicant endowments, to employ mendicants as confessors, and to use them in civil administration and for diplomatic missions.[72] On several occasions, Louis dressed like a friar,[73] and after his capture at Mansourah, Louis reportedly wanted to abdicate and become a friar.[74]

But Louis was merely continuing a tradition started by his grandfather Philip Augustus of attempting to find a royal solution to an inter-university problem to re-establish peace at Paris. Louis' intervention into the conflict could have had wide-ranging effects on the continued development of the

70 Erfurt, Amplon. Q.170, f.174r-v. Clasen has studied and printed this sermon in "Kampfpredigten," 88-95. Dufeil partially transcribed it and Little published this transcription in "Saint Louis' Involvement with the Friars," *Church History* 23 (1964):147-8.

71 *Chart.* I, No. 230, 254-5.

72 On Louis' relationship with the friars, see Little, "Saint Louis," 125-148; J. Richard, *Saint Louis* trans. J. Birrell (Cambridge: University Press, 1992), 228-30.

73 W.C. Jordan, *Louis IX and the Challenge of the Crusade: A Study in Rulership* (Princeton, NJ: University Press, 1979), 129.

74 Geoffrey of Beaulieu, *Vita Ludovici noni* in *Recueil* 20:7; Matthew of Paris, *Chronica maiora* ed. H. Luard (London, 1872-1882), 5:466. All of the contemporary accounts of Louis mention the simplicity of his clothing. On at least one occasion, he was addressed as "Frater Ludovicus". Reference in G.G. Coulton, *From Saint Francis to Dante* 2nd ed. (Philadelphia: University of Pennsylvania Press, 1972), 315.

studium at Paris as it had, over the past fifty years, balanced the often conflicting demands of popes, kings, and bishops to establish a large degree of self-autonomy. But Pope Alexander IV quickly quashed Louis' royal initiatives, guaranteeing that the University would, for the time being, continue to remain under papal supervision. William's Pentecost sermon against Louis would ensure that the king would support Alexander in this matter.

Louis first intervened directly into the conflict in January 1256 by requesting that a committee of French prelates arbitrate a peaceable solution to the university problem;[75] two months later, Louis and four archbishops produced the peace agreement *Noverit universitas vestra* to reintegrate the friars into the theological faculty to which all parties upheld.[76] Although Pope Alexander later nullified this agreement, Louis still continued to pursue a policy of reconciliation in other ways. He refused Alexander's initial requests to have William incarcerated or expelled from France.[77] And according to William's account of the controversy, Louis also permitted him an opportunity to defend himself publicly at Paris before the archbishop of Tours in 1256.[78] The poet Rutebeuf explained that Louis had met William personally and promised him assistance in establishing a workable compromise with the mendicants.[79]

On balance, Louis had also assisted the Parisian friars. By the summer of 1255, Louis had provided the Dominicans protection from harassment by means of royal archers.[80] And Louis had, at Pope Alexander's request, began to investigate into the state of affairs of the Dominicans at Paris in mid-April 1256.[81] Louis' influence must have had some effect in calming anti-Dominican sentiment, as the Master General of the Order, Humbert of Romans, reported two months later that the situation for the Preachers at Paris seemed to have improved.[82]

But after the delivery of the Pentecost sermon, one can detect a change in policy towards Louis's dealings with William; Louis began to work in closer cooperation with Alexander. Shortly after William preached this sermon, Louis sent two envoys, along a copy of *De periculis* to Alexander for examination.[83] Louis' response may not only have been in retaliation for

75 DuBoulay, *Historia universitas parisiensis*, III:294-5; *Resp.*, 353-6.
76 *Chart.* I, No. 268, 304-5.
77 *Cf. Chart.* I, Nos. 280, 282, 319-23, 324-6.
78 *Resp.*, 346-53.
79 "Li Dit de Guillaume de Saint-Amour," in *Oeuvres complètes de Rutebeuf* edd. E. Faral and J. Bastin 8th ed. (Paris: A. Picard, 1985), I:246.
80 *Chart.* I, No. 273, 312.
81 *Chart.* I, No. 275, 314-5.
82 *Chart.* I, No. 279, 318-9.
83 *Chart.* I, No. 289, 334.

William's untimely comments; he had also been presented with a *cedula* of errors contained in William's works.[84] Alexander acknowledged receipt of *De periculis* and commissioned a group of cardinals to study it. When Alexander formally condemned it, he asked Louis on the same day to assist the French episcopacy to help detect and destroy copies of it.[85] Alexander then requested Louis' assistance to ensure that all masters subscribe to a series of papal provisions governing the re-integration of the friars into the University.[86] And when Alexander excommunicated William, he notified him that he would need, at the express request of King Louis, a papal license to enter France.[87]

It therefore appears that although Louis had entered the university conflict personally, William forced him to change his course of careful arbitration and instead, pushed him into the arms of Alexander IV. After the delivery of the Pentecost sermon, Louis made sure that William's writings were examined, and after they were condemned, he made certain that his punishment would be severe.

As his theme for this sermon, William chose John 14:23: Anyone who loves me will heed what I say. He immediately announces the tripartite structure of the sermon: 1) what it means to love God truly; 2) how one can know who truly loves God; and 3) what gain is acquired in loving God. William concentrates the bulk of *Si quis diligit me* on responding to the first question. William proclaims three ways in which one can truly love God. One must desire above all to fulfill the will of God and devote every labor and thought to attaining this goal.[88] To love God means to bind oneself fully to him in love. Unless one is joined to God in this manner, he cannot be considered religious, even if he wears a humble habit. Religion, William continues, can be feigned under the external garments of a robe, a sack or woolen cloth. William alludes to the subject of a future sermon, *De pharisaeo et publicano*, by stating that anyone who sports exteriorly the appearance of religion, yet has no interior religion, is called a Pharisee.[89]

William explains that the Pharisees were rich and powerful men who donned humble garments in order to be recognized as holy. But all those who wear base clothing solely for worldly renown ought to be identified as hypocrites. Although Satan manifests himself through all forms of sin, he seems to have particular success in the sin of hypocrisy. And for this

[84] *Resp.*, 354.
[85] *Chart.* I, No. 289, 333-5.
[86] *Chart.* I, No. 313, 361-2.
[87] *Chart.* I, No. 315, 363.
[88] *SQD, infra*, n. 5.
[89] *SQD, infra*, n. 5.

reason, Christ and the Apostles have attacked hypocrisy more than any other sin.[90]

While William remarks that hypocrisy used to be very rare, he also grieves that it has in his days made great strides throughout Christendom. It has broken down all social boundaries and has permeated the ranks both of ecclesiastical and secular prelates, nobles, city-dwellers, and even women.[91] William then, having poorly appraised his influence at the Palais Royal, discusses at length the problem of hypocrisy within royal courts. How deplorable it is, he states, that kings arise in the middle of the night to say matins and hear six pairs of masses a day. These kings are so partial to the poor that they often approve their cases in court even without hearing them. Moreover, they imitate the poor in their manner of dress. While unduly concerning themselves with the plight of the poor, these kings extort money from their towns and villages, with no intention of paying it back,[92] in order to wage a war in which a thousand Christians could be killed. But none of these activities are condoned in Scripture; rather, the office of kingship consists in preserving justice and procuring peace.[93] William notes that Jerome had advised a king to use his wealth for his kingdom rather than himself, and this included having beautiful clothes for the purpose of maintaining royal dignity and impressing others.[94]

William next directs his sermon at Louis' entourage. Kings should not surround themselves with "good men";[95] nor should they be overly disturbed about the proper distribution of alms. They should concern themselves with the administration of justice and dress as befits their station. The Church has commanded that the pope use the best red and gold bridle available when he rides; knights always wear silk capes while on horseback.[96] Similarly, clerics do not vest themselves in the raiment of barons and knights. William argues that everyone ought to dress according to one's condition, neither exceeding it nor diminishing it in clothing.[97]

He next asserts that France,[98] more than any other place in the world, is inundated with a multiplicity of religious habits. Moreover, it has been so

90 *SQD*, *infra*, n. 5.

91 *SQD*, *infra*, n. 5.

92 *SQD*, *infra*, n. 5.

93 In reference to Ps. 118:121.

94 *SQD*, *infra*, n. 5; *Cf.* Hier., *Epist.* 79 in *CSEL* 55:96.

95 "...homines boni..." *SQD*, *infra*, n. 5. It is unlikely that William is intentionally linking the familiar nickname of the Cathars with the mendicants, as he refers to these good men as *beguini*. William's point was that kings should not seek counsellors who have taken religious vows.

96 *SQD*, *infra*, n. 5.

97 *SQD*, *infra*, n. 5.

98 *SQD*, *infra*, n. 6.

plagued since ancient times.[99] Although some of these habits are legitimate, William confesses that he has come to believe that this multiplication has been instigated by the devil, so that he might thereby more easily deceive the faithful.[100]

It is not difficult to imagine how King Louis would have reacted to this sermon. As a devoted friend of the friars, who always wore simple, unostentatious garb, Louis himself would have interpreted William's diatribe on hypocrisy as a direct attack on his inviolate royal person.[101] Moreover, William's mention of a war in which thousands of Christians were killed, could only bring to mind Louis' recent unsuccessful crusade.

William then examines mendicant infringements upon parochial prerogatives. In the second section, William discusses how one may know those who truly love the Lord. He splits this section into five divisions which describe the ways in which one can serve the Lord's word. While his first way is seemingly innocuous–to serve the Lord's mandates–his second is aimed directly against the friars: not to sell the word of the Lord. William next condemns all who preach who are not bishops, priests nor archdeacons and continues by prohibiting the laity from confessing to one who is *non vocatus*.[102]

William's admonitions to the faithful grow in intensity. He claims that one who dies after having confessed to a preacher without the prerequisite *licentia praedicandi*, will, along with the confessor, go to hell.[103] Some, he claims, have already been damned by not having confessed to their parish priest even once in their life.[104] Others make out their wills on their deathbeds to the benefit of *tales fratres*, and are still sent to perdition by the

99 "Et hoc habet ab antiquo." William claims that for the past twelve hundred years, priests and clerics have striven to distinguish themselves by constantly diversifying their religious attire. He demonstrates this assertion by citing a spurious decretal of Pope Celestine (422-32) directed to the bishop of Paris which was intended to stop this needless proliferation. *SQD, infra*, n. 6. This decretal can be found in Pope Celestine's *Registrum* in *PL* 50:431B and Dionysius Exiguus' *Collectiones* in *PL* 50:431B. It may in fact derive from part of the Pseudo-Isidorean collection which was not incorporated into Gratian's *Decretum*. It can be found in Migne's edition, *PL* 130:755, but not in that of Hinschius. Even Aquinas had noted the difficulties of locating this source: "...quod mandatum papae in registro romanae ecclesiae habetur, ut dicunt, quamvis in corpore Decretorum non contineatur." *Contra impugnantes* in *Opera*, 41A:125.

100 *SQD, infra*, n. 6.

101 While William never mentioned Louis by name, at least one mendicant, the Dominican Thomas of Cantimpré, viewed this statement as an attack on the king. *Bonum universale de apibus* (Douai, 1627), II, c.57, § 63-4, 588-9.

102 *Vocatus* refers to Heb. 5:4; "Nec quisquam accipiat sibi potestatem, sed qui vocatus est a Deo tanquam Aaron." *SQD, infra*, n. 9.

103 *SQD, infra*, n. 9.

104 *SQD, infra*, n. 9.

counsel of the same brothers.[105] In a reaffirmation of canon twenty-one of the Council of Lateran IV, William asserts that salvation depends on annual confession to a parish priest.

William's third way of serving the word of the Lord is to preach without the expectation of gain. To those who preach to acquire worldly possessions for themselves or their order, William repeats the story of Giezi.[106] The Prophet Elisha, after having cured the general Naaman of leprosy, refused to accept money for his services. Yet Elisha's servant Giezi pursued Naaman and requested money in the name of his master. Giezi returned home, deceived his master as to his own whereabouts, and was instantly punished by leprosy. William therefore asserts that accepting money for spiritual services is perilous since it distorts our vision,[107] causes us to serve the world,[108] binds us to worldly concerns,[109] makes us indebted to the giver,[110] and ultimately forces us to relinquish our freedom.[111]

Another way of serving the word of God is by using it for the salvation, and not the damnation, of the faithful. William has directed his recommendation against those who claim:

> Confess to me, not to your parish priest.[112]

Such an interloper is a *ribaldus*, and will undoubtedly lead the laity to damnation, since he has no power to absolve them.

The fourth and fifth ways to serve the word of God are to maintain and to defend the Gospel against those who try to destroy it. For fifty-five years, some, inspired by Joachim,[113] have labored to destroy the teachings of Christ. Naturally all of those involved in this undertaking are tainted by sin–but so too are those who know of this effort and have the ability, although have done nothing as yet, to oppose it.[114] These enemies of the Church proclaim that the law of God will only endure until the year 1260.

105 "...et in morte fit totaliter testamentum eius per tales fratres, nihil sciente sacerdote, qui totum debet scire, et sic mittitur in infernum ille confessus per consilium istorum fratrum." *SQD, infra*, n. 9.

106 William repeatedly argued that accepting offerings for administering the sacraments was *ipso facto* simony. The Giezi story was perhaps his favorite biblical *exemplum*. Through the canon C.1 q.1 c.11 *Qui studet*, William makes an effective connection between Giezi and the friars. This story not only appears in *SQD, infra*, n. 10, it can also be found in *DVM*, 340, *QDM, infra*, n. 141, *DP*, 64; and *Resp.*, 350-1.

107 Ex. 23:8; *SQD, infra*, n. 11.

108 Gal. 1:10; *SQD, infra*, n. 12.

109 Iac. 4:4; *SQD, infra*, n. 13.

110 Pr. 22:7; *SQD, infra*, n. 14.

111 Pr. 22:9; *SQD, infra*, n. 15.

112 "Confitere mihi, non sacerdoti tuo." *SQD, infra*, n. 16.

113 *SQD, infra*, n. 18.

114 *SQD, infra*, n. 18.

Moreover, they assert that both the priesthood and the sacraments will lose their validity in 1260; after this time, they claim, Christ's Gospel will lose its efficacy and only those who proceed barefoot may preach.[115]

Si quis diligit me concludes by returning to the threefold division made at the outset of the sermon to describe what is to be gained by loving God. One who truly loves God and has lived without sin will be rewarded with perfect happiness. However, as a nasty stab at the Dominicans, William notes that one who lives in such a manner will not receive perfect knowledge of the Trinity, since this cannot be attained during mortal existence. William is refuting the error of the Dominican Stephan of Vénizy–"quod divina essentia in se nec ad homine nec ab angelo videbitur"–condemned by the Faculty of Theology in 1241, and by the Dominican Chapter of 1256.[116] The Faculty declared that Stephan's statement was erroneous because the glorified soul will see *Deus in sua essentia.* William continues that after having lived a sinless life, one can attain after death knowledge both of the Trinity and of the humanity assumed in the Virgin Mother.[117] A listener must have been left with the impression that not only were the Dominicans tainted by error, but also that their assistance in pastoral concerns was surely the fastest route to damnation.

William's Pentecost sermon continues the trend of *De periculis* and *Qui amat periculum* by warning both of the friars' ministerial activities and of the dangers prophesied in Gerard's *Eternal Gospel.* William erred, however, by using this sermon as a vehicle to attack both the lifestyle and the dress of King Louis IX. Louis was prepared to give both parties involved in the conflict impartiality; but when verbally assaulted by William, Louis assisted Pope Alexander, and let him dictate the terms of the restoration of the university. These terms included the excommunication of William, his expulsion from the University, and his banishment from France.

De pharisaeo et publicano

William's sermon for the tenth day after Pentecost, *De pharisaeo et publicano,* survives in two early modern printings and one manuscript.[118] In it, William expands upon two themes raised earlier in *Si quis diligit me*:

115 *SQD, infra,* n. 18.

116 *Chart.* I, No. 128, 170-1; *Chart.* I, No. 285, 328. *SQD, infra,* n. 19; Dufeil, *Guillaume de Saint-Amour,* 230.

117 The allusion to the Virgin Mother is another reference to Stephan's errors. Stephan had claimed that glorified souls were not located in the same heaven as Angels, but were rather in a lower one. The Blessed Mother is also situated in this lower heaven. *Chart.* I, No. 128, 170-1.

118 *Appendix ad fasciculum rerum,* II:43-7; *Opera,* 7-15. The only known manuscript is Wolfenbüttel, Guelf. 367 Helmst., ff. 78v-81r.

hypocrisy and Pharisees.[119] William employs the parable of the Pharisee and Publican in Luke 18:9-14 to four ends: 1) to explain what both of these figures represent; 2) to compare and contrast them; 3) to report the Lord's opinion as to their relative merits; and 4) to interpret the intent of the parable: *Quia qui se exaltat, humiliabitur.*[120]

William first notes that the Pharisees were members of a religious order among the Jews, comparable to contemporary regular orders.[121] But in habit, in austerity of life, and in spiritual observances, some of these Pharisees displayed a show of sanctity which they lacked in their hearts and were therefore hypocrites.

William describes their hypocrisy in their outward appearance. These Pharisees possessed small pieces of parchment (*membranulas*) upon which the precepts of the Decalogue were written.[122] They wore these *membranulas* on their foreheads to convey the impression that they were always meditating on the Law.[123] They also carried them in their hands to convince others that they were always operating according to the Law. To demonstrate further their austere way of life, these Pharisees would tie sharp thorns to the tassels of their cloaks. Thus whether they were walking or sitting, the thorns would pierce them and continually remind them of their service to God. William observes that they would have had to have walked barefoot since if they had walked otherwise, they would not have been pricked by the thorns.[124] The barefoot *topos* is obviously intended to recall the memory of Gerard's *Introductorius*.

William then describes some aspects of the Pharisees in order that their modern-day counterparts, or those whom William identifies as the "hypocrites of our own times" may more easily be recognized by his listeners.[125] William first provides an etymology of the word "Pharisee",

[119] This sermon is discussed in Dufeil, *Guillaume de Saint-Amour*, 242, 251-2, and Szittya, *The Origins of the Antifraternal Tradition in Medieval Literature* (Princeton, NJ: University Press, 1986), 34-41. The content of this sermon was captured and popularized first by William's contemporary Rutebeuf in his poems "Du pharisien ou C'est d'hypocrisie" and "Dit des règles" and later by Jean de Meun. *Rutebeuf*, I:249-55, 269-276; *Roman de la Rose* ed. E. Langlois, III (Paris: Honoré Champion, 1921), ll. 11,605-36; A. Serper, "L'influence de Guillaume de Saint-Amour sur Rutbeuf," *Romance Philology* 17 (1963-4):391-402.

[120] Luc. 18:14.

[121] *Dephar., infra*, n. 3.

[122] These *membranulas* are William's interpretation of the *phylacteria* mentioned in Matt. 23:5. *Dephar., infra*, n. 3.

[123] *Dephar., infra*, n. 3. William's description comes almost entirely from the ordinary gloss. *Cf. ord.* in Matt. 23:5 in *Ed. pr.* 4:71A; Hier., *Comm. in Matt.* in *CCSL* 77:211. Rutebeuf epitomized the theme and popularized it in his "Dit des regles" in *Rutebeuf*, I:271, ll. 33-5: "Mais il croient ces ypocrites; Qui ont les enseignes escrites; Einz vizages d'estre preudoume."

[124] *Dephar., infra*, n. 4.

[125] *Dephar., infra*, n. 5.

defining it as "those divided from the people".[126] He then paraphrases Matthew 23:6-7, writing that these Pharisees desire the place of honor at feasts, they want the chief seat in their synagogues, to be greeted respectfully *in foro*, and to be addressed always as rabbi. These four features of the Pharisees constitute the four infallible signs with which the Lord provided us in order to identify these hypocrites.

The first sign, that these hypocrites desire to sit at the head of the table at the banquets of kings, princes, and prelates, is especially true for the contemporary Pharisees. And like *De periculis* and *Qui amat periculum*, William contrasts this aspect of the Pharisees with that of true preachers.[127] The Pharisees flatter the nobility, linger in royal courts, and profess a desire to live by the Gospel while eschewing manual labor. They involve themselves in the affairs of others, while serving their own God–their stomachs.[128]

They desire the first seat in the synagogue so that they may dine in the homes of the powerful and involve themselves in the affairs of others. And by sitting in the prime location of the Synagogue, they may also be more easily called upon to preach, often by a secular lord.[129] Yet their sermons are not concerned with the moral edification of the faithful. Rather, they provide these hypocrites with an opportunity to exhibit their wisdom and eloquence in the presence of everyone. The Pharisees seek glory for themselves in their sermons, while usurping the power of the local bishops and prelates by preaching in defiance of canon law.[130]

They love to be warmly received in the forum, which as Isidore has described, signifies a place where lawsuits are brought.[131] These religious love to be called to the consistories of kings and prelates to fulfill the function of judge or legal assistant.[132] They covet this position so that the litigants might show them judicial reverence and greet them with a bowed head. However, William notes that the Apostle had forbidden legal aspirations for those serving God.[133]

[126] *Dephar.*, *infra*, n. 4; *ord.* in Matt. 3:7 in *Ed. pr.* 4:11B (*PL* 114:80B); Hrab. Maur., *Comm. in Matt.* in *PL* 107:770B; *cf. SQD*, *infra*, n. 5.

[127] *Dephar.*, *infra*, n. 6. This sign is a amalgamation of many different signs enumerated in *DP*. See signs 2, 9, 11, and 29 in *DP*, 57, 60, 61, 68.

[128] *Dephar.*, *infra*, n. 7; sign 29 in *DP*, 68. This claim also appears in *DVM*, 342.

[129] *Dephar.*, *infra*, n. 8. This sign consists of excerpts from signs 6, 7, 10, 11 and 13 in *DP*, 58, 59, 60, 61, 62.

[130] C.9 q.2 c.7 *Episcopum non debere*; C.7 q.1 c.38 *Episcopi vel Presbyteri*; *Dephar.*, n. 8.

[131] "Forum, ut dicit Isidorus, est exercendarum litium locus." *Etymologiarum* II, XVIII c.15, 402; *Dephar.*, *infra*, n. 10.

[132] This sign has no direct parallel in *DP*, but it conveys the spirit of signs 8, 17, and 22 in *DP*, 59, 60, 63, 65.

[133] "Nemo militans Deo implicat se saecularibus negotiis, ut ei placeat, cui se probavit." II Tim. 2:4; *Dephar.*, *infra*, n. 10.

In sign four, William proclaims that these hypocrites love to be called rabbi, or by its Latin equivalent *magister.*[134] This assertion would have had particular relevance for the mendicants and their theological masters at Paris. These modern-day Pharisees have provoked many excommunications and a great deal of scandal simply to obtain the title of master.[135]

William concedes that someone could object to this statement and claim that these hypocrites have sought the title of master not on account of the name itself, but for the benefit of souls, since one would be more prone to believe a master than a non-master in matters concerning salvation.[136] After William has expressed his inability to grasp this reasoning, [137] the imaginary opponent explains that masters are not only known to be wiser than non-masters, but they can also teach better and preach more articulately. William retorts that neither a magisterial position nor a familiarity with learning can make one good or bad. For Arius, Sabellius, Eutyches, and Nestorius were all masters of divine letters and are now recognized as heresiarchs.

Although Christ kept company with learned converts such as Nathanael and Nicodemus, he did not send them to preach.[138] Instead, he sent his simple and unlettered followers. The title of master should therefore have no effect on one's ability to perform pastoral care. Rather, William notes, that the Apostle had highlighted the qualities necessary for preaching. And while these included patience, works of virtue, and the ability to perform miracles, he had mentioned neither a magisterial license nor an inordinate display of wisdom and eloquence as prerequisites.[139]

Having described the signs by which the Pharisees may be recognized, William next defines a *Publicanus.* He is a secular who recognizes himself as a sinner and does not simulate sanctity. The remainder of the sermon contrasts the specific characteristics of the Pharisee and the Publican. William first identifies five examples of the Pharisee's proud, hypocritical demeanor. He then opposes these qualities to those of the Publican.

The Pharisee begins his prayers by thanking God that he is not like "other men". He claims to be just and immune from sin although he is a hypocrite. He claims that it is the Publican, rather than himself, who sins. He has usurped the name of goodness for himself, he has unjustly

[134] This sign repeats the charges made against the mendicants in the University's 1254 *Apologia*: "Nolite vocari rabbi" and "Ne vocemini magistri." *Chart.* I, No. 230, 253; Matt. 23:8, 23:10.

[135] *Dephar., infra,* n. 11.

[136] *Dephar., infra,* n. 12.

[137] William writes: "Sed quaero, quare est hoc?" *Dephar., infra,* n. 13.

[138] Ioan. 1-3.

[139] II Cor. 12:12; *Dephar., infra,* n. 13.

appraised his neighbor the Publican, and is reputed to be an adulterer since he has appropriated the glory of the Lord as his own.[140]

The Publican, on the other hand, admits that he is unworthy, reverently keeps his distance from the altar during mass, detests sin but acknowledges that he is sinner and is not embarrassed to confess his sins before God. As in Pope Innocent IV's bull *Etsi animarum*, William acknowledges that shame and embarrassment play an essential role in the sacrament of confession.[141]

Following this comparison, William abruptly ends this sermon by explaining the Lord's purpose for this parable. Christ was attempting to show that it is better to be humble than to be proud, since he who exalts himself will be humbled and he who humbles himself will be exalted.

William's line of attack in *De pharisaeo et publicano* was to highlight the similarities between the Pharisees and their contemporary equivalents, the friars. Like the Pharisees, the friars are preoccupied by legal concerns, zealously crave the title of master, and seek to display their knowledge in their sermons. And although William does not mention the mendicants by name, the parallels would not have been lost on contemporaries. Unlike his other two extant sermons, *De pharisaeo et publicano* has little recourse to Gerard's *Introductorius*. Nevertheless, the themes which William emphasizes, including hypocrisy, vanity, and feigned sanctity, appear in various degrees throughout the other two as part of William's stock repertoire and would have served as readily identifiable signifiers for the friars to William's audience.

THE *RESPONSIONES*

The *Responsiones* were probably written in late fall 1256, shortly after William's examination by the cardinals at Anagni delegated to investigate his works. They were published by Alithophilius in 1632 under the rather cumbersome title "Casus et articuli super quibus accusatus fuit magister Guillielmus de Sancto Amore a Fratribus Praedicatoribus cum responsionibus ad singula."[142] Edmond Faral prepared its critical edition in 1950 and shortened the title to "Responsiones". The document itself is not simply a *procès-verbaux* of the cardinals' deliberations, but is rather an extensive report of the accusations brought against William and his replies. Glorieux has labelled it, quite appropriately, a "mémoire-justificatif".[143]

[140] *Dephar., infra*, n. 17-20.
[141] *Chart.* I, No. 240, 269; *Dephar., infra*, n. 24.
[142] In *Opera*, 88-110.
[143] *Répertoire des maîtres*, I:345.

The text could not have been prepared by William before his examination, since it is much too detailed in the types of questions which he would have encountered at Anagni. Nor, as Faral suggests, could it have been prepared by the Anagni tribunal following William's condemnation to present the arguments used at the examination to both the parties of the accused and the defense.[144] It seems more likely that the document was composed after the interrogation either by William or one of his circle as a form of propaganda. This assertion becomes particularly evident in section five of this work in which William states certain theses which he proceeds to reject using the standard scholastic style: *Dicet autem aliquis.*[145] One wonders why William would have had to employ an imaginary opponent when he was being questioned by a papal commission. The obvious intent of this work, as witnessed by William's adroit responses to the committee's questions, his complete acceptance of papal authority to license preachers,[146] and his willingness to correct all statements considered erroneous,[147] was clearly to persuade readers that he had been wrongfully condemned.

The document consists of six sections: a recapitulation of William's denunciation at Mâcon in early 1256, a detailed discussion of William's role at the 1 March assembly sponsored by Louis IX to restore order to the University, extracts of William's Parisian sermons which the commission judged erroneous, a summary of his defense before the archbishop of Tours in July 1256, a narrative of the Dominican Humbert of Romans' condemnation of him before the archbishops of Reims and Sens in summer 1256, and a defense of *De periculis.* Since the publication of Faral's critical edition, scholars have concentrated on interpreting the events of 1256 in a new chronological perspective.[148] The document lends itself to this form of analysis, since the material contained therein is presented more or less in an accurate chronological order.

It begins with the thirteen errors William was accused of having preached in Mâcon either in January or early February 1256. The fact that these errors had been submitted to the papal commission suggests that the Dominicans were the prime movers behind William's examination. As William explains, he had already purged himself of these errors earlier in the year when the Preachers had presented a similar list of errors to the

144 *Resp.,* 361.

145 *Resp.,* 356-8.

146 Article 24, *Resp.,* 349.

147 *Resp.,* 360-1.

148 Douie, "St. Bonaventure," 588-92; Dufeil, *Guillaume de Saint-Amour,* 287-8; idem, "Gulielmus de Sancto Amore," 218-9; Faral, *Resp.,* 369-74; Glorieux, "Le Conflit de 1252-1257," 366-70; Marrone, "Ecclesiology," 54-6; McKeon, "Status of the University," 659-75.

bishop of Mâcon.[149] These questionable statements are mainly a reiteration of points made in his disputed questions and his responses to Bonaventure's *De mendicitate.* He was charged with having stated that preachers who solicit and accept offerings from those to whom they preached have mortally sinned,[150] that one who relinquishes all for God and afterwards begs is not in a state of salvation,[151] and that one who lives by alms instead of manual labor has similarly sinned.[152] It is clear from the context that William was still deliberating upon the issues of the previous year during his preaching stint in Mâcon.

The second portion of the text concerns William's role in the events leading up to the peace agreement *Noverit universitas vestra.* William reports that he had been requested to return to Paris to assist in the composition of a peace agreement between the students and the friars.[153] But according to the cardinals, William's role in these deliberations consisted entirely of proposing arguments against the friars' entrance into the University. The committee identified five reasons William had advanced as to why the academic consortium should not readmit the friars. These reasons are noteworthy in themselves because they parallel the objections which the University published in fall 1255 to reintegrating the friars into the theological studium.[154] William had argued that an association ought to be voluntary and not coerced,[155] that the friars could be *penetrantes domos,*[156] that the friars are excessively concerned with the affairs of others and spiritual works,[157] that they desire to be called master,[158] and that their religious profession is simply not consistent with the office of teaching.[159] William does not admit to any of the charges, but merely downplays his role in the formation of an accord.

The third section of the *Responsiones* details excerpts from William's Parisian sermons which the commission had judged to be in error. And while the specific errors culled from these sermons follow a vague topical organization, they themselves are not arranged chronologically. The

[149] *Resp.*, 345.

[150] *Resp.*, 340; *DVM*, 342.

[151] *Resp.*, 341; *DQE*, 328-9.

[152] *Resp.*, 342; *DQE*, 330; *QDM*, n. 99.

[153] "...per litteram suam patentem me revocaverat, retentus a quibusdam magnis viris ut ad compositionem faciendam inter Fratres, et Scholares iuvarem, sicut et feci, tractatui illius compositionis interfui." *Resp.*, 346.

[154] Found in Du Boulay, *Historia universitatis parisiensis,* III:287-8 and Wolfenbüttel, Guelf 367, Helmst., f. 77va.

[155] *Resp.*, 345. This was an argument which naturally played a large role in the University's dissolution threat. *Chart.* I, No. 256, 293.

[156] *Resp.*, 345.

[157] *Resp.*, 345.

[158] *Resp.*, 345-6.

[159] *Resp.*, 346.

sermons discussed in this section are those for Palm Sunday, Holy Thursday, Saints James and Philip, the fifth Sunday after Easter, Ascension, and Pentecost: all of William's sermons preached between 9 April and 4 June 1256.

Of specific interest is the material condemned in William's sermons which are no longer extant. Although his sermon for Palm Sunday no longer exists, we know some of its content as the *Responsiones* lists four incorrect statements from it.[160] Similarly, the cardinals questioned William on three propositions culled from his lost Ascension sermon,[161] two from that for Holy Thursday,[162] and four from his sermon for the fifth Sunday after Easter.[163]

The cardinals compiled a miscellany of questionable statements from these sermons, but a surprisingly large number of them concern proper dress. Six of the twenty-three suspect articles discuss clothing;[164] only two of these stem from his Pentecost sermon and only one of them pertains to the apparel of royalty. Yet with his constant preoccupation upon matters of dress, William probably would have angered King Louis even if he had not insulted him directly.

Four of the articles are not localized to any particular sermon. Article thirty-five, which accused William of having stated that he was prepared to suffer death for what he had preached, is written to have been said *frequenter.*[165] His entreaty for his followers to carry on his struggle if they should hear of his capture, imprisonment, or decapitation, was merely a reminder for them to confirm the truth of his preaching in their hearts. And his call for a general council simply meant that he was prepared to defend his teachings before an ecclesiastical tribunal.[166]

The next portion of the document describes the denunciation of the archbishop of Tours. In the presence of King Louis, the bishop of Paris, and a great multitude of people, Archbishop Peter of Lamballe charged William of having preached many *falsitates.* William had concurrently been given a *cedula,* by someone he did not know, which listed various errors in his works and had been delivered to King Louis. William then refuted the errors recorded in this *cedula* and defended his teachings without anyone, not even Archbishop Peter, raising a word against him.

[160] Articles 16, 17, 21, and 22 in *Resp.,* 347-8.

[161] Articles 15, 23, and 27 in *Resp.,* 346-350.

[162] Articles 18 and 33 in *Resp.,* 347, 351-2.

[163] Articles 28, 30, 31, and 32. The committee even referred to this sermon by its incipit *Si quis se religiosum putat. Resp.,* 350-1.

[164] Articles 17, 19, 20, 21, 22, and 33 in *Resp.,* 347-352.

[165] *Resp.,* 352.

[166] *Resp.,* 353. But the secular theologians had already called for a provincial or general council as early as October 1255. *Chart.* I, No. 256, 293.

This denunciation can be placed with certainty to July 1256. While asking specific questions about the events surrounding Peter's accusation, William admits to having heard rumors of Pope Alexander's letter demanding that he and his cohorts be deprived of their benefices. This proclamation was not issued until 17 June 1256[167] and there must have been at least a two-week time lag before it reached Paris. King Louis was known to have been present at Paris for most of July and thus would have been available to attend this gathering. Furthermore, William's judges mention that only three of the seven secular theologians at the University were in Paris for this assembly. As Faral has commented, their absence would be readily explainable if the gathering took place in July when classes were not formally in session.[168]

In the following section, William discusses the intervention of the archbishops of Reims and Sens into the academic quarrel at Paris.[169] At Paris, the prelates had heard the Dominicans' Master General, Humbert of Romans, charge that certain theologians had preached false doctrine publicly which denigrated his Order directly. The archbishop of Sens summoned William to appear before him to answer Humbert's complaint. When asked if this accusation was true, William staunchly denied it. Moreover, he declared that he was prepared to defend everything that he preached, and correct his statements, if they were found to need emendation. Impressed with his response, the archbishop proposed the idea of a council to settle the issue. William immediately accepted the proposal but Humbert was unreceptive to the plan. He argued that whatever such a council would pronounce would be applicable only in the province of Sens and not the whole kingdom.[170]

The cardinals then pose specific objections to William's preaching matter, of which the most notable was the question of timing. As some have observed, William started to preach about the Last Times during the conflict between the University and the friars. Could not one therefore conclude that he was preaching on account of the friars and perhaps against the friars?

William responds to this criticism *tripliciter*. First, he notes that the peace agreement between the friars and the University had already gone into effect when he began his preaching. Second, he claims to have never preached anything derogatory to the friars and only concentrated on *Pseudo-Praedicatores* and *penetrantes domos*. William finds it highly unusual that the friars think they have been inculpated in his sermons. He does not understand how they could have made this connection; unless, that is,

[167] *Chart.* I, No. 280, 319-23.
[168] *Resp.*, 354, 373.
[169] *Resp.*, 356.
[170] *Chart.* I, No. 287, 330.

these dangers have started to manifest themselves through the friars' deeds. But William dismisses this possibility as unimaginable.[171] Third, William writes that even if the struggle between the University and the friars had not ended in March, he could still preach about *Pseudo-Praedicatores* without them being understood as the friars. A quarrel should not prevent someone from speaking the truth. As an example, William notes that even the Apostle preached openly about the Pseudo-Prophets when they flagrantly challenged him.[172]

William next discusses *De periculis* directly. He confesses that many French prelates wanted to warn their congregations about the impending perils. To this end, they solicited the University to compose a list of these dangers. William, along with other masters and students of theology and doctors of law, collected these scriptural signs and produced them in *De periculis*. However, William admits, the work had undergone several revisions. He knows that the papal commission had been examining the third version; but he does not know whether this version contains falsified additions or eliminations of the original text.[173] He is ready to present the committee with a copy of the fourth or fifth version, which he can testify as truthful and promises would be met with instant approbation.[174] Repeating his profession to the archbishops of Reims and Sens, William states that he and his coauthors are prepared to emend all contained within the work which the commission judges to need correction.

But William's offer to emend *De periculis* was blatantly ignored. Instead, Pope Alexander condemned it and quickly ended his tenure as a master of theology. Although near the end of his pontificate, Alexander eased some of his sanctions against William's supporters,[175] and ensuing popes would relax some of their predecessor's decrees against the master, he still remained banished and excommunicated the rest of his life.

Although their leader had been exiled, William's followers continued their literary activities. Throughout the 1250s and into the 1260s, the poet

[171] "...cum hoc esse vix potest, ut estimo, nisi in eis talia opera (quod absit!) modo aliquo appareren t." *Resp.*, 359.

[172] Phil 1:15; Phil 2:17; *Resp.*, 358-9.

[173] "Nec scio tamen utrum per vitium falsitatis in isto volumine quicquam additum fuerit vel subtractum." *Resp.*, 360.

[174] "...credens firmiter quod, si quartam vel quintam compilationem earundem auctoritatem vidisset (cum in eis nihil contineatur quod offendere debeat animarum christianum), non eas reprobasset, sed potius approbasset." *Resp.*, 360.

[175] On 27 September 1257 he granted the bishop of Paris the power to absolve all those scholars from excommunication who had complied with *Quasi lignum vite*. *Chart.* I, No. 329, 377-8. Three years later, he gave Bishop Reginald authority to absolve those from excommunication who had the works of William in their possession. Absolution for this crime could previously come only from Alexander himself. *Chart.* I, No. 366, 414.

Rutebeuf popularized William's attacks on the friars in the vernacular;[176] in his poetry, he emphasized the friars' hypocrisy,[177] he created the characters of *Faus Semblant* and *Morte Color* to parody the friars,[178] and he denounced Louis IX's preferential treatment of the friars.[179]

While in exile, William continued to write. In the early 1260s, he published his eschatalogical *Liber de antichristo* to broadcast the fact that the year 1260 had passed without the occurrence of any of the *Eternal Gospel's* predictions.[180] And in October 1266, Pope Clement IV acknowledged receipt of the *Collectiones catholicae*, William's encyclopedic reply to all the mendicant critics of *De periculis*. And while Clement admitted that he had not as yet read the work thoroughly, he noted that it seemed to be of the same substance of *De periculis*.[181] Clement then stated that he feared too much learning had made its author mad.[182]

William also seems to have kept abreast of university affairs. During the papal interregnum of 1268-1271, the secular masters Gerard of Abbeville and Nicholas of Lisieux renewed their mentor's fight against the friars. The latter, in 1270, sent William a copy of his *De perfectione et excellentia status clericorum* along with an introductory letter.[183] Heartened by his disciple's undertaking, but saddened by his own absence, William explained to him that "more than I could ever express, I want to see you and to rejoice in your conversation."[184] His death occurred two years later.

The years 1255-6 witnessed a polemical struggle for survival between the Parisian secular theologians and the mendicant orders. The mendicants, through the aggressive decisions of Alexander IV, managed to emerge as

[176] On Rutebeuf's role in the conflict and his use of *De periculis*, see Faral, *Rutebeuf*, I:65-93; C.M. Pugh, "*Le Roman de la rose*: The *Contraire* Allegory of Jean de Meung" unpublished Ph.D. dissertation, Louisiana State University, 1999; A. Serper, "L'influence de Guillaume," 391-402; Szittya, *Antifraternal Tradition*, 184-6.

[177] See, for examples, "La Complainte de Maistre Guillaume de Saint Amour" ll. 91-6 in *Rutebeuf*, I:262; "La Chanson de Pouille," ll. 33-40 in *Rutebeuf*, I:434; "La Discorde de l'université et des Jacobins," ll. 41-8 in *Rutebeuf*, I:240, and " Le Dit d'hypocrisie," ll. 235-8 in *Rutebeuf*, I:295.

[178] "La Complainte de Maistre Guillaume de Saint Amour" in *Rutebeuf*, I:258-66. The character of Faus Semblant would be immortalized by Jean de Meung in *Le Romance de la rose*, III:316-29.

[179] "La Complainte de Constantinople," ll. 133-44 in *Rutebeuf*, I:429 and "La Bataille des vices contra les vertus," ll. 107-11, 136-46 in *Rutebeuf*, I:309-10.

[180] *Liber de antichristo et eius ministris* edd. E. Martène and U. Durand in *Veterum scriptorum et monumentorum historicum dogmaticorum moralium amplissima collectio* (Paris, 1731), IX:1271-1445. On William's authorship of this work, see Lerner, "Refreshment of the Saints," 125-6, n. 93 and Traver, "*Liber de Antichristo*," 87-98.

[181] *Chart.* I, No. 412, 459.

[182] "Te multe littere faciunt insanire." *Chart.* I, No. 412, 459; Act. 26:24

[183] *Chart.* I, No. 439, 495-498.

[184] "...quod plus quam velim exprimere desidero vos videre ac vestro colloquio congaudere." *Chart.* I, No. 440, 498-9.

victors; they were reincorporated into the University and remained an integral part of the studium. Yet the university conflict had left their reputations tarnished. Opposition to their ministry perdured and would once again erupt into open conflict at the University following the death of Pope Clement IV. This next phase of the conflict would be led by Gerard and Nicholas, but watched very closely by their master *in absentia*.

William was pivotal in constructing a set genre of academic antifraternalism. Even after its condemnation, his *De periculis* would continue to retain an almost "eternal" quality. The later controversies between the mendicants and seculars remained especially indebted to it, since all subsequent defences or detractions of the mendicant life were simply responses to, or elaborations upon, arguments initially advanced by William.

MANUSCRIPT DESCRIPTIONS AND THE RELATIONSHIP OF MANUSCRIPTS

DE MENDICITATE

William's responses to Bonaventure's disputed question *De mendicitate* survive in three manuscripts (*CLP*). Manuscript descriptions are contained below:

MANUSCRIPTS

C = Cambridge, Corpus Christi College, ms. 103.[1]
De mendicitate = pp. 95a-105b.

Vellum. 290 x 195 mm. 214 pp. *C* was written in two late fourteenth- and fifteenth-century hands in two columns. It contains a variety of theological works including sermons, Robert Kilwardby's commentary on book three of the *Sentences*, Richard FitzRalph's *De pauperie salvatoris*, and several works by John Wyclif. *C* also includes a number of documents relating to the secular/mendicant conflict at the University of Paris including Pope Innocent IV's restrictive decree on the mendicants' activities in 1254 (pp. 107-8),[2] the secular theologians' 1254 *Apologia* (pp. 109-11),[3] the secular theologians' threat to dissolve the University in 1255, *Radix amaritudinis*, (p. 107),[4] and the interim peace agreement *Noverit universitas vestra* made between the friars and the University in 1256 (p. 112).[5]

1 Bougerol, "Reportatio," 58-9; Dufeil, "Universitaire parisien réactionnaire," 248; M.R. Rhodes James, *A Descriptive Catalogue of the Manuscripts in the Library of Corpus Christi College* (Cambridge: University Press, 1912), I:198-201; Traver, "Reportatio," 288.

2 *Chart.* I, No. 240, 267-70.

3 *Chart.* I, No. 230, 252-8.

4 *Chart.* I, No. 256, 292-6.

5 *Chart.* I, No. 268, 304-6.

The *incipit* of the *reportatio* on page 95a reads:

> Quaestio disputata a Fratre Bonaventura super mendicitatem et obiectiones Magistri Guillelmi de Sancto Victore(!) qua <continentur> eiusdem fratris solutiones et solutiones Magistri Guillelmi ad eiusdem fratris obiectionis. Unde ubi invenies in margine *Magister Guillelmus,* scias hoc a Magistro Guillelmo dictum esse; cetera dicta sunt fratris. Hanc quaestionem nullus habet Parisius praeter unum vel duos; circa huius acquisitionem multum laboravi.

The *explicit* on page 105b reads:

> Et sic patet <solutio> totius quaestionis et argumentorum ostendentium quod mendicare non sic de perfectione christianae religionis. Cetera conceduntur. Hanc quaestionem determinavit magister bonus eventus de ordine fratrum minorum, secundum quod a quodam clerico potuit reportari.

C identifies the arguments of Bonaventure and William by the marginal referents of ff. b. (*Frater Bonaventura*) or m. g. (*Magister Guillelmus*). William's annotations usually begin with the word *Respondeo,* though apart from the *incipit* and the marginal notes, there is no way to identify who is responding. The top of p. 97 contains the header written in a hand other than that of the scribe: "Hic respondet Magister Guillelmus ad argumenta Bonaventura." The bottom of p. 100, immediately preceding Bonaventure's solution, a phrase written in a hand other than that of the scribe notes: "Hic respondet Bonaventura ad argumenta Magistri Guillelmi."

L = Florence, Biblioteca Medicea Laureniziana, ms. Plt. 36 dextr. 12.[6]
De mendicitate = ff. 124r-129v.

Parchment. 238 x 158 mm. iv + 131 ff. Written in various fourteenth-century hands, *L* contains several Franciscan theological works on poverty including treatises by Richard of Conington and John Pecham. Folio 7v reads: "Liber Sanctae crucis de Florentia ordinis minoris de evangelica paupertate No. 413."

[6] Bougerol, "Reportatio," 58; Dufeil, "Universitaire parisien réactionnaire," 248; A. Heyesse, "Fr. Richardi de Conington, O.F.M., Tractatus de paupertate Fratrum Minorum et Abbreviatura inde a Communitate extracta," *AFH* 23 (1930):62-4; Traver, "Reportatio," 289.

The *explicit* of the *reportatio* on f. 129v reads:

> Hanc quaestionem determinavit ita Magister Bonaventura de ordine fratrum minorum secundum quod a quodam clerico potuit reportari. Deo gratias et amen.

William's marginal notes begin on f. 125r; they are in a similar, though smaller script than the rest of the text. These notes make no mention of William–nor is William mentioned anywhere in the colophon. Most of them commence with the word *Respondeo*, although the respondent is never identified. On ff. 125r-v, the annotations are accompanied by a corresponding letter to indicate which argument William is refuting; the letter has a counterpart within the text. After f. 125v, the letter is no longer included in the marginal note and is instead placed in the opposite margin, always on the same line as a paragraph marker, to show where William's argument should be inserted.

P = Paris, Bibliothèque Nationale, ms. lat. 15850.[7]
De mendicitate = ff. 2r-4v.

Parchment. 280 x 187 mm. i + 325 folios; copied before 1310. *P* is written in several thirteenth-century hands, in two columns. The volume is composed of two separate books, ff. 1-44, 45-325; the writing on ff. 1-7v is extremely small. *P* contains William of Saint-Amour's disputed questions along with quodlibets of Henry of Ghent and Godfrey of Fontaines. *P* was once in the possession of the Parisian secular master Nicholas of Bar-le-Duc as revealed on f. 1v.

On f. 2rb, immediately preceding William's first objection, *P* contains the following introductory preface:

> Respondet Magister Guillelmus de Sancto Amore sustinens partem oppositam non sui auctoritate, sed per sacram paginam etc., tota universitate magistrorum parisiensium contra Praedicatores et Minores et ordines consimiles...

William's name is further revealed throughout the text as each objection begins with a phrase such as *Respondet Magister Guillelmus*, *Respondet Magister Guillelmus dicens quod* or *Respondet Magister Guillelmus et dicit quod*, rather than the more familiar *Respondeo* of *CL*. The *explicit* on f. 4va exposes the identity both of the opponent and the respondent. It reads:

7 *Bibliotheca manuscripta Henrici de Gandavo* ed. R. Macken O.F.M. (Leiden: E.J. Brill, 1979), I:634-5; Bougerol, "Reportatio," 59; Dufeil, "Universitaire parisien réactionnaire," 248-9; Traver, "Reportatio," 289-90; idem, "William of Saint-Amour," 309.

> quaestionem ita determinavit Magister Bonaventura emeritus de ordine fratrum minorum ... et ita respondet Magister Guillelmus de Sancto Amore ad omnia supradicta.

C, *L*, and *P* all derive from a common *reportatio*. *P* is the oldest manuscript, yet *L* is the closest witness to the original report and it contains William's objections in their original form–as marginal notes.

The manuscripts of the *reportatio* are divided into two families: *β*, consisting of manuscript *L*, and *δ*, consisting of manuscripts *C* and *P*. The manuscript *L* of *β* provides the better text and forms the basis for this edition.

The *β* family, consisting solely of manuscript *L*, can be characterized by two features. First, as we have seen, it includes William's responses as marginal notes. Second, it contains many significant errors, most of which are homeoteleutic in nature. In these instances of omission, *δ* corrects *L*. Some of these omissions are noted below:

infra, n. 31, ll. 3-7:	Item, in Psalm. 108: *Et persecutus est hominem inopem et mendicum.* Glossa Augustini: Iudas, Iesum Christum; et ita fuit Christus mendicus. Sed sequi Christum non est opus imperfectionis et peccati; ergo mendicare pro Christo non est peccatum sed potius opus perfectionis. *om. L*
infra, n. 70, ll. 5-6:	Ergo qui spiritualibus insistunt nihil in mundo habentes debent a domino vel ab eius ministris sustentari *om. L*
infra, n. 81, l. 4-5:	nec quo veniunt relictis divitiis suis dominum praedictum ibi sint rustici delicati. Et *om. L*
infra, n. 101, ll. 18-19:	ACT. 4 ET 12, Q. 1, *VIDENTES*. *om. L*
infra, n. 144, ll. 11-13:	sicut Ordo Minorum et Praedicatorum; et ideo praedicti Ordines potestative accipere non debent. Sed quia habent subauctoritatem *om. L*
infra, n. 149, ll. 7-8:	SED MENDICARE EST CONTRA VOLUNTATEM CHRISTI *om. L*

The common ancestor of manuscripts *C* and *P*, *δ*, originally contained William's objections as marginal notes. This can be seen as both *C* and *P* occasionally differ on where they have inserted the notes into the text proper. The marginal objections were interpolated into the text of *P* at a very early date, quite possibly by *P*'s scribe himself. The tendency in *P* is to provide an introductory preface to each response. Thus most of the objections in *P* begin with the phrase "Respondet Magister Guillelmus dicens" or a similar introductory marker rather than *Respondeo*.[8] *P* explicitly mentions William thirty times by name. The frequency with which *P* identifies William, as well as the claim at *infra*, n. 22 that William was using

[8] For examples see *infra* and Traver, "Reportatio," 294-5.

Scripture and not himself to refute Bonaventure quite possibly suggests that *P* was copied by a supporter.

While William's responses in *C*, *L*, and *P* usually immediately follow Bonaventure's argument, *P* occasionally groups several of William's arguments into one unit. As examples, his responses at *infra*, nn. 36 and 38 are conjoined and form one unit. This same tendency appears throughout *P*; William's responses at *infra*, nn. 79 and 82 are conjoined and comprise one unit as they are at nn. 90 and 92, nn. 99 and 101, nn. 111 and 113, and nn. 119, 121, and 123. Because of this restructuring *P* had to add key phrases such as "Ad hoc quod dicit" to redirect the reader to which argument William was refuting. As an example, *P* has joined William's responses at nn. 111 and 113. To clarify to which argument William is responding, *P* has added the prefatory phrase at n. 113 "Ad hoc quod dicit de Chrysostomo 'adularia oportet' etc., ipse dicit" to direct the reader to the Chrysostom citation cited by Bonaventure in n. 112. Other examples of these key phrases can be found *infra* at nn. 36, 101, 113, and 123[9].

It is unclear when the responses were inserted into the text in *C*, but they were done so without regard to grammar or syntax. Several of the responses in *C* were incorporated into the text intersententially. As an example, William's argument at *infra* n. 99 was inserted into Bonaventure's argument at n. 98 thus separating the word "omittenda" from the rest of Bonaventure's text. In *infra*, n. 101 William's argument was interpolated into the final sentence of n. 100 thereby severing the words "omnibus sunt secuti" from the Augustine passage which Bonaventure had cited. William's responses in *C* were also imported into Bonaventure's text mid-sentence at *infra*, nn. 110 and 111, nn. 118 and 119, and nn. 120 and 121.[10]

Both *C* and *P* had difficulty determining exactly where to insert William's arguments at nn. 101, 111, 119 and 121. This indicates that it was probably unclear in their common ancestor δ to which of Bonaventure's arguments the marginal notes at these locations referred. *P* solved this problem by joining William's responses at these locations to their closest marginal counterpart and then inserted them as a unit into the text after Bonaventure's nearest argument. *P* then provided a key phrase to redirect the reader to the appropriate argument of Bonaventure. *C*, or more likely its exemplar, simply tried to interpolate the marginal responses immediately after Bonaventure's closest argument; but in so doing, it fragmented Bonaventure's text in all four of these instances.

9 Traver, "Reportatio," 296.
10 Traver, "Reportatio," 297.

On one occasion, *C* presents the correct ordering of Bonaventure's text and William's arguments against the readings of manuscripts *LP*. Both *L* and *P* place Bonaventure's response to *contra* statement eight and William's rebuttal to it at *infra*, nn. 114 and 115 after William's response to Bonaventure's reply to *contra* statement nine at *infra*, n. 117.[11] Since this error is contained in both *L* and *P*, it was very likely contained in the autograph. It is extremely unlikely that *C*'s scribe corrected the transposed textual order. *C* contains such a large number of unique variants it is difficult to imagine its scribe deliberately restructuring the text in this instance. Rather, this correction was made by an ancestor of *C* probably before the marginal notes were interpolated into the text.

Manuscript *P* is the best witness of the *δ* tradition and it usually presents a faithful rendering of the text. On a few occasions, *P* can correct manuscripts *CL* when they are in error.

infra, n. 6, ll. 3-4:	Sed omnis mendicus compellatur necessaria petere *om. CL*
infra, n. 68, l. 21:	in² *om. CL*
infra, n. 82, l. 15:	CIBUS] omnibus *CL*
infra, n. 115, ll. 21-2:	EX EGESTATIS COMPULSIONE ET ISTE DICIT QUOD PROHIBETUR PETERE *om. CL*
infra, n. 127, l. 17:	NE] nec *CL*
infra, n. 128, l. 7:	sanciendum] sciendum *CL*
infra, n. 128, l. 8:	Spritus induxit *om. CL*

P also bears witness to several stages of glossing. Some of these glosses remain marginal notes while others have been incorporated directly into the text.

infra, n. 39, l. 14:	*ei*] scilicet mulieri *add. in mg.* P^c
infra, n. 67, l. 18:	CONCULCABATUR] *add.* quae satis vilificat se *P*
infra, n. 83, l. 5:	mendicus] pauper et *praem. P*
infra, n.84, l. 7:	OPERANDO] operari vel *praem. P*
infra, n. 74, l. 4:	et amplius] *add.* quam frustra vel buccelam panis *P*: quod maius est *add. in mg.* P^c
infra, n. 96, l. 18:	PAUPERIS] pauperum vel *praem. P*
infra, n. 133, l. 9:	FAMIS] *add.* et fame *P*
infra, n. 141, l. 19:	ACCIPERET] *add.* nihil enim exinde sperabat et volebat habere cum esset spirituale bonum *P*

Manuscript *C* is the weaker member of the *δ* tradition. *C* is a late manuscript and presents a large number of unique variants in the form of transpositions, omissions, and scribal errors. In particular, *C* contains a significant number of lengthy omissions. A few of these are noted below:

[11] *Cf*, *QDM*, *infra*, nn. 114-117.

infra, n. 11, ll. 7-11: secundum decreta Sanctorum, et maxime quia in fine illius decreti dicitur: Si aliquis existiterit modernis vel futuris temporibus qui contra nitatur, iam dicta damnatione feriatur. Ergo omnis qui mendicus est vel indigens per istud decretum excommunicatus est et sic in peccato mortali. Sed nullus talis est in statu perfectionis *om. C*

infra, n. 23, ll. 22-3: vel tamquam perfectis. Non tamquam praelatis *om. C*

infra, n. 23, l. 24: praelatis, et ita datur eis tamquam *om. C*

infra, n. 25, l. 12: Glossa: Puerum, id est pauperem. Ergo qui recipit pauperes, recipit *om. C*

infra, n. 31, ll. 2-3: ergo mendicare pro Christo est opus perfectionis *om. C*

infra, n. 31, ll. 4-5: et ita fuit Christus mendicus. Sed sequi Christum *om. C*

infra, n. 36, ll. 4-6: SUPPLE QUOD DEEST, SCILICET ET ITA NULLI ADULATUS ETC. QUI ERGO DE FACILI INVENIUNT, VIDETUR QUOD SINT ADULATORES. *om. C*

infra, n. 42, l. 4: et ita ii qui perfecte ipsum sequuntur *om. C*

infra, n. 117, l. 1: OMNE CONSILIUM SIT SUPEREROGATIONIS ET *om. C*

There are very few instances in which *C* corrects *LP*, namely it supplies the word *opus* omitted in *LP* at *infra,* n. 15, l. 1, and, as we have seen, it presents the correct ordering of Bonaventure's responses to contra statements eight and nine at nn. 114-117.

Stemma Codicum

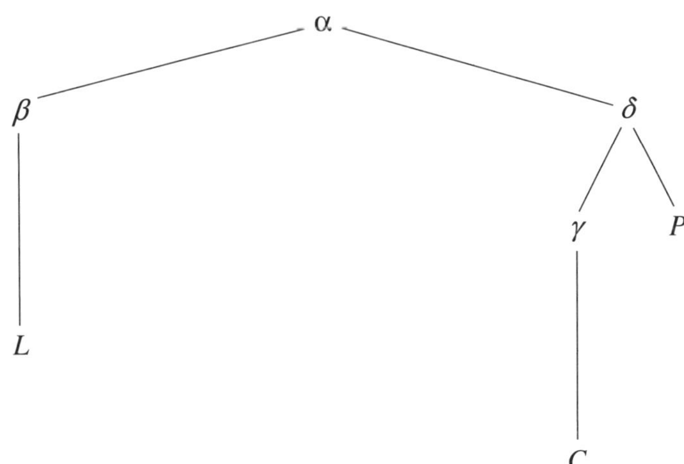

QUI AMAT PERICULUM, SI QUIS DILIGIT ME, AND *DE PHARISAEO ET PUBLICANO*

William's three sermons survive in eight manuscripts (*BDEMNSVW*) and three printed editions (*APR*). The sermon *Qui amat periculum* exists in all eight manuscripts and all three printed editions. *Si quis diligit me* survives in one manuscript, *E*, while the sermon *De pharisaeo and publicano* is extant in one manuscript, *W*, and two early modern printings (*AP*). A list and a description of the manuscripts are contained below:

MANUSCRIPTS

B = Vienna, Österreichische Nationalbibliothek, ms. lat. 4941.[12]
De periculis = ff. 167r-194v.
Qui amat periculum = ff. 194v-203v.

Fifteenth century (1431); 203 x 140 mm. 277 ff. *B* consists of a miscellany of texts both in Latin and Czech against John Wyclif and John Huss. Folios 1r-141v comprise an admixture of treatises against Huss and Wyclif including excerpts from the Council of Constance. Folios 1r-2r include a series of *propositiones* made against Wyclifites at Constance (1414) and ff. 2v-9v contain determinations by the Faculty of Theology at the University of Prague against Wyclif. On ff. 25r-26r is Huss' *Littera directa dominis baronibus Boëmie in quattuor temporibus ante Nativitatem Domini anno 1412* (in Czech) and ff. 26v-141v form a compendium of documents relative to Huss' teachings, including many of his letters. Folio 142 is blank while ff. 143r-166v contain an assortment of treatises on communion in both kinds. William of Saint-Amour's *De periculis* is found on ff. 167r-194v; *Qui amat periculum* follows on ff. 194v-203v. While neither work is identified, the running header "De periculis" written in the same hand as the text spans ff. 167r-203v. An attempt to differentiate the texts was made at some point, for a later hand has placed the rubric "Sermo magistri Guillelmi doctoris Parisiensis contra hypocrisim" between the two texts at f. 194v. A work entitled "Auctoritates contra communionem infantium" follows *De periculis* spanning ff. 204r-229v; ff. 229v-236v contains Jean Gerson's *Regulae contra haereses* and ff. 237r-238v consist of extracts about heresy from Isidore of Seville. The remainder of the manuscript comprises a mixture of documents about Wyclif, Huss, and the Council of Constance.

[12] *Tabulae codicum manu scriptorum praeter graecos et orientales in Biblioteca Palatina Vindobonensi asservatorum* ed. Academia caesarea vindobonensis (Vienna, 1869) [rpt Graz: Akademische Druck- u. Verlagsanstalt, 1965), III:433-436.

D = Naples, Biblioteca nazionale Vittorio Emanuele III, ms. VII.D.9.[13]
De periculis = ff. 164r-189r.
Qui amat periculum = ff. 189r-196v.

Fifteenth century; 305 x 203 mm. 259 ff. Although f. 1r *in calce* identifies this ms. as *Guillelmus, Contra haereses, D* is primarily a compilation of documents relative to the Council of Constance. Ff. 1r-54r include a sermon by John Wyclif and a series of forty-five articles by him condemned at Constance. *D* also contains a description of the errors of Wyclif and Huss, an analysis of communion in both kinds, and a discussion of Thomas Aquinas' position on heretics. Huss' treatise *De corpore Christi* is found on ff. 145r-153v and is followed by *dicta de corpore Christi* and *de statu monachorum.* William of Saint-Amour's *De periculis* is contained on ff. 164r-189r. The *incipit* identifies the work as an anti-heretical, or perhaps anti-Wyclifite in nature:

> Liber Magistri Guillelmi Parisiensis de Sancto Amore contra hereticos seu falsos viclefistas in cognoscendo sectas eorum.

Ff. 189r-196v contain *Qui amat periculum.* A later hand has sought to distinguish the two texts by adding the phrase "Sermo de praedicta" on f. 189r. In the *explicit,* on f. 196v, the scribe again assumes that the work was intended to be anti-Wyclifite.

> Explicit liber scriptus Parisius contra hypocritas et falsos viglifistas a magistro Guillelmo de Sancto Amore burgundo anno domini MCCCCXVII.

Ff. 196v-259v consist of material relating to both Wyclif and Huss both in Latin and Czech.

E = Erfurt, Amplonianische Bibliothek, ms. Q 170.[14]
De periculis = 168r-173v.
Si quis diligit me = f. 174r-v.
Qui amat periculum = ff. 174v-175v (ends at n. 29).

226 ff; 240 x 155 mm. Contains various texts, mainly theological in nature, written in a series of late-thirteenth to mid-fourteenth-century hands. Folios 1r-116r contain Hugh of St. Cher's *Speculum ecclesiae* (ff. 1r-8r), Robert Holcoth's *Lectura primo sententiarum* (ff. 9r-83v) and Hugh of

[13] *Inventario generale di tutti codici manoscritti della biblioteca nazionale* handwritten catalogue microfilmed by Library of Congress [Washington D.C.], 1986, II:311.

[14] *Beschreibendes Verzeichniss der Amplonianischen Handschriften-Sammlung zu Erfurt* ed. Wilhelm Schum (Berlin: Weidmannsche Buchhandlung, 1887), 425-427.

Saint Victor's *Liber sententiarum* (*Summa sententiarum*) (ff. 84v-116r). Ff. 116r-118r comprise a *Tractatus de moribus vitae monasticae* and ff. 118r-39r consist of postills on Mark and Matthew. Ff. 140r-160v comprise excerpts of Augustine's *Confessions* and *Homilies on John*; f. 161r contains excerpts of Seneca's *De causis*, and ff. 161v-167v includes extracts from three of Augustine's works, *De divinatione daemonum*, *super Genesim ad litteram*, and *De disciplina Christiana*. William of Saint-Amour's *De periculis* is found on ff. 168r-173v. The *incipit* on f. 168r reads:

> Libellus Guillelmi de Sancto Amore de futuris et instantibus periculis ecclesiae

Folio 174r-v, contains his sermon *Si quis diligit me*. The *incipit* on f. 174r reads:

> Sermo de Magistri Guillelmi de Sancto Amore in die pentecosten Parisius.

The sermon *Qui amat periculum* follows on ff. 174v-175v. The *incipit* on f. 174v reads:

> Sermo eiusdem in festo Philippi et Jacobi.

The sermon abruptly ends at the end of f. 175v (n. 29) where William announces seven signs to identify true preachers from false ones. The scribe has inserted the rubric "quare supra c. fi. (capitulo finali)" to redirect the reader back to the final chapter of *De periculis* in which William tabulates the signs to identify true Apostles from pseudoapostles. Ff. 176r-200v contain Giles of Rome's *De intellectu et intelligibili* and ff. 201r-222v comprise Jacobus de Aesculo, *Quaestiones quaesdam circa sententias*. The remaining folios (ff. 222v-226v) contain various *quaestiones astronomicae*.

M = Munich, Bayerische Staatsbibliothek, ms. Clm. 14635.[15]
De periculis = 146ra-168ra.
Qui amat periculum = ff. 168ra-174ra.

Parchment; 190 x 130 mm. 203 ff. written in various fourteenth- and fifteenth-century hands. The first sixty-eight folios contain decrees of a variety of Church councils between 1267 and 1418. Ff. 69ra-72vb contain excerpts of the Council of Constance. Ff. 73ra-111vb constitute material

[15] *Catalogus codicum latinorum bibliothecae regiae monacensis* edd. C. Halm and G. Meyer (Munich, 1876) [rpt Wiesbaden: Otto Harrassowitz, 1968], II, pt. 2, 207-8.

relative to the Augustinians, including the *Vita S. Augustini*, the Rule of St. Augustine, and sermons by Augustine and others. William of Saint-Amour's *De periculis* is found on ff. 146ra-168ra. *Quia amat periculum* begins on f. 168ra and ends at f. 174ra. This sermon is followed by an exposition of the Lord's prayer.

N – Nurenberg, Stadtbibliothek, ms. Cent. I, 80.[16]
De periculis = ff. 88ra-98rb.
Qui amat periculum = ff. 98rb-101rb.

Parchment. 355 x 265 mm. i + 146 ff. *N* was written in the second half of the fifteenth century in one textualis hand in two columns of 48 lines. Once in the possession of the Dominican convent in Nurenberg. The flyleaf reads:

> Anno domini MCCCCLIII ligatus est iste liber per fratres Conradum Forster et Johannem Lorhatub conventus Nurembergensis ordinis praedicatorum.

N contains a report about the Church Councils at Florence and Basel (ff. 2ra-14va), the Franciscan Roger Conway's *Contra Armacanum* (ff. 17ra-25ra), the treatise of Richard FitzRalph (*Armacanus*) *Contra privilegia ordinis fratrum mendicantium*. *N* also includes three works by the Dominican Johannes de Dambach, *Tractatus de moderatione quartae* (ff. 30ra-67va), *De quarta* (ff. 67vb-81ra), and *De quantitate indulgentiarum* (ff. 81ra-87va). Folios 88ra-101rb contain William of Saint-Amour's *De periculis* to which is appended the sermon *Qui amat periculum*. The *incipit* reads:

> Incipit libellus condemnatus per papam Alexandrum quartum de periculis quae instabunt temporibus novissimis false compilatus per quosdam Parisius sed iuste condemnatus per ecclesiam dei editus in confusionem mendicantium.

Qui amat periculum begins on f. 98r with no break between it and *De periculis*. The *explicit* on 101rb identifies William:

> Explicit Libellus de periculis quae instabunt temporibus novissimis Magistri Guillelmi de Amore Parisius false compilatus in confusionem religionum mendicantium sed iuste per Alexandrum papam quartum condemnatus.

16 *Die Handschriften der stadtsbibliothek Nürnberg.* Band III: *Die lateinischen mittelalterlichen Handscriften. Juristische Handschriften* ed. Ingeborg Neske (Wiesbaden: Otto Harrassowitz, 1991), 19-22.

N concludes with Thomas Aquinas' *Contra impugnantes Dei cultum et religionem* (ff. 101rb-146vb).

S = Stuttgart, Württemberg, Landesbibliothek, ms. HB I 91.[17]
De periculis = pp. 293r-325r.
Qui amat periculum = pp. 325v-333r (incomplete ends at n. 38).

Paper. 215 x 150 mm. 354 pages. *S* contains a variety of theological and historical texts copied in the first and second half of the fifteenth century. Included amongst its contents are Innocent III's *Expositio missae* and several chronicles including those by Honorius of Autun, Heinricus de Heimburg, and Jacques de Vitry's *Historia orientalis seu Hierosolymitana* (pp. 48r-177r). *S* also contains treatises on wine, medicine, and agriculture (pp. 178r-231r) along with articles from the Council of Constance against John Huss (pp. 233r-292r). William of Saint-Amour's *De periculis* can be found on pp. 293r-325r. It is identified by a rubric written in a different hand on f. 293r:

Incipit Guillelmus de sacro fonte de periculis mundi futuris.

Qui amat periculum follows on pp. 325v-333r. An attempt to separate the two texts was made in a later hand at the top of f. 325v and reads: "Sermo de periculis ecclesiae." Following *Qui amat periculum*, *S* contains prophecies attributed to Hildegard of Bingen (pp. 333v-335r), and a collection of documents relative to the Council of Constance (pp. 341r-354v).

V = Biblioteca apostolica vaticana, ms. vat. lat. 1160.[18]
De periculis = ff. 1-47v.
Qui amat periculum = ff. 47v-60v.

Parchment. 60 ff. 205 x 140 mm. Folios 1-60r are written in one hand of the late-thirteenth/early fourteenth century. Folio 60v contains two geometrical theorems written in a fifteenth-century hand. Folios 1-47v contain William's *De periculis* while ff. 47v-60r contain *Qui amat periculum*. The word *explicit* on f. 47v separates William's two texts but the sermon has no *incipit* and could easily be construed as an additional chapter of *De periculis*. The *explicit* on f. 60r seems to do precisely that as it reads:

[17] *Die Handschriften der Württembergischen Landesbibliothek Stuttgart. Die Handscriften der Ehemaligen Hofbibliothek Stuttgart.* I *Codices ascetici* edd. J. Autenrieth, V.E. Fiala (Wiesbaden: Otto Harrassowitz, 1968), 163-7.

[18] *Biblioteca apostolica vaticana. Codices vaticani latini* ed. M.-H. Laurent. (Vatican, 1958), 3:33.

> Explicit liber scriptus Parisius contra hypocritas et falsos religiosos a Magistro Guillelmo de Sancto Amore Burgundo anno domini MCCLV Deo Gratias.

W = Wolfenbüttel, Bibliothek Herzog-August, ms. Guelf. 367 Helmstedt.[19]
De pharisaeo et publicano = ff. 78vb-81ra.
Qui amat periculum = ff. 81ra-86vb.

Paper and parchment. 285 x 210 mm. 83 ff. *W* is a miscellany codex containing an assortment of texts written in eleven different fourteenth- and fifteenth-century hands. The majority of the contents are fifteenth-century works written in fifteenth-century hands, with the exception of Alan of Lille's *De fide catholica* and William's sermons all of which were composed much earlier and whose texts are contained in *W* in two different fourteenth-century hands. Ff. 1r-2v contain fragments of letters between Eusebius Burgus and Isote Nogarole (c. 1438) while ff. 3r-8v (fourteenth c.) consist of parts of books two (*Against the Waldensians*) and three (*Against the Jews*) of Alan of Lille's *De fide catholica.* Folios 9r-13v preserve a brief speech by John Huss and fragments of Hussite letters while ff. 14r-15v contain a bull of Gregory XI against Johannem Militium, archdeacon of Prague. Ff. 16r-17r contain two low German poems; ff. 18r-26v comprise a treatise of Nicholas of Cusa against the Council of Basel (1442). Articles for the reformation of the Church and the calling of a new Church council follow on ff. 27r-31r, and ff. 31v-38r detail prophecies of Hildegard about the Antichrist. Ff. 39r-75r preserve Dietrich of Niem's three books *De schismate* while ff. 75r-76r contain a letter of Charles I of Sicily to Peter of Aragon, and the latter's response. Folio 76v enumerates a list of popes while f. 77v-78ra contains the University of Paris' 1255 letter explaining why the friars should not be readmitted into that institution.[20] *De pharisaeo et publicano* is found on ff. 78vb-81ra; William is identified on f. 78vb in a notation written in the same hand as the text: "Sermo Magistri Guillelmi." *Qui amat periculum* follows on ff. 81ra-86vb. The *incipit* on f. 81ra notes: "Sermo Magistri Guillelmi de Sancto Amore." The *explicit* on f. 86vb again identifies William:

> Sermo ab heretico praedicationis Guillelmo de Sancto Amore Explicit.

[19] *Die Handschriften der Herzoglichen Bibliothek zu Wolfenbüttel* ed. Otto von Heinemann (Wolfenbüttel, 1884) [rpt as *Die Helmstedter Handschriften beschrieben von Otto von Heinemann* (Frankfurt am Main: Vittorio Klostermann, 1963), 295-6.

[20] Du Boulay, *Historia universitatis parisiensis*, III:287-8.

W is the only manuscript of William's sermons which does not contain *De periculis.*

PRINTED EDITIONS

A = *Appendix ad fasciculum rerum expetendarum et fugiendarum* ed. E. Brown. 2 voll. London, 1690 [reprint Tucson, AZ: Audax Press, 1967].
De periculis = II:18-41.
Qui amat periculum = II:48-54. Printed edition based on ms. *W.*
De pharisaeo et publicano = II:43-47. Printed edition based on ms. *W.*

P = *Opera omnia quae reperiri poterunt* ed. Alithophilius. Constance [Paris],1632.
De periculis = 17-72.
Qui amat periculum = 491-506. Printed edition based on *A.*
De pharisaeo et publicano = 7-16. Printed edition based on *A* and another unknown ms.

R = *Matěje z Janova Mistra Pařižského, Regula veteris et novi testamenti* ed. V. Kybal. Innsbruck,1911.
De periculis = III:256-314.
Qui amat periculum = III:315-332. Printed edition based on an unknown ms. closely related to *M.*

Qui amat periculum

The manuscripts and printed editions of *Qui amat periculum* can be divided into two groups: *α*, containing manuscripts *EW* and the printed editions *AP*, and *β*, containing the manuscripts *BDMNSV* and the printed edition *R.* The manuscripts *EW* of α provide the better manuscript tradition and will form the basis for this edition.

Manuscripts *BDMNSV* all derive from a common ancestor, *β. V* is the oldest extant relative of *β; BDMNS* are much more distant relations. With the exception of *V,* all of the manuscripts of the *β* family are late manuscripts, copied in the fifteenth century. *V* is not only the oldest member of the *β* family, it is also the oldest manuscript containing any of William's sermons. The printed edition in the *β* group, *R,* was printed from an unidentified late manuscript very closely related to *M.*

A characteristic feature all of all the manuscripts in *β* is that they have copied the texts *De periculis* and *Qui amat periculum* in the same order; *Qui amat periculum* follows *De periculis* in every manuscript and in the printed edition *R*. In manuscript *V*, near the head of the *β* family, *De periculis* ends at the middle of f. 47v and contains the word *explicit* on the work's concluding line of text. After a one-line space, *Qui amat periculum* begins without any *incipit* or introductory material. Apart from the word *explicit*, *Qui amat periculum* would appear to be a continuation of *De periculis*. And indeed, the scribe who copied these two works apparently thought that they were one text as the *explicit* following *Qui amat periculum* on f. 60r reads: "Explicit liber." Nowhere in *V* is *Qui amat periculum* identified as a sermon.

In *N*, no differentiation is made between *De periculis* and *Qui amat periculum*. Although *De periculis* has an *incipit*, its *explicit* begins after the conclusion of *Qui amat periculum* and reads "Explicit libellus de periculis." Similarly in *D*, the *incipit* of *De periculis* on 164r introduces a "Liber Magistri Guillelmi." *De periculis* and *Qui amat periculum* form one unit in *D* and at f. 196v the *explicit* following *Qui amat periculum* again refers to a *liber*. All three manuscripts present the sermon in a way which makes it virtually indistinguishable from *De periculis*. *D* differs from *V* and *N* in that on f. 189r, a later hand inserted the phrase "Sermo de praedicta" to separate the two texts. Of these three manuscripts, only *D* identifies it as a sermon and even in this case, this observation was made by a hand other than that of the scribe.

The two texts are joined in *B* by the running reader "De periculis." But, like *D*, a later hand sought to make a distinction between the texts by adding the rubric "Sermo Magistri Guillelmi doctoris Parisiensis contra hypocrisim" between them at f. 194v. The two texts in *S* form one unit and are only separated by a rubric *in calce* on f. 325v made by a hand other than that of the scribe that reads: "Sermo de periculis ecclesiae." In *M*, the two texts simply run together without any differentiation. Of these three manuscripts, both *B* and *S* identify *Qui amat periculum* as a sermon; but like *D*, this identification is made by a hand other than that of the scribe.

Thus all of the manuscripts of the *β* family treat *De periculis* and *Qui amat periculum* as one unit; three of them (*DNV*) refer to them together as a *liber* or *libellus*. One of them (*B*), has the heading "De periculis" throughout both texts. In three of them (*BDS*), *Qui amat periculum* is only identified as a work separate from *De periculis* by notations made in hands different from that of the text. In two manuscripts (*MN*), no attempt is made to distinguish between these texts at all.

The *explicit* of *V* claims that William wrote the *liber* in 1255. As Dufeil has shown, *V* is the oldest member of the family of manuscripts that contain the third or "Roman version" of *De periculis*.[21] What seems to have happened is that an early ancestor of *V* contained a copy of both *De*

[21] Dufeil, *Guillaume de Saint-Amour*, 271, n. 95.

periculis and *Qui amat periculum.* There probably was initially some type of division between the two texts in *β* and *V* preserves a vestigial form of this division in the location of the word *explicit* on f. 47v between the two texts. Nevertheless, its *explicit* on f. 60r already assumes that the two works were in fact one work. So the process of fusing the two works had already begun in *V.* The date 1255 contained in *V*'s *explicit* on f. 60r thus refers to *De periculis* rather than to *Qui amat periculum.*

Therefore, at a very early date, the two works came to be perceived as one work. Whatever division existed between the two texts disappeared and *Qui amat periculum* became an additional chapter of *De periculis.* Later readers of the sermon in manuscripts *B, D,* and *S* realized that *Qui amat periculum* was a sermon and made marginal annotations to indicate that it was something separate from *De periculis.*

The confusion between the two texts becomes more understandable when one considers the relationship between them. *Qui amat periculum* is in many ways a summarized version of *De periculis.* It abbreviates large portions of chapters one, two, four, thirteen, and fourteen, it reiterates the errors of the *Eternal Gospel,* and it tabulates seven different ways to identify true preachers from false ones. The sermon could have easily been construed as an additional chapter of *De periculis* as it provides a convenient summary of the work.

Since *V* is the oldest surviving member of the "Roman" version of *De periculis,* one might well wonder if the feature of combining both *De periculis* and *Qui amat periculum* into one text was a characteristic of the manuscripts of this version. According to Dufeil, it was not. He lists nine manuscripts of the Roman version which he examined.[22] Of these, only three contain *Qui amat periculum.*[23] Moreover, not all of the *β* manuscripts contain what Dufeil identified as the Roman version of *De periculis.*[24] *N* contains the fifth version,[25] although this may be due to contamination.[26]

In terms of its content, with the exception of manuscripts *N* and *V,* all of *β*'s members circulated with decrees of the Council of Constance (1414-8), and even *N* contains decrees from the Councils of Basel (1431-9) and Florence (1438-45).

The *β* family is marred by omissions, faulty readings, and homeoteleutic errors. Some of the more significant omissions are noted below:

22 *Guillaume de Saint-Amour,* 271, n. 95.

23 Manuscripts *B, M,* and *V* all contain the third version of *De periculis. Guillaume de Saint-Amour,* 271, n. 95.

24 The manuscripts Vatican, B.A.V., vat. lat 1160, Prague, Chapter, ms. 538, Vienna, Naz. Bib., ms. 1528, Vienna, Naz. Bib. ms. 3971, Oxford, Bod., Bodley 158, Brussels, Bib. Roy., ms. 1467, and Olomouc, C.O., ms. 211 contain the third version of *De periculis* but not *Qui amat periculum.*

25 *Guillaume de Saint-Amour,* 278, n. 182.

26 *Guillaume de Saint-Amour,* 252-3.

infra, n. 3, ll. 14-15:	ego habeo veritatem mecum. Unde si me derident *om. β*
infra, n. 7, ll. 8-9:	quod debent venire *om. β*
infra, n. 10, ll. 13-16	Et isti erunt pleni peccato, et praetendentes speciem pietatis. Glossa: Id est religionis. Sed quomodo scietur hoc, quod plus honorem suum quam Dei laudem quaerunt? *om. β*
infra, n. 15, ll. 5-6:	sicut patet in Francia in duobus locis. Per mortem Sancti Dionysii, ecclesia apud Sanctum Dionysium ditata est, et ipse] et *BDMNSV: om. R*
infra, n. 17, ll. 13-15:	veris Apostolis causa accurati sermonis, quia Apostoli non nisi veritatem quaerebant dicere *om. β*
infra, n. 19, ll. 19-20:	sed quomodo? Mediante securi? Immo franget domum *om. β*
infra, n. 20, ll. 5-6:	sicut illi sunt ordinati in hierarchia angelica, quod *om. β*
infra, n. 27, l. 10:	ut magis specificemus. Multi enim sunt litterati Parisius *om. β*
infra, n. 33, ll. 5-7:	In longa oratione. Glossa: Qui ex vestra superstitione nihil aliud quaeritis, nisi etc., qui comeditis domos viduarum. *om. β*

β also bears witness to a glossed hyparchetype.

infra, n. 15, l. 2:	subvertant] decipiant et *praem. β*
infra, n. 17, l. 14:	episcopi] praelati sive *praem. β*
infra, n. 30, l. 2:	accipiant] acquirant et *praem. β*
infra, n. 30, l. 2:	fructu] lucro vel (et *S: om. N*) *praem. β*

There are three main groupings within the *β* family, manuscripts *BS* (*δ*), manuscripts *DN* (*γ*), and manuscript *M* and the printed edition *R* (*λ*). All of these manuscripts and the version printed in *R* have descended directly from *V*.

The most independent manuscript within the *β* family is manuscript *B*. *B* is the product of a very intelligent and resourceful scribe who sought to repair damage and correct the errors and misreadings found throughout the *β family*. Some examples of these corrections are noted below:

infra, n. 3, l. 14:	et detrahunt mihi] me *B: om. γλSV*
infra, n. 11. l. 2:	Augustinus] *E:* Glossa *B:* Dominus *γλSV*
infra, n. 19, 1. 14:	*quemadmodum*] sicut *B: om. γλSV*
infra, n. 20. l. 9:	Christiani] laici *B: om. γλSV*
infra, n. 30, l. 6:	pecuniaria] pecuniarum *B:* pecuniam *γRSV:* pecunias *M*

Many of the corrections found in *B* correspond to readings found in α. Some examples are noted below:

infra, n. 5, l. 23: activis] *αB:* actibus *γMSV:* artibus *R*
infra, n. 11, l. 2: sunt] *post* Domini *B: om. γλSV*
infra, n. 12, l. 9: quia[1]] *αB: om. γλSV*
infra, n. 15, l. 11: videns] *αB: om. γλSV*
infra, n. 16, l 17: est] *αB: om. γλV:* quod *S*
infra, n. 19, l. 7: scilicet] *αB:* sed *γλSV*
infra, n. 19, l. 18: in] *αB: om. γλSV*
infra, n. 19, l. 22: Antichristum] *αB: om. γλSV*
infra, n. 19, l. 22: pravae] *αB:* paternae *γλSV*
infra, n. 20, l. 7: et] *αB: om. γλSV*
infra, n. 20, l. 1: Dominus] *αB: om. γλSV*
infra, n. 20, l. 9: scilicet] *αB: om. γλSV*
infra, n. 20, l. 10: et] *αB:* vel *γλSV*
infra, n. 22, l. 6: Glossa] *αB: om. γλSV*
infra, n. 23, l. 2: enim] *αB: om. γλSV*
infra, n. 25, l. 15: *ascendentem*] *αB:* descendentem *γλSV*
infra, n. 27, l. 15: credentur] *αB:* creduntur *γλSV*

It is extremely unlikely that *B* had access to an α manuscript as it makes no attempt to correct the severe homeoteleutic errors found throughout the *β* tradition. If one examines these corrections, it becomes readily apparent that the majority of them were supplied for the sake of sense. Most of these emendations involve the insertion of a conjunction or a preposition or a word needed to complete the sentence. The vast majority of *B*'s corrections are grammatical in nature; *B*'s readings do not reveal any contact with an α-related manuscript and one most conclude that *B*'s scribe arrived at these corrections independently.

Manuscript *S* is closely related to manuscript *B*. Some of their shared significant variants are listed below:

infra, n. 5, l. 1: commendatione] communi delectatione (declaratione *δ*) *β*
infra, n. 8, l. 18: Dicit] *praem.* Unde *W: add.* enim *δ*
infra, n. 15, l.2: Si videamus quod faciant miracula et virtutes, numquid est eis credendum. *om. δ*
infra, n. 17, l. 11: enim *om. δ*
infra, n. 17, l. 13: Glossa *om. δ*
infra, n. 22, l. 14: foraminata] forata *δ*
infra, n. 32, l. 20: *videte om. δ*

In a few instances, manuscripts *B* and *S* read in agreement with members of α against the entire *β* tradition. Some examples of this are noted below:

infra, n. 11, l. 5: evenient] *αδ*: eveniant *γλV*
infra, n. 20, l. 4: vidimus non nisi] *γλV:* non v. nisi *E:* vidimus non *δW*

infra, n. 28, l. 1:	*consiliarium*] αδ: consilium *γλV*
infra, n. 33, l. 2:	super] *δW*: secundum *γλV*

Although related to *B,* manuscript *S* also shows signs of contact with a manuscript from the α tradition. *S* supplies the passage "Sed periculum quod omnibus et toti ecclesiae imminet maximum est periculum;" at n. 4, ll. 7-9 that is missing in all of the other manuscripts of the *β* family. *S* also provides the word "omnium" at n. 5, l. 20 which is not found in the other *β* manuscripts. The contamination that *S* received from the *α* family may be isolated to a manuscript closely related to *E*:

infra, n. 5, l. 17:	infirmitate] *add.* sicut in febre acuta vel aliqua (*om. S*) alia (*add.* magna *S*) infirmitate *ES*
infra, n. 13, l. 1:	venient pericula] p. v. *transp. ES*
infra, n. 17, l. 11:	*sint om. ES*
infra, n. 17, l. 12:	Christo] *add.* quia soli reprobi separantur a Christo *ES*
infra, n. 20, l. 10:	adhuc] *ante* per *BDMNRV: om. ES*
infra, n. 20, l. 13:	isti *om. ES*

The *α*-based exemplar to which *S* had access was not *E* itself as *S* occasionally agrees with α against *β* after n. 29 where *E* has ended.

infra, n. 35, l. 3:	quod (quoniam *S*) digni (*om. S*) habiti sunt pro nomine Iesu contumeliam (contumelias *S*) pati *SW: om. BDλV:* etc. *N*

Although *S* had contact with an α manuscript related to *E,* it only made one attempt to repair the homeoteleutic damage, and as we have seen, that is at Sed ... periculum" at n. 4, ll. 7-9.

S or one of its ancestors had two exemplars of *Qui amat periculum.* One of them was a manuscript that had been contaminated by α, the other one was an ancestor of *B* perhaps even *δ* itself. *S*'s scribe thus selected most of its readings from its *δ* exemplar, although he occasionally followed some of the readings in its exemplar contaminated by α. In so doing, he created a hybrid text.

Manuscript *S* is also incomplete. It ends at the word credatis at n. 37 and has omitted the remaining three paragraphs of text, extending from Audivi (n. 38) to carentes (n. 40).

Within the *β* family, manuscripts *D* and *N* (*γ*) are very closely related and are often in agreement. Together, they share thirty-three unique variants in the form of omissions, transpositions, and altered word order. Some of their significant errors are noted below:

infra, n. 4, l. 9:	quod] pro *γ*
infra, n. 5, l. 19:	gravi infirmitate] i. g. *transp. γ*
infra, n. 7, l. 15:	pericula venient] v. p. *transp. γ*

infra, n. 8, l. 19: *fiduciam*] fidem *γ*
infra, n. 13, l. 21: dicet] diceret *γ*
infra, n. 13, l. 3: scripturarum] scripturas *W: post* explanatores *γ*
infra, n. 15, l. 4: illorum] eorum *δλV: om. γ*
infra, n. 15, l. 5: magis *ante* non *γ*
infra, n. 17, l. 11: fine] interim *γ*
infra, n. 19, l. 22: nos recipiamus] non recipiamus *γ*

Manuscript *N* shares a large omission with *B*; this passage is, however, contained in *D*. Manuscripts *BN* omit the passage from Audivi (n. 38) to protulisse (n. 39), in which William relates the story from the *Vita S. Dominici* about the religious who claimed that his Order had been founded at the express request of the Virgin Mary.[27] But apart from this large omission, *N* shares very few significant errors with *B*.

infra, n. 4, l. 1: *habuit*] *αδN*: habet *DλV*
infra, n. 7, l. 10: *scito*] *αBN*: scitote *DλSV*
infra, n. 11, l. 18: tacere] *BEN*: arcere *DSVW*: alicere *M*: licere *M*^{C}

Similarly, *N* shares very few significant errors with manuscript *S*, and almost all of them are omissions:

infra, n. 18, l. 8: *incidat*] incidant *NS*
infra, n. 18, l. 2: *est om. NS*
infra, n. 19, l. 4: et *om. δN*
infra, n. 20, l. 15: quae] *αδN:* quod *DλV*
infra, n. 23, l. 1: de veritate *om. NS*
infra, n. 28, l. 12: enim *om. NS*
infra, n. 30, l. 6: honorum] honorem *NS*

Almost all of the errors that *N* shares with the constituent members of *δ* are random and could have occurred independently. The only exception to this rule is the case of the large omission at nn. 38 and 39 in both *BN*. But since manuscripts *BN* share so few other significant errors, one must conclude that these two omitted paragraphs cannot be attributed to some type of relationship between them and must have rather occurred in each manuscript independently. As we have seen, the two paragraphs in question recount the story from the *Vita S. Dominici* of Theodore of Apolda. Apart from William's purposefully vague references to *falsi religiosi* and *falsi fratres*, they are the only part of the sermon that explicitly suggests that the intended targets of the sermon are members of a religious order;

[27] *B*'s relative *S* of *δ* also omits these two paragraphs. But *S* also omits the following paragraph n. 40 which manuscript *B* contains and which would have therefore been contained in *δ*.

moreover, since they contain content from a *vita* of St. Dominic, they help to identify the Dominicans as the possible false Preachers mentioned therein. As this shared omission cannot be explicated paleographically, the only possible explanation is that they were intentionally deleted in both manuscripts independently as editorial interventions. The scribes of *B* and *N* deliberately omitted these passages in order to remove any possible inference that the perils threatening the Church would be ushered in by means of a religious order, quite possibility the Dominicans if they were familiar with Theodore of Apolda's *Vita.* And through this editorial emendation, both *B* and *N* gave the pseudoprophets and hypocrites mentioned throughout the sermon a little more anonymity.

Manuscript *M* is a late manuscript and is extremely corrupt. It has a very large number of unique variants, usually in the forms of homeoteleutic errors or simple mistranscriptions. It, however, descends from *V*, although very distantly related to it. The printed edition *R* was based on a still unidentified manuscript very closely related to *M.* The conjunction of *MR* allows us to reconstruct their common ancestor λ.

R shares many of *M*'s errors, usually in the form of omissions, transpositions, and the addition of supplementary material. Some examples of these shared errors are noted below:

infra, n. 13, l. 21:	per tales] *ante* venient λ
infra, n. 13, l. 22:	*speciem*] *add.* dignitatis et λ
infra, n. 15, l. 13:	falsos] *add.* contra sanctum ordinem et λ
infra, n. 15, l. 13:	fratres] *add.* sanctos inique et perverse et dolose agentes et λ
infra, n. 15, l. 13:	perturbent] perturbant *β*: *add.* venenum ipsorum maledictum effundunt in fratres probos (parvos *M)* honestos et discretos et sanctos λ
infra, n. 17, ll. 3-4:	potest alium vocare, aliter alius in sua diocesi non potest praedicare *om.* λ
infra, n. 20, l. 13:	et non alii] alii vero non λ
infra, n. 22, l. 10:	sed religiosi] nec saeculares λ
infra, n. 26, ll. 6-7:	accusabunt quia ipsi accusant apud principes *om.* λ
infra, n. 28, ll. 9-10:	quia etiam diabolus creatura Dei est *om.* λ

Many of the members of *β*, especially manuscripts *M* and *S*, contain a large number of unique variants. While the following edition will note the readings of the three branches of the *β* family, it only notes the readings of *β*'s individual members to indicate contamination or a corrupted passage or error in the *α* tradition.

The *α* family of *Qui amat periculum,* containing *AEPW,* only contains two manuscripts. Both manuscripts, however, derive from a common ancestor *α*. William's works in both *E* and *W* were copied in the fourteenth century; the printed edition *A* is based on manuscript *W*; the printed edition *P* is based on *A* but reveals heavy editorial intervention on the part of Alithophilius, primarily in the form of expanded biblical citations.

The *α* family does not have the same "set" pattern of transmission which characterized *β*. In *E*, William's *De periculis, Si quis diligit me*, and *Qui amat periculum* all circulated as a unit, though the latter sermon is incomplete, ending at the point where William repeats the signs from *De periculis* to distinguish true preachers from false ones.[28] In *W, De pharisaeo et publicano* and *Qui amat periculum* circulated together.

In terms of what the sermons circulated with, *E* is a theological miscellany containing works by Hugh of Saint Victor, Giles of Rome, and Robert Holcoth. In its content, *W* somewhat resembles *β-V* in that it contains some conciliar material from the fifteenth century. However, the portion of the manuscript which contains William's sermons (ff. 77r-86v) is written in a clearly identifiable fourteenth-century hand; this section was then added to other works before *W* was bound as a volume.[29]

The constituent members of *α* usually agree on readings. However, as noted above, *E* contains a few readings that are likewise found in *S*, most notably the two passages:

infra, n. 5: infirmitate] *add.* sicut in febre acuta vel aliqua (*om. S*) alia (*add.* magna *S*) infirmitate *ES*
infra, n. 17: Christo] *add.* quia soli reprobi separantur a Christo *ES*

These passages were added to an ancestor of *E* to which *S* had recourse to in the fifteenth century. They serve to prove that *E* was not contaminated by the *β* family, rather, an ancestor of *E* contaminated *S*.

E occasionally supplies a passage which *W* has omitted. Near the end of n. 11 at l. 2, *βE* read:

> quod exponit (exponens *E*) Augustinus (Augustinus] Glossa *B*: Dominus *DMNRSV*) dicens (dicit *E*) qui videntur quasi (enim *β*) nuntii Dei = *βE*

W has omitted this passage, most probably due to homeoteleuton. *W* jumps from *Domini* on the preceding line to the word *per* immediately after *Dei*. Likewise, at the end of n. 17, ll. 14-6, *E* reads:

> …quia Apostoli non nisi veritatem quaerebant dicere; sed praelati modo tantum veritatem dicere curant, alii vero ornant verba sua.

28 According to Dufeil, *E* contains the second version of *De periculis*. *Guillaume de Saint-Amour*, 271, n. 94.

29 *Die Handscriften der Herzoglichen Bibliothek zu Wolfenbüttel*, 296.

In this instance of homeoteluton, *W* jumps from *veritatem* to *dicere*² thereby omitting the phrase "quaerebant dicere sed praelati modo tantum veritatem."

As we have seen, *Qui amat periculum* in *E* is incomplete, ending at the portion of the sermon where William announces the seven ways to identify false preachers from true ones (n. 29). All of the constituent members of *β* except *S* contain supplementary material at the end of *Qui amat periculum* not found in *W*. At n. 40, immediately after the sentence "Unde, carissimi, ab istis falsis Apostolis valde est cavendum," *β-S* contains the following addition:

> Volunt homines (homines] enim (*om. D*) h. (humiles *γ*) *Bγ*) esse sine despectu, pauperes sine defectu, bene (bene induti] bene in divitiis *M*) induti sine sollicitudine, (solutione *M*) cibos electos, exquisitos et lauciores habere, tamen (tamen] cum *λ*; tamen ... mala *om. N*) in via mala in manifesto adulantes, (*om. λ*) in (et *M:* ab *R*) occulto detrahentes, exterius asperam (asperam] alternam *M*: alteram *R*) vitam praetendentes, interius (*add.* etiam *λ: add. ult.* ad *M*) delicias quaerentes, mordaces ut canes, dolosi ut vulpes, superbi ut leones, illusores ut dracones, intrinsecus sunt (*om. B*) lupi rapaces, exterius (extrinsecus *B*) mel laudis humanae (*add.* propinantes *N*) ut ursi (*add.* id *N*) amantes, sine cognitione volunt esse iudices, testes sine visu, falsi accusatores, omni veritate carentes. (*add.* etc. *BDR: add. ult.* Amen *M*).

The conjuction of *EW* permits us to reconstruct *α*; the conjunction of *Wβ* or *Eβ* allows us to construct the autograph. Throughout roughly four-fifth of the sermon, the edition relies upon the superior witnesses *E* and *W*. *E* acts as a control over potential copying errors in *W;* but the control is lost after *E* drops out. For the remainder of the sermon, only *W* represents the tradition of *α*.

One cannot say with certainty whether the passage cited above was contained in *α* as it is not contained in the sole representative of its tradition. It has been included in this edition as it is present in five manuscripts of the *β* family and very possibly could have been in *α* and simply omitted in *W*.[30]

Qui amat periculum gained a success, as witnessed by manuscript dissemination, which none of William's other sermons ever attained. Its popularity can partially be explained by the fact that it circulated immediately after *De periculis* in the *β* family; it thus seems to have been understood to be an additional chapter of *De periculis* throughout the *β*

[30] One possible explanation for its omission in *W* could be the conflation of the abbreviations for *cavendum* and *carentes* at n. 40.

tradition. Therefore, the success of *Qui amat periculum*, judging by the extant manuscripts, rather reflects the success of *De periculis*.

The manuscript tradition of *Qui amat periculum*, especially within the *β* family, is intimately connected to that of *De periculis*. Dufeil made several conclusions about the manuscript tradition of *De periculis* which also hold true for *Qui amat periculum*. First, of the manuscripts of *De periculis* that Dufeil dated, that is, thirty-one of the fifty-one, twenty-eight date from the fifteenth century.[31] Similarly, five of the eight extant manuscripts of *Qui amat periculum*, all from the *β* family, date from the fifteenth century. This would seem to suggest a renewed interest in *De periculis* in the beginning of the fifteenth century; the revival of *De periculis* translated into a proliferation of copies of *Qui amat periculum*, for as we have seen, the two texts were fused within the *β* tradition.

Dufeil also noted the success of *De periculis* in central and eastern Europe in the fifteenth century.[32] Of the twenty-eight fifteenth-century manuscripts of *De periculis* Dufeil examined, nine are presently located at Prague, two at Olomouc, four at Wroclaw, five at Vienna, four at Munich, two at Nuremberg, one at Trebon.[33] Although a manuscript's actual location is never a good indicator of where a manuscript was copied or where it circulated, the present evidence–with such a large number of manuscripts housed at archives in central Europe, would seem to indicate a widespread circulation of *De periculis* in these areas in the fifteenth century. Furthermore, three archives in Prague contain more manuscripts of *De periculis* than any other European city; in fact, the number of *De periculis* manuscripts housed at Prague is equal to those held at Paris and Oxford, as listed by Dufeil, combined.[34] Dufeil has also made mention of its success, especially of the second version, in areas under Hussite influence.[35]

Of the eight extant manuscripts of *Qui amat periculum*, six are currently housed in central European archives. With the exception of two manuscripts (*E* and *V*), all of the manuscripts circulated with material relative to the Church councils of the fifteenth century. *BDMS* circulated with decrees of the Council of Constance, manuscripts *NW* include decrees from the Councils of Basel and *N* contains matter relating to the Council of Florence. Manuscripts *BD* contain material concerning Wyclif while four manuscripts (*BDSW*) contain matter about Huss.

[31] *Guillaume de Saint-Amour*, 269, n. 75; 271, nn. 92-5; n. 276, nn. 157, 159, 278, n. 182.

[32] *Guillaume de Saint-Amour*, 271, n. 93; 278, n. 182.

[33] Dufeil assigns most of these manuscripts to the second and fifth versions of *De periculis*. *Guillaume de Saint-Amour*, 269, n. 75; 271, nn. 92-5; n. 276, nn. 157, 159, 278, n. 182.

[34] *Cf. Guillaume de Saint-Amour*, 269, n. 75; 271, nn. 92-5; n. 276, nn. 157, 159, 278, n. 182.

[35] *Cf. Guillaume de Saint-Amour*, 271, n. 94.

Since six of the eight extant manuscripts of *Qui amat periculum* circulated with early fifteenth-century conciliar material or works both by and against Wyclif and Huss, it would appear that in the fifteenth century, *Qui amat periculum* (and *De periculis* in the *β* family) came to be understood as works which were somehow concerned with and/or directed against Wyclif and Huss. The *explicit* of *D* openly states that *De periculis* was directed *contra hypocritas et falsos Wiglifistas,* and both *B* and *D* form compendia of anti-Wyclif and anti-Huss thought.

Perhaps the popularity of *De periculis* and *Qui amat periculum* in the fifteenth century can be explained by the fact that William's stock motifs against the mendicants could be recycled and reused against other groups who seemingly threatened the Church: in the case of manuscript *D*, the followers of Wyclif. And even if there was an understanding that *De periculis* and *Qui amat periculum* had been written centuries earlier for a different purpose, there was nevertheless some understanding that the texts could still be used, in the fifteenth century, both to support the decrees of Constance and to cast doubt upon the activities of the followers of Wyclif and Huss.

Because of the complexity involved in the manuscript circulation of *Qui amat periculum* and its relationship with *De periculis* only a probable *stemma codicum* can be offered here. First, there are two families of manuscripts: *α* (*EW*) and *β* (*BDMNSV*). There are three subgroupings within *β* consisting of manuscripts *B* and *S* (*δ*) , manuscripts *DN* (γ) and manuscript *M* and the printed version *R* (*λ*); all five manuscripts and the version transcribed by Kybal have descended from *V*. *B* is the most independent member of *β*; although copied from a descendant of *V*, it was heavily corrected. Many of the common grammatical errors and omissions found throughout the *β* family have been repaired in *B*. Manuscript *S* is closely related to *B* but reveals contamination from a manuscript from the *α* tradition and a probable ancestor of *E*. Manuscripts *D* and *N* (γ)are closely related. *M* is the most corrupt manuscript of *Qui amat periculum*; it contains dozens of unique variants and many scribal errors. The printed edition *R* was based on a manuscript very closely related to *M*.

Probable Stemma Codicum

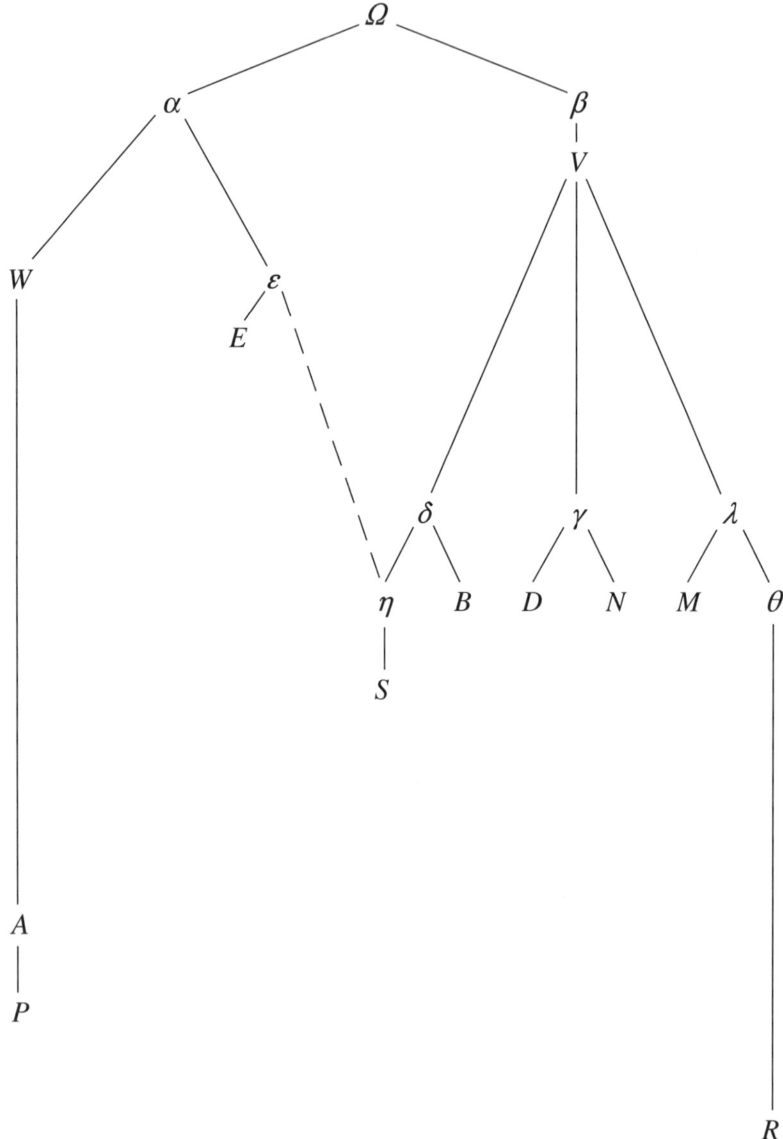

Si quis diligit me

William's sermon *Si quis diligit me* survives only in *E*. The edition presented here contains the text as preserved in *E* with minimal editorial interventions, most notably at n. 5 containing a corrupted passage:

> Caritas est vere diligere Deum [et caritas Dei de cherte].

E also bears witness to numerous corrections. Most of the corrections made in *E* are of an explanatory nature.

infra, n. 5:	*suas*] E^C: scilicet *E*
infra, n. 5:	robam] *add.* id est vestem *sup. lin.* E^C
infra, n. 5:	id est vili panno] *add. sup. lin.* E^C
infra, n. 5:	robas] *add.* id est vestes *sup. lin.* E^C
infra, n. 6:	robam] *add.* id est vestem *sup.* E^C
infra, n. 10:	etiam] *add. sup. lin.* E^C
infra, n. 16:	Tertius] vel alius *add. sup. lin.* E^C

However, at least one of these corrections shows an attempt to emend what probably was a homeoteleutic error. *E*'s scribe skipped from the word *suae* preceding *sine* near the middle of n. 9 to the "non potest absolvi" phrase following the *suae* after anima.

> n. 9: sine licentia illius qui habet curam animae suae *add. in cap.* E^C

De pharisaeo et publicano

William's sermon *De pharisaeo et publicano* survives in *W* and the printed editions *A* and *P*. As with the sermon *Quia amat periculum*, the printed edition in *A* is based on manuscript *W*. The version printed in *P*, however, is based both on *A* and a still unidentified manuscript. Alithophilius used *A* and an unknown manuscript of *De pharisaeo et publicano* when preparing his edition; this can be seen as Alithophilius' printing is able to supply a missing passage when *W* is in homoteleutic error. Near the end of n. 7, ll. 2-5, *P* provides a reading lost in *W*.

> ...ne cuiquam onerosus esset vel adulari necesse haberet. Illi ergo qui potestatem apostolicam non habent utpote qui non praesunt regimini animarum non de evangelio debent vivere sed potius de labore manuum suarum.

In this instance of obvious homeoteleuton, *W* has jumped from the *suarum* on line 2 to its counterpart on line 5.

P is also able to correct *W* when it provides inferior text or a corrupted passage, as can be seen at *infra*, n. 19, ll. 13-5:

> Talis enim est natura huius (natura huius] naturalis *W*) morbi, quod cum fuerit radicatus, (dedicatus *W*) ignorat eum morbosus, (morbus *W*) quia credit (quia credit] eorum est *W*) se sanctum apud Deum, sicut apud homines sanctus reputatur (deputatur *W*).

Although a printed edition, *P*, is an important witness in that it reflects readings from a manuscript which no longer survives and is thus able to help correct and clarify readings in *W*. The edition presented here is based on *W* but relies on *P* when *W* is in omission or in manifest error.

Editorial technique

In the following editions emendations have been kept to the minimum required to correct obvious errors or to help clarify the text; these emendations have been adopted in the text itself and indicated in the *apparatus*. Both punctuation and capitalization are in accord with modern practice.

All significant variant readings have been noted in the *apparatus*. Expunctions and marginal notes which have been considered significant are similarly listed in the *apparatus*. Words or letters located within square brackets are extraneous or redundant and are to be disregarded for the sake of sense. Angle brackets surround words or letters which must be supplied for the understanding of a sentence. The superscript *c* (^{c}) designates emendations by a corrector or a later hand.

All scriptural citations within the edition are in italics, while their respective references in the *apparatus fontium* are given in the standard Roman font. All non-biblical sources cited in the *fontes* are italicized. All citations from the biblical *Glossa ordinaria* are noted either by *int.* (interlinear gloss) or *ord.* (ordinary gloss); they are cross referenced to readings in the *Editio princeps* of the *Glossa* (*Ed. pr.*) and to the edition in the *Patrologia latina* (*PL* 113-4). A complete listing of source materials used by William can be found in the *conspectus fontium*.

In the following editions, the *reportatio* of *De mendicitate* is based on manuscript *L* yet relies on manuscripts *CP* (δ) when *L* is manifestly in error. William's responses to Bonaventure's arguments have been centered and placed in small capitals to differentiate them from Bonaventure's text. The edition of *Qui amat periculum* is based on the two manuscripts of the α family (*EW*). The edition of *Si quis diligit me* is based on the sole surviving manuscript of the sermon, *E*, while the edition of *De pharisaeo et publicano* is based on *W* yet relies on the printed edition *P*, which reflects the readings of a lost manuscript, when *W* is in omission or error.

CONSPECTUS FONTIUM

AB =
Analecta Bollandiana

"Acta fabulosa S. Dionysio," =
"Acta fabulosa S. Dionysio areopagita afficta," in *AS* 52. t. 4 Oct. Paris: Victor Palmé, 1860, 792-7.

AF =
Analecta Franciscana

Amb. Aut., *Expo. in Apoc.* =
Ambrosius Autpertus, *Expositio in Apocalypsin* in *CCCM* 27, 27A. Ed. R. Weber O.S.B. Turnhout: Brepols, 1975.

Amb., *Comm. in Epist. ad Col.* =
S. Ambrosius, *Commentarius in Epistolam ad Colossenses* in *PL* 17. Ed. J.-P. Migne. Paris, 1879, 443-66.

Amb.,
Amb., *Comm. in Epist. ad Cor.* =
S. Ambrosius, *Commentarius in Epistolas ad Corinthios* in *PL* 17. Ed. J.-P. Migne. Paris, 1879, 193-358.

Amb., *Comm. in Epist. ad Eph.* =
S. Ambrosius, *Commentarius in Epistolam ad Ephesios* in *PL* 17. Ed. J.-P. Migne. Paris, 1879, 393-426.

Amb., *Comm. in Epist. ad Phil.* =
S. Ambrosius, *Commentarius in Epistolam ad Philippenses* in *PL* 17. Ed. J.-P. Migne. Paris, 1879, 425-44.

Amb., *Comm. in Epist. ad Rom.* =
S. Ambrosius, *Commentarius in Epistolam ad Romanos* in *PL* 17. Ed. J.-P. Migne. Paris, 1879, 47-192.

Amb., *Comm. in Epist. ad Thess.* =
S. Ambrosius, *Commentarius in Epistolas ad Thessalonicenses* in *PL* 17. Ed. J.-P. Migne. Paris, 1879, 465-86.

Amb., *Comm. in Epist. ad Tim.* =
S. Ambrosius, *Commentarius in Epistolas ad Timotheum* in *PL* 17. Ed. J.-P. Migne. Paris, 1879, 487-526.

Amb., *Epist.* =
S. Ambrosius, *Epistolae* in *CSEL* 82, pars 2, 1-2. Edd. M. Zelzer et O. Faller S.J. Vienna: Tempsky, 1968-90.

Amb., *Expo. in Luc.* =
S. Ambrosius, *Expositio evangelii secundum Lucam* in *CCSL* 14. Ed. M. Adriaen. Turnhout: Brepols, 1957, 1-400.

Arist., *Ethica* =
Aristoteles, *Ethica Nicomachea. Translatio Roberti Grosseteste Lincolniensis sive 'Liber Ethicorum'*. *Aristoteles latinus* XXV 1-3 fasc. 3. Ed. R. A. Gauthier. Leiden: E.J. Brill, 1973.

AS =
Acta sanctorum

Auct. Arist. =
Les Auctoritates Aristotelis. Un Florilège médiéval: étude historique et édition critique in Philosophes médiévaux XVII. Ed. J. Hamesse. Louvain: Publications universitaires, 1974.

Aug., *Contra Faust.* =
S. Aurelius Augustinus, *Contra Faustum libri XXXIII* in *CSEL* 25, sect. 6, pars 1. Ed. J. Zycha. Vienna: F. Tempsky, 1891, 249-797.

Aug., *De bono coniug.* =
S. Aurelius Augustinus, *De bono coniugali* in *CSEL* 41, sect. 5, pars 3. Ed. J. Zycha. Vienna: F. Tempsky, 1900, 187-231.

Aug., *De civ. Dei* =
S. Aurelius Augustinus, *De civitate Dei* in *CCSL* 47-8. Edd. Bernard Dombart et Alphonse Kalb. Turnhout: Brepols, 1955.

Aug., *De op. mon.* =
S. Aurelius Augustinus, *De opere monachorum* in *CSEL* 41, sect. 5, pars 3. Ed. J. Zycha. Vienna: F. Tempsky, 1900, 531-596.

Aug., *De serm. Dom.* =
S. Aurelius Augustinus, *De sermone Domini in monte* in *CCSL* 35. Ed. Almut Mutzenbecher. Turnhout: Brepols, 1967.

Aug., *De vera rel.* =
S. Aurelius Augustinus, *De vera religione* in *CCSL* 32. Ed. J. Martin. Turnhout: Brepols, 1962, 169-260.

Aug., *Enarr. in Ps.* =
S. Aurelius Augustinus, *Enarrationes in Psalmos.* in *CCSL* 38, 39, 40. Edd. D. E. Dekkers O.S.B. et Iohannes Fraipont. Turnhout: Brepols, 1956.

Aug., *Epist.* =
S. Aurelius Augustinus, *Epistulae* in *CSEL* 34 pars 1, 2. Ed. A. Goldbacher. Vienna: F. Tempsky, 1895-1898.

Aug. *Serm.* =
S. Aurelius Augustinus. *Sermones* in *PL* 38, 39. Ed. J.-P. Migne. Paris, 1841-65.

Aug., *Serm. de vet.* =
S. Aurelius Augustinus, *Sermones de vetere testamento (I-L)* in *CCSL* 41. Ed. C. Lambot O.S.B. Turnhout: Brepols, 1961.

Aug., *Spec.* =
S. Aurelius Augustinus, *Liber qui appellatur speculum* in *CSEL* 12, sect. 3 pars 1. Ed. F. Weihrich. Vienna: C. Geroldi bibliopolam academiae, 1887, 1-285.

Aug., *Tract. in Ioan.* =
S. Aurelius Augustinus, *In Ioannis evangelium Tractatus CXXIV* in *CCSL* 36. Ed. D. R. Willems O.S.B. Turnhout: Brepols, 1954.

Beda, *Expl. Apoc.* =
Beda Venerabilis, *Explanatio Apocalypsis* in *PL* 93. Ed. J.-P. Migne. Paris, 1862, 129-206.

Beda, *Expo. Act.* =
Beda Venerabilis, *Expositio Actuum Apostolorum* in *CCSL* 121. Ed. M.L.W. Laistner. Turnhout: Brepols, 1983, 1-99.

Beda, *Expo. in Luc.* =
Beda Venerabilis, *In Lucae evangelium expositio* in *CCSL* 120. Ed. D. Hurst O.S.B. Turnout: Brepols, 1960, 1-425.

Beda, *Expo. in Marc.* =
Beda Venerabilis, *In Marci evangelium expositio* in *CCSL* 120. Ed. D. Hurst O.S.B. Turnhout: Brepols, 1960, 427-648.

Beda, *Hom. evang.* =
Beda Venerabilis, *Homelarium evangelii* in *CCSL* 122. Ed. D. Hurst O.S.B. Turnhout: Brepols, 1955, 1-378.

Benz, "Exzerptsätze," =
Ernst Benz, "Die Exzerptsätze der Pariser Professoren aus dem Evangelium Eternum," *Zeitschrift für Kirchengeschichte* 51 (1932):415-55.

BF =
Bullarium Franciscanum. Ed. J.H. Sbaralea. 4 voll. Rome, 1759. [rpt. Assisi: Tipographica Porziuncola, 1983].

Cass., *Expo. Psalm.* =
M. Aurelius Cassiodorus, *Expositio Psalmorum* in *CCSL* 97, 98, 99. Ed. M. Adriaen. Turnhout: Brepols, 1958.

CCCM =
Corpus Christianorum Continuatio Mediaeualis

CCSL =
Corpus Christianorum series latina

Cel., *Epist.* =
S. Coelestinus I Papae. *Epistolae et decreta* in *PL* 50. Ed. J.-P. Migne. Paris, Migne, 1865, 418-566.

Chart. =
Chartularium universitatis parisiensis edd. Heinrich Denifle et Emile Chatelain. 4 voll. Paris: Delalain, 1889-97.

Chrys., *Hom. in Matt.* =
S. Ioannis Chrysostomus, *Homiliae in Mattheum* in *PG* 57, 58. Ed. J.-P. Migne. Paris, 1862.

Chrys., *Serm.* =
S. Ioannis Chrysostomus, *Sermones panegyrici in solemnitates* in *PG* 49, 50. Ed. J.-P. Migne. Paris, 1862.

Codex =
Codex Iustinanus in *Corpus iuris civilis* II. Ed. Paul Krueger. Zurich: Weidmann, 1877. [rpt. 1967].

CSEL =
Corpus scriptorum ecclesiasticorum latinorum

Cyp., *Lib. de lapsis* =
S. Thascius Caecilius Cyprianus, *Liber de lapsis* in *PL* 4. Ed. J.-P. Migne. Paris, 1891, 477-510.

De ecc. dog. =
De ecclesiasticis dogmatibus in *PL* 42. Ed. J.-P. Migne. Paris, 1886, 1213-22.

De reg. iur. =
De regula iuris in *Corpus iuris canonicis* II. Ed. Aemilius Friedberg. Leipzig, 1879. [rpt. Graz: Akademische Druck-U. Verlagsanstalt, 1955], 1122-24.

Dephar. =
Sermo de pharisaeo et publicano

Digesta =
Digesta in *Corpus iuris civilis* I. Ed. Paul Krueger. Zurich: Weidmann, 1877. [rpt. 1967], 29-926.

Dion. Ex., *Coll.* =
Dionysius Exiguus, *Collectio decretorum pontificorum romanorum* in *PL* 67. Ed. J.-P. Migne. Paris, 1865, 229-346.

DP =
William of Saint-Amour, *De periculis novissimorum temporum* in *Opera omnia quae reperiri poterunt*. Ed. Alithophilius. Constance [Paris], 1632, 17-72.

DQE =
William of Saint-Amour, *De quantitate eleemosynae* in A. G. Traver, "William of Saint-Amour's Two Disputed Questions *De quantitate eleemosynae* and *De valido mendicante*," *AHDL* (1995): 323-332.

DVM =
William of Saint-Amour, *De valido mendicante* in A. G. Traver, "William of Saint-Amour's Two Disputed Questions *De quantitate eleemosynae* and *De valido mendicante*," *AHDL* 62 (1995): 333-342.

Ed. pr. =
Biblia latina cum glossa ordinaria. Ed. Adolph Rusch. Strassburg, 1480-1. [rpt. 4 voll. Turnhout: Brepols, 1992].

"Evangelium aeternum," =
P. Heinrich Denifle O.P., "Das Evangelium aeternum und die Commission zu Anagni," in *Archiv für Litteratur- und Kirchengeschichte des Mittel Alters* 1 (1885): 49-142.

Expo. reg. =
Fr. Angelo Clareno, *Expositio regulae fratrum minorum* Ed. P. Livarius O.F.M. Quaracchi: Collegium S. Bonaventurae, 1912.

Extra. =
Decretalium Gregorii Papae IX compilatio in *Corpus iuris canonicis* II. Ed. Aemilius Friedberg. Leipzig, 1879. [rpt. Graz: Akademische Druck-U. Verlagsanstalt, 1955], 2-928.

"Gesta S. Ludovici," =
"Gesta sancti Ludovici noni, Francorum regis, auctore monacho Sancti Dionysii anonymo," in *RHGF* 20. Paris: Imprimerie royale, 1840, 45-57.

Grat. =
Decretum magistri Gratiani in *Corpus iuris canonicis* I. Ed. Aemilius Friedberg. Leipzig, 1879. [rpt. Graz: Akademische Druck-U. Verlagsanstalt, 1955].

Greg., *Dial.* =
S. Gregorius Magnus, *Dialogorum libri IV* in *SC* Nos. 251, 260, 265. Ed. A. de Vogüé. Paris: Les Éditions du Cerf, 1978-9.

Greg., *Hom.* =
S. Gregorius Magnus, *Homiliae in evangelia* in *CCSL* 141. Ed. R. Étaix. Turnhout: Brepols, 1999. (*PL* 76: 1075-1314).

Greg., *Mor.* =
S. Gregorius Magnus, *Moralia in Iob* in *CCSL* 143, A, B. Ed. M. Adriaen. Turnhout: Brepols, 1979-85.

Greg., *Reg. past.* =
S. Gregorius Magnus, *Règle pastorale* in *SC* No. 381. 2 voll. Ed. F. Rommel O.S.B. Paris: Les Éditions du Cerf, 1992.

Hier., *Adv. Iov.* =
S. Hieronymus, *Adversus Iovinianum libri duo* in *PL* 23. Ed. J.-P. Migne. Paris, 1883, 221-368.

Hier., *Comm. in Matt.* =
S. Hieronymus, *Commentariorum in Matthaeum libri IV* in *CCSL* 77. Edd. D. Hurst O.S.B. et M. Adriaen. Turnhout: Brepols, 1969.

Hier., *Epist.* =
S. Hieronymus, *Epistulae* in *CSEL* 54, 55, 56. Ed. I. Hilberg. Vienna: F. Tempsky, 1910-18.

Hier., *Lib. inter.* =
S. Hieronymus, *Liber interpretationis Hebraicorum nominum* in *CCSL* 72. Ed. P. De Lagarde. Turnhout: Brepols, 1959, 57-161.

Hild., *Epist.* =
Hildebertus Cenomonesis, *Epistolae* in *PL* 171. Ed. J.-P. Migne. Paris, 1893, 142-312.

Hrab. Maur., *Comm. in Eccli.* =
B. Rabanus Maurus, *Commentariorum in Ecclesiasticum libri decem* in *PL* 109. Ed. J.-P. Migne. Paris, 1864, 763-1126.

Hrab. Maur., *Comm. in Matt.* =
B. Rabanus Maurus, *Commentariorum in Mattheum libri octo* in *PL* 107. Ed. J.-P. Migne. Paris, 1864, 727-1156.

Hrab. Maur., *Expo. in Epist. ad Thess.* =
B. Rabanus Maurus, *Expositio in Epistolas ad Corinthios* in *PL* 112. Ed. J.-P. Migne. Paris, 1878, 539-580.

int. =
Glossa interlinearis

Ioan. Cass., *Coll.* =
Ioannes Cassianus, *Collationum XXIV Collectio* in *PL* 49. Ed. J.-P. Migne. Paris, 1874, 478-1328.

Isid., *Etymol.* =
San Isidore de Sevila, *Etimologías.* 2 voll. Edd. J. O. Reta et M. A. M. Casquero. Madrid: Biblioteca des auctores cristianos, 1973.

Leg. ant. =
La Legenda antiqua S. Francisci: texte du ms. 1046 (M. 69) de Pérousse. Ed. P. Ferdinand-Marie Delorme O.F.M. Paris: Éditions de la France Franciscaine, 1926.

Leg. aur. =
Jacobus de Voragine (Iacopo da Varazze), *Legenda aurea.* Ed. G.P. Maggioni. 2 voll. Florence: Edizioni del Galluzzo, 1998. (*Leg. aur.* = *Legenda aurea.* Ed. T. Graese. 1890. [rpt. Osnabrück: O. Zeller, 1969]).

Leg. maior =
S. Bonaventura, *Legenda sancti Francisci* in *Opera omnia* VIII. Quaracchi: Collegium S. Bonaventurae, 1898, 504-549 (*AF* 10.557-652).

"Martyrologium romanum" =
"Martyrologium romanum" in *Propylaeum ad Acta Sanctorum Decembris* in *AS*, Dec., Brussels: 1940.

MGH =
Monumenta Germaniae Historiae

ord. =
Glossa ordinaria

Pasc. Rad., *Expo. in Mat.* =
Pascasius Radbertus, *Expositio in Matheo libri XII* in *CCCM* 56, A, B. Ed. B. Paulus O.S.B. Turnhout: Brepols, 1984.

PG =
Patrologia graeca

PL =
Patrologia latina

Potthast =
Registra pontificum romanorum inde ab anno post Christi natum 1198 ad annum 1304. 2 voll. Ed. A. Potthast. Berlin, 1874-5. [rpt. Graz: Akademische Druck- und Verlagsanstalt, 1957].

Prim., *Comm. in Apoc.* =
Primasius Hadrumentinus, *Commentarius in Apocalypsin* in *CCSL* 92. Ed. A.W. Adams. Turnhout: Brepols, 1985.

Pseudo-Aug., *De spiritu et anima* =
Pseudo-Augustinus, *De spiritu et anima* in *PL* 40. Ed. J.-P. Migne. Paris, 1887, 779-832.

Pseudo-Dion., *Eccl. hier.* =
Pseudo-Dionysius Areopagita, *Ecclesiastica hierarchia* in *Opera.* Ed. Jacobus Faber Stapulensis. Strassburg, 1503 [rpt. Frankfurt: Minerva, 1970], ff. 21v-46v.

Pseudo-Isid., *Decret. coll.* =
Pseudo-Isidorus, *Decretalium Collectio* in *PL* 130. Ed. J.-P. Migne. Paris, 1880, 1-1178.

QAP =
Qui amat periculum

QDM =
Quaestio de mendicitate

Recueil =
Recueil des historiens des Gaules et de la France

Resp. =
"Les *Responsiones* de Guillaume de Saint-Amour," Ed. E. Faral in *AHDL* 25-26 (1950-1): 337-394.

Rich., *In Apoc.* =
Richardus a Sancto Victore, *In Apocalypsin Ioannis* in *PL* 196. Ed. J.-P. Migne. Paris, 1880, 683-888.

Rom. ord. =
Romani ordines in *PL* 78. Ed. J.-P. Migne. Paris, 1895, 935-1406.

Rutebeuf =
Rutebeuf, *Œuvres complètes de Rutebeuf.* Edd. E. Faral et J. Bastin. 2 voll. 8th ed. Paris: A. et J. Picard, 1977-85.

Sal., *Chronica* =
Salimbene de Adam, *Chronica* in *MGH* 32. Ed. O.H.-Egger Hannover, 1905-1913.

SC =
Sources chrétiennes

Sext. =
Liber sextus decretalium Domini Bonifacii Papae VIII in *Corpus iuris canonicis* II. Ed. Aemilius Friedberg. Leipzig, 1879. [rpt. Graz: Akademische Druck- U. Verlagsanstalt, 1955], 934-1124.

SQD =
Si quis diligit me

Test. =
Testamentum sancti Francisci in *Die opuscula des Hl. Franziskus von Assisi.* Spicilegium Bonaventurianum 13. Ed. Kajetan Esser O.F.M. Grottaferrata: Collegium S. Bonaventurae, 1976, 438-444.

Theo., "Acta ampliora S. Dominici," =
Theodoricus de Appoldia. "Acta ampliora S. Dominici Confessoris," in *AS* 35. t. 1 Aug. Paris: Victor Palmé, 1883, 558-629.

Tract. de Mir. =
Thomas de Celano, *Tractatus de miraculis B. Francisci* in *AF* 10. Quaracchi: Collegium S. Bonaventurae, 1926-41, 269-331.

"Vie de Saint-Louis," =
"Vie de saint-Louis par le confesseur de la reine Marguerite," in *RHAF* 20. Paris: Imprimerie royale, 1840, 58-121.

Vita I =
Thomas de Celano, *Legenda prima B. Francisci* in *AF* 10. Quaracchi: Collegium S. Bonaventurae, 1926-41, 1-126.

Vita II =
Thomas de Celano, *Legenda secunda B. Francisci* in *AF* 10. Quaracchi: Collegium S. Bonaventurae, 1926-41, 127-268.

"Vita S. Alex." =
"Vita S. Alexii confessoris," in *AS* 31. t. 4 Iul. Paris: Victor Palmé, 1868, 251-70.

"Vita S. Dom." =
"Vita de S. Dominico confessore fundatore ordinis fratrum praedicatorum," in *AS* 35. t. 1 Aug. Paris: Victor Palmé, 1867, 359-541.

"Vita S. Dom. auct. Petro Ferrando" =
"Vita S. Dominici auctore Petro Ferrando O.P." in "Pierre Ferrand O.P. et les premiers biographes de S. Dominique fondateur de l'ordre des Frères Prêcheurs," in *Analecta Bolandiana* 30 (1911): 54-87.

CONSPECTUS SIGLORUM

De mendicitate

C = Cambridge, Corpus Christi College, 103, pp. 95a-105b.
L = Florence, Biblioteca Medicea Laureniziana, Plt. 36 dextr. 12, ff. 124r-129v.
P = Paris, Bibliothèque Nationale, lat. 15850, ff. 2r-4v.

δ = consensus codd. CP

Qui amat periculum

Semper laudantur:
E = Erfurt, Amplonianische Bibliothek, Q 170, ff. 174v-175v.
W = Wolfenbüttel, Bibliothek Herzog-August, Guelf. 367 Helmstedt, ff. 81ra-86vb.

α = consensus codd. EW

Raro laudantur:
B = Vienna, Österreichische Nationalbibliothek, lat. 4941, ff. 194v-203v.
D = Naples, Biblioteca nazionale Vittorio Emanuele III, VII.D.9, ff. 189r-196v.
M = Munich, Bayerische Staatsbibliothek, Clm. 14635, ff. 168ra-174ra.
N = Nurenberg, Stadtbibliothek, Cent. I, 80, ff. 98rb-101rb.
R = *Matěje z Janova Mistra Pařižského, Regula veteris et novi testamenti* ed. V. Kybal. Innsbruck,1911, III, pp. 315-332.
S = Stuttgart, Württemberg, Landesbibliothek, HB I 91, pp. 325v-333r.
V = Biblioteca apostolica vaticana, vat. lat. 1160, ff. 47v-60v.

β = consensus codd. BDMNRSV
δ = consensus codd. BS
γ = consensus codd. DN
λ = consensus codd. MR

A = *Appendix ad fasciculum rerum expetendarum et fugiendarum* ed. E. Brown. London, 1690 [reprint Tucson, AZ: Audax Press, 1967] II, pp.48-54.

P = *Opera omnia quae reperiri poterunt* ed. Alithophilius. Constance [Paris], 1632, pp. 491-506.

Si quis diligit me

E = Erfurt, Amplonianische Bibliothek, Q 170, f. 174r-v.

De pharisaeo et publicano

W = Wolfenbüttel, Bibliothek Herzog-August, Guelf. 367 Helmstedt, ff. 78vb-81ra.

A = *Appendix ad fasciculum rerum expetendarum et fugiendarum* ed. E. Brown. London, 1690 [reprint Tucson, AZ: Audax Press, 1967] II, pp. 43-47.

P = *Opera omnia quae reperiri poterunt* ed. Alithophilius. Constance [Paris], 1632, pp. 7-16.

<QUAESTIO DE MENDICITATE>

Quaestio est de mendicitate: Utrum mendicare pro Christo sit perfectionis christianae.

1. **Et videtur quod non**, in Psalm. 33: *Timete Dominum, omnes sancti eius,* 1
quoniam non est inopia timentibus eum.[1] Sed omnis mendicus est inops; ergo nullus mendicus est timens Deum. Sed timor Dei est de perfectione religionis christianae; ergo etc.

2. Item, in Psalm. 36: *Iunior fui, etenim senui, et non vidi iustum derelictum* 2
nec semen eius quaerens panem.[2] Sed omnis mendicus quaerit panem; ergo nullus mendicus iustus. Sed iustitia est de perfectione christiana; ergo mendicare non est de perfectione eiusdem.

3. Item in Psalm. 108: *Nutantes transferantur filii eius et mendicent et eiciantur* 3
de habitationibus suis.[3] Hic propheta loquitur per Spiritum Sanctum; ergo Spiritus Sanctus maledicit mendicantes, et ita mendicare non est opus perfectionis christianae.

4. Item, Eccli. 40: *Fili, in tempore vitae tuae non indigeas, melius est enim mori* 4
quam indigere.[4] Sed constat quod loquitur Salomon per Spiritum Sanctum; ergo Spiritus Sanctus inhibet mendicationem, ergo etc.

5. Item, Act. 20: *Beatius est dare quam accipere,*[5] et ita dare est perfectionis; 5
ergo accipere, eius oppositum, non est perfectionis. Sed mendicare est accipere vel velle accipere; ergo mendicare non est perfectionis, immo potius imperfectionis.

2 Quaestio] Quaestio disputata a Fratre Bonaventura super mendicitatem et obiectiones Magistri Guillelmi de Sancto Victore qua <continentur> eiusdem fratris solutiones et solutiones Magistri Guillelmi ad eiusdem fratris obiectionis. Unde ubi invenies in margine "Magister Guillelmus", scias hoc a Magistro Guillelmo dictum esse; cetera dicta sunt fratris. Hanc quaestionem nullus habet Parisius praeter unum vel duos; circa huius acquisitionem multum laboravi. *praem. C* 4 33] 13 *C*: 23 *LP* 5 *quoniam*] quia *P* | inops] *add.* est *P* 7 religionis christianae] c. r. *transp. P* 9 Sed ... panem *om. P* 12 108 *om. C* 16 *tuae*] suae *C* | *non*] *ante in P:* ne *P* | *est enim*] enim est *transp. C* 17 Salomon] Salamon *L* 18 inhibet] *add.* scilicet *C* | mendicationem] mendicari eis *L* | ergo etc. *om. C* 21 immo] sed *C*

[1] Ps. 33:10.
[2] Ps. 36:25.
[3] Ps. 108:10.
[4] Eccli. 40:29.
[5] Act. 20:35.

6 6. Item, II ad Thess. 3: *Si quis non vult operari, non manducet.*[6] Glossa: "Vult enim Apostolus servos Dei corporaliter operari, ut non compellantur egestate necessaria petere."[7] Sed omnis mendicus compellatur necessaria petere; ergo omnis mendicus facit contra Apostolum. Sed qui facit contra Apostolum non habet perfectionem christianam; ergo nec qui mendicat.

7 7. Item, in eodem capitulo super illud: *Ut formam vobis daremus nosmetipsos.*[8] Glossa: "Qui enim ad alienam mensam frequenter accedit otio deditus, aduletur necesse est pascenti se."[9] Sed omnis mendicus frequenter ad alienam mensam accedit; ergo omnis mendicus otio deditus adulatur. Sed nullus in perfectione christianae religionis existens adulatur, cum adulatio sit peccatum mortale; ergo nullus mendicus est in perfectione christianae religionis.

8 8. Item, I Thess. 4: *Operemini manibus, ut nullius aliquid desideretis.*[10] Glossa: "Nedum rogetis vel tollatis."[11] Sed omnis mendicus rogat sive petit; ergo omnis mendicus facit contra Apostolum. Sed qui facit contra Apostolum, non est in perfectione christiana; ergo etc.

9 9. Item, I Thess. 5: *Rogamus vos, fratres*[12] etc. Glossa: "Sicut divitiae negligentiam pariunt salutis, ita egestas, dum saturari quaerit, a iustitia declinat."[13] Sed a iustitia declinare non est perfectionis christianae; sed omnis mendicus est egenus; ergo etc.

10 10. Item, Luc. 12: *Vendite quae possidetis et date eleemosynam.*[14] Glossa: "Ut omnibus vestris semel pro Domino spretis, postea labore manuum

1 ad Thess.] Tim *P* 3 Sed … petere] *om. CL* 4 omnis mendicus *om. P* | contra Apostolum *om. P* 5 habet … christianam] est in statu perfectionis christianae *P* 6 illud] istud *C* | *vobis daremeus*] d. v. *transp. P* 7 *nosmetipsos om. P* | frequenter *ante* ad *L* 8 frequenter *post* mensam *P* 9 mendicus] mendicans *C* 11 peccatum mortale] m. p. *transp. C* 12 christianae religionis] r. c. *transp. P* 13 *Operemini*] Operamini *L* | *manibus*] *add.* vestris *P* 17 etc. *om. P* 22 semel] simul *C* | Domino] Deo *P* | labore] laboretis *P* | manuum] manibus *P: add.* vestris *P*

[6] II Thess. 3:10; *DQE*, 329; *DVM*, 336; *SQD*, n. 17.

[7] *ord.* in II Thess. 3:10 in *Ed pr.* 4.403B (*PL* 114.624B); Aug., *De op. mon.* in *CSEL* 41.5.3, 535-6; *DVM*, 336; *SQD*, n. 17.

[8] II Thess. 3:9; *DQE*, 327, 329, *DVM*, 339; *DP*, 49, 69.

[9] *ord.* in II Thess. 3:9 in *Ed. pr.* 4.403B; Amb., *Comm. in Epist. ad Thess.* in *PL* 17.485C; *DQE*, 327; *DVM*, 339; *DP*, 49, 69; *Dephar.*, n. 7.

[10] I Thess. 4:11; *DQE*, 327; *DVM*, 337; *DP*, 52; *SQD*, n. 17.

[11] *ord.* in I Thess. 4:11 in *Ed. pr.* 4.398A (*PL* 114.618C); Hrab. Maur., *Comm. in Epist. ad Thess.* in *PL* 112.554B; *DQE*, 327; *DVM*, 337.

[12] I Thess. 5:12; *DQE*, 326; *DP*, 48.

[13] *ord.* in I Thess. 5:12 in *Ed. pr.* 4.399B (*PL* 114.619D); Amb., *Comm. in Epist. ad Thess.* in *PL* 17.477B; *DQE*, 326.

[14] Luc. 12:33; *DQE*, 323, 328; *DP*, 50.

operemini unde vivatis et eleemosynam faciatis."[15] Perfectionis ergo christianae est omnia vendere et postea ad suum victum laborare; non ergo mendicare.

11. Item, 12, q. 1, c. *Videntes summi pontifices*, dicitur quod "nullus 11
communem vitam ducens sit in christiana religione indigens."[16] Sed omnis mendicus indiget; ergo nullus mendicus est in perfectione christianae religionis secundum decreta Sanctorum, et maxime quia in fine illius decreti dicitur: "Si aliquis existiterit modernis vel futuris temporibus qui contra nitatur, iam dicta damnatione feriatur." Ergo omnis qui mendicus est vel indigens per istud decretum excommunicatus est et sic in peccato mortali. Sed nullus talis est in statu perfectionis; ergo etc.

12. Item, *De consecratione episcopi*,[17] inhibetur quod ecclesia non fundetur 12
nisi dotetur; ergo qui volunt habere ecclesiam non dotatam, faciunt contra statuta ecclesiae. Sed communitas mendicantium est huiusmodi; ergo omnis in communitate mendicus facit contra ecclesiae statuta. Sed omnis talis peccat mortaliter; ergo omnis mendicus est in peccato mortali. Sed nullus talis est in statu perfectionis, immo potius in statu demeriti; ergo etc.

13. Item, ius civile inhibet hoc iis qui sunt sub iure civili, c. *De* 13
mendicantibus validis, L. *Cunctis quos in publicum*[18] etc. Sed maioris perfectionis et nobilitatis est ius divinum; ergo multo magis debet mendicationem inhibere, et ita qui vult mendicare, facit contra ius divinum. Nullus talis est in perfectione religionis christianae; ergo etc.

14. Item, videtur hoc per rationes. Opus indifferens cum hac additione 14
'pro Christo' non est opus perfectionis: sicut ire ad monasterium est opus indifferens, sed ire ad monasterium sive ad ecclesiam pro Christo non est opus perfectionis. Sed mendicare est opus indifferens, quia competit et bonis et malis et bene et male potest mendicare. Ergo cum hac additione 'pro Christo' non est opus perfectionis, et sic mendicare pro Christo non est opus perfectionis.

1 operemini] operamini *L*: *om. P* 3 mendicare] *add.* ergo etc. *C* 6 christianae religionis] r. c. *tranp. L* 7 secundum … perfectionis *om. C* 8 temporibus *om. P* 9 nitatur] *Gratianus*: utatur *LP* 10 istud] illud *P* | excommunicatus est] est e. *transp. P* 12 quod] ut *P* 14 mendicantium] mendicandi *C* 15 Sed *om. δ* 17 immo] sed *P* | in statu *om. P* | demeriti] detrimenti *C* 18 sub] subiecti *L* 20 perfectionis … nobilitatis] n. … p. *P* | magis] *add.* inhibebit sive *C* 21 mendicationem inhibere] i. m. *transp. C* 23 videtur hoc] hoc v. *transp. C* 24 ire] ut *C* 25 ire] ite *C*: ut *L* 26 et *om. δ* 27 et[3] *om. C* 28 et … perfectionis] ergo etc. *P*: *om. C*

[15] *ord.* in Luc. 12:33 in *Ed. pr.* 4.187A (*PL* 114.297D); Beda, *Expo. in Luc.* in *CCSL* 120.254-5; *DQE*, 328; *DVM*, 337; *DP*, 50.

[16] C.12 q.1 c.16 *Videntes*; *DQE*, 328, 330; *DP*, 50.

[17] *De con.* D.1 c.9 *Nemo ecclesiam.*

[18] *Codex* 11.26(25).1; *DVM*, 340.

15 15. Item, in pluribus obligari non est opus perfectionis, quia qui obligatur, tenetur de iure, non voluntarie. Sed qui eleemosynas recipit, dantibus in multis se obligat, scilicet ad orandum pro ipsis, ad erudiendum eos; ergo recipere eleemosynas non est opus perfectionis; ergo multo fortius nec petere. Sed qui mendicat petit, et ita nec mendicare erit opus perfectionis.

16 16. Item, qui mendicant et sunt validi ad laborandum, aut hoc faciunt quia pauperes aut quia praedicatores. Si quia pauperes, tales enim faciunt contra Augustinum in libro *De opere monachorum* per totum.[19] Si quia praedicatores evangelii, ergo faciunt evangelium venale. Sed tales peccant mortaliter; ergo validi mendicantes peccant mortaliter, et ita mendicare non est opus perfectionis, immo imperfectionis.

17 17. Item, IV Reg. 5,[20] dicitur quod Giezi, servus Elisei prophetae qui sanaverat Naaman Syrum a lepra, insciente domino suo petiit a Naaman, sanato a domino suo, vestes et pecuniam, et ob hoc dicit Gregorius Nazianzenus quod commisit simoniam.[21] Ergo multo fortius illi qui praedicant evangelium et postea, per se vel per suos fratres vel famulos sive per alias personas, nomine ipsorum ab eis petunt aliquid quibus praedicaverant, simoniam committunt. Sed nullus simoniacus est in statu perfectionis, sed peccati mortalis; ergo nullus praedicator evangelii petens sive mendicus est in statu perfectionis.

18 18. Item, perfectorum est se *abstinere ab omni specie mala*.[22] Sed mendicare est *species mala*, quia multi latrones et sanctitatis simulatores sunt in statu mendicationis; ergo perfecti a mendicatione se debent abstinere, et ita mendicitas non est perfectionis christianae.

19 19. Item, qui petunt eleemosynas et sunt validi ad laborandum, aut hoc faciunt habentes auctoritatem aut non. Si non, faciunt contra Apostolum in multis locis[23] et contra Augustinum in libro *De opere monachorum*,[24] et contra

1 opus *om. LP* | qui *om. C* 5 erit] est *P* 7 laborandum] mendicandum *P* 8 Si] Non *δ* | tales *bis L* 12 immo *om. δ* | imperfectionis] *add.* sive peccati *L* 13 5] 6 *LP* 14 lepra] *add.* sua *P* 15 a] pro *P* 16 Ergo] Tunc *praem. C* 18 nomine ipsorum] i. n. *transp. L* 19 Sed] Ergo *P* 22 *mala*] mali *C* 23 *mala*] mali *C* | sanctitatis simulatores] simul. sanct. *transp. P* 24 debent abstinere] a. d. *transp. C* | ita *om. L* 28 locis *om. L*

19 Aug., *De op. mon.* in *CSEL* 41.5.3, 531-596.
20 IV Reg. 5:20-23; *DVM*, 340; *SQD*, n. 10.
21 C.1 q.1 c.11 *Qui studet*; *DVM*, 340; *SQD*, n. 10.
22 I Thess. 5:22; *DVM*, 342.
23 *Cf. supra*, nn. 6, 7, 8.
24 *Cf. supra*, n. 16.

ius civile.[25] Si habentes auctoritatem et petant, male faciunt, quia ex auctoritate accipere possunt; non ergo debent petere per mendicitatem.

20. Item, persona praedicatoris debet esse discreta et nobilis sive 20
honorabilis, non vilis. Sed nulla vilior persona quam persona mendicantis; ergo persona praedicantis vel praedicatoris non debet esse mendicans. Et sic mendicare praedicantibus non est opus perfectionis christianae.

Ad oppositum sunt rationes istae quae sequuntur:

1. Matt. 10: *Nolite possidere aurum neque argentum neque pecuniam in zonis* 21
vestris.[26] Glossa: "Nec ipsa necessaria nec cellarium secum habeant, nihil praeter indumentum, quo contenti esse possunt."[27] Cum ergo necessaria a Domino discipulis gerere inhibeatur, eisdem accipere ab eis quibus praedicant conceditur sive petere. Sed hoc est mendicare; ergo Dominus praecepit mendicationem, et ita erit perfectionis christianae pro Christo mendicare, maxime quia illa praecepta sunt non parabolice, sed ad litteram intelligenda.

RESPONDEO: ILLUM QUI HABET POTESTATEM MINISTRANDI SPIRITUALIA 22
PETERE NON EST MENDICITAS, SED POTESTAS, UT DICIT AUGUSTINUS IN LIBRO *DE OPERE MONACHORUM* ET IN GLOSSA II TIM. 2 SUPER ILLUD: *LABORANTEM AGRICOLAM.*[28]

2. Item, Marc. 6: *Praecepit eis ut nihil tollerent in via nisi virgam tantum, non* 23
peram, non panem neque in zona aes.[29] Istud praeceptum datum Apostolis aut datur eis a Domino tamquam praelatis vel tamquam perfectis. Non tamquam praelatis, quia si sic, praelati hoc deberent facere; ergo cum non faciant, non datur Apostolis tamquam praelatis, et ita datur eis tamquam perfectis; ergo istud quilibet perfectus potest facere. Sed per hoc

1 habentes] habent *P* | petant] petans *C*: peccant *L* 4 vilior persona] p. v. *transp. P* 5 praedicantis vel *om. P* 6 praedicantibus] praedicatoribus *P* 7 **rationes istae**] i. r. *transp. P* 10 quo] *add.* homo *P* | contenti] contentus *δ* | possunt] potest *δ* | a Domino] ad non *C*: *post* discipulis *C* 13 christianae *om. C* 16 RESPONDEO] Respondet Magister Guillelmus de Sancto Amore sustinens partem oppositam non sui auctoritate, sed per sacram paginam etc., tota universitate magistrorum parisiensium contra Praedicatores et Minores et ordines consimiles huic rationi sic *P* 17 SED POTESTAS] *om. L*: *add.* potius *P* 18 2] et *C*: *om. P* 20 *eis*] *add.* Dominus *C* | *tollerent*] tollerarent *L* | *in via om. P* 21 Istud] Illud *C* 22 eis *om. L* | a Domino *om. C* | vel … praelatis *om. C* 23 praelati *post* facere *P* | deberent] debent *C* 24 Apostolis] eis *C* | praelatis … tamquam *om. C* | eis] ei *P* 25 istud] illud *C* | perfectus *post* facere *L* | per *om. C*

[25] *Cf. supra,* n. 13.

[26] Matt. 10:9; *DP,* 63.

[27] *int.* in Matt. 10:9 in *Ed. pr.* 4:38a,b; Hier., *Comm. in Matt.* in *CCSL* 77.66.

[28] *ord.* in II Tim. 2:6 in *Ed. pr.* 4.414A (*PL* 114.634C); Aug., *De op. mon.* in *CSEL* 41.5.3, 558; *DQE,* 331k; *DP,* 51.

[29] Marc. 6:8.

praeceptum conceditur petitio sumptuum; ergo perfectionis est petere sumptus, hoc est mendicare; ergo etc.

24 RESPONDEO: PRAECIPITUR EIS AMOVERE IMPEDIENTIA PRAEDICATIONIS OFFICIUM, QUOD EST PRAELATORUM. UNDE PRAECIPITUR TAMQUAM PRAELATIS IN STATU ECCLESIAE PRIMITIVAE EXISTENTIBUS; ADHUC ETIAM TENENTUR PRAELATI AMOVERE IMPEDIMENTA SUAE PRAEDICATIONIS. EX HOC ETIAM ARGUITUR QUOD PRAELATI VISITANTES ET PRAEDICATIONIS OFFICIUM EXERCENTES RECIPERE DEBENT PROCURATIONES; QUOD NON POSSUNT, QUI NON SUNT PRAELATI. SED HOC NON EST MENDICITAS, SED POTESTAS, UT DICTUM EST SUPRA.[30]

25 3. Item, Luc. 9: *Quicumque susceperit puerum in nomine meo, me recipit.*[31] Glossa: "Puerum, id est pauperem;"[32] ergo qui recipit pauperes, recipit Christum. Sed nemo magis pauper quam mendicus; ergo pauperes mendicantes a fidelibus sunt maxime recipiendi. Sed non essent a fidelibus recipiendi, si peccatum facerent mendicando; ergo mendicare pro Christo non est peccatum, immo opus perfectionis.

26 RESPONDEO QUOD SI MENDICARE IN CASU LICITO, UTPOTE QUIA NON POTEST OPERARI VEL QUIA SUBITO FACTUS EST PAUPER, MAXIME SINE CULPA SUA, VEL NESCIT AUT NON POTEST OPERARI NEC POTEST ALIUNDE HABERE VICTUM SUUM, SINE PECCATO, SICUT DICIT AMBROSIUS IN LIBRO *DE OFFICIIS*,[33] TUNC DEBET SUSCIPI PROPTER CHRISTUM, SI PETAT IN NOMINE CHRISTI. ALIOQUIN DEBET REPELLI ET CORRIGI, UT DICIT GLOSSA SUPER ILLUD MATT. 5: *QUI PETIT A TE, DA EI.*[34] GLOSSA: "ET SI NON QUOD PETIT, SED MELIUS CUM INIUSTE PETENTEM CORREXERIS."[35]

27 4. Item, Luc. 16: *Facite vobis amicos de mammona iniquitatis.*[36] Glossa: "Non quoslibet pauperes, sed eos qui *vos* possunt *in aeterna tabernacula recipere.*"[37]

1 sumptum] summum *C* 3 RESPONDEO] Respondet Magister Guillelmus secundum Glossam *P*: *om. C* | EIS] *add.* per hoc *P* | IMPEDIENTIA] *δL:* impedimenta P^c | PRAEDICATIONIS *om. P* 4 OFFICIUM *post* est *P* | PRAECIPITUR] *add.* eis *P* 8 QUI] quando *L* 11 9] 8 *P* 12 Glossa … recipit *om. C* 16 immo] sed *C* | opus] potius *L* 17 RESPONDEO] Respondet Magister Guillelmus *P* | MENDICARE] mendicant *C* 19 SUUM] *om. δ* 21 PROPTER] per *C* | CHRISTI *om. C* 22 ILLUD *om. C* 23 ET] Etiam *P*: *om. L* 25 Luc. *om. C* | *vobis amicos*] a. v. *transp. L*

[30] *Cf. supra*, n. 22.

[31] Luc. 9:48.

[32] *int.* in Luc. 9:48 in *Ed. pr.* 4.178a.

[33] D.86 c.17 *Consideranda*; *DVM*, 336.

[34] Matt. 5:42; *DVM*, 333, 341; *DP*, 52.

[35] *ord.* in Matt. 5:42 in *Ed. pr.* 4.23A (*PL* 114.97C); *cf.* Hier., *Comm. in Matt.* in *CCSL* 77.34; *DVM*, 341.

[36] Luc. 16:9.

[37] *int.* in Luc. 16:9 in *Ed. pr.* 4.198a; Beda, *Expo. in Luc.* in *CCSL* 120.298.

Sed isti sunt *pauperes spiritu*;[38] ergo pauperibus spiritu debent fideles necessaria ministrare et ab eis necessaria recipere. Sed nullus magis *pauper spiritu* quam qui in omnibus et in proprio et in communi renuntiavit; ergo talis potest recipere eleemosynas; et qui potest recipere, et petere supplicando potest. Sed hoc est mendicare; ergo mendicare non est peccatum, immo opus perfectionis.

RESPONDEO: VERUM EST, SI NON POTEST OPERARI VEL ALIUNDE VIVERE SINE 28
PECCATO. SED DUM SIC VICTUM POTEST HABERE, SI PETAT, NON EST *PAUPER SPIRITU*; SED VULT PAUPERTATEM SUAM ESSE LUCROSAM, ET SI EST RELIGIOSUS, EXPONIT SANCTITATEM VENALEM. ET HAEC DUO DICIT AUGUSTINUS, IN LIBRO *DE OPERE MONACHORUM*.[39] UNDE NON EST PERFECTUS VIR, SED PECCATOR.

5. Item, II ad Cor. 8: *Vestra abundantia illorum inopiam suppleat, ut et illorum* 29
abundantia vestrae inopiae sit supplementum.[40] Glossa: "*Vestra abundantia* terrenorum *suppleat inopiam illorum* et e converso *abundantia* meritorum *illorum* spiritualium, qui divinis vacant, *sit supplementum vestrae inopiae*."[41] Ergo illi, "qui vacant divinis," possunt recipere a divitibus. Sed pauperes mendicantes pro Christo "vacant divinis"; ergo tales possunt recipere eleemosynas et etiam petere supplicando, et ita idem quod prius.

RESPONDEO: POSSUNT VACARE DIVINIS ET NIHILOMINUS OPERARI PROPTER 30
VICTUM, ET SI NON SUFFICIT EORUM OPUS AD VICTUM ET NON POSSUNT ALIUNDE VICTUM HABERE, TUNC DANDUM EST EIS PRO CHRISTO. ET HOC DICIT GLOSSA SUPER ILLUD II THESS. 3: *VOS AUTEM, FRATRES, NOLITE DEFICERE BENEFACIENTES*.[42] GLOSSA: "PAUPERIBUS, QUONIAM, ETSI OPERENTUR, POSSUNT TAMEN NONNULLIS INDIGERE."[43]

6. Item, videtur quod mendicare sit opus perfectionis, exemplo Domini 31
nostri Iesu Christi in Psalm. 39: *Ego autem mendicus sum et pauper*.[44] Glossa:

2 necessaria ministrare] m. n. *transp. L* 3 in] et *L: om. C* | in² *om. L* 6 immo] sed *C* 7 RESPONDEO] Respondet Magister Guillelmus *P* | OPERARI VEL *om. C* 8 VICTUM POTEST] p. v. *transp. P* | PETAT] petit *L* 9 SED] si *L* | SUAM *om. L* 12 *suppleat*] impleat *P* | *et om. L* 17 recipere eleemosynas] e. r. *transp. P* 19 RESPONDEO] Respondet Magister Guillelmus et dicit quod *P* | OPERARI] *add.* etiam *C* 21 EIS] illis *P* 23 QUONIAM] Glossa *C* 26 Glossa] Et cum *praem. C*

[38] Matt. 5:3; *DQE*, 323.

[39] Aug., *De op. mon.* in *CSEL* 41.5.3, 585.

[40] II Cor. 8:14; *DVM*, 333.

[41] *int.* in II Cor. 8:14 in *Ed. pr.* 4.348a; Amb., *Comm. in Epist. ad Cor.* in *PL* 17.327D; Aug., *Spec.* in *CSEL* 12.3.1, 225; *DVM*, 333.

[42] II Thess. 3:13; *DVM*, 341.

[43] *int.* in II Thess. 3:13 in *Ed. pr.* 4.403b (*PL* 114.624C); *DVM*, 341.

[44] Ps. 39:18; *DQE*, 323.

"Hoc Christus dicit de se ex forma servi;"[45] et sic Christus mendicavit. Sed sequi Christum est opus perfectionis; ergo mendicare pro Christo est opus perfectionis. Item, in Psalm. 108: *Et persecutus est hominem inopem et mendicum.*[46] Glossa Augustini: "Iudas, Iesum Christum;"[47] et ita fuit Christus mendicus. Sed sequi Christum non est opus imperfectionis et peccati; ergo mendicare pro Christo non est peccatum sed potius opus perfectionis.

32 RESPONDEO: CHRISTUS DICITUR '*MENDICUS*' NON QUIA MENDICARET VICTUM, HOC ENIM NON LEGITUR,[48] SED PROPTER MISERIAS HUMANAS ASSUMPTAS INDIGEBAT AUXILIO DEI, ET PETEBAT AUXILIUM DEI NON TANTUM PRO SE QUANTUM PRO MEMBRIS SUIS. UNDE AEQUIVOCATUR HOC NOMEN '*MENDICUS*'.

33 7. Item, Luc. 19: *Zachaee, festinans descende, quia hodie in domo tua oportet me manere.*[49] Glossa: "Non invitatus invitat."[50] Dominus ergo petiit hospitium; ergo qui sequuntur Christum hoc facere possunt. Sed hoc est mendicare; ergo mendicare possunt pro Christo perfecti imitatores Christi.

34 RESPONDEO PER HOC QUOD SEQUITUR: "QUIA ETIAMSI NONDUM AUDIERAT VOCEM INVITANTIS, AUDIERAT AFFECTUM."[51] UNDE PRAEVENIT EUM SEIPSUM INVITANDO APUD EUM EX CAUSA DILECTIONIS.

35 8. Item, Marc. 11: *Circumspectis omnibus, cum iam vespera esset hora, exiit Bethaniam.*[52] Glossa: "Si quis eum hospitio susciperet."[53] Circumspiciebat ergo aut ut de hospitio impetraret aut ut hospitium conduceret aut ut sibi hospitium dari vellet. Non primo modo, quod patet per Glossam: "Si quis

1 Christus dicit] d. C. *transp. P* | ex] in *P* | et sic] ergo *P* 2 ergo … perfectionis *om. C* 3 Item ... perfectionis *om. L* 4 et … Christum *om. C* 6 peccatum] opus imperfectionis *C* | opus *om. C* 7 RESPONDEO] Respondet Magister Guillelmus dicens quod *P* 8 MISERIAS HUMANAS] h. m. *transp. L* 9 DEI] *add.* nundum *P* 10 AEQUIVOCATUR] – vocabat *C:* -vocat *P* 11 *descende*] *add.* in domum *C* 12 hospitium] respitium *C* 13 Christum *om. C* 15 RESPONDEO] Respondet Magister Guillelmus *P* | QUIA] quod *C: om. P* | ETIAMSI] si *C:* etsi *P* 16 EUM] ipsum *P* 17 EX] et *C* 18 11] 10 *L* 20 aut] autem *L* | impetraret] inpertaret *C: om. L* | ut[2] *om. C* | sibi *om. P* 21 Non] Si *L* | quod] ut *C*

45 *ord.* in Ps. 39:18 in *Ed. pr.* 2.503B (*PL* 113.903C); Aug., *Enarr. in Ps.* in *CCSL* 38.444; Cass., *Expo. Psalm.* in *CCSL* 97.371.

46 Ps. 108:17.

47 "Pro eo quod non est recordatus [*int.* Iudas] facere misericordiam. Et perfectum est hominem [*int.* Christum] inopem et mendicum." *int.* in Ps. 108:17 in *Ed. pr.* 2.597b; *cf.* Aug., *Enarr. in Ps.* in *CCSL* 40.1594.

48 "Sed quod mendicaverit panem, non lego..." *DQE*, 330.

49 Luc. 19:5.

50 *int.* in Luc. 19:5 in *Ed. pr.* 4.205a; Amb., *Expo. in Luc.* in *CCSL* 14.330-1.

51 *int.* in Luc. 19:5 in *Ed. pr.* 4.205a; Amb., *Expo. in Luc.* in *CCSL* 14.331.

52 Marc. 11:11.

53 *ord.* in Marc. 11:11 in *Ed. pr.* 4.119A.

eum hospitio susciperet," non dicit 'ut alicui de hospitio impetraret'. Non secundo modo, per Glossam ibidem: "Tantae enim paupertatis fuit ut in tanta urbe nullum hospitium inveniret."[54]

36 <RESPONDEO>: SUPPLE QUOD DEEST, SCILICET "ET ITA NULLI ADULATUS"[55] ETC. QUI ERGO DE FACILI INVENIUNT, VIDETUR QUOD SINT ADULATORES.

37 8[2]. Ergo ut volens hospitium sibi dari gratis circumspiciebat, et ita petebat signo et voluntate, licet non verbo. Sed sic petere est mendicare; ergo Christus mendicavit, et ita perfecti ipsum sequendo sine peccato possunt mendicare.

38 RESPONDEO: CHRISTUS, QUI ERAT *MISSUS AD OVES QUAE PERIERANT DOMUS ISRAEL*,[56] POTUISSET PETERE, SED TAMEN NOLUIT UT ALIIS FORMAM DARET NON PETENDI.

39 9. Item, Ioan. 4: *Dixit ei Iesus: Da mihi bibere.*[57] Et exponit Augustinus in Homilia 15 *Super Ioannem*: "Dominus eget ut accepturus, affluit ut daturus;"[58] et ita Dominus petiit aquam. Sed petere est mendicare; ergo mendicavit. Sed perfectionis est ipsum in omnibus quae possibilia sunt homini sequi; ergo perfectionis christianae est mendicare.

40 Si dicatur quod istud intelligitur de aqua spirituali, contrarium dicit Hieronymus, *Ad Rusticum*.[59]

41 <RESPONDEO:> RIDICULOSUM EST DICERE QUOD PETERE AQUAM AD PUTEUM VEL AD FONTEM SIT MENDICARE, CUM SIT COMMUNIS USUS AQUARUM ET CUM SECUNDUM GLOSSAM: "EXIGEBAT AQUAM SPIRITUALEM, ID EST FIDEM."[60]

1 susciperet] susceperit *L*: *om.* *P* | impetraret] imperaret *δL* 2 Tantae enim] e. T. *transp.* *L* 4 SUPPLE] Respondet Magister Guillelmus quod quando accipit illam glossam "tantae paupertatis fuit" etc. *P* | SUPPLE ... ADULATORES] *ante* ut *L*: *post* mendicare[2] *P*: *om.* *C* | QUOD DEEST] obmittit de glossa *P* | ITA] *om.* *P* 5 ADULTATUS] adultatur *P* | INVENIUNT] inveniuntur *P* 7 gratis *om.* *P* 11 RESPONDEO] Praeterea *P*: *om.* *C* 12 PETERE *om.* *C* | formam daret] d. f. *transp.* *P* 14 *ei*] scilicet mulieri *add. in mg.* *P*[C] 15 Dominus] dicens *P* 19 istud] illud *C* 20 *Rusticium*] Iustitiam *C*: *add.* monachum *P* 21 RIDICULOSAM] Respondet Magister Guillelmus et dicit quod *praem.* *P* | QUOD] et *C* 22 CUM] tamen *δL*

[54] *ord.* in Marc. 11:11 in *Ed. pr.* 4.119A; Hier., *Comm. in Matt.* in *CCSL* 77.190; *cf.* Beda, *Expo. in Marc.* in *CCSL* 120.576.

[55] *ord.* in Marc. 11:11 in *Ed. pr.* 4.119A; Hier., *Comm. in Matt.* in *CCSL* 77.190; *cf.* Beda, *Expo. in Marc.* in *CCSL* 120.576.

[56] Matt. 15:24.

[57] Ioan. 4:7.

[58] Aug., *Tract. in Ioan.* in *CCSL* 36.155.

[59] Hier., *Epist. 125* in *CSEL* 56.1.3, 119.

[60] *int.* in Ioan. 4:7 in *Ed. pr.* 4.232b.

42 10. Item, Christus mendicabat per hospitia Iudeorum[61] aut tamquam ex potestate accipiens aut tamquam mendicans. Non primo modo, quia neminem ad hoc compellebat, quod facere posset si ex potestate acciperet; ergo tamquam mendicans, et ita ii qui perfecte ipsum sequuntur, exemplo eius possunt et debent mendicare, et sic mendicare est opus perfectionis et non peccati.

43 RESPONDEO: CHRISTUS PETERE POTUISSET TAMQUAM POTESTATEM HABENS, SED TAMEN NON PETEBAT UT DARET NOBIS FORMAM; SED INVITATUS RECIPIEBAT, QUOD NULLATENUS EST MENDICARE.

44 11. Item, ad Heb. 11: *Circuierunt in melotis et in pellibus caprinis, egentes, angustiati, afflicti, quibus dignus non erat mundus.*[62] Sancti ergo propter egestatem commendantur et Deum meruerunt. Sed nullus est magis egens quam pauper mendicans pro Christo; ergo mendicare pro Christo debet commendari et Deum meretur, qui sic mendicat, et sic non est peccatum sed opus perfectionis.

45 <RESPONDEO:> NULLA EST MAGIS EGENS QUAM QUAE MANDUCAT FILIUM SUUM PRAE NIMIA EGESTATE;[63] ERGO MANDUCARE FILIUM EST OPUS PERFECTIONIS.

46 12. Item, exemplo Eliae, III Reg. 17: *Dixit Dominus ad Eliam: Surge, et vade in Sarepta Sidoniorum et manebis ibi; praecepi enim mulieri viduae ut pascat te;*[64] et sequitur: *Da mihi paululum aquae ut bibam;*[65] et post: *Affer mihi, obsecro, buccellam panis in manu tua.*[66] Et ita praecepto Domini Elias aquam et panem petiit et ita mendicavit; ergo similiter sine peccato de praecepto Domini possunt viri in statu perfectionis mendicare. Unde Augustinus de hoc in quodam sermone: "Numquid Deus <non> poterat pascere servum suum"[67] etc.

3 acciperet] reciperet *L* 4 et … sequuntur *om. C* | perfecte ipsum] i. p. *transp. L* 5 et[2] … peccati *om. C* 7 RESPONDEO] Ad hoc respondet Magister Guillelmus dicens quod *P* 10 *Circuierunt*] Circumerunt *C* 11 *angustiati*] angustiam *C* 13 pauper *om. C* 16 NULLA] Nihil *C:* Nullus *P:* Item instantia *praem. C:* Ad hoc dat instantiam Magister Guillelmus dicens quod *praem. P* | EST MAGIS] m. est *transp. C* | QUAE] qui *P* 17 SUUM] scilicet *L: om. C* 19 III] 1 *C:* 2 *L: om. P* | 17] 10 *δL* | *et om. δ* 20 *Sarepta*] *-am L* 21 *aquae*] aquam *δ* | *Affer*] Affert *C* 22 *manu tua*] tua m. *transp. P* | praecepto *om. C* 23 ita *om. L* | similiter *om. P* 24 de hoc *om. C* 25 pascere] patere *C*

[61] *Cf.* Luc. 7:36; Luc. 11:37; Luc. 14:1.
[62] Heb. 11:37-8.
[63] IV Reg. 6:29; Bar. 2:3.
[64] III Reg. 17:9.
[65] III Reg. 17:10.
[66] III Reg. 17:11.
[67] Aug., *Serm. de vet. 11* in *CCSL* 41.161 (*PL* 38.98); Aug., *Serm. 103* in *PL* 38.613.

<RESPONDEO:> RIDICULOSA ARGUMENTATIO. SCIEBAT ENIM ELIAS QUOD 47
MULIER EX PRAECEPTO DOMINI VOLEBAT VEL DEBEBAT PASCERE ILLUM. ERGO NON MENDICAVIT, SED DEBITUM EXEGIT EX PRAECEPTO DOMINI.

13. Item, in Legenda Beati Ioannis. Duo honorati viri, omnibus suis 48
relictis sive pauperibus erogatis, secuti sunt Beatum Ioannem. Cum non post longum tempus reversi sunt ad civitatem de qua fuerant, tentati sunt a diabolo eo quod viderent se egentes; et ita Beatus Ioannes et ipsi egebant.[68] Sed nullus magis est egens quam pauper mendicus pro Christo; ergo tales maxime sunt in statu perfectionis.

<RESPONDEO:> FALLACIA CONSEQUENTIS, INSTANTIA SICUT PRIUS, VEL 49
'SICUT FURARI SEQUITUR AD EGESTATEM SICUT MENDICARE, ERGO FURARI EST OPUS PERFECTIONIS.'

14. Item, Ioannes Chrysostomus, *De laudibus Pauli*: "Paulus pecuniam 50
non accepit;"[69] et sequitur de ipso et illis sanctis, qui cum ipso erant: "Egentes et pauperes, in fame et egestate." Egere ergo perfectionis christianae est; ergo cum mendicare pro Christo sit maxima egestas, perfectionis christianae erit mendicare.

RESPONDEO: MENDICARE, LICET SEQUI POSSET EX EGESTATE SICUT FURARI, 51
NON TAMEN EST OPUS BONUM, SICUT NEC FURARI; POTEST ENIM ALIUNDE VIVERE SINE PECCATO.

15. Item, Beatus Benedictus perfectus fuit et in II *Dialogorum* scribitur 52
quod quidam Romanus in spelunca quadam, ubi orabat, per triennium eum sustentavit ei necessaria ministrando.[70] Sustentari ergo ab alio exemplo praedicti Sancti est perfectionis. Sed qui petit eleemosynas pro Christo et accipit, ab alio sustentatur; ergo petere ab alio sive mendicare, quod idem est, erit perfectionis.

RESPONDEO: NON QUICQUID FACIT PERFECTUS EST PERFECTIONIS, NAM 53
COMEDIT ET EGERIT, ET TAMEN HAEC NON SUNT OPERA PERFECTIONIS, SICUT NEC MENDICARE.

1 RIDICULOSA] Respondet Magister Guillelmus dicens quod haec est *praem. P* 2 MULIER *post* Domini *L* 3 DOMINI] Dei *C* 4 honorati] honorifici *L* | suis relictis] r. s. *transp. C* 7 eo *om. C* | viderent] vident *C* | se] illos *P* 9 statu] status *C* 10 FALLACIA] Respondet Magister Guillelmus et dicit hic est *praem. P* | CONSEQUENTIS] *add.* et *P* | INSTANTIA] instantiam *P*: *add.* est *C* 11 SICUT] sic *δ*: ficum *L* | SICUT²] sic *L* 14 ipso] Christo *C* 18 RESPONDEO] Respondet Magister Guillelmus dicens quod *P* | MENDICARE LICET] l. m. *transp. P* | POSSET] posit *P* 24 petit *om. C* 27 RESPONDEO] Respondet Magister Guillelmus dicens quod *P* | NAM] iam *C* 28 TAMEN *om. C* | SICUT] sic *C* 29 NEC *om. C*

[68] *Leg. aur.* I:69-70 (*Leg. aur.* c. 9, 57-8).

[69] Chrys., *Serm. 4* in *PG* 50.491.

[70] Greg., *Dial.* II c. 1-4 in *SC* No. 260.128-32.

54 16. Item, Beatus Alexius, contempto patrimonio et patre et matre et muliere relictis, ivit per mundum mendicando et sanctus fuit.[71] Sed si mendicare pro Christo esset peccatum, sanctus non fuisset; ergo exemplo eius viri in statu perfectionis possunt mendicare.

55 RESPONDEO: PROBA. ITEM, EXEMPLUM UNIUS NON INDUCIT LEGEM COMMUNEM, QUIA FORSAN PRIVATO DEI CONSILIO DUCEBATUR, CUM MENDICARE COMMUNITER SIT CONTRA DOCTRINAM APOSTOLI.

56 17. Item, hoc videtur exemplo novorum Sanctorum, quod non reputo minimum testimonium, immo magnum, quisquis minimum reputet. Primo exemplo Beati Dominici, qui imprecatus est maledictionem in morte sua ei qui divitias in Ordine suo poneret, immo fratres suos voluit per mundum universum mendicare.[72] Item, exemplo Beati Francisci, qui mendicavit et fratres suos mendicare praecepit et hoc etiam a summo pontifice fecit confirmari,[73] et etiam post eius mortem fuit hoc in concilio generali approbatum.[74]

57 RESPONDEO: NON EST CREDENDUM QUOD DOMINUS PAPA MENDICARE PRAECIPERET, CUM HOC SIT CONTRA DOCTRINAM APOSTOLI, "SED POTIUS ERRARE CONVICERETUR, QUOD ABSIT," 25, Q. 1, *SUNT QUI DICUNT*.[75] QUOD AUTEM DICIT BEATUM FRANCISCUM HOC PRAECEPISSE, NON VALET AD PROPOSITUM; NAM SICUT DICIT BEATUS CYPRIANUS, "MANDANT MARTYRES ALIQUA FIERI, SED SI IN LEGE SCRIPTA NON SUNT EA QUAE MANDANT, PRIUS NECESSE EST UT EA SE PROBENT A DEO IMPETRASSE, QUAE POSTULANT SIVE MANDANT."[76]

58 18. Item, dictus Sanctus Franciscus istud miraculis confirmavit. Quia cum vellet transire ultra mare, naute, quia non habebat victum, ipsum recipere noluerunt;[77] et petiit eleemosynas et habuit parum ad victum. Postea ingressus navem cum aliis, cum navigarent per mare, defecerunt victualia

5 RESPONDEO] Respondet Magister Guillelmus *P* | LEGEM COMMUNEM *om. C* 8 non *om. L* 9 testimonium *om. P* 10 Primo *om. P* 11 morte sua] s. m. *transp. P* | fratres] sanctus *L* 12 Item] *add.* hoc *P* 13 praecepit] –eperat *C* | etiam *om. C* 14 fuit hoc *om. C* 15 generali *om. L* 16 RESPONDEO] Respondet Magister Guillelmus et dicit quod hoc *P* 18 1]2 *C* | *SUNT ... DICUNT om. C* 20 BEATUS *om. C* 24 dictus] *add.* etiam *P* | istud] illud *C*

[71] *Cf.* "Vita S. Alex.," in *AS* 31, t. IV Iul., 252

[72] *Cf.* "Vita S. Dom. auct. Petro Ferrando," in *AB* XXX (1911):78; "Vita S. Dom.," in *AS* 35, t. I Aug., 515.

[73] *Solet annuere* in *BF* I, No. 14, 15-19.

[74] *Cf. Leg. ant.* No. 39, 39; *Expo. reg.* 6, 16 n.3.

[75] C.25 q.1 c.6 *Sunt qui dicunt*.

[76] D.50 c.27 *Si quis praepostera*; Cyp., *Lib. de lapsis* in *PL* 4.481.

[77] *Vita I*, No. 55, 42; *Tract. de mir.* No. 33, 284-5; *Leg. maior* in *Opera* VIII c. 9, n. 5, 531 *(AF* 10.599).

aliorum; victus autem praedicti Sancti supererat, unde alios sustentavit. Et ita Dominus voluit et fecit ut alii de mendicatione sustentarentur per miraculum et ita mendicatio per miraculum fuit approbata.

RESPONDEO: PROBA. SED ESTO QUOD SIT VERUM, DICO QUOD MIRACULA 59
NON PROBANT HOMINEM SANCTUM ESSE, QUIA MULTI MALI MIRACULA FACIUNT, 1, Q. 1, *TENEAMUS*.[78] MATT. 24: *SURGENT PSEUDOPROPHETAE ET DABUNT SIGNA ET PRODIGIA MULTA*.[79] ITEM, DE PANE MENDICATO POTEST FIERI MIRACULUM, NEC TAMEN SEQUITUR QUOD MENDICITAS SIT BONA; SICUT DE PANE FURATO POSSET FIERI MIRACULUM, NON TAMEN SEQUITUR QUOD FURTUM SIT BONUM. VEL POTEST DICI QUOD FRANCISCUS IN ALIQUO CASU LICITO MENDICAVIT; UNDE NON EST "TRAHENDUM AD CONSEQUENTIAM,"[80] MAXIME CUM SCIAMUS FRATRES EIUS AB INITIO VIXISSE DE LABORE MANUUM SUARUM.[81]

19. Item, Chrysostomus, 41 Homilia: "Multus a te numerus sanctorum 60
sustentatur, sed melius faceres si inter sanctos indigens communiter viveres."[82] Ergo perfectius est indigere quam sua pauperibus erogare. Sed nullus est magis indigens quam pauper mendicus pro Christo; ergo perfectionis christianae est mendicare pro Christo.

RESPONDEO: FALLACIA CONSEQUENTIS VEL ACCIDENTIS 'EGERE EST BONUM, 61
ERGO MENDICARE EST BONUM, QUOD SEQUITUR AD EGERE'; NON ENIM NECESSARIO SEQUITUR SED CONTINGENTER.

20. Item, istud videtur per rationes. Quod mihi est difficile nec mihi 62
prohibitum est, perfectionis et est hoc facere.[83] Sed mendicare difficile est et utile, nec prohibitum invenitur in lege naturae vel scripturae vel gratiae; ergo mendicare pro Christo est perfectionis christianae.

2 mendicatione] *add.* eius *C* 3 ita *om. L* | approbata] *C:* approbatum *L:* comprobata *P* 4 RESPONDEO] Respondet Magister Guillelmus *P* 5 SANCTUM ESSE] sanctum *C:* e. s. *transp. P* 6 24] 13 δL 9 NON] nec *P* | SEQUITUR] sequeretur *L* | SIT] esset *L* 10 FRANCISCUS] Beatus *praem. P* 13 Multas] *add.* autem *P* | a te *post* sanctorum *P* | sanctorum sustentatur] s. sanct. *transp. L* 15 perfectius] perfectionis *C* | indigere] *add.* potius indigere *C* | sua] *add.* bona *C* 16 pauper *om. L* 17 perfectionis christianae est mendicare pro Christo] m. pro Christo est p. christianae *P* 18 RESPONDEO] Respondet Magister Guillelmus *P: om. C* | FALLACIA] per fallaciam *P* 19 NON] si *L* | ENIM NECESSARIO] n. e. *transp. P* 20 SED *om. L* | CONTINGENTER] *add.* ex hoc *L* 22 et *om. P* | est² *om. C* | facere ... vel *om. L* 23 naturae *om. C* | vel ... vel] nec ... nec *C*

[78] C.1 q.1 c.56 *Teneamus*; Aug., *Tract. in Ioan.* in *CCSL* 36.140.

[79] Matt. 24:24.

[80] "Quae a iure communi exorbitant, nequaquam ad consequantiam sunt trahenda." *Sext.* V, t. 12 *De reg. iur.*, reg. 28.

[81] *Vita I*, No. 39, 31; *Vita II*, No. 161, 223; *Test.*, No. 20, 440.

[82] Hier., *Epist. 118* in *CSEL* 55.1.2, 443.

[83] "Circa difficilia semper est ars et virtus." in *Auct. Arist.*, 235; Arist., *Ethica* in *AristL* XXVI³ B2 1105a 9.

63 RESPONDEO PER INTEREMPTIONEM, QUIA PROHIBITUM EST AB APOSTOLO, I THESS. 4: *OPEREMINI MANIBUS VESTRIS SICUT PRAECIPIMUS VOBIS, UT NULLIUS ALIQUID DESIDERETIS.*[84] GLOSSA: "NEDUM ROGETIS".[85] ITEM, PROHIBITUM EST CAPITULO *DE MENDICANTIBUS VALIDIS* L. UNICA.[86]

64 21. Item, ecclesia imponit poenam mendicationis. Sed neque peccatum neque peccati occasionem imponit; ergo nec mendicare est peccatum nec peccati occasio.

65 RESPONDEO: FALSUM EST, NAM ECCLESIA HOC PRAECIPIENDO ERRARET.[87]

66 22. Item, contemptus sui est laudabilis; ergo magis contemptus magis laudabilis. Sed mendicare pro Christo est contemptus maximus sui; ergo mendicare pro Christo est laudabile. Nullum peccatum est laudabile; ergo mendicare pro Christo non est peccatum, immo bonum et perfectionis opus.

67 RESPONDEO: FALSUM EST. MENDICARE ENIM EST CURA SUI NON CONTEMPTUS SUI, ET APPELLAT AUGUSTINUS MENDICARE "LUCROSAM EGESTATEM,"[88] *DE OPERE MONACHORUM.* ITEM, NON QUAELIBET VILIFICATIO SUI EST BONA, SED POTEST ESSE PECCATUM, SICUT APPARET IN MULIERE MERETRICE, QUAE *TAMQUAM STERCUS IN VIA* AB OMNIBUS *CONCULCABATUR.*[89]

68 23. Item, plus placet Deo paupertas voluntaria quam coacta. Sed paupertas coacta placet Deo; ergo multo fortius paupertas voluntaria. Sed qui omnia relinquit nihil retinendo in communi vel in proprio pro Christo, et postea voluntarie mendicat, est in paupertate voluntaria; ergo placet Deo, et ita mendicare sic non est peccatum, sed magis perfectionis opus. Quod paupertas coacta placeat Deo, habetur Luc. 16 de Lazaro: *Factum est ut moreretur mendicus et portaretur ab angelis in sinum Abrahae*[90] etc. Et erat mendicus coactus, cum esset *ulceribus plenus,*[91] ut dicitur ibidem.

1 RESPONDEO] Respondet Magister Guillelmus *P* | QUIA] quod *C* 2 *OPEREMINI*] operamini *L* | *VESTRIS om. L* 4 CAPITULO *om. L* | L. UNICA] VI *C*: L. ita *L* 5 poenam] poenitentiam *CL* 8 RESPONDEO] Respondet Magister Guillelmus dicens quod *P* 10 maximus] maxime *C* 11 est[2] *om. P* 12 non *om. C* | peccatum immo *om. C* 14 RESPONDEO] Respondet magister Guillelmus dicens quod *P* | NON] *add. in mg.* C^C 15 SUI *om. L* 16 EGESTATEM] *add.* in libro *P* 18 OMNIBUS] hominibus *P* | *CONCULCABATUR*] conculcatur *L*: *add.* quae satis vilificat se *P* 19 paupertas *om. C* 20 paupertas *om. C* 21 relinquit] derelinquit *P* | in[2] *om. CL* 23 sed magis] immo *C* | opus *om. C* 24 placeat] placet *C* | Deo] *add.* haec *C* | 16] 17 *C* 25 *sinum*] sinu *δL* | etc. *om. C* 26 esset] erat *C*

[84] *Cf. supra,* n. 8.
[85] *Cf. supra,* n. 8.
[86] *Cf. supra,* n. 13.

RESPONDEO: IMMO CREDENDUM QUOD ERAT VOLUNTARIA, ALITER ENIM NON 69
ESSET MERITORIA EIUS PAUPERTAS. SED MENDICITAS EIUS ERAT COACTA, QUIA *ULCERIBUS PLENUS*, UNDE LICEBAT EI MENDICARE.

24. Item, qui servit alicui domino, debet ab ipso vel ab eius ministris 70
sustentari. Ergo qui spiritualibus insistunt nihil in mundo habentes debent a domino vel ab eius ministris sustentari; ergo possunt petere a fidelibus, qui Dei sunt ministri. Sed hoc facere est mendicare, et ita qui spiritualibus insistunt, sine peccato possunt mendicare.

<RESPONDEO:> SECUNDUM HANC RIDICULOSAM RATIONEM POSSUNT OMNES 71
DE MUNDO MENDICARE, CUM OMNES POSSINT ORARE. SED SECUNDUM AUGUSTINUM, INTERMITTENDA SUNT SPIRITUALIA PRO VITAE NECESSARIIS ACQUIRENDIS,[92] UT DICIT IN LIBRO *DE OPERE MONACHORUM*. ILLOS ENIM, QUI POSSUNT OPERARI, PASCIT DEUS UT HOMINES ADICIENDO SCILICET NECESSARIA, QUAE PROMISIT PER LABOREM EORUM, QUI EIS DEDIT UT LABORARE POSSINT. ILLOS AUTEM, QUI LABORARE NON POSSUNT, PASCIT UT AVES, UT DICITUR IN EODEM LIBRO.[93]

25. Item, qui servit altari, iuste ab altari debet sustentari secundum 72
Apostolum;[94] ergo petere possunt sustentationem, qui spiritualibus insistunt. Sed hoc est mendicare; ergo etc.

RESPONDEO: FALSUM EST, QUIA PETERE PRAELATUM A SUBDITO, CUI 73
MINISTRAT SPIRITUALIA, NON EST MENDICITAS, SED POTESTAS, UT DICIT QUAEDAM GLOSSA ET AUGUSTINUS, *DE OPERE MONACHORUM*.[95] SED PETERE A NON SUO SUBDITO, CUI NON LICET MINISTRARE SPIRITUALIA, EST MENDICITAS, NON POTESTAS, ET QUI HOC FACIT MINISTRANDO SPIRITUALIA, PSEUDO EST.

1 RESPONDEO] Respondet Magister Guillelmus dicens quod *P* | QUOD] *add.* paupertas eius *C* | ERAT *om. L* 3 *ULCERIBUS PLENUS*] p. u. *transp. C* | UNDE] et ideo *C* 4 alicui *om. C* 5 Ergo ... sustentari *om. L* | nihil] *add.* id est *C* 6 petere *post* fidelibus *P* 9 SECUNDUM] Item *praem C:* Respondet Magister Guillelmus dicens quod *praem. P* 11 INTERMITTENDA] interimenda *L* | SUNT] *add.* opera *C* | VITAE] luce *C* 12 DICIT] *add.* Augustinus *P* 13 HOMINES] haberent *C* | SCILICET] illis *L* 14 LABOREM] labores *P* 15 LABORARE] operari *P* | PASCIT] pascet *L* 17 altari[2]] altario *δL* 19 ergo etc. *om. C* 20 RESPONDEO] Respondet Magister Guillelmus dicens quod *P* 21 SPIRITUALIA] spiritualiter *L*

[87] *Cf. supra* n. 57.
[88] Aug., *De op. mon.* in *CSEL* 41.5.3, 585.
[89] Eccli. 9:10.
[90] Luc. 16:22; *DQE*, 323.
[91] Luc. 16:22; *DQE*, 331.
[92] Aug., *De op. mon.* in *CSEL* 41.5.3, 564.
[93] Aug., *De op. mon.* in *CSEL* 41.5.3, 584; *DQE*, 332.
[94] I Cor. 9:13; I Cor. 10:18.
[95] *Cf. supra*, n. 22, 24.

74 26. Item, si licet recipere quod maius est, licet recipere quod minus est.[96] Sed maius est recipere centum millia marcarum reditus quam frustra vel buccellam panis; ergo, si viri sancti potuerunt recipere et receperunt centum millia marcarum reditus et amplius in ecclesiis in universo orbe diffusis sine peccato, multo fortius perfecti viri possunt recipere victualia sine peccato.

75 RESPONDEO: DEBERET CONCLUDERE DE PETENDO ET CONCLUDIT DE RECIPIENDO. RECIPERE ENIM ELEEMOSYNAM, SI OFFERATUR ECCLESIAE, NON EST PECCATUM, CUM RES ECCLESIAE SINT RES PAUPERUM, 16, Q. 1, *QUONIAM QUICQUID*.[97] SED SI SUB PRAETEXTU PAUPERTATIS PETUNT INDEBITUM, MENDICITAS EST QUAE AB APOSTOLO PROHIBETUR, I THESS. 4 ET II THESS. 3: *SI QUIS NON VULT OPERARI, NON MANDUCET*. GLOSSA: "VULT APOSTOLUS SERVOS CHRISTI CORPORALITER OPERARI UNDE VIVANT, NE COMPELLANTUR EGESTATE NECESSARIA PETERE."[98]

76 27. Item, qui dat maiora, potest recipere minora; sed praedicatores evangelii dant maiora scilicet spiritualia. Ergo possunt recipere minora scilicet temporalia, et ita petere temporalia ab eis, quibus tribuuntur spiritualia, non est peccatum.

77 RESPONDEO: VERUM EST DE ILLO QUI HABET POTESTATEM MINISTRANDI SPIRITUALIA; SED DE ALIIS NON EST VERUM.[99] IMMO SI MINISTRARENT, PSEUDO ESSENT.

78 28. Item, praedicans auctoritate secundum Apostolum potest sumere sumptus potestative. Dicit enim Apostolus: *Qui evangelium annuntiant, de evangelio vivere debent*.[100] Ergo qui habet subauctoritatem potest sumere sumptus supplicative, hoc est petere ex gratia nomine Christi. Sed petere ex gratia nomine Christi est mendicare; ergo qui habent praedicandi subauctoritatem, sine peccato possunt mendicare.

1 recipere] accipere *C* | maius] magnum *P* | minus] nullius *C* 2 maius] magis *C*: magnum *P* | reditus] et maius *P* | frustra] *add.* panis *C* 3 si] cum *L* | receperunt] recapere *L* 4 et amplius] *add.* quam frustra vel buccelam panis *P*: *add.* quod maius est *in mg.* P^C 6 sine peccato *ante* perfecti *P* 7 RESPONDEO] Respondet Magister Guillelmus dicens quod ipse *P* | DE^2 *om. C* 9 ECCLESIAE] ecclesiastice *L* | RES *om. L* 10 SI *mg.* P^C | SUB *om. C* 11 ET ... 3 *om. L* 12 *NON*^{2}] nec *P* 13 OPERARI] laborare *L* 19 RESPONDEO] Respondet Magister Guillelmus dicens quod *P* 24 habet] *add.* potestatem *C* | subauctoritatem] δL^C: auctoritatem *L*

96 *Sext.* V, *De reg. iur.*, reg. 53.

97 C.16 q.1 c. 68 *Quoniam quidquid*.

98 *Cf. supra*, n. 6, 8.

99 *Cf. supra*, n. 73.

100 I Cor. 9:14; *DQE*, 331.

Et haec argumenta sufficiant ad istius partis ostensionem.

RESPONDEO: ISTA VERBA "QUI HABET SUBAUCTORITATEM PRAEDICANDI, 79
POTEST SUMERE SUMPTUS SUPPLICATIVE" NON SUNT VERBA SCRIPTURAE, SED INVENTA *AD EXCUSANDUM EXCUSATIONES IN PECCATIS.*[101] NAM HABERE SUBAUCTORITATEM AUT EST HABERE POTESTATEM AUT NON. SI NON, ERGO SUMPTUS SUMERE NON DEBET SECUNDUM APOSTOLUM ET AUGUSTINUM.[102] SI AUTEM SUBAUCTORITAS DICIT POTESTATEM, AUT DICIT POTESTATEM PROPRIAM AUT ALIENAM: SI DICIT POTESTATEM PROPRIAM SIC SUMERE POTEST SUMPTUS TAMQUAM PRAELATUS; SI DICIT POTESTATEM ALIENAM, TUNC SUMPTUS POTEST PETERE NON A PLEBE, SED A MITTENTE. EXTRA, *DE OFFICIO ORDINARII*, § *INTER CETERA.*[103]

Solutio:

Ad istam quaestionem respondeo per distinctionem mendicationis: 80
tripliciter enim contingit mendicare, scilicet ex necessitate naturae, ex vitiositate culpae, ex supererogatione iustitiae. Primus modus tolerabilis, sicut patet de Lazaro, Luc. 16, qui ex necessitate naturae *erat mendicus,* ut dicitur ibidem, quia *ulceribus plenus,* et postea *mortuus est et ab angelis in sinum Abrahae deportatus.*[104]

Secundus modus vituperabilis, quod fit tripliciter, scilicet pro otio 81
fovendo, et pro lucro augmentando, vel pro utroque. Qui illis modis volunt mendicare, reprehensibiles sunt; quos Augustinus reprehendit in libro *De opere monachorum,* et solum ibi contra tales loquitur in toto libro. Quod potest perpendi per hoc quod dicit ibidem: "O servi Dei, milites Christi"[105] etc., et sequitur: "Tam multos hypocritas sub habitu monachorum usquequaque dispersos, circumeuntes provincias, nusquam missos, nusquam fixos, nusquam stantes, nusquam sedentes;"[106] et sequitur: "Omnes petunt, omnes exigunt aut sumptus lucrosae egestatis aut

1 istius ... ostensionem] hanc partem *P* 2 RESPONDEO] Respondet Magister Guillelmus dicens ad argumentum quod *P* | RESPONDEO ... *CETERA post* utrumque facere (n. 81) *P* | ISTA] illa *P* 6 SUMPTUS SUMERE] s. sump. *transp. L* 7 AUTEM *om. L* 8 ALIENAM] alteram *L* | DICIT] dicat *C* | POTEST SUMPTUS] s. p. *transp. L* 9 DICIT] dicat *C* | SUMPTUS *om. C* 10 *ORDINARII*] ordinis *C* 11 *CETERA*] *add.* Hic respondet Bonaventura ad argumenta Magistri Guillelmi *in calce C* 15 tolerabilis] *add.* est *P* 16 qui ex necessitate *om. L* | *mendicus om. P* 17 *sinum*] sinu *L* 19 quod] qui *P* 24 Tam] Cum *P* | sub *om. L* 25 circumeuntes] circuentes *δL* 26 nusquam fixos *om. C*

101 Ps. 140:4.

102 *Cf. supra,* n. 22.

103 *Extra.* I, t. 31, c. 15 *Inter cetera*; *DP*, 26; *QAP*, n. 17.

104 Luc. 16:20-22; *DQE*, 323.

105 Aug., *De op. mon.* in *CSEL* 41.5.3, 585; *DQE*, 329.

106 Aug., *De op. mon.* in *CSEL* 41.5.3, 585; *DQE*, 329.

simulatae pretium sanctitatis."[107] Et similiter in eodem libro: "Neque propterea in christiana militia ad pietatem divites humiliantur, ut pauperes extollantur. Nullo enim modo decet ut in ea vita ubi senatores sunt laboriosi, ibi fiant opifices otiosi, nec quo veniunt relictis divitiis suis dominum praedictum ibi sint rustici delicati."[108] Et sic per verba Augustini potest perpendi quod loquitur contra tales qui volebant otium fovere vel lucrum augmentare sive utrumque facere.

82 <RESPONDEO:> QUOD DICIT: "AUGUSTINUM LOQUI CONTRA ILLOS QUI MENDICANT PRO OTIO FOVENDO VEL PRO LUCRO CAPTANDO," DICO QUOD ETSI LOQUITUR CONTRA ILLOS QUIA FORTE TALES ERANT, QUOD TAMEN NON HABETUR EX LIBRO NIHILOMINUS TAMEN LOQUITUR CONTRA OMNES MENDICARE VOLENTES, CUM POSSINT OPERANDO QUAERERE VICTUM VEL ALIUNDE SINE PECCATO HABERE, LICET SINT INTENTI OPERIBUS SPIRITUALIBUS. UNDE DICIT QUOD SICUT INTERMITTENDA SUNT OPERA SPIRITUALIA UT MANDUCETUR VEL CIBUS PARETUR SIVE COQUATUR, ITA DIMITTENDA SUNT AD TEMPUS UT VICTUS OPERANDO QUAERATUR.[109] ET RATIONEM SUBIUNGIT, VIDELICET NE QUIS CHRISTIANUS MENDICARE COMPULSUS VENDAT LIBERTATEM CHRISTIANAE PROFESSIONIS, VIDELICET UT FIAT ADULATOR VEL DETRACTOR VEL CADAT IN ALIUD PECCATUM VEL VIDEATUR SUAM SIMULATAM VENDERE SANCTITATEM.[110]

83 Tertius vero modus mendicandi est perfectionis christianae sequendo Dominum nostrum Iesum Christum, qui fuit verus contemptor sui ut apparuit in sua passione, quia vilissimam mortem elegit et tantam habuit paupertatem quod non habuit in sua passione unde se tegeret. Item, verus cultor fuit Dei, sicut patet in omnibus factis suis et in morte se Deo commendavit dicens: *In manus tuas, Domine, commendo*[111] etc. Item, verus fuit dilector proximi, quod in sua passione maxime apparuit, qua tam vilem mortem pro nobis dignatus est sustinere offerens se Deo *hostiam viventem,*

3 ubi] tibi *C* | senatores] cenatores *L* 4 otiosi] curiosi *C* | nec ... sic *om. L* 5 dominum praedictum] domini praedictorum *C* | sint] sunt *C* | delicati] deligati *C* 8 QUOD] Ad aliud Magister Guillelmus *praem. P* | AUGUSTINUM *om. P* 9 QUOD *om. P* | ETSI] primo *L* 10 TAMEN] cum *C* 13 LICET] sed *L* | SINT] *om. C: add.* sicut *L* 14 QUOD *om. C* | INTERMITTENDA] interimenda *L* 15 CIBUS] omnibus *CL* 17 LIBERTATEM] paupertatem *L* 18 UT *om. L* 21 mendicandi *om. C* | christianae] *add.* scilicet *C* 22 nostrum *om. C* 26 *commendo*] *om. P: add.* spiritum *L* | fuit *om. L* 27 quod] quia *P* | qua] qui *C*

[107] Aug., *De op. mon.* in *CSEL* 41.5.3, 585; *DQE,* 329.

[108] Aug., *De op. mon.* in *CSEL* 41.5.3, 580.

[109] *Cf. supra,* n. 71.

[110] *Cf. supra,* n. 28.

[111] Luc. 23:46.

immaculatam, *Deo placentem.*[112] Qui ergo verus est contemptor sui, cultor Dei, dilector proximi, perfecte agit. Unde Augustinus, in quodam sermone quadragesimali: "In isto tempore quantum Deus"[113] etc. In imitando ergo Christum opus est perfectionis mendicare, quia nullus magis se contemnit quam qui propter Christum de divite fit mendicus.

HIC RESPONDEO QUOD FIERI PAUPER PRO CHRISTO OPUS EST PERFECTIONIS; 84
SED PAUPEREM MENDICARE, CUM POSSIT OPERANDO VICTUM ACQUIRERE VEL ALIUNDE SINE PECCATO VIVERE, NON EST OPUS PERFECTIONIS, SED OPUS PECCATI, QUIA CONTRA DOCTRINAM APOSTOLI.[114] NEC CHRISTUS UMQUAM MENDICAVIT NEC HOC LEGITUR IN SCRIPTURA; SED BENE LEGITUR QUOD PAUPER FUIT, SED NON MENDICANS VICTUM CORPORALITER, LICET '*MENDICUS*' DICATUR ALIO MODO, UT DICTUM EST SUPRA.[115]

Item, non solum mendicare perfectionis est pro Christo imitando, sed 85
etiam pro Christo evangelizando, quia ex hoc tripliciter commodum elicitur. Primum ex parte eius quod praedicatur, quia contemptus mundi praedicatur; nemo magis contemnit mundum quam pro Christo mendicans.

HIC DICO QUOD CONTEMNERE DIVITIAS EST CONTEMNERE MUNDUM. SED 86
MENDICARE NON EST CONTEMNERE SICUT NEC MANDUCARE, IMMO EST CURAM HABERE SUI.[116]

Secundum est ex parte eius a quo praedicatur. Quia modo multi sunt 87
praedicatores qui, si non acciperent eleemosynas, non praedicarent in multis locis in quibus praedicant. Et ideo in concilio generali provisum fuit:[117] quod mundus, licet in istis partibus sacra doctrina valde sufficienter esset illustratus, tamen in aliis partibus sacra doctrina deficiebat. Et ideo isti Ordines duo scilicet Praedicatorum et Minorum, missi fuerunt eleemosynas petentes. Quia pro eleemosynis petendis nomine Christi ibant multi, qui

3 quadragesimali] quadragesimalis *L* | In *om. P* 4 Christum] Christo *L* 5 mendicus] pauper et *praem. P* 6 HIC RESPONDEO] Respondet Magister Guilelmus dicens *P* | EST] et *C* 7 OPERANDO] operari vel *praem. P* 8 ALIUNDE] alium tamen *C* 9 UMQUAM] necquam *C* 10 SCRIPTURA] scriptum *C* 12 ALIO] aliquo *L* 13 perfectionis est pro Christo] pro Christo est p. *P* 15 Primum] *add.* quia *P* 17 mendicans] mendicus *L* 18 HIC DICO] Respondet Magister Guillelmus dicens *P* 21 Secundum] Item *praem. L* 23 ideo] *add.* cum *C* | concilio] consilio *L* | generali *om. L* 24 quod] quia *L* | mundus] *add.* per eleemosynas eos petentes sustentaret *P* 26 Praedicatorum ... Minorum] Minorum ... Praedicatorum *P*

[112] Rom. 12:1.
[113] Aug., *Serm. de vet. 11* in *CCSL* 41.161.
[114] *Cf. supra,* nn. 6-9, 55, 57, 63, 75. 79.
[115] *Cf. supra,* n. 32.
[116] *Cf. supra,* n. 67.
[117] *Extra.* I, t. 31, c. 15 *Inter cetera.*

non ivissent pro praebendis minoribus vel etiam forte maioribus habendis, immo citius in suis partibus morarentur.

88 HIC DICO QUOD PRAEDICARE NON DEBENT NISI MISSI, ET SI MISSI PRAEDICANT, DEBET EIS A MITTENTIBUS PROVIDERI, *EXTRA*, *DE OFFICIO ORDINARII*, *INTER CETERA*.[118]

89 Tertium commodum est ex parte eorum a quibus tales recipiuntur et eleemosynas accipiunt, quia per hoc *in aeterna tabernacula*[119] deferuntur. Unde Ioannes Chrysostomus, Homilia 33 *Super Mattheum*: "Manifestum est quoniam discipulos Domini ab eis quibus praedicaverunt cibari oportebat, ut neque ipsi magna saperent"[120] etc. Et in Glossa super illud Psalm. 103, *Producens foenum iumentis*[121] etc., "<Herbam>, id est temporalia, *servituti hominum*, id est praedicatorum, scilicet servi hominum facti pro Christo,"[122] ubi multum loquitur de ista materia etc.

90 HIC DICO QUOD *QUI RECIPIT PROPHETAM IN NOMINE PROPHETAE, MERCEDEM PROPHETAE ACCIPIT*.[123] SED TAMEN ILLE PROPHETA, SI NON HABET POTESTATEM A DEO, POTEST DAMNARI ET DAMNATUR.

91 Sic ergo concedendum quod mendicare pro Christo imitando et evangelizando non solum est bonum, sed etiam est de perfectione christianae religionis. Et argumenta hoc probantia concedantur.

92 HAEC CONCLUSIO SUPPONIT FALSUM DICENDO CHRISTUM IMITANDUM IN MENDICANDO, QUIA CHRISTUS SIC NON MENDICAVIT; VEL SI ETIAM CHRISTUS MENDICASSET NON ESSET "TRAHENDUM AD CONSEQUENTIAM,"[124] CUM HOC PROHIBEAT APOSTOLUS, IN QUO LOQUEBATUR CHRISTUS.[125]

2 citius] *add.* forte *P* 3 HIC DICO] Respondet Magister Guillelmus et dicit *P* 6 tales recipiuntur] r. t. *transp. P* 8 33] 3 *δ*: tertia *L* | Manifestum est] Et *C* | Manifestum … etc. *post* DAMNATUR (n. 90) *C* 9 praedicaverunt] praedicaverit *C*: praedicaverant *P* 10 saperent] seperent *L* | super … 103 *post* materia *P* | 103] 102 *C* 12 Christo] proximo *C* 14 HIC DICO] Respondet Magister Guillelmus dicens *P* | HIC … DAMNATUR *post* concedantur (n. 91) *P* | QUOD *om. C* 15 *ACCIPIT*] recipit *L* 17 concedendum] *add.* est *P* 18 de *om. C* 20 HAEC] Postea ipse dicit quod *P* | CONCLUSIO] *add.* argumenti *P* | DICENDO] *add.* quod *P* | IMITANDUM] imitando *P* | IN *om. L* 21 sic *om. C* 23 LOQUEBATUR] sequebatur *C*

[118] *Cf. supra*, n. 79.

[119] Luc. 16:9.

[120] Chrys., *Hom. in Matt.* in *PG* 57.382.

[121] Ps. 103:14.

[122] *int.* in Ps. 103:14 in *Ed. pr.* 2.586b; Aug., *Enarr. in Ps.* in *CCSL* 40.1506; Cass., *Expo. Psalm.* in *CCSL* 98.931.

[123] Matt. 10:41.

[124] *Cf. supra*, n. 59.

[125] II Cor. 13:3; *cf.* nn. 6-9, 55, 57, 63, 75, 79.

Ad argumenta in oppositum respondendum est:

Primo, <ad 1> ad primum: *Timete Dominum* etc., sic dicendum quod 93
intelligitur de mendicitate spirituali, non corporali; quod perpenditur per hoc quod sequitur: *Divites eguerunt et esurierunt*[126] etc. Sed obicitur de corporali; ideo non valet obiectio illa.

Ad secundum <ad 2> quod obicitur: *Iunior fui*, etc., dicendum quod 94
Glossa solvit ita dicens: "*panem* scilicet spiritualem, id est indigere panem verbi Dei, quia verbum Dei semper est cum eo."[127] Et sic intelligitur de pane spirituali, non corporali, sicut ratio procedebat.

Ad aliud <ad 3> de Psalm.: *Nutantes* etc., dicendum quod duplex est 95
mendicitas: voluntaria, quae perfectionis est, ut ostensum est supra,[128] et de hac non loquitur auctoritas; alia involuntaria, quae non est perfectionis, immo aliquando maledictionis, de qua auctoritas est intelligenda.

Contra: Licet paupertas debeat esse voluntaria, quia aliter non 96
esset meritoria; tamen mendicitas non debet esse voluntaria, quia si mendicet quis, nisi egestate compulsus, peccat fraudando pauperes quibus eleemosynae debentur. Unde Augustinus, *De verbis Domini*, 14, q. 5, *Immolans*: "Panis egentium vita est pauperis; qui defraudat illum, homo est sanguinis."[129] Et alibi: "Qui de bonis suis sustentari possunt, si quod pauperum est accipiunt, sacrilegium profecto incurrunt et per abusionem talium *iudicium sibi manducant et bibunt*,"[130] 16, q. 1, *Quoniam quicquid*.[131]

Ad aliud <ad 4> de Eccli. 40: *Fili* etc., dicendum quod Glossa solvit: 97
Melius est mori quam indigere. Glossa: "Virtutibus vel bonis moribus,"[132] et ita loquitur de indigentia spirituali.

Ad aliud <ad 5> de Act.: quod *beatius est* etc., dicendum quod 98
intelligendum est de illis, qui omnia bona sua pauperibus erogant vel dividunt et postea operantur manibus unde vivunt et eleemosynas

1 **est**] et *C*: *om. P* 2 *Timete Dominum*] Timere Deum *C* 3 spirituali] *add.* et *P* 4 Sed] Et si *C* | obicitur] obiciatur *C* 5 ideo] quod *praem. L* | valet] neque *C* 6 *fui*] *add.* etenim senui *L* 9 procedebat] praecedebat *L* 10 *Nutantes*] *add.* transferentur *P* 12 involuntaria] non voluntaria *P* 14 Contra] *add.* hoc est Magister Guillelmus dicens quod *P* 16 fraudando] fraudendo *L* 18 pauperis] pauperum vel *praem. P* | illum] eum *L* 20 pauperum est] e. p. *transp. L* | et] vel *P* 23 *Fili*] Filii *L* 26 *est om. C* 27 sua *om. C* 28 manibus] *add.* suis *P*

[126] Ps. 33:11.

[127] *int.* in Ps. 36:25 in *Ed. pr.* 2.498b.

[128] *Cf. supra*, n. 68.

[129] C.14 q.5 c.2 *Immolans*; *DQE*, 324.

[130] I Cor. 11:29.

[131] C.16 q.1 c.68 *Quoniam quidquid*.

[132] *int.* in Eccli. 40:29 in *Ed. pr.* 2.786b.

largiuntur.[133] Quod facere perfectissimum est, si secundum quod debent tales spiritualibus insistant; sed adhuc solum spiritualibus prout debemus insistere non sufficimus, et ideo nec laborem manuum sustinere debemus, quia propter temporalia non sunt spiritualia omittenda.[134]

99 HIC DICO QUOD NON SUNT SPIRITUALIA OMNINO OMITTENDA, SED SECUNDUM AUGUSTINUM, PROPTER QUAERENDUM VICTUM SUNT SPIRITUALIA INTERPONENDA.[135]

100 Unde spiritualibus, dimissis omnibus nihil penitus retinendo, perfectius est insistere quam sua pauperibus erogare. Et hoc dicit Augustinus, in libro *De bono coniugali*, in haec verba: "Bene faciebant mulieres, quae de sua substantia Domino ministrabant, sed melius et perfectius Apostoli, qui *eum relictis omnibus sunt secuti*."[136]

101 ILLUD NON FACIT AD PROPOSITUM, QUIA BENE CONCEDIMUS QUOD MELIUS EST PRO CHRISTO OMNIA RELINQUERE QUAM ALIQUID RETINERE; SED EX HOC NON SEQUITUR QUOD OPORTEAT MENDICARE, SED DEBET OPERANDO VICTUM QUAERERE, UT DICIT GLOSSA PRAEALLEGATA LUC. 12: "UT OMNIBUS SEMEL PRO DEO SPRETIS, POSTEA *OPEREMINI MANIBUS VESTRIS* UNDE VIVATIS,"[137] VEL DEBET INTER COMMUNEM VITAM DEGENTES DE BONIS ECCLESIAE SUSTENTARI, ACT. 4 ET 12, Q. 1, *VIDENTES*.[138]

102 Et ideo dicitur, *De ecclesiasticis dogmatibus*: "Bonum est facultates"[139] etc.

103 Ad aliud <ad 6> de Glossa <II> ad Thess. 3: *Si quis*, dicendum est quod per Glossam solvitur dicentem: "ut non compellantur," et ita non voluntarie

1 debent] *add.* largiuntur *P* 2 tales *om. C* | spiritualibus insistant] s. insistunt *C: om. P* | adhuc solum] nos *P* 3 nec laborem] ne clamorem *C* 4 omittenda *post* INTERPONENDA (n. 99) *C* 5 HIC DICO] Respondet Magister Guillelmus dicens *P* | HIC ... INTERPONENDA *post* facultates etc. (n. 102) *P* | NON SUNT SPIRITUALIA] s. sunt non *P* | OMITTENDA] dimittenda *CL* 8 dimissis omnibus] o. d. *transp. P* | perfectius] perfectionis *C* 11 perfectius] *add.* qui scilicet *P* | qui *om. P* 12 *omnibus ... secuti post VIDENTES* (n. 101) *C* 13 ILLUD] Ad aliud quando dicit "melius et perfectius" etc., dicit Magister Guillelmus quod *praem P:* Istud *L* | ILLUD ... *VIDENTES post* facultates etc. (n. 102) *P* 14 EST *om. C* | PRO CHRISTO OMNIA] omnia pro Christo *L* 15 NON *om. C* 16 PRAEALLEGATA] praeallegatur *C* | SEMEL] simul *C: post* DEO *P* 17 DEO] Christo *L* | *OPEREMINI*] operamini *L* 18 SUSTENTARI *post VIDENTES P* | ACT ... *VIDENTES om. L* 21 *Si quis*] sic δ: sicut *L* | est *om. C* 22 non[2] *om. L*

[133] *Cf. supra*, n. 10.
[134] *ord.* in Act. 20:35 in *Ed. pr.* 4.498A (*PL* 114.464B); Beda, *Expo. Act.* in *CCSL* 121.84.
[135] *Cf. supra*, n. 71.
[136] Aug., *De bono coniug.* in *CSEL* 41.5.3, 199; Matt. 4:22; Luc. 5:11.
[137] *Cf. supra*, n. 10; I Thess. 4:11.
[138] Act. 4:32-5; *cf. supra*, n. 11.
[139] *De ecc. dog.* c. 38 in *PL* 42.1219.

petant. Sed mendicantes pro Christo voluntarie petunt, ideo de talibus mendicantibus non intelligitur Glossa illa.

RIDICULOSA SOLUTIO ET CONTRA DEUM, QUIA SI PETUNT NON COMPULSI 104
EGESTATE, PECCANT, UT DICTUM EST SUPRA.[140]

Item, <ad 6> dicit: "Vult Apostolus servos Dei" etc. Non ergo praecepit, 105
sed consulit, et ita qui hoc non facit, non facit contra Apostolum.

HIC FALSUM DICIT, IMMO PRAECEPIT HOC APOSTOLUS, I THESS. 4: *OPEREMINI* 106
MANIBUS VESTRIS, SICUT PRAECEPIMUS VOBIS.[141] SED CERTE NON POTEST NON MENTIRI, QUI VULT SUSTINERE FALSUM CONTRA SACRAM SCRIPTURAM.

Item, <ad 6> si ligat ex praecepto, non nisi eos de quibus locutus est 107
supra dicens: *Audivimus inter vos quosdam inordinate ambulantes, curiose agentes*[142] etc. Tales non sunt qui pro Christo mendicant Christum imitando et evangelizando, quia non sunt curiosi vel inordinati sive otiosi, sed spiritualibus insistunt, quod melius est quam temporali lucro insistere. Unde Glossa Ambrosii, super illud Luc. 9: *Tu autem vade et annuntia regnum Dei.*[143] Glossa: "Dominus docet minora bona pro utilitate maiorum esse praetermittenda; est enim maius animas mortuorum praedicando suscitare quam corpus mortuum in terra abscondere."[144]

HIC LOQUITUR AMBROSIUS DE ILLIS QUI A DOMINO SUNT MISSI. 108

Et ita quod praecipit Apostolus de labore manuum, praecipit illis qui 109
maiora et utiliora facere non possunt.

Ad aliud <ad 7> de alia Glossa ibidem posita, dicendum quod ipsa Glossa 110
solvit quando dicit: "otio deditus," id est fovens otium, talis enim sine adulatione vivere non potest. Sed tales non sunt qui mendicant omnibus suis spretis evangelizando et imitando Christum, quia spiritualibus insistunt.

1 petant] petunt *L* 3 RIDICULOSA SOLUTIO] Respondet Magister Guillelmus dicens quod ista solution ridiculosa est *P* 4 EST *om. C* | SUPRA *om. P* 5 dicit] *add.* Glossa *P* | Vult Apostolus] A. v. *transp. L* 7 HIC] Ad hoc dicit Magister Guillelmus quod *P* | DICIT] est *P* | *OPEREMINI*] Operamini *CL* 9 SACRAM *om. P* 10 non] *add.* ligat *P* 11 dicens *om. L* | *vos*] nos *L* 12 etc. *om. C* | mendicant] mendicans *C* 14 melius est] est m. *transp. P* 15 illud] istud *C* 19 HIC] Respondet Magister Guillelmus et dicit hoc quod *P* | HIC ... MISSI *post* possunt (n. 109) *P* 20 Apostolus *om. P* | qui] quod *C* 22 Glossa[2] *om. L* 25 spretis] scriptis *C* | evangelizando ... insistunt *post* EGESTAS (n. 111) *C*

[140] *Cf. supra*, n.11, 12, 19, 28, 75.

[141] I Thess. 4:11; *DP*, 52.

[142] II Thess. 3:11; *DP*, 48; *Dephar.*, n. 8.

[143] Luc. 9:60.

[144] *ord.* in Luc. 9:60 in *Ed. pr.* 4.177A; Beda, *Expo. in Luc.* in *CCSL* 120.213; *cf.* Amb., *Expo. in Luc.* in *CCSL* 14.226-7.

111 HIC DICO QUOD QUANTUMCUMQUE PRO CHRISTO SPREVERIT BONA SUA, NIHILOMINUS TAMEN, CUM HOMO SIT, PECCARE POTEST ET ADULARI, ET DETRAHERE, QUANDO COMPELLIT EGESTAS.

112 Unde paupertas non est adulatrix sicut divitiae, secundum quod dicit Ioannes Chrysostomus, ultima homilia super Mattheum: "Adulari oportet multos principes et nobiles et supplicare et timere; sed non paupertas est aliquid tale."[145] Unde per totam illam homiliam ostendit mirabiliter bene qualiter paupertas non adulatur, sed divitiae adulantur ut habeantur et non amittantur.

113 HIC DICO QUOD LOQUITUR CHRYSOSTOMUS DE DIVITIBUS ET DE PAUPERIBUS SIBI SUFFICIENTIBUS, DE QUIBUS APOSTOLUS, II COR. 9: *UT IN OMNIBUS SEMPER OMNEM SUFFICIENTIAM HABENTES ABUNDEMUS IN OMNE OPUS BONUM.*[146] GLOSSA: "QUI SOLAM SUFFICIENTIAM ELIGIT, POTERIT *IN OMNE OPUS BONUM* ABUNDARE."[147]

114 Ad aliud <ad 8> de I ad Thess. 4: *Operamini* etc., dicendum quod petere dupliciter est: aut ex cupiditate, et hoc inhibet Apostolus, ut in illa Glossa perpenditur, aut propter salvationem animarum, ut dantes sanctorum orationibus in *aeterna tabernacula recipiantur.*[148] Hoc Apostolus non inhibet, hoc modo petunt pauperes pro Christo mendicantes.

115 HIC VIDE QUALITER DICIT APERTISSIME CONTRA GLOSSAM! DICIT ENIM GLOSSA QUOD PROHIBETUR PETERE EX EGESTATIS COMPULSIONE ET ISTE DICIT QUOD PROHIBETUR PETERE EX CUPIDITATE, CONSTAT QUOD HOC EST PEIUS QUAM PRIMUM. SED TAMEN NON HIC PROHIBETUR PETERE EX CUPIDITATE, SED PROHIBETUR PETERE EX EGESTATIS NECESSITATE. ITEM QUOD DICIT: "MENDICARE LICET PROPTER SALVATIONEM ANIMARUM" NIHIL EST, QUIA MENDICARE NON SALVAT MENDICANTEM, IMMO POTIUS DAMNAT, CUM SIT PROHIBITUM NISI IN CASU; NEC SALVAT ILLOS QUIBUS PRAEDICAT HOMO

1 HIC DICO] Respondet Magister Guillelmus et dicit *P* | HIC ... EGESTAS *post* amittantur (n. 112) *P* | CHRISTO] *add.* quis *P* 2 ET *om. L* 6 supplicare] supplicari *δ* | non paupertas] p. non *transp. P* 7 tale *om. C* 10 HIC DICO] Ad hoc quod dicit de Chrysostomo "adularia oportet" etc., ipse dicit *P* | QUOD] *add.* ibi *P* | DIVITIBUS] *add.* cupidis *P* | DE *om. C* 11 II] I *δL* | *SEMPER*] super *L:* sicut *P* 12 *OMNEM SUFFICIENTIAM*] s. o. *transp. P* | *OPUS BONUM*] b. o. *tranp. L* 15 Ad ... ACCIDENTIS (n. 115) *post* ALIMONIA EGENTES (n. 117) *LP* 16 dupliciter] duplex *C* | ex *om. L* | illa *om. L* 20 HIC] Respondet Magister Guillelmus dicens *P* 21 EX ... PETERE *om. CL* 22 QUOD] quam *C* | HOC] hic *C* 24 ITEM] Ita *C:* Sed *L* 25 LICET *om. P* 26 NON] nihil *C:* nec *P* 27 ILLOS] eos *L*

145 Chrys., *Hom. in Matt.* in *PG* 58.791.

146 II Cor. 9:8.

147 *int.* in II Cor 9:8 in *Ed. pr.* 4.348b-349a; Amb., *Comm. in Epist. ad Cor.* in *PL* 17.331.

148 Luc. 16:9.

MENDICUS, LICET EIUS PRAEDICATIO *PER OCCASIONEM*[149] SALVARE POSSIT. SED IN HAC ARGUMENTATIONE 'PRAEDICATOR MENDICUS SALVAT, ERGO MENDICITAS SALVAT', EST FALLACIA ACCIDENTIS.

Ad aliud <ad 9> de Glossa I Thess. 5, dicendum quod per ipsam Glossam 116
solvitur, per hoc quod dicitur: "egestas dum saturari quaerit, a iustitia declinat." Sed mendicantes pro Christo praedicando et evangelizando egestatem suam saturari non quaerunt, et ideo de talibus non est intelligenda.

HIC DICO QUOD LICET ELIGERUNT EGERE PRO CHRISTO, NIHILOMINUS 117
TAMEN, QUANDO ESURIUNT, SATURARI QUAERUNT; ADHUC ENIM ANIMALES SUNT, ID EST ALIMONIA EGENTES.

Ad aliud <ad 10> quod obicitur: *Vendite* etc., dicendum quod in illa 118
Glossa duae sunt partes. Prima est de integritate consilii, scilicet spernere omnia sua; ad hanc partem faciendam tenentur omnes viri, qui volunt esse in statu perfectionis secundum consilium Domini in evangelio: *Si vis esse perfectus, vade et vende omnia quae habes et da pauperibus et sequere me,*[150] 'non partem',[151] sicut dicit Glossa. Secunda vero pars illius Glossae non est de integritate consilii, sed supererogationis; quod perpenditur per hoc quod alii Apostoli a Beato Paulo hoc non fecerunt, ut ipse Paulus testatur in epistolis suis,[152] et aliquando fecit hoc Paulus, aliquando non,[153] et tamen *omne consilium Dei*[154] fecerunt alii Apostoli, cum perfectissimi fuerunt. Et ideo perfecti viri bene facerent si hoc facerent, non tamen ad hoc quantum ad perfectionem sunt obligati. Non enim eos laborare de consilio est necesse.

VIDE MIRABILEM DISTINCTIONEM ET SOPHISTICAM ET IDEO ODIBILEM, 119
VIDELICET QUOD PARS GLOSSAE EST DE INTEGRITATE CONSILII, PARS VERO EST

1 MENDICUS] mendicans *L* | SED] Unde *C* 4 dicendum] *add.* est *L* 5 quod *om.* *δ* | dicitur] dicit *P* 6 praedicando] CLP^{C}: mendicando *P* 7 egestatem suam saturari] saturari e. suam *P* | talibus] tali *C* 9 HIC DICO] Respondet Magister Guillelmus dicens *P* | LICET] qui *L* 10 ADHUC] ad hoc *P* 13 sunt partes] p. s. *transp.* *P* 17 vero *om.* *P* 18 supererogationis] *add.* est *P* | quod[2]] et *C* 19 Beato] Bono *C* 23 est necesse] est n. *transp.* *C: post* I Cor. 9 (n. 119) *C* 25 VIDE] *add.* Magister Guillelmus respondens *P* | VIDE ... I COR. 9 *post* responsio ad illud (n. 122) *P* | DISTINCTIONEM ET SOPHISTICAM] et est sophisticam distinctionem *C* | IDEO] *add.* Deo *P* 26 VERO] autem *P*

[149] Phil. 1:18; *DP*, 60; *QAP*, n. 30; *SQD*, n. 9; *Dephar.*, n. 9.

[150] Matt. 19:21; *DQE*, 323.

[151] *int.* in Matt. 19:21 in *Ed. pr.* 4.62b; Hier., *Comm. in Matt.* in *CCSL* 77.170; *DQE*, 323.

[152] I Cor. 4:12; I Cor. 9:4; II Thess. 3:7

[153] Act. 18:3.

[154] Act. 20:27.

SUPEREROGATIONIS, CUM OMNE CONSILIUM SIT SUPEREROGATIONIS ET TOTA GLOSSA UNIUS EST TEXTUS ET PENDET ETIAM CONSTRUCTIO ET SENTENTIA ILLIUS USQUE IN FINEM. ET QUOD DICIT QUOD 'ALII APOSTOLI A PAULO' NON SUNT OPERATI MANIBUS, FALSUM EST, SICUT LEGITUR IOAN. 21, QUOD AD PISCATIONEM PISCIUM REDIERUNT "CUM UNDE VIVERENT NON HABERENT,"[155] UT DICIT GLOSSA IBIDEM. ET TAMEN POTERANT NON OPERARI ET VIVERE DE EVANGELIO, CUM AD HOC MISSI ESSENT, UT PROBAT APOSTOLUS, I COR. 9.[156]

120 Unde Glossa, super illud Luc. 12: *Considerate corvos*[157] etc., Glossa: "Sancti merito avibus comparantur, qui nihil in mundo habentes nec laborantes, sola contemplatione aeterna petunt, iam similes angelis."[158]

121 HIC DICO QUOD LOQUITUR DE SANCTIS COMMUNEM VITAM DEGENTIBUS, QUI ETSI NON OPERENTUR CORPORALITER, TAMEN VIVUNT DE BONIS ECCLESIAE COMMUNIBUS, UT ACT. 4 ET 12, Q. 1, *VIDENTES*;[159] VEL LOQUITUR DE ILLIS QUI LABORARE NON POSSUNT, QUIA TALES PASCIT DOMINUS SICUT AVES UT DICIT AUGUSTINUS, *DE OPERE MONACHORUM*.[160]

122 Et in Glossa Luc. 10: *Nolite portare*[161] etc. "Tanta praedicatoris debet esse fiducia in Deo ut praesentis vitae sumptis, et si non provideat sibi, tamen certissime non defecturos sciat, ne dum occupatur mens ad temporalia, minus praedicet aeterna."[162] Et sic apparet responsio ad illud.

123 HIC DICO QUOD LOQUITUR DE PRAEDICATORIBUS MISSIS A DEO, QUIBUS LICET VIVERE DE EVANGELIO, ET HOC EXPRESSE DICIT GLOSSA.

1 OMNE … ET *om. C* 2 UNIUS EST] sit unius *C* | TEXTUS] contextus *P* | PENDET] pendeat *C* | ETIAM *om. C* 3 IN] ad *C* 4 FALSUM EST] est f. *transp. C* | 21] 19 *L* 8 illud] istud *C* | 12] 13 *P* 9 qui] quia *C* 10 angelis *post* MONACHORUM (n. 121) *C* 11 HIC DICO] Ad quod dicit de illa Glossa "Considerate corvos" etc., respondet Magister Guillelmus et dicit *P* | HIC … MONACHORUM *post* responsio ad illud (n. 122) *P* 12 OPERENTUR] operantur *L* 13 ET *om. L* 14 SICUT AVES *om. L* | UT] sicut *C*: et *L* 16 etc.] et cum *C* 17 tamen] cum *L* 18 certissime *om. P* | ne] nec *L* 19 minus] unus *L* 20 HIC DICO] Ad aliud de illa Glossa "Nolite portare" etc, respondet dicens *P*

155 Ioan. 21:3; *DVM*, 338; *ord.* in Ioan. 21:3 in *Ed. pr.* 4.269B (*PL* 114.424B); Aug., *Tract. in Ioan.* in *CCSL* 36.669; *DVM*, 338.

156 I Cor. 9:13-4.

157 Luc. 12:24.

158 *ord.* in Luc. 12:24 in *Ed. pr.* in 4.186B (*PL* 114.296D); *cf.* Aug., *De op. mon.* in *CSEL* 41.5.3, 584-5.

159 Act. 4:32; *cf. supra*, nn. 11, 101.

160 *Cf. supra*, n.73.

161 Luc. 10:4.

162 *ord.* in Luc. 10:4 in *Ed. pr.* 4.177B (*PL* 114.284C); Beda, *Expo. in Luc.* in *CCSL* 120.215; Beda, *Expo. in Marc.* in *CCSL* 120.504; Greg., *Hom.* in *CCSL* 141.119.

124 Ad aliud <ad 11> de decreto, dicendum est quod tangit episcopos, quod episcopi debent invenire necessaria indigentibus. Et etiam ibi loquitur Sanctus Urbanus de indigentia non voluntaria; sed pauperes mendicantes pro Christo voluntarie indigentes sunt, et ideo eos non ligantur.

125 VIDE QUOMODO DICIT CONTRARIUM VERITATI! IMMO LOQUITUR DE ILLIS QUI OMNIBUS RELICTIS VITAM COMMUNEM DEGERE ELEGERUNT SCILICET IN COLLEGIIS.

126 Item, <ad 11> non tangit pauperes mendicantes nec eos ligat, quia quod posterius confirmatum est, vim debet obtinere et priori statuto debet derogare. Sed quia religiones pauperum mendicantium post illud decretum fuerunt confirmatae a papa[163] et a concilio generali approbatae, ideo non ligantur per istud decretum.

127 VIDE QUOD NON ATTENDIT VERBA DECRETI. URBANUS ENIM EX PROPRIO MOTU NIHIL IBI STATUIT, SED RECITAT VERBUM CONTENTUM ACT. 4: *ERANT ILLIS OMNIA COMMUNIA ET NULLUS ERAT EGENS INTER EOS,*[164] ET ILLUD STATUTUM APOSTOLORUM DECLARAT. UNDE NON EST STATUTUM URBANI, SED APOSTOLORUM; CONTRA QUOD STATUTUM NEC PAPA SCIENTER FACERET NE "ERRARE CONVINCERETUR," 25, Q. 1, *SUNT QUI DICUNT*.[165]

128 Sed si dicatur quod Sanctus fuit qui decretum composuit, non qui istos Ordines mendicantes confirmavit, et dictis Sancti citius et magis credendum est. Dicendum quod Beatus Hieronymus solvit unam quaestionem per cuius simile solvi potest hoc. Quaerit enim quare monachi non comedant carnes, cum ante adventum Christi et in adventu comedantur ab omnibus carnes. Et respondet quod in primo tempore, ante dilivium, non comederunt homines carnes; post dilivium et in tempore legis permissum est eis comedere carnes, quod est medium temporis. In fine vero temporum, scilicet in tempore gratiae, cum Christus incarnatus est, passus et resurgens in caelum ascendit, "revolavit ω ad α;" et ideo sicut in primo tempore non comedebantur carnes, ita nec modo in tempore

1 aliud] *add.* autem *L* | de *om. C* 2 etiam *om. L* 4 eos] eo *L: post* ligantur *L* | ligantur] ligat *C* 5 VIDE … DICIT] Respondeo Magister Guillelmus dicens quod hoc est *P* 9 confirmatum] ligatum *C* 11 decretum] determinatum *C* | concilio] consilio *L* 13 VIDE] Respondet Magister Guillelmus dicens *P* 14 IBI] emiti *C* 15 *EOS*] illos *P* | ET] vel *P* 16 EST STATUTUM] s. est *transp. C* 17 NE] nec *CL* 19 Sed] Item *P* | si *om. C* 20 Sancti] sanctis *P* 21 est *om. P* | Dicendum] Et *praem. C* | solvit unam quaestionem] u. q. s. *P* 24 comedantur] comdebant *C:* comedebantur *P* 25 et] *add.* etiam *C* 27 cum … gratiae *om. P*

[163] *Solet annuere* in *BF* I, No. 14, 15-9; *cf. supra*, 56.

[164] Act. 4:34; *cf. supra*, n.11.

[165] *Cf. supra*, n. 57.

gratiae, quod est finis temporum.[166] Et hoc dicitur 35 Dist., c. *Ab exordio.*[167] Similiter, dico quod primitiva ecclesia fuit in maxima paupertate per voluntatem Dei, deinde medio tempore ditata Spiritu Sancto operante. Sed in fine revolabit ω ad α, id est ecclesia in quibusdam erit in maxima paupertate. Et hoc similiter operatione Spiritus Sancti. Dico ergo quod, sicut in tempore ditatae ecclesiae Spiritus Sanctus induxit Beatum Urbanum ad illud decretum sanciendum,[168] similiter idem Sanctus Spiritus induxit dominum papam in fine ecclesiae ad tales Ordines mendicantes confirmandos.

129 VIDE PERICULOSUM VERBUM ET SUSPICIONE NON CARENS, QUOD DICIT ECCLESIAM REDITURAM IN QUIBUSDAM ORDINIBUS AD PRISTINAM PAUPERTATEM! HOC ENIM SAPIT SENTENTIAM IOACHIM, QUI PONIT IMPERIUM PETRI ET ECCLESIAE ROMANAE IMPERIUM BABILONICUM EO QUOD DITATA EST ECCLESIA ET IMPERIUM ROMANUM HABERE MERUIT.[169] NEC CREDENDUM EST QUOD DECRETUM URBANI, IMMO APOSTOLORUM, FUIT TEMPORALE, CUM IN FINE DICATUR: "SI QUIS EXTITERIT MODERNIS AUT FUTURIS TEMPORIBUS QUI HOC EVELLERE NITATUR, IAM DICTA DAMNATIONE FERIATUR."[170]

130 Unde Gregorius papa et Innocentius,[171] qui istos Ordines confirmaverunt, multum nobiles fuerunt et magni animi et multas habebant divitias. Et ideo non est praesumendum quod istos pauperes Ordines et viles habitu confirmassent nisi instigati Spiritu Sancto.

131 Ad consequens argumentum <ad 12> est similiter respondendum.

132 Ad aliud argumentum <ad 13> de iure civili, sic dicendum quod illa lex introducta fuit tempore famis, quae fuit in Lombardia, quia tunc volebant multi esse mendicantes, qui alio modo vivere nolebant, et ita per illos vere mendicantes fame peribant.

1 dicitur] dicit *P* 3 Spiritu Sancto] Sancto Spiritu *transp. L* 4 id est] scilicet *L* 5 maxima] maxime *C* | Spiritus Sancti] Sancti Spiritus *transp. C* 7 illud] istud *C* | sanciendum] sciendum *CL* 8 Spritus induxit *om. CL* 10 VIDE] *add.* dicit Magister Guillelmus *P* | VIDE … FERIATUR *post* Spiritu Sancto (n. 130) *P* 13 ECCLESIAE ROMANAE] r. e. *transp. C* | BABILONICUM] babiloniam *C* 15 FUIT] fuerit *δ* | CUM] et *C* 20 habebant] hababunt *C* | non *om. C* 22 est *om. C* 23 aliud] istud *C* | dicendum] respondendum *P* 24 introducta fuit] f. i. *transp. L*

[166] Hier., *Adv. Iov.* in *PL* 23.247.

[167] D. 35 c.2 *Ab exordio.*

[168] C.25 q.1 c.6 *Sunt quidam.*

[169] *Cf.* "Evangelium aeternum," 118-20.

[170] "Ideo si aliquis extiterit modernis aut futuris temporibus qui hoc avellere nitatur, iam dicta damnatione feriatur." C.12 q.1 c.16 *Videntes.*

[171] *Extra.* V, t. 31, c. 17 *Nimis prava*; Gregorius: (Potthast, Nos. 8786a, 8787-9, 9063b); Innocentius: (Potthast, Nos. 11746, 11811-2, 11842, 11877, 11878a, 11942, 12104, 14591).

Item, introducta fuit quia tales scilicet mendicantes, de consuetudine et usu sunt libenter fures et latrones, qui debent a iuribus civilibus evitari. Tales autem non sunt pro Christo mendicantes, ideo nec ista iura ligant eos.

Item, homines religiosi sive perfecti a multis sunt civilibus iuribus absoluti, et ideo ad istud observandum non sunt ligati.

VIDE QUALITER IMPONIT RABIEM LEGI QUOD "FACTA FUIT TEMPORE FAMIS!" 133
CUM DE HOC LEX NON FACIAT MENTIONEM NEC APPARATUS EIUS. SED ESTO QUOD ILLA CAUSA, SCILICET FAMIS, IMPELLENTE FACTA FUERIT, NIHILOMINUS TAMEN LEX PERPETUA EST ET GENERALIS ET CONTINET IUS COMMUNE, QUIA CESSANTE CAUSA IMPLETIVA CONSTITUTIONIS, NON TAMEN CESSAT CONSTITUTIO, SICUT APPARET DE CARFANIA, "QUAE DEDIT CAUSAM EDICTO, CUM ESSET IMPROBISSIMA MULIER."[172] NON TAMEN CESSAT LEX *DE POSTULANDO* FACTA PROPTER EIUS IMPROBITATEM FF. *DE POSTULANDO*, L. 1, § *SEXUM*.

Ad aliud <ad 14> quod 'opus indifferens' etc., dicendum quod 134
mendicare est opus indifferens, sed mendicare omnibus suis abrenuntiando non est opus indifferens. Et ideo cum hac additione 'pro Christo' est opus perfectionis, et ita mendicantes pro Christo omnibus suis abrenuntiantes sunt in statu perfectionis.

HIC DICO QUOD MENDICARE NON EST OPUS INDIFFERENS, IMMO OPUS 135
PROHIBITUM NISI IN CASU. UNDE PROPTER CIRCUMSTANTIAM NON FIT BONUM VEL MERITORIUM, SED PROPTER CIRCUMSTANTIAM EXCUSARI POTEST.

Ad aliud <ad 15> quod 'in pluribus obligari', dicendum est quod duplex 136
est obligatio, scilicet ex reatu poenae: talis obligatio est imperfectionis; de tali obicitur. Alia est ex vinculo caritatis perfecte; haec est perfectionis. Hoc modo obligatur, qui ab aliis eleemosynas recipit, scilicet ad orandum pro illis, ut eius orationibus *in aeterna tabernacula recipiantur.*[173]

1 Item *om. C* 2 libenter fures] f. l. *transp. P* 3 pro Christo *ante* non *P* | nec *om. P* 5 Item … ligati *post Sexum* (n. 133) *C* | sunt *om. P* | civilibus iuribus] c. viribus *C:* i. c. *transp. L* 7 VIDE] Respondet Magister Guillelmus dicens ita *praem. P* | QUOD *om. L* | FUIT] *add.* in *P* 9 SCILICET] sit *P* | FAMIS] *add.* et fame *P* 10 TAMEN] cum *L* 11 IMPLETIVA] C^cP: implere vis *C*: impulsiva *L* 12 CAUSAM *om. C* 16 omnibus suis] *s. o. transp. P* 17 additione] adiectione *L* 18 mendicantes] mendicare *C* 20 HIC DICO] Respondet Magister Guillelmus dicens *P* | OPUS^2 *om. P* 22 VEL] neque *C*: *om. P* 23 obligari] *add.* etc. *P* | est *om. P* 24 poenae] *add.* et *C* 25 ex *om. C*

172 "...origo vero introducta est a Carfania improbissima femina, quae inverecunde postulans et magistrum inquietans causam dedit edicto." *Digesta* III, t. 1, § 5.

173 Luc. 16:9.

137 VIDE QUID DICIT, SCILICET QUOD QUI RECIPIT ELEEMOSYNAS, OBLIGATUR EX CARITATE. SED SI NON HABET CARITATEM, NUMQUID OBLIGATUR? CONSTAT QUOD SIC. ERGO PERICULOSUM EST RECIPERE, CUM NON SEMPER POSSIT SOLVERE; NEC EST NECESSE QUOD OMNIS QUI RELINQUIT OMNIA PRO CHRISTO, SEMPER SIT IN CARITATE.

138 Ad aliud <ad 16> quod obicitur: 'Qui mendicant' etc., dicendum quod non solum quia pauperes, neque simpliciter quia praedicatores, sed quia pauperes praedicatores evangelizantes verbum Dei. Nec faciunt evangelium venale, quia propter hoc non praedicant scilicet propter eleemosynas, sed propter salutem animarum.

139 SED CONTRA: SI NON POSSUNT MENDICARE QUIA PAUPERES NEC QUIA PRAEDICATORES, ERGO NEC QUIA PAUPERES PRAEDICATORES.

140 Ad aliud <ad 17> de Giezi, dicendum quod qui praedicat fingendo intentionem suae praedicationis, ut reportet commodum temporale vel per se vel per suos vel per alienos nomine ipsius, est giezita: qui vero praedicat non propter victum, sed propter zelum animarum, et ab eis quibus praedicat petit vel recipit victum, non est giezita.

141 SED CONTRA: CONSTAT QUOD ELISEUS NON GEREBAT IN ANIMO, QUANDO SANAVIT NAAMAN, QUOD ALIQUID AB EO ACCIPERET. SED PONE QUOD POSTEA MANDAVIT PETI AB EO VEL RATAM HABUIT PETITIONEM PUERI SUI, NONNE SIMONIAM COMMITTERET? CONSTAT QUOD SIC, SICUT GIEZI, QUI EX POST FACTO PETIIT A NAAMAN EO QUOD VIDIT EXENNIA DOMINO SUO PRAESENTARI. ERGO ET ILLE QUI POST PRAEDICATIONEM PERMITTIT SUOS PETERE AB ILLIS QUIBUS PRAEDICAVIT, SI PROHIBERE POSSIT, VIDETUR COMMITTERE SIMONIAM. PRAETEREA, ETSI ILLE QUI PRAEDICAVIT NON COMMITTIT SIMONIAM, QUIA NON PETIT NEC MANDAT PETI NEC PLACET EI QUOD PETATUR, TAMEN PUER SUUS VEL SOCIUS SUUS, QUI PETIT, VIDETUR COMMITTERE SIMONIAM.

142 Ad aliud, <ad 18> dicendum quod multi mali sunt sub specie mendicationis; tamen mendicare propter Christum imitandum et evangelizandum non est *species mala*, immo perfectionis opus. Et ideo a mendicatione viri perfecti non debent abstinere.

1 VIDE] Respondet Magister Guillelmus dicens sic *praem P* 2 SI *om. P* | HABET *om. P* | NUMQUID] *add.* non *P* 4 NECESSE] verum *P* | OMNIS] omnes *L* | RELINQUIT] relinquunt *L* 5 SIT] sint *L* 8 verbum] verbis *C* 9 propter hoc *om. P* | scilicet *om. P* 11 SED CONTRA] Ad hoc dicit Magister Guillelmus quod *P* 13 dicendum quod *om. L* 18 SED CONTRA] Contra hoc respondet Magister Guillelmus dicens quod *P* | CONSTAT] stat *L* 19 ALIQUID] quid *P* | ACCIPERET] *add.* nihil enim exinde sperabat et volebat habere cum esset spirituale bonum *P* 20 HABUIT] habuerit *P* 23 SUOS] in nos *C* 25 NON[2]] nec *P* 27 COMMITTERE] comittunt *C* 28 dicendum] dicitur est *C* | sunt] sicut *C* 30 *mala*] mali *C* 31 viri perfecti] p. v. *transp. P*

CONTRA: MENDICARE EST SIMPLICITER PECCATUM NISI ALIQUATENUS 143
EXCUSETUR, QUIA EST CONTRA DOCTRINAM APOSTOLI. SED QUOD EST SIMPLICITER PECCATUM, FIERI NON POTEST PROPTER CHRISTUM, QUIA IPSE PECCATIS NOSTRIS NON EGET;[174] ERGO MENDICARE NON POTEST ESSE OPUS PERFECTIONIS.

Ad aliud <ad 19> quod obicitur: 'Qui petunt eleemosynas' etc., 144
dicendum quod verus praedicator debet habere ista tria, scilicet quod sit missus, quod veritatem praedicet, quod utilitatem faciat; et si ab aliqua istarum conditionum deficiat, non est verus praedicator. Dico ergo quod praedicatores mendicantes dictorum Ordinum auctoritatem habent non principalem, sed delegatam sive subauctoritatem, sicut Ordo Minorum et Praedicatorum; et ideo praedicti Ordines potestative accipere non debent. Sed quia habent subauctoritatem ideo supplicative petere possunt, et ita mendicare.

CONTRA: HOC DICTUM EST SUPRA, SCILICET QUOD SUBAUCTORITAS AUT DAT 145
POTESTATEM SUMENDI AUT NON. SI DAT POTESTATEM, ERGO NON MENDICAT QUIA POTESTAS NON EST MENDICITAS, UT DICIT GLOSSA II TIM. 2.[175] SI VERO NON DAT POTESTATEM, ERGO NON POTEST SUMERE QUIN MENDICET, QUOD EST CONTRA APOSTOLUM ET AUGUSTINUM.[176]

Item, <ad 19> dato quod accipere possent, quia evangelium annuntiant; 146
tamen maioris humilitatis et perfectionis est petere ex gratia quod debetur de iure quam accipere potestative quod ex iure debetur. Et ideo adhuc perfectius est mendicare quam potestative accipere.

HOC EST CONTRA GLOSSAM PRAEDICTAM, QUIA POTESTATEM HABENS NON 147
POTEST MENDICARE ILLUD QUOD EX POTESTATE SIBI DEBETUR.

1 CONTRA] *add.* hoc respondet Magister Guillelmus dicens quod *P* | PECCATUM *bis P* | ALIQUATENUS] aliquantulum *P* 6 quod obicitur *om. C* 7 debet] oportet *L* 8 missus] *add.* et *C* | utilitatem faciat] f. u. *tranp. L* 10 praedicatores] veri *praem. L* 11 sicut ... subauctoritatem *om. L* | Minorum ... Praedicatorum] Praedicatorum ... Minorum *C* 15 CONTRA] Respondet Magister Guillelmus dicens quod *praem. P* 16 POTESTATEM] *add.* sumptus *P* 18 POTEST] *add.* potestatem *L* | QUIN] quando *C* 20 dato] dico *L* 21 tamen] cum *C* 22 de] ex *C* | quod] quia *C* | ideo] ita *P* | adhuc *post* est *P* 23 perfectius] perfectus *C* | potestative] potestatem *P* 24 HOC] Respondet Magister Guillelmus et dicit quod *praem. P* 25 ILLUD] istud *C*

[174] *Cf.* Iob 13:7; Greg., *Mor.* in *CCSL* 143A.607.

[175] *Cf. supra*, n. 22.

[176] *Cf. supra*, n. 22.

148 Ad ultimum <ad 20> quod 'persona praedicatoris' etc., dicendum quod si aliquis se vilificat pro Christo, non tamen vilis est persona, immo honorabilis, quia vilificare se pro Christo est de perfectione christianae religionis, cuius exemplum in David invenitur, II Reg. 6: *Ita Iudam*, inquit, *et vilior fiam plus quam factus sum et ero humilis in oculis meis*[177] etc.

149 Bene concedo quod se vilificare pro Christo ex humilitate bonum est, dum tamen illa vilitas non sit contra voluntatem Christi. Sed mendicare est contra voluntatem Christi in Apostolo loquentis, II Cor.: *An experimentum quaeristis eius, qui loquitur in me Christi?*[178] Et ideo talis vilificatio non est bona, sed potius est peccatum.

150 Et sic patet solutio quaestionis et argumentorum ostendentium quod mendicare non sit de perfectione christianae religionis. Cetera conceduntur.

151 Hanc quaestionem determinavit ita Magister Bonaventura de Ordine Fratrum Minorum, secundum quod a quodam clerico potuit reportari.

1 ultimum] *add.* dico *C* | persona] per *L* | dicendum] *add.* est *P* 2 vilificat] vileficat *L* | immo] sed *P* 4 *Ita Iudam*] David *P* | inquit] *add.* Iudam *δ* 5 *fiam*] fieram *C* | *quam om. L* 6 Bene concedo] Respondeo contra *C:* Respondet Magister Guillelmus et concedit *P* | Bene … peccatum *post* Minorum *P* | se] *add.* humiliare *C* 7 vilitas] humilitas *P* | Sed … Christi *om. L* 8 loquentis] *add.* scilicet *C* 11 solutio] conclusio *C* | et … conceduntur *om. P* 14 determinavit ita] determinavit *C:* ita d. *transp. P* | Bonaventura] bonus eventus *C: add.* emeritus *P* 15 secundum … reportari] et ita respondet Magister Guillelmus de Sancto Amore ad omnia supradicta *P* | reportari] *add.* Deo gratias et amen *L*

[177] II Reg. 6:22.
[178] II Cor. 13:3.

<QUI AMAT PERICULUM>

Qui amat periculum peribit in illo.[1] *Factus est sermo Domini in corde meo quasi* 1
ignis exaestuans.[2]

Verbum secundo propositum scribitur in Ieremia, qui propter verbum 2
Domini quod annuntiabat, multa opprobria et tribulationes habuit, et ipse omnia sustinuit, et tandem prorupit in haec verba dicens: *Factus est sermo Domini etc.* Et subdit: *Audivi multorum contumelias et terrores.*[3] *Dominus autem mecum est, tamquam bellator fortis.*[4]

Haec verba sunt ipsius Prophetae et haec verba pro me possum dicere. 3
Ego scio ecclesiae quaedam pericula imminere, et non potest esse quin eveniant; unde non possum tacere, sed oportet ut ea manifestem secundum quod possum elicere ex scripturis. Sed quia non placet omnibus audire huiusmodi pericula, ideo quidam audientes me de his loqui derident et detrahunt mihi; sed ego habeo veritatem mecum. Unde si me derident, hoc est ad utilitatem meam; et ideo non dimittam dicere veritatem, quae est utilis toti ecclesiae. Et ut hoc possim ardentius et diligentius facere, in principio rogemus etc.

Qui amat periculum peribit in illo. Verbum istud scribitur in Ecclesiastico, in 4
quo ostenditur quod illi qui pro posse suo amant et quaerunt periculum, necesse habent perire in illo. Et hoc est quod dicit Isaias: *Propterea ductus est*

2 *Qui*] Sermo magistri Guillelmi doctoris Parisiensis contra hypocrisim *praem* B^C: Sermo de praedicta *praem.* D^C: Sermo eiusdem in festo Philippi et Iacobi *praem. E*: Sermo de periculis ecclesiae *praem. in cal.* S^C*:* Sermo Magistri Guillelmi de Sancto Amore *praem. W* 5 habuit … omnia] *E*: et ipse omnia *W*: *om. β* 6 sustinuit *ante* et tribulationes *β* 10 ecclesiae *post* pericula *β* 11 ut] quod *β* 12 possum] *add.* ea *E* | elicere] *post* scripturis *β* 13 loqui *om. β* 14 et ... mihi] me *B: om. γλSV* | ego ... derident *om. β* 15 dimittam] omittam *β* | dicere veritatem] v. d. *transp. λ* 16 utilis *post* ecclesiae *β* | hoc *om. β* | possim] possum *δM* 17 in … etc. *om. N* | rogemus] *add.* dominum *DδλV* 18 istud scribitur] s. i. (illud *R*) *transp. λ* 19 quod] quomodo *λ* 20 dicit] dicitur *BDλV*

[1] Eccli. 3:27; *DP*, 35, 37.
[2] Ier. 20:8-9.
[3] Ier. 20:10.
[4] Ier. 20:11.

populus meus in captivitatem, quia non habuit scientiam;[5] anima enim sine scientia perit. Salomon: *In iniquitate sua morietur, quia non habuit disciplinam, et in multitudine stultitiae suae decipietur.*[6] Peccator, scilicet *qui non habet disciplinam*, quia si non habet scientiam de vitandis periculis, peribit. Omnia peccata mortalia pericula sunt; nec quaelibet pericula, sed pericula mortis aeternae. Sed inter pericula parva et magna, illud quod est periculum duorum vel trium vel decem vel centum, hoc est magnum periculum. Sed periculum quod omnibus et toti ecclesiae imminet, maximum est periculum; et ideo de tali periculo, quod est omnibus commune, maxime est curandum.

5 Unde quidam mirantur quare ego non praedicem de luxuria, superbia, avaritia et gula, sed de peccato hypocrisis specialiter. Et etiam detrahunt mihi apud magnates et in curia Domini Papae. Et dicunt quod ego non praedico contra pompam mundi nec contra luxuriam, sed contra hypocritas tantum. Sed haec est ratio quare ego facio: quia si medicus aliquis esset, qui totum mundum haberet in cura sua, et videret quod fere omnes essent in una magna infirmitate, et duo vel tres ex omnibus haberent unam modicam infirmitatem, non reputaretur ille bonus medicus nisi maiorem curam et sollicitudinem adhiberet illi gravi infirmitati omnium, quam modicae infirmitati istorum duorum vel trium. Sic et in hac parte dico quod omnia peccata mortalia, quotquot sunt, pericula sunt; sed tamen totus mundus haec peccata non facit, quia in bonis religiosis non regnat luxuria, nec in bonis activis regnat avaritia, et sic de aliis. Et ideo periculum aliorum peccatorum non est commune omnibus sicut peccatum hypocrisis, quo fere tota ecclesia vel pro maiori parte infecta est. Et ideo de tali periculo valde est utile praedicare, ut illi qui audiunt, ab hoc se possint

1 *habuit*] habet *DλV* 2 perit] peribit *β* | *In om. λ* | *habuit*] habet *DλSV* 4 si] is (hiis *M* hii *RS*) qui *β* | habet] habent *λS* peribit] peribunt *λS* 5 peccata mortalia] m. p. *transp. β* 6 illud] id *β* | periculum] *om. β* 7 hoc *om. BγλV:* non *S* | Sed ... periculum² *om. BγλV* 8 maximum est] est magnum *S* 9 quod] pro *γ* | est *post* omnibus *BγSV: post* commune *M* | maxime est curandum] est (est] *post* timendum *B: om. MN*) maxime timendum *β* 13 dicunt *om. β* | ego] *add.* hoc *E* 15 quare] quia *DλV: om. N* 16 mundum haberet] h. m. *transp. DλSV* 17 infirmitate *add.* sicut in febre acuta vel aliqua (*om. S*) alia (*add.* magna *S*) infirmitate *ES* | ex omnibus *om. β* 19 gravi infirmitate] i. g. *transp. γ* 20 omnium *om. BγλV* | Sic] Sed *W* 21 pericula sunt] s. p. *transp. DδRV:* pericula *M* 22 tamen *om. β* | non regnat] *ante* in *β* 23 activis] actibus *γMSV:* artibus *R* 24 sicut *add.* est *β* 25 est *om. DW* 26 se possint] p. s. *transp. λ*

[5] Is. 5:13; *DP*, 34-5.

[6] Prov. 5:22-3; *DP*, 35.

custodire. Unde omissa commendatione et laude Sanctorum Apostolorum Philippi et Iacobi, quorum hodie est festum, de istis periculis videamus.

Circa haec pericula, quinque possunt notari.

Primo enim ostendendum est quod haec pericula debent venire. 6
Secundo, quae sint haec pericula. Tertio, per quos venient haec pericula. Quarto, quibus modis illi mittent haec pericula in mundum. Quinto, quomodo isti per quos venient sint cognoscibiles.

Primo ergo videndum est quod haec pericula debent venire. Et quod 7
debent venire, ostendo per has auctoritates, scilicet per Apostolum et ipsum Christum. Apostolus enim dicit ad Tim.: *Hoc autem scito, quod in novissimis temporibus instabunt tempora periculosa;*[7] ergo pericula venient. Sed Christus dicit in evangelio: *Erit autem tanta tribulatio, qualis non fuit ab initio mundi;*[8] et dicit haec inter pericula quae numerat debere evenire ante ipsum Antichristum. Et posset probari hoc per alios testes, sed isti sufficiunt. Unde constat quod pericula venient.

Secundo videndum, quae sint haec pericula quae venient. Dicam autem 8
vobis quae sint haec pericula, et nihil addam de meo, sed per scripturas ostendam. Dicit Ieremias: *Unusquisque a proximo suo se custodiat, et in fratre non habebit fiduciam.*[9] Nonne hoc est magnum periculum?; nec solum corporis, sed etiam animae, quia de salute animae in nullo se potest homo certificare. De hoc periculo dicitur etiam in Mich.: *Noli credere amico, noli confidere in carne: ab ea quae dormit in sinu tuo custodi claustra oris tui.*[10] Nonne ergo hoc erit magnum periculum, quod vir uxori suae, cum qua ipse est corpus unum, suum secretum manifestare non poterit? Unde Glossa super illud *Noli credere amico*: "id est pseudoprophetis, qui fingunt se amicos et non sunt; pseudo sunt falsi prophetae."[11] Ad idem dicit Dominus in evangelio

1 commendatione] communi delectatione (declaratione *δ*) *β* 2 hodie *om. β* 5 quae] quot *γSV:* quod *λ* | sint] sunt *λS* 6 illi *om. δγλ* 7 sint] sic *E:* sunt *λS* 8 quod[2] ... venire *om. β* 9 debent] debeant *W* | has *om. α* 10 *scito*] scitote *DλSV* 12 evangelio *add.* quod *β* | *autem*] ante *β* 13 haec *om. β* | evenire] venire *β* 14 Antichristum] Christum *W* | probari hoc] hoc p. *transp. λW:* haec p. *S* 15 pericula venient] v. p. *transp. γ* 16 Dicam] Dico *β* 17 scripturas] scripturam *β* 18 Dicit] Unde *praem. W: add.* enim *δ* | *custodiat*] custodiet *W* | *fratre*] fratrem *γ: add.* suo *EλS* 19 *fiduciam*] fidem *γ* | Nonne *om. Eλ* 20 se potest] p. s. *transp. λ* 21 dicitur] dicit *DMSV: om. N* | etiam in *om. β* 22 *carne*] duce *P et Vulgata* 23 ergo *om. β* | erit] est *β* | est *post* unum *β* 25 *amico add.* tuo *β*

[7] II Tim. 3:1; *DP*, 18, 20.

[8] Matt. 24:21; *DP*, 31-2.

[9] Ier. 9:4; *DP*, 31.

[10] Mich. 7:5; *DP*, 31.

[11] *int.* in Mich. 7:6 in *Ed pr.* 3.411a.

Matt.: *Frater tradet fratrem in mortem, et pater filium: et insurgent filii in mortem patris.*[12] Nonne ergo istud erit magnum periculum? Et impossibile est hoc non evenire, quia hoc Veritas dicit; et ideo oportet quod eveniant. Multa erunt alia pericula, sed haec ad praesens dico vobis.

9 Tertio videndum, per quos haec pericula venient. Sed numquid venient haec pericula per principes et barones primo? Certe non principaliter; tamen illi per quos venient, multos habebunt principes et barones pro se. Vel numquid venient per milites armatos vel per burgenses bene vestitos? Certe non, sed per illos qui praetendunt *speciem sanctitatis*[13] exterius, intus vero sunt pleni dolo et malitia.

10 Et quod ita sit, ostendo per Apostolum, qui dicit postquam enumeravit multa pericula ventura, dicit quod per illos evenient, qui plus de suo honore quam de Dei laude quaerunt.[14] Et isti erunt pleni peccato, et praetendentes *speciem pietatis.*[15] Glossa: "Id est religionis."[16]

11 Sed quomodo scietur hoc, quod plus honorem suum quam Dei laudem quaerunt? Unum signum est ad hoc, *quod plus se quam veritatem diligunt,*[17] quia etiam non possunt pati, quod veritas de ipsis dicatur. Unde dicit Gregorius in Past.: "Qui perverse vult agere, et ad ea ceteros vult tacere, ipse sibi testis est, quod plus se quam veritatem vult diligi quam contra se non vult defendi."[18] Et Apostolus dicit: *quod amabunt plus honorem suum quam veritatem,*[19] et nolunt quod de eis malum dicatur. Unde super illud Apostoli ad Cor.: *In caritate non ficta.*[20] Glossa Augustini: "Pseudo simulant caritatem, ut facilius decipiant."[21] Ergo haec pericula venient per illos, qui pietatem et caritatem simulant. Unde dicit Apostolus: *Nolite seduci in religione angelorum,*[22]

1 *et*^{2} *om.* α 2 ergo *om.* β | istud] illud *Eλ* | erit *ante* istud λ 3 hoc Veritas] V. hoc *transp.* *δλV* | hoc Veritas dicit] V. d. hoc γ 4 erunt] erint *W*: *om.* β | dico vobis] v. d. *transp.* *δλV* 5 videndum] *add.* est β 6 haec *om.* α | et] vel *γλS* | primo *om.* β 7 et barones *om.* β 8 Vel] Sed β | per^{2} *om.* β 10 sunt pleni] p. s. *transp.* *δγV* 12 evenient] venient α 13 Et ... quaerunt *om.* β 16 Unum] Unde β 17 pati] audire β 18 perverse] perversa *W* | tacere] *BEN*: arcere *DRSVW*: alicere *M*: licere *M*^{C} 19 quod] *ES*: quando *W*: quoniam *BγλV* | se *om.* γ 20 *amabunt plus*] p. a. *transp.* β | *honorem suum*] se β 21 Apostoli *om.* β 23 venient] sunt ventura β

[12] Matt. 10:21.
[13] *Cf.* II Tim. 3:5; *DP*, 28, 54-5; *Dephar.*, n. 3.
[14] *Cf.* II Tim. 3:2-4.
[15] II Tim. 3:5; *DP*, 28, 54-5.
[16] *int.* in II Tim. 3:5 in *Ed. pr.* 4.416a.
[17] II Tim. 3:2; *DP*, 22.
[18] Greg., *Reg. past.* in *SC* 381, I.234; *DP*, 21.
[19] II Tim. 3:2-4; *DP*, 21-2.
[20] II Cor. 6:6; *DP*, 29, 54.
[21] *int.* in II Cor. 6:6 in *Ed. pr.* 4.345a; Aug., *De serm. Dom.* in *CCSL* 35.132; *DP*, 29, 54.
[22] Col. 2:18; *DP*, 29.

scilicet “in illis qui videntur esse angeli,”[23] per honestam conversationem exterius. “Angeli enim sunt nuntii Domini,”[24] quod exponit Augustinus dicens “qui videntur quasi nuntii Dei per speciem et sanctitatem religionis, facile possunt homines decipere.”[25] Sic ergo patet per praedicta Sanctorum, quod pericula per illos evenient, qui foris *speciem sanctitatis* praetendunt ad hoc ut facilius decipiant.

Sed quoniam aliqui sunt qui melius credunt verbis Christi quam 12
Sanctorum, unde testimonium Christi ad hoc inducam. Et tamen Sanctis ita credendum est sicut Christo, quia quod Sancti dicunt, Christus dicit, quia sicut dicitur in evangelio: *Non vos estis qui loquimini, sed Spiritus Patris vestri qui loquitur in vobis.*[26] Sed ad maiorem confirmationem videte quid Christus ipse dicit, ubi loquitur de periculis quae ventura sunt ante tempora Antichristi. Dicit enim sic: *Multi Pseudoprophetae surgent et seducent multos.*[27] Glossa: “Qui in humilitate et falsa religione ambulant;”[28] et isti multos decipient. Unde dicit Apostolus: *Nam eiusmodi pseudo sunt Apostoli,*[29] *operarii subdoli et transfigurantes se in Apostolos Christi. Et non est mirum: ipse enim angelus Satanae transfiguravit se in angelum lucis.*[30] *Non est ergo magnum, si ministri eius transfigurant se in Apostolos,*[31] qui sunt ministri Dei. Super illud verbum *subdoli*, dicit Glossa Augustini: “callide sub specie religionis decipientes.”[32]

Sed dicet aliquis: “Bene videmus quod pericula venient per tales qui 13
praetendunt *speciem sanctitatis*; sed tamen de bonis, hoc non est verum.”

1 esse *om. β* | angeli] *add.* scilicet *λ* 2 enim *om. W* | sunt] *post* Domini *B: om. γλSV* | quod ... Dei] = *βE: om. W* | exponit] *β:* exponens *E* | Augustinus] *E:* Glossa *B:* Dominus *γλSV* 3 dicens] *β:* dicit *E* | quasi] *E:* enim *β* 4 facile] quibus faciliter *E* | patet] pati *E* | per *om. MN* | praedicta] dicta *BEγMV* 5 evenient] eveniant *γλV* 8 inducam] induci volunt *B*: inducere *DλV*: adducere *N*: inducere volo *S* | Et] Cum *B:* Sed *S: om. N* | ita *om. β* 9 quia *om. γλSV* 10 *vestri om. γ* 11 quid] quod *β* 15 *eiusmodi*] huiusmodi *β* | *pseudo s. Apost.*] Pseudo sunt *E:* pseudoapostoli sunt (*om. B*) *BR* 16 *et om. E* 17 *transfiguravit*] transfigurat *W* | *Non … magnum*] Nec magnum mirum *β* 18 *transfigurant*] transfigurat *NR* 19 *subdoli* dicit *om. β* 21 dicet] diceret *γ* | aliquis] *add.* Domine *β* | venient] evenient *γ* | per tales *ante* venient *λ* 22 *speciem*] *add.* dignitatis et *λ* | tamen de] mente *β*

[23] *int.* in Col. 2:18 in *Ed. pr.* 4.391b.

[24] *int.* in Col. 2:18 in *Ed. pr.* 4.391b; *DP*, 17.

[25] *int.* in Col. 2:18 in *Ed. pr.* 4.391b; Amb., *Comm. in Epist. ad Col.* in *PL* 17.456B-C; *DP*, 29.

[26] Matt. 10:20; *SQD*, n. 17.

[27] Matt. 24:11; *DP*, 40, 59; *Dephar.*, n. 14.

[28] *int.* in Matt. 7:15 in *Ed. pr.* 4.30b.

[29] II Cor. 11:13; *DP*, 29, 57.

[30] II Cor. 11:14.

[31] II Cor. 11:15.

[32] *int.* in II Cor. 11:13 in *Ed. pr.* 4.351b; Aug., *De op. mon.* in *CSEL* 41.5.3, 585; *DP*, 29.

Bene concedo hoc; sed tamen istorum per quos venient pericula, erunt opera de genere bonorum. Nec miremini, quod Prophetas Praedicatores voco, quia dicit Glossa: "Prophetas, id est, scripturarum explanatores."[33] Quod[34] autem ipsi faciunt opera de genere bonorum, hoc dicit Dominus: *A fructibus eorum cognoscetis eos.*[35] Glossa: "Per fructus perdurabiles."[36] Sed dicit alia Glossa quod "non debent attendi opera quae ostendunt."[37] Unde Glossa: "In conspectu hominum similes sunt ministris iustitiae, dum ieiunant, orant, eleemosynas dant; sed isti non sunt fructus eorum, quia hoc faciunt ut decipiant."[38]

14 Sed tunc dicet aliquis: "Nonne credendum est omnibus qui bene praedicant de peccatis?" Certe non omnibus talibus est credendum, quia dicit Dominus in evangelio: *Multi venient in die illa, dicentes Domine, nonne in nomine tuo praedicavimus, daemones eiecimus, virtutes fecimus?*[39] Et Dominus respondebit eis: *Discedite a me qui operamini iniquitatem*;[40] et hoc dicet talibus in iudicio. Non ergo omnibus est credendum qui bene de peccatis praedicant.

1 venient pericula] p. v. *transp. ES* 2 Nec] Non *β* 3 quia dicit *om. β* | scripturarum] scripturas *W: post* explanatores *γ* 4 ipsi *om. β* 8 sunt *om. DSV* 10 tunc] nunc *β* | est] *add.* eis *β* | qui] quoniam *λ* 14 respondebit] *B*: respondet *EγλSV*: respondit *W* | eis *om. β* | hoc] *om. β*

[33] *int.* in Eph. 4:11 in *Ed. pr.* 4.375b; Amb., *Comm. in Epist. ad Ephes.* in *PL* 17.409C; *DP*, 17.

[34] *Cf. Resp.*: 352: "Item, dixit in sermone Qui amat periculum quod non est reputandus bonus qui bona opera exterius praetendit, et cavendum est ab illis, quia per tales maior pars catholicae fidei oportet quod pereat, et quod tales persequentur Ecclesiam et eorum persecutio gravior erit quam haereticorum et tyrannorum." "Respondeo: Hoc non dixi, sed dixi quod illi pseudo et penetrantes domos, qui procurabunt pericula novissimorum temporum, venient sub habitu religionis et tantam sanctitatem praetendent, quod videbuntur electa membra Ecclesiae. Unde in Apocalypsi 6:7: Et cum aperuisset sigillum quartum, audivi vocem quarti animalis dicentis: Veni et vide. Et ecce equus pallidus, etc. (Glossa: Videns diabolus nec per apertas tribulationes nec per apertas haereses posse proficere, praemittit falsos fratres, qui sub habitu religionis naturam obtinent et rufi equi et nigri pervertendo fidem). Id est: tantam facient persecutionem quantam fecerunt aperte tyranni, quos appellavit rufum equum supra, eodem capitulo, et quantam fecerunt aperte haeretici, quos appellavit nigrum equum supra, eodem capitulo. Item, Iob 13 [30:12] super illud Ad dexteram Orientis, etc., dicit Glossa: ad dexteram Orientis illico calamitates insurgunt, quia hic ad persecutionem Ecclesiae prosiliunt qui electa membra Ecclesiae videbantur. Et ideo huiusmodi homines maxime nocebunt Ecclesiae Dei, quia, sicut dicit Gregorius in Pastorali [1, 2] nemo plus nocet in Ecclesia Dei quam qui, perversa agens, nomen habet sanctitatis vel ordinis."

[35] Matt. 7:16; *DP*, 29, 36.

[36] *int.* in Matt. 7:16 in *Ed. pr.* 4.30b.

[37] *ord.* in Matt. 7:16 in *Ed. pr.* 4.30B (*PL* 114.111B); Aug., *De serm. Dom.* in *CCSL* 35.178.

[38] *ord.* in Matt. 7:15 in *Ed. pr.* 4.30B (*PL* 114.110C); Aug., *De serm. Dom.* in *CCSL* 35.179; *DP*, 29, 36-7; *Dephar.*, n. 5.

[39] Matt. 7:22.

[40] Matt. 7:23.

Sed tunc adhuc dicet aliquis: "Si videamus quod bene praedicent, non est eis credendum? Si videamus quod faciant miracula et virtutes, numquid est eis credendum?" Certe non, quia Dominus, quandoque per tales bene miracula facit propter conversionem et utilitatem illorum quibus praedicant, sed tamen propter hoc non est eis magis credendum. Unde super illud verbum[41] dicit Glossa: "Maxime cavendum est ab his, qui miracula faciunt propter nomen Christi, quae propter perfidos Dominus fecit; nec putemus ibi esse invisibilem sapientiam, ubi est visibile miraculum."[42] "Quam mundo ergo et simplici oculo opus est, ut inveniatur sapientia inter tot deceptiones hypocrisis."[43] Et tales habebunt habitum sanctitatis. Unde super illud Apocalypsis: *Et apertum est quartum sigillum, et audivi vocem quartae bestiae, et dixit, veni et vide: et ecce equus pallidus, et qui sedebat super eum, nomen illi mors.*[44] Glossa dicit quod "Ioannes ponit duas prophetias et ponit triplicem persecutionem ecclesiae, signatam per triplicem equum quem vidit, scilicet equum rubeum, nigrum et pallidum."[45] Sensus est et non verba. Et dicitur ibi quod per equum rufum significatur persecutio ecclesiae facta per tyrannos, qui saevitiam suam in Apostolos et sanctos martyres exercuerunt.[46] Per nigrum equum significatur persecutio ecclesiae facta per haereticos tempore Beati Augustini et Hilarii;[47] tempore enim illorum magnam sustinuit ecclesia persecutionem ab haereticis. Sed equus pallidus significat persecutionem ecclesiae imminentem per hypocritas.[48] Unde dicit ibi Glossa: "Videns diabolus per apertos tyrannos et

1 tunc] tamen *γ* | adhuc] ad hoc *DRV* 2 est eis] eis est *transp. λ* | Si] Sed si *E* | Si … credendum *om. δ* | Si … non *om. γλV* | faciant] faciunt *E* 3 eis *om. W* | quandoque] quando *DR* | bene *om. β* 4 miracula facit] f. m. *transp. BW* | illorum] eorum *δλV: om. γ* 5 est eis *om. γλSV* | magis *ante* non *γ* 6 super … verbum *om. BλNV* 8 fecit] facit *E* 10 tot deceptiones] *α et Augustinus*: tantos deceptores *β* 11 super illud *om. β* 13 *eum*] illum *EγRSV:* illud *M* 14 signatam *om. β* 16 est *om. β* | significatur] intelligitur *B:* signatur *αNS* 18 significatur] signatur *αNS* 19 haereticos] *add.* manifestos *E* 21 significat] signat *αNS* 22 ibi *om. λ* | per] se per *BγV*: se *λ:* semper *S*

[41] Matt. 7:22.

[42] *ord.* in Matt. 7:22 in *Ed. pr.* 4.31A (*PL* 114.111C); Aug., *De serm. Dom.* in *CCSL* 35.184.

[43] *ord.* in Matt. 7:22 in *Ed. pr.* 4.31A (*PL* 114.111C); Aug., *De serm. Dom.* in *CCSL* 35.186.

[44] Apoc. 6:7-8; *DP*, 29.

[45] *Cf. ord.* in Apoc. 6:1 in *Ed. pr.* 4.556B (*PL* 114.721C).

[46] *Cf. ord.* in Apoc. 6:1, 6:4 in *Ed. pr.* 4.556B (*PL* 114.721C-D); Amb. Aut., *Expo. in Apoc.* in *CCCM* 27.277; Aug., *Enarr. in Ps.* in *CCSL* 38.70; Prim., *Comm. in Apoc.* in *CCSL* 92.95; Rich., *In Apoc.* in *PL* 196.762.

[47] *Cf. ord.* in Apoc. 6:1, 6:5 in *Ed. pr.* 4.556B (*PL* 114.721C, 722A); Amb. Aut., *Expo. in Apoc.* in *CCCM* 27.279-80; Aug., *Enarr. in Ps.* in *CCSL* 38.70; Prim., *Comm. in Apoc.* in *CCSL* 92.95; Rich., *In Apoc.* in *PL* 196.764

[48] *Cf. ord.* in Apoc. 6:1 in *Ed. pr.* 4.556B (*PL* 114.721C, 722C); Amb. Aut., *Expo. in Apoc.* in *CCCM* 27.281-2; Aug., *Enarr. in Ps.* in *CCSL* 38.70; Beda, *Expl. Apoc.* in *PL* 93.147C; Prim., *Comm. in Apoc.* in *CCSL* 92.97; Rich., *In Apoc.* in *PL* 196.767.

manifestos haereticos se non posse proficere, praemittit falsos fratres, qui sub habitu sanctitatis homines subvertant."[49] In veritate diabolus per tyrannos ecclesiam destruere conabatur, in hoc quod Apostolos et alios sanctos morti tradebant. Sed in veritate in hoc, magis ecclesia exaltata est et sublimata, sicut patet in Francia in duobus locis. Per mortem Sancti Dionysii, ecclesia apud Sanctum Dionysium ditata est, et ipse rex cum omnibus suis ad fidem conversus est.[50] Hoc etiam patet in ecclesia Remensi, quae per mortem Sancti Nicasii ditata est et sublimata.[51] Unde cum videret diabolus quod per tyrannos fides ecclesiae multiplicaretur et confirmaretur, misit postea haereticos in quos Sanctus Hilarius et Sanctus Augustinus fidem defenderunt in tantum, quod haeresis ablata est. Sed videns quod per istos duos equos nihil proficeret, ultimo misit equum pallidum, "id est hypocritas, falsos fratres,"[52] qui sub habitu sanctitatis ecclesiam perturbent. Et haec persecutio tertia hypocritarum maior erit aliis duabus praecedentibus, sicut dicit Augustinus in Glossa super Psalterium, super primum *Confitebor*.[53]

16 Quid ergo faciendum est, cum non sit credendum habitui eorum, nec miraculis, nec ieiuniis, nec orationibus eorum? Certe hoc idem quaeritur in Glossa. Et respondetur: "Quam mundo ergo et simplici oculo opus est, ut inveniatur sapientia inter tot deceptiones."[54] Magnum ergo est periculum, quod pericula ecclesiae imminentia per tales evenient, quibus omnes credent. Gregorius: "Nemo plus nocet in ecclesia Dei quam qui perverse agens, habet dignitatem vel honorem."[55] Et Augustinus dicit de falsis

1 se non posse] nil *β* 2 subvertant] decipiant et *praem. β* 3 destruere conabatur] subvertere nitebatur *β* 4 morti tradebant] sub morte perdidit *β* | hoc] se *W* | magis ecclesia] e. m. (magna *S*) *transp. λS* 5 sicut ... ipse] et *δγMV: om. R* | mortem] *add.* enim *W* 7 in *om. λ* 9 fides ecclesiae *om. β* 10 in quos] inter *E:* iniquos *β* 11 Sed] Et *δλNV:* Et sic *D* | videns *om. γλSV* 12 istos] illos *β* | proficeret] posset proficere *β* 13 falsos] *add.* contra sanctum ordinem et *λ* | fratres] *add.* sanctos inique et perverse et dolose agentes et *λ* | sanctitatis] superbiae *λ* | perturbent] perturbant *β: add.* venenum ipsorum maledictum effundunt in fratres probos (parvos *M)* honestos et discretos et sanctos *λ* 14 haec *om. W* | aliis duabus] d. a. *transp. γ* 16 *Confitebor*] Confiteor *W* 17 est *om. γλV:* quod *S* | sit] sic est *λ* 18 eorum] *ante* nec² *γλSV: om. B* | quaeritur] loquitur *β* 20 deceptiones] deceptores *β* | ergo est] *transp. β* 21 quod] cum *β* | evenient] eveniant *δλV:* veniant *γ* | omnes credent] homines credunt *β*

49 *ord.* in Apoc. 6:5 in *Ed. pr.* 4.557A (*PL* 114.722A); Rich., *In Apoc.* in *PL* 196.764D; *DP*, 29.

50 *Cf.* "Acta fabulosa S. Dionysio," in *AS* 52, t. IV Oct., 792; *Leg. aur.* II:1048-50 (*Leg. aur.* c. 153, 684-6).

51 "Martyrologium romanum" in *AS*, Dec., 582.

52 *ord.* in Apoc. 6:1 in *Ed. pr.* 4.556B (*PL* 114.722C); Rich., *In Apoc.* in *PL* 196.767.

53 Ps. 9:2; *ord.* in Ps. 9:7 in *Ed. pr.* 2.466B; Aug., *Enarr. in Ps.* in *CCSL* 38.70.

54 *ord.* in Matt. 7:22 in *Ed. pr.* 4.31A (*PL* 114.111C); Aug., *De serm. Dom.* in *CCSL* 35.186; *cf. supra*, n. 15.

55 Greg., *Reg. past.* in *SC* 381, I.134.

religiosis: "Sicut non inveni meliores quam qui in monasterio profecerunt, sic non inveni deteriores quam qui in claustro defecerunt."[56] Patet ergo quod pericula sunt ventura, et quae sint, et per quos venire debent, quoniam per illos quibus omnes credent. Et in hoc maxime consistit periculum.

Quarto videndum est quomodo venient isti qui pericula inducent. Et 17
Apostolus ostendit in multis locis,[57] quod isti erunt qui non habebunt curam animarum et per totum mundum praedicabunt et pugnabunt pro praelaturis et dignitatibus habendis. Isti sunt falsi Apostoli, qui praedicabunt non missi, quia sicut dicit Apostolus: *Quomodo praedicabunt, nisi mittantur?*[58] Ibi dicit Glossa: "Non sunt veri apostoli, nisi sint missi."[59] Duo enim tantum genera praedicatorum missa sunt,[60] videlicet duodecim Apostoli Luc. 9 et septuaginta duo discipuli Luc. 10.[61] Et dicit Glossa quod "Apostoli sunt episcopi, discipuli presbyteri."[62] Unde dicit Glossa: "Apostolorum formam episcopi tenent, sed discipulorum formam tenent presbyteri."[63] Verum est, quod alii sunt vicarii, sicut archidiaconi vicarii episcoporum, et isti possunt supplere vicem episcoporum. Unde Apostolus

3 et *om. E* 4 quoniam] quam *EM* | omnes credent] homines credunt (credent *B*) *β* | maxime] maximum *E* 6 videndum] considerandum *E* | venient isti] i. v. *transp. γ* | inducent] inducunt *DλV* 7 habebunt] habent *β* | curam animarum] curam in animabus *E*: *corr.* E^c 9 qui] quia *δEγV* 11 Glossa] ergo *W* | sint *om. ES* 12 tantum genera] g. t. *transp. γλ* | missa sunt] s. m. *transp. E* 13 Luc. 9] *E*: Luc. 10 *γλSW*: *om. B* | Luc. 10] *E*: Luc. *βW* 14 episcopi] praelati sive *praem. β* | Unde] ut *γ*: et *S* 15 episcopi tenent] episcopi *E*: t. e. *transp. W* | Verum est quod] Verumtamen *δγRV*: Tamen *M* 16 alii] aliqui *E*

56 Aug., *Epist. 78* in *CSEL* 34.2, 344-5: "Quo modo difficile sum expertus meliores, quam qui in monasteriis profecerunt, ita sum expertus peiores, quam qui in monasteriis cediderunt..."

57 *Cf.* Rom. 10:15; Rom. 16:18; II Cor. 11:13.

58 Rom. 10:15; *DP*, 24, 36, 58; *Dephar.*, n. 9.

59 *int.* in Rom. 10:15 in *Ed. pr.* 4.296b; Amb., *Comm. in Epist. ad Rom.* in *PL* 17.152B; *DP*, 24, 36, 58-9.

60 *Cf.* Luc. 9:1; *Cf. Resp.*: 348-9: "Item, dixit in sermone Qui amat periculum quod qui praedicant et non sunt episcopi, qui sunt successores apostolorum, vel sacerdotes et curati, qui sunt successores septuaginta duorum discipulorum, vel nisi vocentur a presbyteris curatis, sunt pseudo apostoli, non facientes mentionem de commissione episcoporum vel papae vel legationem eius." "Respondeo: Dixi quod illi qui non sunt episcopi aut curati, vel missi ab eis, si se ingerant praedicationi, pseudo sunt. Rom. 10:15: Quomodo praedicabunt nisi mittantur? (Glossa: non sunt veri Apostoli nisi missi). Et ibidem expresse adieci quod, loquendo de missis ab episcopis, maxime intelliguntur missi a domino papa, qui est sumus episcoporum."

61 *Cf.* Luc. 10:1; *DP*, 24.

62 Luc. 9:1; Luc. 10:1; *ord.* in Luc. 10:1 in *Ed. pr.* 4.177A; Beda. *Expo. in Luc.* in *CCSL* 120.213-4; *DP*, 24.

63 *ord.* in Luc. 10:1 in *Ed. pr.* 4.177A (*PL* 114.284A); Beda, *Expo. in Luc.* in *CCSL* 120.213-4; *DP*, 24; *cf. SQD*, n. 9.

ad Cor.: *Opitulationes.*[64] Glossa: "id est, opem maioribus ferentes, ut archdiaconi episcopis."[65] Episcopus enim, si non vult in sua diocesi praedicare, potest alium vocare, aliter alius in sua diocesi non potest praedicare, sicut nec ipse in diocesi alterius, nisi vocatus. Et de hoc habetur 9 q. 2 per totum[66] et in decreto *Hortamur* 6 q. 3, quia nullum officium episcopus extra suam diocesim exercere potest, nisi requisitus,[67] sic nec presbyter extra suam parochiam. Et quod dico de episcopis, intelligendum est de archiepiscopis et maioribus praelatis.[68] Unde dicit Apostolus: qui vult praedicare non missus, sua praedicatio non est propter honorem Dei, sed se honorari quaerit, quia, *non quem homines commendant, ille probatus est, sed quem Deus commendat.*[69] Glossa: "Qui praedicat non missus; talis enim non est idoneus,[70] sed praesumptor et reprobus;"[71] et tales separantur a Christo. Unde super illud Cor. 2: *Qui gloriatur, in Domino glorietur.*[72] Glossa Augustini: "*In Domino glorietur,* quod non potest qui non est missus; talis enim, si praedicat, gloriam suam quaerit."[73] Sed isti qui sic praedicabunt non missi, quomodo poterunt decipere, cum ipsi bona dicant, quia videtur quod fides ex hoc potius confortetur quam debilitetur? Et ad hoc ego dico, quod

1 *Opitulationes*] Opitulatores *β* | est] *add.* eis *B: add.* episcopis *γλSV* | maioribus] *E:* maiorem *W: om β* 2 diocesi] *add.* non potest *λ* 3 potest … praedicare *om. λ* | vocare] praedicare *W: corr.* W^c | aliter] alter *λSV: add.* enim *DδV* | alius] alter *B: om. DSV* | non potest] *ante* in *M: post* praedicare *S* 4 ipse] episcopus *N: om. DλV* | Et … habetur] ut *B* | habetur *om. γλSV* 5 2] *add.* ut *γλS* | 6] 5 *β* 7 episcopis] ipsis *MV* 8 est] *add.* etiam *E* | et *om. γ* | Unde] Ut *λ* | qui] quod *praem. BR* 9 sua praedicatio] p. s. *transp. β* 10 honorari] honorare *BEγλV* 11 *commendat*] *add. vel rep.* ille probatus est *α* | praedicat] praedicaret *γ* | enim *om. δ* 12 Christo] *add.* quia soli reprobi separantur a Christo *ES* 13 Glossa ... potest] in se nunc (vero *B*) gloriatur (glorietur *R*) *β* 16 fides *post* hoc *λ* 17 ad *om. γ*

64 I Cor. 12:28; *DP*, 24.

65 *int.* in I Cor. 12:28 in *Ed. pr.* 4.329a; Amb. *Comm. in Epist. ad Cor.* in *PL* 17.263C; *DP*, 24.

66 C.9 q.2 c.9 *Non invitati; DP*, 25.

67 C.9 q.2 c.6 *Nullum episcopum.*

68 C.9 q.2 c.3 *Nullus primas.*

69 II Cor. 10:18.

70 "Unde cum saepe contingit, quod episcopi propter suas occupationes multiplices vel invaletudines corporales aut hostiles incursus, seu occasiones alias, ne dicamus defectum scientiae, quod in eis reprobandum est omnino, nec de cetero tolerandum, per se ipsos non sufficiunt ministrare populo verbum Dei, maxime per amplas dioceses et diffusas: generali constitutione sancimus, ut episcopi viros idoneos ad sanctae praedicationis officium salubriter exsequendum assumant, potentes in opere et sermone, qui plebes sibi commissas vice ipsorum, cum per se idem nequiverint, sollicite visitantes, eas verbo aedificent et exemplo, quibus ipsi, cum indiguerint, congrue necessaria subministrent, ne pro necessariorum defectu compellantur desistere ab incepto." *Extra.* I, t. 31, c. 15 *Inter cetera*; *QDM*, n. 79; *DP*, 26.

71 *int.* in II Cor. 10:17 in *Ed. pr.* 4.350b; Amb., *Comm. in Epist. ad Cor.* in *PL* 17.337D.

72 I Cor. 1:31; II Cor. 10:17; *DP*, 61; *SQD*, n. 9; *Dephar.*, n. 9.

73 *int.* in II Cor. 10:17 in *Ed. pr.* 4.350b (*PL* 114.521C); Aug., *Enarr. in Ps.* in *CCSL* 39.840-1; *DP*, 61; *SQD*, n. 9; *Dephar.*, n. 9.

quando praedicabunt, in suis praedicationibus tantum laborabunt ad bene loquendum; et praedicabunt quod ipsorum praedicatio ipsis laicis plus placebit quam praedicatio praelatorum, licet tamen ipsi non dicant aliud quam praelati. Sed quia habebunt verba magis polita ct ornata, ideo magis diligetur eorum praedicatio. Sic et Apostoli simpliciter praedicabant, sed pseudoapostoli tantum circa ornatum verborum laborabant, quod carius audiebantur quam ipsi Apostoli. Unde dicit Apostolus ad Cor.: *Existimo me nihil minus fecisse a magnis Apostolis.*[74] Glossa: "Quidam favebant pseudo a quibus idem audiebant, sed verbis compositis, quod ab Apostolis verbis incompositis."[75] Et iterum: "Horum nuntii iam quidam sunt, sed plures in fine futuri sunt."[76] Et dicit Augustinus super illud: *Etsi imperitus sermone, non tamen scientia.*[77] Glossa: "Non erant eloquentes Apostoli, sed pseudo verba componebant."[78] Glossa: "Corinthii praeferebant pseudo veris Apostolis causa accurati sermonis,"[79] quia Apostoli non nisi veritatem quaerebant dicere; sed praelati modo tantum veritatem dicere curant, alii vero ornant verba sua. Unde super illud: *Non sumus quaerentes ab hominibus gloriam.*[80] Glossa: "Tangit pseudo, qui se magis quam doctrinam Dei commendare volebant; Apostolus autem qui non ad praesens sed in futuro gloriam quaerebat, se humilem faciebat ut eius praedicatio exaltaretur."[81] Et est Glossa Augustini: "Quia quando Apostolus multos convertit ad fidem Christi, noluit quod hoc attribueretur scientiae et eloquentiae huius mundi, sed divinae potentiae et bonitati."[82]

1 praedicabunt] ipsi *praem.* *β* | praedicabunt] bene *praem.* *E*: praedicandum *α*: *om.* *B* 2 ipsorum] eorum *β* | ipsis *om.* *β* 3 placebit … praelatorum *om.* *λ* 4 magis polita] p. m. *transp.* *β* 5 diligetur] diligitur *δMSV* | Sic et] Sicut *β* 6 quod] ut *D*: et ideo *E*: quia *W* 7 ipsi *om.* *W* | *me om.* *γλSV* 8 *minus fecisse*] aliud dixisse (dixisses *M*) *β* | Quidam favebant] *P*: Quaedam faciebant *αβ* 9 verbis incompositis] i. v. *transp.* *β* 10 iterum] verum *γλSV* 11 fine] interim *γ* | sunt] erunt *γλSV* | illud] *add.* Apostoli *β* 12 *tamen*] tantum *BγRV* | eloquentes Apostoli] loquentes A. *γ* 13 Glossa *om.* *δ* | Corinthii ... pseudo] Eorum (Eorum quae] Eorumque *D*) quae proferebant pseudo (*om.* *B*: per se *S*) *β* | veris … dicere *om.* *β* 14 quaerebant … veritatem *om.* *W* 15 modo tantum] tantummodo *γ* | veritatem … curant] dicere (curant dicere *transp.* *MS*) curant veritatem *β* 19 quaerebat] quaerit *α* | Et] *add.* etiam *β* 21 noluit] noluerit *λ*

74 II Cor. 11:5; *Dephar.*, n. 10.

75 *ord.* in II Cor. 11:5 in *Ed. pr.* 4.351A (*PL* 114.566D); Amb., *Comm. in Epist. ad Cor.* in *PL* 17.339B; *Dephar.*, n. 10.

76 *int.* in II Tim. 3:6 in *Ed. pr.* 4.416a; *DP*, 21.

77 II Cor. 11:6; *DP*, 34, 61; *Dephar.*, n. 10.

78 *ord.* in II Cor. 11:6 in *Ed. pr.* 4.351A; Amb., *Comm. in Epist. ad Cor.* in *PL* 17.339C; *DP*, 61.

79 *ord.* in II Cor. 11:6 in *Ed. pr.* 4.351B (*PL* 114.566D); Amb., *Comm. in Epist. ad Cor.* in *PL* 17.339B; *DP*, 34, 61; *cf.* *Dephar.*, n. 10.

80 I Thess. 2:6; *DP*, 60; *Dephar.*, n. 9.

81 *ord.* in I Thess. 2:5 in *Ed. pr.* 4.395B (*PL* 114.616D); *sub nomine Augustini in Glossa, potius Ambrosius, Comm. in Epist. ad Thess.* in *PL* 17.469C; *DP*, 60; *Dephar.*, n. 9.

82 *Cf.* *ord.* *in* I Cor. 1:17 in *Ed. pr.* 4.308A; Amb, *Comm. in Epist. ad Cor.* in *PL* 17.198B.

18 Sed multi sunt qui plus desiderant quod dicatur de eis: “Iste bene praedicavit,” quam quod dicatur, “Iste fructum fecit Deo.” Sed Apostolus dicit: *Non in doctis humanae sapientiae verbis*[83] etc. Et per hunc ornatum verborum facient, quod nobiles et magnates laici et clerici etiam, pro magna parte eis obedient et adhaerebunt. Unde tunc erit tempus, quando subditi suos praelatos non diligent, nec praelati subditos. Et ideo dicit Apostolus ad Tim.: *Oportet episcopum testimonium bonum habere ab eis qui foris sunt, ut non incidat in contemptum, et odium et in laqueum diaboli.*[84] Glossa Augustini: “Ut non incidat in contemptum apud fideles, et ex hoc sequitur odium contra illos;”[85] et tunc erit magnum periculum.

19 Sed numquid isti facient plus? Certe sic. Unde dicit Apostolus in prophetia sua, et bene dico in prophetia, quod haec est prophetia Apostoli, quae revelat per Spiritum Sanctum futura. Et ibi dicit Apostolus: *Ex his sunt qui penetrant domos, et captivas ducunt mulierculas.*[86] “Quia laborabunt ad hoc, ut sciant conscientias hominum, et primo muliercularum et per illas, conscientias virorum; sicut diabolus seducendo Evam, Adam seduxit.”[87] Glossa ad litteram: *Domos ingredientur.* “Qui enim vult violenter intrare domum, non facit viam per quam locum intret, dummodo intret.”[88] Franget ergo domos; sed quomodo? Mediante securi? Immo franget domum, id est conscientiam. Quod autem domus sit conscientia dicit Ecclesiasticus: *Praecurre prior in domum tuam.*[89] Glossa: “Id est, in domum conscientiae nos recipiamus.”[90] Ille autem frangit domum, qui in conscientiam aliter quam per ostium intrat. Ostium conscientiae est ille qui habet curam animarum; et qui aliter quam per illum in conscientias

1 bene] *add.* praedicat vel *λ* 2 quod dicatur] illi quantum *N: om. DδλV* | Iste] Praedicator *praem. β* 5 obedient] obediunt *DV* | Unde] *add.* et *W* | tempus *om. E* 6 quando] quod *β* 7 *testimonium*] nomen *β* | *ab eis*] ad eos *β* 8 *ut non*] ne *β* | *incidat*] incidant *NS* 9 ncidat] incidatis *λ* | fideles] fides *W* 12 quod] quia *B:* quae *γRSV* | quod … prophetia *om. M* | haec *om. δγRV* 15 primo] prius *γ* 16 muliercularum] mulierum *βW* 17 *ingredientur*] penetrant *B:* ingrediuntur *γλSV* | Qui] Quando *α* | enim] vero *W: add.* aliquis *E* 18 vult violenter] violenter vult *transp. β* | viam] *AP:* vim *αβ* | quam] *AP:* quem *αβ* | locum intret] i. l. *transp. λS* 19 Franget] Frangent *E* | sed ... domum *om. β* 21 Id est *om. W* 22 nos recipiamus] non recipiamus *γ* 23 in *om. βE* | per *mg. W*

[83] I Cor. 2:13.

[84] I Tim. 3:7; *DP*, 34.

[85] *int.* in I Tim. 3:7 in *Ed. pr.* 4.408b; Aug., *Enarr. in Ps.* in *CCSL* 39.1267; *cf.* Amb., *Comm. in Epist. ad Tim.* in *PL* 17.496A; *DP*, 34.

[86] II Tim. 3:6; *DP*, 20, 22, 32, 46; *SQD*, n. 16.

[87] *ord.* in II Tim. 3:6 in *Ed. pr.* 4.416A; Amb., *Comm. in Epist. ad Tim.* in *PL* 17.521A-B; *DP*, 32-3.

[88] *Cf.* ord. in Ioan. 10:1 in *Ed. pr.* 4.249A (*PL* 114.396B); Aug., *Sermo 137* in *PL* 38.756-7; Aug., *Tract. in Ioan.* in *CCSL* 36.389-90.

[89] Eccli. 32:15; *DP*, 23, 33.

[90] *ord.* in Eccli. 32:15 in *Ed. pr.* 2.777B ; Hrab. Maur., *Comm. in Eccli.* in *PL* 109.996C; *DP*, 23, 33.

hominum intrat, latro est, testimonio Domini: *Qui non intrat per ostium, ille fur est et latro.*[91] De hac domo, quam isti sic penetrabunt et frangent, dicitur alibi: *Ne recipias omnem hominem in domum tuam: multae enim sunt insidiae dolosi,* et est in Ecclesiastico.[92] Non cuilibet conscientiam vestram manifestare debetis in confessione, quia quidam sunt dolosi qui plus de sua laude quam de salute animarum curant. Unde sequitur ibidem: *Admitte alienigenam et subvertet te, et alienabit te a viis propriis,*[93] scilicet, si confiteris illi qui non habet clavem de conscientia tua, nec ipse potest absolvere animam tuam, quia talibus plus credent homines quam suis episcopis et presbyteris. Isti ergo frangent domos. Sed quare? Ratio huius sequitur statim post: *Et captivas ducunt mulierculas oneratas peccatis per varia desideria,*[94] quando scilicet subditos extra potestatem sui praelati ducent, et hoc est satis magnum periculum. Et hoc dicit Apostolus et Spiritus Sanctus per ipsum. Sed numquid plus facient? Certe sic, quia *quemadmodum Iamnes et Mambres restiterunt Moysi, sic et ipsi veritati resistant.*[95] Isti enim fuerunt duo incantatores, et restiterunt Moysi in Aegypto et fecerunt miracula per incantationes suas, ita quod non credebat rex Moysi; sic et isti resistant veritati. Sed postea quid? Erunt homines mali et corruptores fidei, et erunt errantes et in errorem mittentes. Unde dicitur ad Tim. 1: *Spiritus autem manifeste dicit, quod in novissimis temporibus discedent quidam a fide, attendentes malignis spiritibus et erroribus.*[96] Unde super illud Psalmi: *Constitue, Domine, legislatorem super eos,*[97] ut est in primo *Confitebor.*[98] Glossa: "id est, Antichristum latorem pravae

1 testimonio Domini] testimonium Domini *W*: testante Deo *S* | *ostium*] *add.* in ovile ovium *β* | *ille*] etc. *B*: *om. γλSV* 2 *est om. NS* | pen. et frang.] frangunt et penetrant *β* 3 *sunt om. γλSV* 4 et *om. δN* | est *om. β* | vestram] tuam *γ* 6 *Admitte ... te*] Alieni instruent te *β* 7 *alienabit*] alienabunt *β* | scilicet] sed *γλSV* 9 et] *EN*: vel *DδλV*: quam *W* 10 frangent] frangunt *β* | sequitur statim] statim (statim] *mg.* M^{C}: *om. S*: *add.* non *N*) sequitur *β* | statim post] p. s. *transp. E* 13 et *om. γλSV* | per ipsum] per Apostolum *B*: super Apostolum *γλSV* 14 sic *om. γλSV* | *quemadmodum*] sicut *B*: *om. γλSV* 17 rex *ante* non *β* | resistant veritati] v. r. *transp. W* 18 et erunt *om. β* | in *om. γλSV* 19 *quod*] quando *W* 20 *discedent*] discedant *W*: *om. β* | *attendentes*] abscendentes *β* | *malignis spiritibus et om. β* 21 *erroribus*] erunt *β* 22 ut] et *W* | est *om. β* | *Confitebor*] Confiteor *W* | Glossa] *add.* Augustini *β* | id est] scilicet *β* | Antichristum *om. γλSV* | pravae] paternae *γλSV*

91 Ioan. 10:1; *DP*, 23, 33, 35; *SQD*, n. 16.
92 Eccli. 11:31; *DP*, 23, 33.
93 Eccli. 11:36; *DP*, 23, 33.
94 II Tim. 3:6; *DP*, 20, 22, 32, 46; *SQD*, n. 16.
95 II Tim. 3:8; *cf.* Ex. 7:11-22; *DP*, 30, 46.
96 I Tim. 4:1; *DP*, 18, 42.
97 Ps. 9:21; *DP*, 38.
98 Ps. 9:2.

legis."[99] Nec solum Antichristus faciet malam legem, sed etiam membra sua multas malas leges facient.

20 De istis novis periculis iam habemus quaedam Parisius, scilicet librum illum qui vocatur *Evangelium sempiternum*. Et nos vidimus non nisi modicam partem illius libri, et audivi quod ubicumque etiam sit, tantum vel plus continet ille liber quam tota Biblia! Et ibi enim docetur quod Christus non est Deus et quod sacramentum ecclesiae nihil est[100] et quod evangelium Christi non sit verum evangelium.[101] Et docetur ibi quod ille liber sit evangelium Spiritus Sancti, et dicitur esse evangelium aeternum.[102] Et dicitur ibi quod tantum per quinque annos adhuc evangelium Christi praedicabitur.[103] Nec sunt ista pericula huius libri penitus nova, immo sunt quinquaginta quinque anni, quod primo fuerant incohata; et ideo dicitur quod illi, per quos haec pericula venient, dabunt aliam legem vivendi, et aliter disponent ecclesiam.[104] Quod est valde exsecrabile et abominabile dictu, quia ecclesia, quae tenet fidem Christi, est disposita ad modum illius

1 faciet] facit *β* | sua] eius *β* 2 facient] faciunt *β* 3 quaedam Parisius *om. β* | scilicet *om. δ* 4 vocatur] dicitur *δγRV:* dicit *M* | vidimus non nisi] *γλV:* non v. nisi *E:* vidimus non *δW* | modicam] mediam *β* 5 quod *om. β* | etiam *om. β* | vel] et *BγλV*: quod *S* 6 ille liber] *ante* sit *β* : l. i. *transp. N:* iste l. *S: om. E* | quam tota] sicut *α* | Et *om. E* | ibi enim] in eo *β* 7 et] *om. γλSV: add.* id est corpus Christi *sup. lin.* E^c 8 Et] Sed *α* | ibi] *add.* et dicitur *W*: *exp.* W^c 9 dicitur esse] *BγV*: debet esse *α:* dicit *M*: dicitur *RS* | aeternum] sempiternum *β* 10 quod *om. β* | quinque] *α*: sex *β* | adhuc] *ante* per *BγλV: om. ES* 11 sunt *om. β* | ista pericula] p. ista *transp. E* | ista ... libri] illius libri pericula *β* 12 fuerant] *ES*: fuerat *BγλV:* sunt *W* | incohata] incohatus *BγλV*: incohati *S* 13 haec] ista] *E*: *om. β* 15 dictu] dictum *β* | quae] quod *DλV*

[99] *Cf. int.* in Ps. 9:21 in *Ed. pr.* 2.467a; Aug., *Enarr. in Ps.* in *CCSL* 38.67-8; Cass., *Expo. Psalm.* in *CCSL* 97.104; *DP*, 38.

[100] "Item in eodem libro in tractatu de historia Iudith invenitur quod sacramenta novae legis non durabunt amodo nisi per sex annos a tempore libri conditi conputandos, videlicet usque ad annum dominice incarnationis MCCLX." Benz, "Exzerptsätze," 425-6; *cf. SQD*, n. 18.

[101] "Secundus est quod evangelium Christi non est evangelium regni ac per hoc nec aedificatorium ecclesiae." Benz, "Exzerptsätze," 416; *cf. DP*, 38.

[102] "Secundus est quod adveniente evangelio spiritus sancti sive clarescente opere Ioachim, quod dicitur evangelium aeternum sive Spiriti Sancti, evacuabitur evangelium Christi." Benz, "Exzerptsätze," 419.

[103] "Primum est, quoniam iam sunt LV anni quod aliqui laborabant ad mutandum evangelium Christi in aliud evangelium quod dicunt fore perfectius, melius et dignus; quod appellant evangelium Sancti Spiriti sive evangelium aeternum quo adveniente evacuabitur ut dictum est evangelium Christi." *DP*, 38.

[104] "Quintus quod illi qui erunt ultra tempus illud non tenentur recipere novum testamentum. Sextus quod evengelio Christi aliud evangelium succedet et ita pro sacerdotio Christi aliud sacerdotium succedet." Benz, "Exzerptsätze," 417.

quem ostendit Dominus Moysi in monte, ubi dicitur: *Inspice et fac secundum exemplar, quod tibi in monte monstratum est.*[105] Haec etiam ecclesia ordinata est ad modum illius coelestis curiae, quia Dominus ostendit Apostolo Paulo ecclesiam triumphantem, ad cuius exemplar et similtudinem ipse ecclesiam militantem ordinavit. Dicit enim Dionysius in *Hierarchia angelica* quod sicut illi sunt ordinati in hierarchia angelica, quod quidam gubernant, quidam gubernantur, sic et in hierarchia ecclesiastica esse debet, quia quidam debent gubernare, quidam gubernari. Illi qui gubernant sunt episcopi vel presbyteri;[106] sed gubernandi sunt in triplici differentia, scilicet Christiani, catechumeni et religiosi. Unde religiosi non debent gubernare, sed gubernari, inquantum religiosi. Verum est, si religiosus fuerit episcopus, potest gubernare, vel si religio habet sibi curam animarum annexam sicut isti canonici regulares, illi regere possunt et non alii. Unde quando veniet ad vos talis qui regi et non regere debet, et dicet alicui vestrum, "Committe te mihi et curae meae," dicas sibi, "Tu non potes, nec debes alios gubernare." Nec dico quod modo sint tales, sed aliquando erunt. Unde in tota scriptura non fit mentio tantum de aliquo vitio sicut de isto. Et ideo praedico vobis haec, ut cum venerint, sciatis vobis cavere. Nec ego praedico hic vel in aliquo loco nisi vocatus. Et miror valde, quod de istis vitiis pauci vel nulli praedicant, et qui haec praedicant, odio habentur, et sunt in periculo corporis.

Quinto et ultimo videndum, per quae signa isti, per quos haec pericula 21
venient, cognoscantur, quia in hoc consistit tota vis, scilicet quomodo isti a veris praedicatoribus discernantur. Quia visum est quod non possunt cognosci in habitu, nec in sermone, nec in miraculorum operatione, quomodo ergo cognosci debent? Dicam vobis quaedam signa per scripturas, per quae cognosci possunt.

1 quem] quam *α* | Dominus *om. γλSV* 2 *est om. W* 3 illius *om. β* | curiae] hierarchiae *β* | quia] quam *E* 5 sicut ... quod *om. β* 7 quia] quod *E* 8 debent gubernare] g. d. *transp. γ: add.* debent *λ* | vel] et *β* 9 differentia] gradu *BγλV: om. S* | scilicet *om. γλSV* | Christiani] laici *B: om. γλSV* 10 et] vel *γλSV* | sed gubernari *om. β* 11 Verum] Verumtamen *γ* | est *om. β* | si] *add.* etiam *γRSV:* etiam si *M* 12 religio] religiosus *DS* | sibi *om. β* 13 isti] sunt *N: om. ES* | et … alii] alii vero non *λ* | veniet] venient *β* 14 talis] tales *β* | regi *om. β* | et] *post* non *M:* etiam *N: om. δR* | debet] debent *β* | dicet] dicent *β* 15 dicas sibi] dicatis *δγRV*: indicatis *M* 16 sint] sunt *EλN* 17 tantum *post* vitio *β* | sicut de isto *om. β* 18 haec] hoc *B: om. RS* | venerint] venerit *BγRV*: *add.* quod *γλSV* | 19 hic] hoc *B*: in hoc *γλSV* | valde] valide *λ* | quod *om. γλSV* | istis] *add.* quod de illis (his *M*) *γλSV* 22 haec pericula] p. haec *transp. β* 23 cognoscantur] cognoscentur *B:* cognoscuntur *γλSV* | scilicet *om. β* 25 nec] vel *R:* et *S* 27 possunt] possint *RW*

[105] Ex. 25:40.
[106] Pseudo-Dion., *Eccl. hier.* in *Opera* f. 39r P; *DP*, 27.

22 Una autem via cognoscendi talis est: primo videamus an tales, per quos haec pericula venient, sint Saraceni vel Iudaei vel Christiani. Et dico quod nec erunt Saraceni nec Iudaei; et hoc ostendo per Apostolum qui dicit quod isti habebunt *speciem sanctitatis* et religionis, et utentur sacramentis nostris ad tempus. Unde super illud quod dicit Ioannes in canonica sua: *A nobis exierunt,*[107] Glossa: "Quia eadem sacramenta nobiscum acceperunt."[108] Relinquitur ergo quod isti nec sunt Saraceni, nec Iudaei; unde quaerendi sunt inter Christianos. Sed inter Christianos sunt laici et clerici, religiosi et saeculares; satis constat ex praedictis, quod non erunt laici nec saeculares clerici, sed religiosi falsi, quia reges et magnates non erunt primo, sed isti multos magnates pro se habebunt. Ergo erunt viri litterati et *speciem sanctitatis* praetendentes. Verum est quod Parisius sunt multi viri litterati, sed non omnibus aequaliter creditur. Si aliquis clericus cum cappa rubea vel foraminata vel cum cappa manicata inciperet vobis aliqua nova praedicare, non de facili crederetur; sed si haberet cappam clausam sicut presbyter, magis crederetur sibi. Si vero in habitu exteriori praetenderet aliquam *speciem sanctitatis*, adhuc magis crederetur sibi, et facilius posset decipere et in errorem ducere. Unde oportet quod isti sint viri *speciem sanctitatis* praetendentes, ut satis ostensum est. Sed eruntne viri sapientes? Certe sic, erunt magnam scientiam habentes; multum enim erunt intenti studio de quibus dicit Apostolus: *Semper addiscentes, et numquam ad scientiam veritatis pervenientes.*[109]

23 Sed quomodo potest hoc esse, quod semper discant et in cognitionem veritatis non deveniant? Et ego dico quod Apostolus non loquitur ibi de

1 talis] tales *E* | est] *add.* de qua *B*: *add.* ut scilicet *E*: *add.* ad quae *γλV*: *add.* ad quod *S* 2 haec pericula] p. haec *transp. β* | venient] *αβ*: veniant W^{c} 3 nec] non *β* | erunt *post* Iudaei *β* | hoc *om. β* 4 et] vel *β* 5 quod *om. β* | dicit *om. Bγ* 6 Glossa] Dicit *praem. B*: *om. γλSV* | Quia] Qui *β* | acceperunt] etiam receperunt *β* 7 isti nec] nec isti *tranp. γλSV* 8 Sed … Christianos] *om. λS* | laici et clerici] c. et l. (*add.* et *λ*) *β* 10 sed religiosi] nec saeculares *λ* 11 Ergo erunt] erunt ergo *transp. E* 12 sunt multi] m. sunt *transp. λS* 14 foraminata] *AP*: forata *δ*: fortanta *D*: foriata *αMV*: formata (?) *N*: fodrata *R* | vobis *om. β* | aliqua nova praedicare] a. n. narrare *β*: p. a. n. *W* 15 sed] ei *β* | si] *add.* autem *β* 16 presbyter] presbyteri *γ* | sibi] ei *β* 17 sibi] ei *EMS* | facilius] facile *β* 18 decipere … ducere] in errorem ducere et decipere (percipere *D*) *β* | ducere] deducere *W* | isti] tales *β* | viri *om. β* 19 eruntne] erunt ut *W* 20 scientiam] sapientiam *E* 21 *et*] sed *β* | *scientiam*] disciplinam *BγλV*: viam *S* | *scientiam veritatis*] v. s. *transp. E* 23 in cognitionem] ad disciplinam *BγλV*: ad cognitionem *S* 24 deveniant] perveniant *β*

[107] I Ioan. 2:19.

[108] *ord.* in I Ioan. 2:19 in *Ed. pr.* 4.537A; *ord.* in II Tim. 3:5 in *Ed. pr.* 4.416A (*PL* 114.636C); Aug., *Tract. in Ioan.* in *CCSL* 36.276; *DP*, 55.

[109] II Tim. 3:7; *DP*, 54.

veritate verborum vel de veritate sermonis, sed loquitur de veritate viae. Ad cognitionem enim veritatis viae non devenient, quia sicut dicitur in Ioan.: *Qui facit veritatem, venit ad lucem; sed qui male agit, odit lucem.*[110] Et de hac veritate hic loquitur Apostolus, scilicet de veritate viae, quia in veritate verborum et scripturae bene habebunt notitiam veritatis. Ergo patet per Apostolum quod erunt viri litterati.

Item, super illud Iob: *Hostis meus terribilibus oculis intuitus est me.*[111] Glossa: 24
"Sicut Christus in sua praedicatione idiotas et simplices elegit, ita e contrario Antichristus ad suam falsitatem astruendam duplices, astutos et huius mundi scientiam habentes electurus est."[112] Et postea: "occident professores fidei Christianae."[113] Nec solum Antichristus tales est electurus, sed etiam membra sua, quia Christus et membra sua, scilicet omnes unum sunt, ita et Antichristus et membra sua unum sunt.

Nec mirum si isti procurabunt quod professores fidei Christianae 25
occidantur, quia dicitur in Apocalypsim: *Vidi bestiam ascendentem de mari, habentem capita septem et cornua decem,*[114] et loquitur ibi Ioannes in figura. Et Glossa dicit quod "bestia est Antichristus et membra sua, qui sunt unum, sicut Christus et membra sua."[115] Et Ioannes in canonica sua dicit: *Iam Antichristus venit de mari.*[116] "Id est de populo multo."[117] Dicit Glossa: *habentem septem capita.* Glossa: "Id est universos principes."[118] *Et cornua decem*: "Quia per principes opponent se decem praeceptis."[119] Et ideo illi qui sunt in lege Christi, bene debent sibi cavere quando viderint tales, quia illi erunt viri litterati et docti, sed quanto doctiores et sapientiores, tanto magis timendi et praecavendi.

1 de veritate *om. NS* 2 enim *om. γλSV* | sicut] sic *γMSV* 3 Et *om. E* 4 hic *om. β* | in *om. E* 7 Item] Iterum *DλV* | Glossa] *add.* dicit W^c 8 Sicut] Ut W^c*: om. W* | Christus] *β*W^c*:* incarnata veritas *E: om. W* | in ... elegit] simplices et idiotas in sua praedicatione elegit *E* | e contrario] contrario *EM: post* Antichristus *β* 10 mundi] saeculi *β* | scientiam habentes] sapientiam h. *E:* h. s. *transp. W* | occident] *BDE:* occidet *W:* occiditur *λSV:* occidetur *N* 11 professores] confessores *λ:* per *praem. λNSV* 11 Nec] Non *γλSV* | Antichristus] Christus *β* 12 Christus] Antichristus *β* 13 et *om. β* | Antichristus] Christus *β* 15 *ascendentem*] descendentem *γλSV* 16 et] etiam *E* 17 quod *om. E* | qui] quae *β* 18 sua] eius *DδV* 20 *septem capita*] c. s. *transp. BγRV* 21 per *om. βW* 22 Christi] Dei *β* | sibi cavere] c. s. *transp. E*

[110] Ioan. 3:20-1; *DP*, 54.
[111] Iob 16:10; *DP*, 55.
[112] *Cf. int.* in Iob 16:10 in *Ed. pr.* 2.406b; Greg., *Mor.* in *CCSL* 143A.676; *DP*, 55.
[113] *ord.* in Iob 16:10 in *Ed. pr.* 2.406B (*PL* 113.801B); Greg., *Mor.* in *CCSL* 143A.676.
[114] Apoc. 13:1.
[115] *ord.* in Apoc. 13:1 in *Ed. pr.* 4.565A; Prim., *Comm. in Apoc.* in *CCCM* 92.193.
[116] Apoc. 13:1.
[117] *int.* in Apoc. 13:1 in *Ed. pr.* 4.565a.
[118] *int.* in Apoc. 13:1 in *Ed. pr.* 4.565a.
[119] *int.* in Apoc. 13:1 in *Ed. pr.* 4.565a.

26 Item, ipsi facient illos occidi qui haec pericula praedicant et manifestant. Unde de eis dicitur in Apocalypsim: *Et cruciabunt cruciatu scorpionum.*[120] "Scorpio est parva bestia, quae blanditur ore et pungit cauda et illa punctura vix percipitur. Sed nisi cito remedium adhibeatur, venenum hominem interficit;"[121] sic et ipsi facient. Unde dicit Glossa quod "per seipsos non tormentabunt, sed apud saeculares principes accusabunt,"[122] quia ipsi accusant apud principes saeculares illos qui veritatem de eis dicunt et praedicant. Sic ergo patet quod erunt viri litterati.

27 Sed quia multi sunt litterati, ideo adhuc sumus satis a remotis; unde accedemus propius ut magis specificemus. Multi enim sunt litterati Parisius, ut iam dixi; sed quibusdam magis, quibusdam minus creditur. Et cum tales debeant homines decipere, unde oportet quod praetendant *speciem sanctitatis*, ut dixi, quia aliter non possent decipere. Unde etiam scriptura dicit quod tales erunt qui reputabuntur esse membra Christi, quia ipsi plus electa membra Christi credentur. Unde super illud Iob, *Ad dexteram orientis*[123] etc., dicit Gregorius: "Hii ad persecutionem ecclesiae prosilient, qui electa membra Redemptoris esse credentur."[124] Et sic patet quod tales erunt qui perfecta membra Christi reputantur.

28 Sed adhuc sumus a remotis; unde accedendum est magis prope, quia ipsi erunt viri magni consilii, et qui poterit eos habere in consilio suo, videbitur ei quod habeat consilium a Deo. Unde dicitur in libro Regum,

2 dicitur *ante* de *E* 4 adhibeatur] adhibentur *W* | venenum] veneno *δγV* 5 quod] *BP:* quia *αγλSV* 6 accusabunt ... principes *om. λ* 7 quia ... de *om. N* | principes *om. DδVW* | de eis *post* dicunt *DδλSV* 8 erunt] *post* literati *N*: *om. DλSV* 9 adhuc sumus] s. a. *tranp. λ* | satis *om. β* 10 accedemus] accedamus *β* | ut ... Parisius *om. β* 11 quibusdam] quibus *λ: add.* vero *β* 12 debeant] debent *W* 13 possent] possunt *MW* | scriptura dicit] d. s. *transp. γ* 14 qui] quod *W* | esse] *om. β*: *add.* electa *E* 15 electa membra] m. e. *transp. λ* | Christi] *om. W* | credentur] creduntur *γλSV* 16 prosilient] prosiliunt *W* 17 esse *om. βW* | credentur] credebantur *β* 18 perfecta] perfecte *γ* | membra] *add.* Redemptoris *E* | reputantur] credentur *BD:* credebantur *MS:* credebuntur *NRV* 19 prope] propius *β* 20 viri] *add.* et etiam *λV: add.* litterati et *S* | et] quia *α* | suo *om. β* 21 habeat] habebat *λ* | libro *om. α*

[120] Apoc. 9:5.

[121] *ord.* in Apoc. 9:5 in *Ed. pr.* 4.560B (*PL* 114.727A); Beda, *Expl. Apoc.* in *PL* 93.158B; Beda, *Expo. in Luc.* in *CCSL* 120.219; Isid., *Etymol.* XII.5.4, 90: "Scorpio vermis terrenus, qui potius vermibus adscribitur, non serpentibus; animal armatum aculeo, et ex eo Graece vocatum quod cauda figat et arcuato vulnere venena diffundat."

[122] *ord.* in Apoc. 9:5 in *Ed. pr.* 4.560B (*PL* 114.727B); Beda, *Expl. Apoc.* in *PL* 93.158B.

[123] Iob 30:12; *DP*, 30, 55.

[124] *ord.* in Iob 30:12 in *Ed. pr.* 2.427A; Greg., *Mor.* in *CCSL* 143A.1039; *DP*, 30, 55.

David *habuit filium qui vocabatur Absalom, qui habuit consiliarium Achitophel.*[125] Et iste Achitophel procuravit per consilium suum quod Absalom patrem suum David de regno eiceret. Et dicitur ibi: *quod fuit cum patre et filio. Consilium Achitophel in diebus suis erat quasi consilium Domini, quando fuit cum David et cum Absalom.*[126] Per David Christus intelligitur, qui interpretatur "manu fortis" et "aspectu desiderabilis."[127] Absalom interpretatur "amaritatio."[128] Achitophel interpretatur "frater meus irruens, vel tractans vel cogitans."[129] Per David ergo Christus significatur; per Absalom Antichristus, qui erit homo et creatura Dei, quia etiam diabolus creatura Dei est. Achitophel sunt isti qui prius se coniungunt Christo, et postea sunt contra Christum, sicut iste Achitophel prius fuit cum David et postea contrarius ei.[130] Quamdiu enim isti erunt nobiscum, pro magnis consiliariis tenebuntur; sed postmodum opponent se fidei Christanae. Et ideo cum videbitis tales, nolite vos eis committere.

Signa septem ad praesens ponam, quibus possint cognosci; licet multa 29
possim ostendere, tamen causa brevitatis temporis haec sufficiant.

Unde primum signum est, quod tales volunt vivere de evangelio et de 30
confessionibus audiendis. Quod autem tales non sunt veri praedicatores patet per Apostolum, qui dicit ad Tim.: *Putantes quaestum esse pietatem.*[131]

1 *consiliarium*] consilium *γλV* 2 procuravit] ordinavit *β* 3 *fuit*] *α*: erat *δλNV*: *om. D* 4 *Consilium om. β* | *quasi*] quando *γ*: quia *λSV* | *consilum*] et filium *λ* | *Domini*] *add.* sui (*om. γSV*) fuit *γλ SV* 5 *cum om. β* 6 et] vel *W* 7 irruens] irroneus *R*: eruens *W* 8 significatur] signatur *αS*: interpretatur *N* | Absalom] *add.* autem *λ* 9 Antichristus] Christus *λ* | quia ... est *om. λ* | creatura Dei est] est c. Dei *δV* 10 est *ante* diabolus *γ* 11 et *om. γ* 12 contrarius ei] contra David *β* | enim *om. NS* 13 tenebuntur] reputabuntur *W* | cum] quando *E*: *om. W* 14 vos eis] eis vos *transp. γRV* 15 Signa] *add.* quare supra c. fi. *E* | septem ... carentes (n. 40) *om. E* | ad praesens *ante* Signa *β* | possint] possunt *β* 16 possim] possem *β* 17 Unde primum] Unum *W* | quod] quia *W* | de *om. λS* 19 *pietatem*] pietatis *γRV*: parietatis *M*

[125] *Cf.* II Reg. 14-6; *DP*, 55

[126] II Reg. 16:23; *DP*, 55.

[127] *int.* in I Reg. 17:23 in *Ed. pr.* 2.28a; Hier., *Lib. inter.* in *CCSL* 72.103: "David fortis manu sive desiderabilis."; Isid., *Etymol.* VII.6.64, 658: "David fortis manu, utique quia fortissimus in proeliis fuit."

[128] *ord.* in II Reg. 17:1 in *Ed. pr.* 2.74A (*PL* 113.575C): "Absalon pax patris dicitur quia pacem pater habuit quam ille non habuit."; Hier., *Lib. inter.* in *CCSL* 72.105: "Abessalon pater pacis."; Isid., *Etymol.* VII.6.67, 660: "Absalon patris pax per antiphasin, eo quod bellum adversus patrem gessisset, sive quod in ipso bello David pacatum fuisse legitur filio, adeo ut etiam magno cum dolore extinctum plangeret."

[129] *ord.* in II Reg. 17:1 in *Ed. pr.* 2.74B (*PL* 113.575B); Hier., *Liber inter.* in *CCSL* 72.105-6: "Ahitofel frater meus cadens sive inruens vel frater meus cogitans sive tractans."

[130] "Isti autem recte significantur per Achitophel, qui prius fuit cum David, et postea adhaesit Absalom; ita enim isti prius adhaerebunt Christo..." *DP*, 55.

[131] I Tim. 6:5.

Glossa: "Opus pietatis faciunt, id est praedicant, ut lucra temporalia accipiant; quia pro quaestu praedicant, non fructu animarum, quia ipsi volunt honorari et laudari."[132] Item, alia Glossa super illud ad Col.: *Quia veritas in dolo est, sive per occasionem sive per veritatem Christus annuntietur, in hoc gaudeo.*[133] "Pseudo ex occasione evangelizant, quaerentes commoda sua, vel pecuniaria, vel honorum vel laudis humanae."[134] Veritas in dolo est quando non praedicant, nisi propter commodum temporale. Dicit Glossa: "Tales enim tria commoda de hoc quaerunt, scilicet de praedicatione, scilicet laudem, fructum et comedere et bibere."[135] Ipsi enim bene praedicant de veritate, sed haec tria quaerunt.

31 Sed dicet aliquis: "Nonne, si ipsi praedicant, debent de evangelio vivere? Quia dicit Apostolus: *Ordinavit Dominus, ut qui praedicant evangelium de evangelio vivere.*"[136] Et ego dico quod hoc verum est de illis qui praedicare tenentur; quia si presbyter vester, qui vos debet regere et docere, esset in tali statu quod vestro subsidio indigeret, deberetis sibi subvenire. Sed Benedictus Deus, ecclesia non est hodie in tali statu quod indigeat subsidio tali.

32 Item, secundum signum, per quod cognoscuntur falsi praedicatores, est si sint impatientes, et non possunt sustinere quod veritas de eis dicatur. Unde Apostolus ad Phil.: *Videte canes, videte malos operarios, videte concisionem.*[137] "Canes, id est pseudo,"[138] dicit Glossa. Qui dicuntur canes, quia secundum Augustinum, "ubi canis est, si videt hominem alienum intrantem domum, latrat."[139] Sic et ipsi, si videant quod aliquis veritatem de eis praedicet, recalcitrant.

2 accipiant] acquirant et *praem.* β | pro quaestu] per quaestum λ | fructu] lucro vel (et *S: om. N*) *praem.* β | animarum *om. W* 6 pecuniaria] pecuniarum *B:* pecuniam *γRSV:* pecunias *M* | honorum] honorem *NS* 8 scilicet] videlicet β 9 et *om.* β 11 dicet] dicit *MNS* | evangelio] *add.* debent *W* | vivere] vivant β 14 vester *om.* β | esset] esse *W* 16 hodie *ante* non β 18 secundum] aliud *W* | est *ante* per β 20 Apostolus *om. W* | *videte om.* δ 21 *concisionem*] *P:* occidentes *γλSV:* concidentes *W: om. B* | id est] enim β 22 secundum Augustinum] dicit Augustinus β | ubi] nam *W* | est] *add.* quod *W* 23 intrantem] intrare λ 24 eis] ipsis λ | praedicet] praedicat *W* | recalcitrant] recalcitrent γ

[132] *Cf. int.* in I Tim. 6:5 in *Ed. pr.* 4.411b.

[133] Phil. 1:18; *QDM*, n. 115;*DP*, 60; *SQD*, n. 9; *Dephar.*, n. 9.

[134] *ord.* in Phil 1:18 in *Ed. pr.* 4.381A; Aug., *Sermo 137* in *PL* 38.757; *DP*, 60-1; *SQD*, n. 9; *Dephar.*, n. 9.

[135] *Cf. ord.* in Phil. 1:18 in *Ed. pr.* 4.381A; Aug., *Sermo 137* in *PL* 38.757.

[136] I Cor. 9:14; *DP*, 26.

[137] Phil. 3:2; *DP*, 63.

[138] *int.* in Phil. 3:2 in *Ed. pr.* 4.384b.

[139] *Cf. int.* in Phil. 3:2 in *Ed. pr.* 4.384b: "contra veritatem latrantes"; Aug., *Serm. 137* in *PL* 38.757; "canes ... tanquam pro suo Domino latrantes;" *DP*, 63.

Item, tertium signum est, scilicet, si habeant verba pulchra et ornata, 33
quibus multos ad partem suam trahunt. Unde super illud ad Cor. 7: *Neminem circumvenimus.*[140] Glossa: "Fraudulenta sermonum adulatione, sicut pseudo qui vestra blande auferunt."[141] De hoc dicit Dominus in Matt.: *Vae vobis Scribae et Pharisaei hypocritae, qui comeditis domos viduarum, in longa oratione.*[142] Glossa: "Qui ex vestra superstitione nihil aliud quaeritis, nisi"[143] etc., *qui comeditis domos viduarum.* Glossa: "Qui ut religiosiores appareant, prolixius orant."[144] Et subdit: "Quorum oratio est in peccatum."[145]

Item, quartum signum est, quod veri praedicatores non vadunt illuc 34
praedicare ubi est abundantia praedicatorum, sed ubi nulli sunt qui verbum Dei annuntient.[146] Unde dicit Apostolus ad Rom.: *Sic autem praedicavi evangelium, ubi Christum annuntiavi, ne super alienum fundamentum aedificarem.*[147] Qui enim habet voluntatem praedicandi debet ire ad Saracenos et infideles ubi nullus est qui praedicet. Et ideo cum videritis tales praedicatores, qui ibi praedicare desiderant ubi est copia praedicatorum, et volunt ibi praedicare ubi non est indigentia et penuria praedicatorum, sciatis eos esse non veros praedicatores.

1 Item *om. BN* | tertium] aliud *W* | est] *add.* ad hoc *W* | scilicet *om. Bλ* | si *om. λ* 2 partem suam] partes suas *β* | super] secundum *γλV* | ad *om. W* | 7 *om. β* 3 *circumvenimus*] circumveniemus *λ* | sermonum adulatione] *DδλV:* suorum ablatione *W:* verborum dulcedine *N* 4 vestra] nostra *γλ* | blande *om. β* | De] Et *β* 5 *in ... viduarum om. β* 7 religiosiores] religiosi *β* 9 Item *om. BN* | quartum] aliud *W* | est *om. SV* | quod] quia *W* 11 ad *om. BN* 13 enim] enim autem *W* | habet voluntatem] habent v. *B:* voluntatem *W* 14 cum] quando *W* 16 volunt] nolunt *β* | non *om. β* 17 non veros praedicatores] malos et non veros praedicatores *δγRV*: malos praed. et non veros *M*

[140] II Cor. 7:2; *DP*, 62.

[141] *int.* in II Cor. 7:2 in *Ed. pr.* 4.346a; *DP*, 62.

[142] Matt. 23:14.

[143] *int.* in Matt. 23:14 in *Ed. pr.* 4.71a.

[144] *Cf. int.* in Matt. 23:14 in *Ed. pr.* 4.71a.

[145] *Cf. int.* in Matt. 23:14 in *Ed. pr.* 4.71a.

[146] *Resp.*: 349: "Item dixit in eodem quod signum falsorum apostolorum est quod vadunt praedicare ubi Christus fuit praedicatus vel praedicatur ab aliis quia Apostolus dixit de se quod ipse praedicavit ubi Christus non fuerat praedicatus." "Respondeo: Cum dicat Apostolus, Rom. 15:20: Sic autem praedicavi evangelium non ubi nominatus est Christus, ne super alienum fundamentum aedificarem (Glossa: ne praedicarem iam per alios conversis), item II Cor. 10:15: Non habentes spem gloriari in aliena regula in hiis quae praeparata sunt (Glossa: ab aliis praedicatoribus, quia hiis praedicabat Apostolus quibus non erat annunciatum, ut gloriam suo labore quaereret), timemendum est ne ili qui vadunt praedicare fidelibus iam conversis et orthodoxis, non ostendentes litteras sive auctoritates suae missionis, non sint veri apostoli, cum in hac parte non imitantur veros apostolos."

[147] Rom. 15:20; *DP*, 26, 65.

35 Item, quintum signum est, quod veri Apostoli patientes erant et contumeliam pro Christo sustinebant,[148] quia, *Ibant Apostoli gaudentes a conspectu concilii, quod digni habiti sunt pro nomine Iesu contumeliam pati.*[149] Unde dicebat eis Dominus in Matt.: *Ecce ego mitto vos sicut oves inter lupos,*[150] quia agnus omnia, quae lupus sibi facit, sustinet. Item: *Sicut misit me Pater, et ego mitto vos.*[151] Glossa: "Non ad gaudia, sed ad passiones."[152] Qui enim praedicationis officium suscipit, mala non debet inferre, sed sustinere; et hoc ipse Christus in se ostendit. Unde Petrus in canonica: *Qui cum malediceretur, non maledicebat; cum flagellaretur, non comminabatur; tradebat autem tradenti se iniuste.*[153] Sic quando videritis tales, qui nihil possunt sustinere, sed si irrogetur eis iniuria vel violentia, current ad curiam Papae et impetrabunt litteras excommunicationis, et ad principes saeculares, ut illi qui eos molestant, incarcerentur, tales debetis falsos religiosos reputare.

1 Item *om. BN* | quintum] aliud *W* | quod] quia *W* | veri *om. λ* | patientes erant] e. p. *transp. β* 2 contumeliam] contumelias *β: add.* libenter *β* | Christo] Christi nomine *β* 3 *quod … pati*] quoniam habiti sunt pro nomine Iesu contumelias pati *S:* etc. *N: om. BDλV* 4 *oves*] agnos *β* 5 lupus sibi facit] s. f. l. *β* | sustinet *ante* quae *β* | Item] Glossa *W* 6 Glossa *om. W* 7 officium] *add.* recipit vel *λ* 8 in canonica] can. iii *N: om. W* 10 *autem*] enim *γ* | Sic] Si *S:* Sed *W* | videritis tales] *DδV:* videtis tales *MN:* videbitis tales *RW* 11 irrogetur] irrogetis *δγMV* | iniuria vel violentia] iniuriam vel violentiam *δγMV* 12 et *om. β* | principes] *add.* et *λ* 13 incarcerentur] incarcerent *λ* | tales] *add.* non *BγλV: add.* enim *S* | debetis … reputare] sunt veri Apostoli *N* | falsos *om. DδλV*

[148] *Cf. Resp.*: 349-50: "Item, dixit in eodem quod signum falsorum praedicatorum est quod de iniuriis sibi factis recurrent ad dominum papam et impetrant litteras." "Respondeo: Non sic dixi, sed dixi quod veri apostoli patientes erant: Matth., 10:16: ecce mitto vos, etc., (Glossa: qui locum praedicationis suscipit, mala inferre non debet, sed tolerare); item II Cor. 12: signa apostolatus mei facta sunt super vos in omni patientia et signis, etc. (Glossa: patientiam primo commemora, quae ad mores praedicationis pertinet, et hoc maxime pertinet viris perfectis): Matth. 5:44: Diligite inimicos vestros et benefacite hiis qui oderunt vos: falsi vero praedicatores impatientes sunt; Matth. 7:16: A fructibus eorum cognoscetis eos (Glossa: maxime autem per impatientiam cognoscuntur, quia non solum laedunt hos quos odiunt, sed etiam diffamant). Unde, super Ierem., 23:15, A prophetis Ierusalem egressa est pollutio super omnem terram, dicit Glossa: Non sufficit eis proximos laedere, sed quod semel oderunt per totum orbem conantur diffamare. Unde illi praedicatores, qui vexant homines vel per litteras apostolicas vel alio modo, videntur esse contrarii veris apostolis, maxime si sint in statu perfectionis. Unde I Cor., 6:7: iam quidem omnino delictum est in vobis, quia iudicia habetis inter vos: quare non magis iniuriam accipitis, quare non magis fraudem patimini (Glossa: Perfectis viris licet sua repetere simpliciter, scilicet sine causa, sine lite, sine iudicio; sed non convenit eis movere causam aut iudicium.)"

[149] Act. 5:41.

[150] Matt. 10:16; *DP*, 65; *Dephar.*, n. 15.

[151] Ioan. 20:21; *DP*, 50.

[152] *ord.* in Matt. 10:16 in *Ed. pr.* 4.39A; *int.* in Ioan. 20:21 in *Ed. pr.* 4.269a; Greg., *Hom.* in *CCSL* 141.219 (*PL* 76.1198B).

[153] I Pet. 2:23; *DP*, 65.

Item, sextum signum est, quia Apostoli Christi in principio fuerunt valde 36
despecti et exosi in tantum, quod etiam occisi sunt. Sed tamen propter ipsorum occisionem et mortem, praelati ecclesiae grati et accepti sunt, quia dixerat hoc Dominus Apostolis: *Eritis odio omnibus hominibus propter nomen meum.*[154] Et in Ioan.: *Erit tempus, quando qui vos interficit, aestimabit obsequium se praestare Deo,*[155] quia illi, qui occidebant sanctos martyres, credebant bene facere et propter deos suos quos colebant. Unde si videritis aliquos, qui se dicant Apostolos Christi, etsi in principio sint grati et accepti, in fine vero cognitis operibus eorum sint despecti, signum est quod non sint veri Apostoli Christi, cum de illis e contrario fuerit. Unde sicut dicit Ioannes in canonica sua: *Omne quod natum est ex Deo,* vincit mundum.[156] Sed isti sunt in principio magis accepti, quam in fine.

Item, septimum signum est, quod veri Apostoli non suum sed Christi 37
honorem quaerebant, quia dicit Psalmus: *Non nobis, Domine, non nobis; sed nomini tuo da gloriam.*[157] Et Dominus: *Cum feceritis omnia quae facere debetis, dicite; Servi inutiles sumus, quod debuimus facere, fecimus.*[158] Sed quando videritis tales, qui suam et non Dei gloriam quaerunt, qui dicunt: “Nos illuminavimus totam ecclesiam, et eiecimus homines de peccatis, et ostendimus viam veniendi ad vitam,” talibus non credatis.

Audivi quod quidam religiosus praedicabat in quadam civitate et 38
dixit: “Ordo noster valde est exaltatus, quia ante Ordinem nostrum totus mundus fuit in tenebris. Sed venit Beata Virgo, et cecidit Filio suo ad pedes, et iacuit ante ipsum per tres dies. Et dixit ei Dominus quod peteret quidquid vellet. Et ipsa tunc dixit, quod vellet quod fieret unus

1 Item *om. BN* | sextum] aliud *W* | quia] quod *S* | fuerunt *ante* in *γ* 2 tamen] cum *λ* 3 ipsorum] illorum *δγV:* eorum *λ* | ecclesiae] *add.* facti sunt *β* | sunt *om. β* 4 *hominibus om. BγV* 5 *interficit*] interfecerit *W* | *obsequium se*] se o. *transp. W* 6 *Deo*] *Domino RW* 8 dicant] dicunt *β* | etsi] et *δγMV om. R* | sint] sunt *γλSV* 9 sint] sunt *MS* | sint veri] sunt veri *γMS*: v. sint *transp. R* 10 Apostoli Christi] C. A. *transp. W* 11 sunt … accepti] magis in p. (*add.* magis *M*) sunt accepti *β* 13 Item *om. BN* | septimum] aliud *W* | quod] quia *W* 15 Et *om. W* | Dominus] *add.* in evangelio *β* | *facere debetis*] praecepta sunt vobis *B:* f. debuisitis *γλSV* 16 *dicite*] dicatis (dicat *R*) quod *γλSV* | *sumus*] fuistis *γλSV* | *quod debuimus*] quae (quod *M*) debuistis *DλV* | *quod … fecimus*] etc. *S: om. N* | *fecimus*] fecistis *DλV* | quando *om. λ* 17 gloriam *ante* et *W* | qui dicunt] quia *W* 18 illuminavimus] illuminamus *λ* | totam *om. W* 19 veniendi] vivendi *λN* 19 credatis] creditis *W: add.* etc. *λS* 20 Audivi ... protulisse *om. BN* | Audivi … carentes *om. S* | praedicabat] praedicavit *DλV* 24 quidquid] quod *W*

154 Matt. 10:22.
155 Ioan. 16:2.
156 I Ioan. 3:9.
157 Ps. 113:1; *DP*, 66.
158 Luc. 17:10; *DP*, 66.

Ordo qui totum mundum illuminaret et Dominus concessit ei; et ipsa dixit tunc cuidam quod faceret Ordinem, et iste est Ordo noster. Unde non est mirum, si sic est exaltatus."[159]

39 Sed iste non fecit sicut Apostoli Christi, quibus dicitur quod debebant dicere, quod *sint servi inutiles.*[160] Unde iste deprehensus fuit quod hoc dixerat et compulsus fuit ab episcopo, quod diceret coram omnibus se mendacium protulisse.

40 Unde, carissimi, ab istis falsis apostolis valde est cavendum. Volunt homines esse sine despectu, pauperes sine defectu, bene induti sine sollicitudine, cibos electos, exquisitos et lauciores habere, tamen in via mala in manifesto adulantes, in occulto detrahentes, exterius asperam vitam praetendentes, interius delicias quaerentes, mordaces ut canes, dolosi ut vulpes, superbi ut leones, illusores ut dracones, intrinsecus sunt lupi rapaces, exterius mel laudis humanae ut ursi amantes, sine cognitione volunt esse iudices, testes sine visu, falsi accusatores, omni veritate carentes.

1 ei *om. DλV* | ipsa dixit tunc] tunc ipsa dixit *DλV* 3 sic est] sit *W* 4 debebant] debent *DλV* 5 quod] quia *DλV* 8 apostolis] prophetis *BγλV* | est cavendum] c. e. *transp. BγλV: add.* Sermo ab haeretico praedicationis Guillelmo de Sancto Amore Explicit *W* | Volunt ... carentes *om. W* 9 homines] enim (*om. D*) h. (humiles *γ*) *Bγ* | bene induti] bene in divitiis *M* 10 sollicitudine] solutione *M* | tamen] cum *λ* | tamen ... mala *om. N* 11 adulantes] *om. λ* | in] et *M:* ab *R* | asperam] alternam *M:* alteram *R* 12 interius] *add.* etiam *λ: add. ult.* ad *M* 14 sunt *om. B* | exterius] extrinsecus *B* | humanae] *add.* propinantes *N* | ursi] *add.* id *N* 16 carentes] *add.* etc. *BDR: add. ult.* Amen *M: add.* Explicit liber scriptus Parisius contra hypocritas et falsos viglifistas a magistro Guillelmo de Sancto Amore burgundo anno domini MCCCCXVII *D: add.* Explicit Libellus de periculis quae instabunt temporibus novissimis Magistri Guillelmi de Amore Parisius false compilatus in confusionem religionum mendicantium sed iuste per Alexandrum papam quartum condemnatus. *N:* Explicit liber scriptus Parisius contra hypocritas et falsos religiosos a Magistro Guillelmo de Sancto Amore Burgundo anno domini MCCLV Deo Gratias *V*

[159] Theo., "Acta ampliora S. Dominici," in *AS* 31, t. I Aug., 570-1.
[160] Luc. 17:10.

<SI QUIS DILIGIT ME>

Si quis diligit me sermonem meum servabit, et Pater meus diliget eum, et ad eum 1
veniemus et mansionem apud eum faciemus.[1] *Paraclitus quem mittet Pater in nomine meo, ille vos docebit omnia, et suggeret vobis omnia, quaecumque dixero vobis.*[2]

Verbum ultimum scriptum est in evangelio hodierno et sumptum est 2
istud evangelium de sermone, quem fecit Dominus discipulis suis in die Coenae, quando debebat recedere, *ut ipsos consolaretur* etc. In istis verbis habetur, quod per Sanctum Spiritum docetur et habetur verbum Dei. Unde dicit Glossa: *ille vos docebit omnia* etc., "ut cognoscatis."[3] *Et suggeret*; Glossa: "ut velitis."[4] Et ideo rogemus ipsum etc.

Primum verbum similiter scriptum est in evangelio hodierno et tractum 3
est de sermone, quem fecit Dominus discipulis suis in die Coenae. Unde in die Coenae, quia debebat mortem pati et ab ipsis recedere, ne ipsi ob hoc desolarentur, promittit eis mittere consolationem. "Paraclitus enim consolator interpretatur"[5] et istud promissum hodie eis reddit. Unde hodie misit eis Spiritum Sanctum sub specie ignis. Unde Lucas in Actibus Apostolorum: *Apparaverunt illis dispertitae linguae tamquam ignis, seditque super singulos eorum.*[6] Et quare magis sub specie ignis quam sub specie alterius elementi? Causa est, quia proprietas ignis est calefacere; item, semper crescere et numquam deficere, si habet sibi subiectam materiam.

Similiter, amor Dei et proximi debet calefacere corda nostra et ignire. Et 4
iste debet semper perseverando crescere, Gregorius in *Homelia:* "Sanctus Spiritus sanctus amor est."[7] Unde amor noster erga Deum numquam debet

2 *Si*] Incipit sermo Magistri Guillelmi de Sancto Amore in die pentecosten Parisius *praem. E*

[1] Ioan. 14:23; *DP*, 40.

[2] Ioan. 14:26.

[3] *int.* in Ioan. 14:26 in *Ed. pr.* 4.259a.

[4] *int.* in Ioan. 14:26 in *Ed. pr.* 4.259a.

[5] Beda, *Hom. evang.* in *CCSL* 122.301: "Paraclitus quippe consolator interpretatur."; Greg., *Hom.* in *CCSL* 141.258 (PL 76.1221D).

[6] Act. 2:3.

[7] Greg., *Hom.* in *CCSL* 141.256 (*PL* 76.1220C).

esse otiosus. Et ideo Gregorius in *Expositione* istius evangelii Ioannis dicit sic: "Amor verus numquam otiosus est; operatur autem magna si sit; et si renuit operari, amor non est."[8] In verbis dictis tria notanda sunt. Primum est, quid sit vere diligere Deum, scilicet cum dicit: *Si quis diligit me.* Secundum, quomodo potest cognosci qui vere Deum diligit, cum dicit: *sermonem meum servabit.* Tertium, quae utilitas et quis fructus acquiritur in diligendo Deum, cum dicit: *et ad eum veniemus et mansionem,* etc.

5 De primo sic notandum, quod qui vere diligit Deum, diligit eum quantum valet. Unde si res aliqua diligitur minus quam valet, non vere diligitur. Caritas est vere diligere Deum. [et caritas Dei de cherte]. Potestne Deus diligi quantum valet? Non a nobis, tamen nos debemus facere totum posse nostrum. Unde debemus dilectionem Dei praeponere omni dilectioni alterius rei. Et ideo in Psalmis super illum locum: *Bonum mihi lex oris tui, super milia*[9] etc. Glossa: "plus diligit caritas Deum et legem Dei quam cupiditas aurum et argentum."[10] Unde ad ipsum debet esse totus amor. Debet etiam in eum verti totum desiderium nostrum, et ideo in Canticis, loquens ecclesia dicit: *Ordinavit in me Deus caritatem.*[11] Unde super omnia Dei voluntas est adimplenda. Et cogitatio magis ad ipsum dirigatur quam ad aliud et curam magis et laborem ad ipsum amandum, ut et ipse nos amet, debemus apponere quam ad aliud. Unde ipse Dominus in evangelio: *Qui non odit patrem, et matrem, et fratres, et sorores, adhuc autem animam suam non potest meus esse discipulus.*[12] Glossa: *Qui non odit* "quidquid obsistere potest in servitio Dei."[13] Unde istae tres chordae, quae sunt quod voluntas Dei super omnia adimpleri desideretur. Secunda est, quod ad hoc apponatur labor omnis, qui apponi poterit. Tertia, quod cogitatio nostra magis ad ipsum sit quam ad aliud. Qui habet ista tria, triplici vinculo Dei ligatus est et unitus sive iunctus. Et istud vinculum bonum est. Salomon: *Triplex funiculus ex difficili rumpitur.*[14] Et sic ligatus quilibet debet esse. Unde Augustinus in libro *De vera religione* ostendens quomodo posset quis Deo coniungi

[8] Greg., *Hom.* in *CCSL* 141.257 (*PL* 76.1221B).

[9] Ps. 118:72; *DP,* 67.

[10] *int.* in Ps. 118:72 in *Ed. pr.* 2.613a; Aug., *Enarr. in Ps.* in *CCSL* 40.1722; *DP,* 67.

[11] Ct. 2:4.

[12] Luc. 14:26; *DP,* 71.

[13] *int.* in Luc. 14:26 in *Ed. pr.* 4.194a; *DP,* 71.

[14] Eccli. 4:12.

per amorem, dicit sic: "Religet ergo nos <religio> uni vero, omnipotenti Deo."[15] Unde qui non ligatus est sic Deo non est religiosus, licet habeat habitum humilem. Et talis religio potest esse ita bene sub scarleto, sicut sub sacco sive sub burello. Unde religio non est in dividendo se ab aliis per habitum, sed in uniendo se Deo per amorem. Qui autem habet habitum religionis, si non sit intus religio, dictus Pharisaeus est, "qui interpretatur divisus,"[16] scilicet per diversum habitum. Isti Pharisaei non habebant istam religionem in corde, sed habebant habitum exteriorem solum, unde erant hypocritae.[17] Si non sit ista religio in saecularibus, non propter hoc sunt hypocritae, quia signum huius non ostedunt populo. Notandum, quod non est aliquis ita mendax sicut hypocrita, quia mentitur toto corde vel corpore; sed alius non mentitur nisi ore. Unde dicitur in libro *De dictis modernorum*: "Se toto mentitur hypocrita habens extra circumque speciem virtutum, nihil intus."[18] Isti Pharisaei erant magni homines et divites et potentes, tamen assumebant habitum humilem et vilem magis quam deceret eorum personas, ut dicerentur sancti a populo. Et ideo Dominus in evangelio de istis dicit: *Exterminant facies suas hominibus ut vultus ieiunantes.*[19] Glossa: *Exterminant facies suas*; "id est extra terminos humanae conditionis adducunt."[20] Et est hypocrita in diminuendo sicut in excedendo. Unde Glossa ibidem: "Sicut ex nimio nitore iactantia est, sic ex nimio squalore."[21] Et plus displicet Deo diminutio quam excessus. Unde Glossa dicit: *Exterminant facies* etc. "Luctuosis sordibus, in quibus iactancia est, et magis sub specie religionis decipiunt vestes luctuosae quam vestes lugubres,"[22] quas secundum leges[23] debent gerere viduae primo anno, quo mortui sunt mariti sui, nec debent illo anno contrahere sponsalia. Unde tales vestes sunt viles. Istas habent falsi hypocritae. Item, alia Glossa ibidem, *Exterminant facies suas:* "ut dissimiles aliis videantur, et ut ex ipsa vilitate

13 circumque] circumquaque *E* 17 *suas*] *E*[C]: scilicet *E*

[15] Aug., *De vera rel.* in *CCSL* 32.259.

[16] *ord.* in Matt. 3:7 in *Ed. pr.* 4.11B (PL 114.80B); Hrab. Maur., *Comm. in Matt.* in *PL* 107.770B; *Dephar.*, n. 4.

[17] *Cf.* Matt. 23:5; Hier., *Comm. in Matt.* in *CCSL* 77.212.

[18] *Cf.* Amb., *Epist. 36* in *CSEL* 82.2, 12: "Multi habent humilitatis speciem, virtutem non habent; multi eam foris praetendunt, et intus impugnant."

[19] Matt. 6:16.

[20] *ord.* in Matt. 6:16 in *Ed. pr.* 4.26B (*PL* 114.103C); Hier., *Comm. in Matt.* in *CCSL* 77.38.

[21] *ord.* in Matt. 6:16 in *Ed. pr.* 4.26B (*PL* 114.103C); Pasc. Rad., *Expo. in Mat.* in *CCCM* 56.410.

[22] *ord.* in Matt. 6:16 in *Ed. pr.* 4.26B (*PL* 114.103C); Pasc. Rad., *Expo. in Mat.* in *CCCM* 56.410.

[23] *Codex* V.9.1-224.

ultra homines praedicentur."[24] Verumtamen, hypocrisis magnum peccatum est, et se ingerit ubi alia peccata non habent locum. Unde ibi operatur diabolus per hypocrisim, ubi per alia peccata non potest operari aliquo modo aliud peccatum. Ideo impugnat eam Dominus magis quam aliud peccatum et Apostoli similiter. Peccatum hypocrisis in paucis esse solebat, modo in tantum crevit quod devenit usque ad episcopos, parochiales sacerdotes, milites, burgenses, reges et principes; et similiter de mulieribus. Unde similiter dolendum est. Unde in media nocte modo reges surgunt ad matutinas dicendas et in die audiunt sex paria missarum ad votum,[25] et dimittunt causas pauperum sequentium curiam suam indiscussas. Et non portarent unam pulchram robam,[26] tamen bene permitterent unum bellum oriri vel fieri, in quo mille Christiani interficerentur.[27] Unde de suis extorsionibus redderent decem solidos vel quinque, sed nullo modo redderent unam comitivam, nec unam villam vel castellum. Et tamen a scripturis non habemus, quod reges debent surgere ad matutinas de nocte etc., et quod debeant induere vestes de umello, id est vili pano. Sed bene invenio, quod debent induere vestes pretiosissimas.[28] Non in talibus consistit officium regis, sed in faciendo *iudicium et iusticiam*,[29] et iudicando abbacias et ecclesias et de sedendo et procurando pacem suae terrae. Hieronymus:

11 robam] *add.* id est vestem *sup. lin.* E^C 16 id ... pano] *add. sup. lin.* E^C

[24] *int.* in Matt. 6:16 in *Ed. pr.* 4.26b.

[25] *Cf.* "Gesta S. Ludovici," in *Recueil* 20.50C-D; "Vie de Saint-Louis," in *Recueil* 20.71B-E.

[26] Sal., *Chronica* in *MGH* 32.222; (*Leg. aur.* c. 213, 916): "Scarleto etiam seu bruneto aut viridi vel alia veste pomposa uti nolebat nec pellibus variis aut nimium sumtuosis..."

[27] Sal., *Chronica* in *MGH* 32.333: "Anno Domini MCCL captus est Lodoycus rex Franciae, et maior pars exercitus Gallici, qui cum rege transfretaverat, a Saracenis est interfecta."

[28] *Cf. Resp.*: pp. 347-8: "Item, dixit in sermone Pentecostes quod maius malum erat si aliquis praetermittit cultum vestium personae suae congruentem, accipiens vestes magis viles quam dignitati congruunt, quam si excedat in pretiositate vestium." "Ad hoc responsum est supra." "Item, dixit in eodem quod ad regem pertinet fere vestes pretiosas ad dandum pro Deo, et iudicium et iustitiam facere; et qui aliter facit, peccat mortaliter: non enim dicit Scriptura quod ad regem pertineat portare burellam vel audire matutinas; et quod magnum periculum imminet illis qui talia suadent regi." "Respondeo: Dixi quod ad regem pertinet ferre habitum congruentem suae dignitati, ne contemptibilis habeatur. Unde Hieronymus: 'Utere deliciis non pro te sed pro regno, ut timorem incutias ad iustitiam exercendam.' Item, dixi quod melius est regibus et principibus facere iudicium et iustitiam, ad quae tenentur, et, si oportet, omissis sollemnitatibus divinorum in diebus profestis, quae ipsos a praedictis impediunt, quam propter dictas sollemnitates dimittere iudiciam et iustitiam, ad quae tenentur. Non enim legi: 'Regum est audire plures missas in diebus profestis, vel matutinas', sed legi 'Regum est facere iudicium et iustitiam', XXIII q. 5 Regum; et credo quod qui contraria eis consulunt peccant."

[29] *Cf.* Ps. 118:121.

"Utere deliciis non pro te sed pro regno, ut timorem incutias ad iusticias exercendas."[30] Ipse loquitur cuidam regi, qui forte beguinus erat. Et ideo ordinavit ecclesia, quod papa equitat cum freno de stria aurata bene et rubea, quae potest inveniri, et ferunt milites semper, quando equitant, unum pannum de serico super caput eius.[31] Non deberent regibus consulere homines boni, qui essent beguini, sed quod facerent eleemosynas et vacarent semper iusticiae et iudicio faciendo. Unde Decretum dicit 23 q. 5: "Regum est facere iustitiam et iudicium."[32] Non invenitur quod rex debeat esse beguinus. De nobis clericis notandum quod clerici non debent gerere robas quae pertinent ad burgenses nec quae pertinent ad milites et barones, sed unusquisque secundum professionis suae conditionem debet se gerere, non diminuendo nec excedendo usum et consuetudinem.

Notandum autem, quod non est terra in mundo, quae ita habundet 6
beguinis hominibus et mulieribus ut ista. Et hoc habet ab antiquo. Unde bene sunt mille et ducenti anni elapsi, quod in Francia erant quidam sacerdotes et clerici, qui magis studebant, ut se diversificarent per habitus humiles. Et ideo Celestinus papa fecit in concilio quoddam decretum reprehendo tales et dirigitur hoc decretum episcopis parisiensibus etc. "Didicimus quosdam magis superstitioso cultui inservire"[33] etc. Item, in Deut.: *Non indues tunicam lino lanaque contextam.*[34] Glossa: "Tunica lino lanaque contexta indutus est, qui inordinate vivit."[35] Et ponit exemplum ut "si monialis acciperet sibi robam, quae pertinet ad puellam saecularem, et saecularis vir robam religiosi"[36] etc. Unde tales habitus, qui sunt legitimi, venerunt credo, ut diabolus melius posset decipere, quia ibi operatur diabolus per hypocrisim ubi nullum aliorum peccatorum potest se ingerere.

1 incutias] id est curias *E* 3 aurata] aurato *E* 10 robas] *add.* id est vestes *sup. lin.* E^C 23 robam] *add.* id est vestem *sup. lin.* E^C

[30] *Cf.* Hier., *Epist. 125* in *CSEL* 56.125; *cf.* Hild. Cen., *Epist.* in *PL* 171.155C: "Vale, atque deliciis pro regina utere, non pro te."

[31] *Cf. Rom. ord. XIV,* c.20 in *PL* 78.1132C-1133A; D.96 c.14 *Constantinus.*

[32] C.23 q.5 c.23 *Regum est.*

[33] Cel., *Epist.* in *PL* 50.430B, *forsan ex* Dion. Ex., *Coll.,* in *PL* 67.274D *vel* Pseudo-Isid., *Decret. coll.* in *PL* 130.755A.

[34] Deut. 22:11.

[35] *ord.* in Deut. 22:11 in *Ed. pr.* 1.403B; Greg., *Mor.,* in *CCSL* 143.451.

[36] *ord.* in Deut. 22:11 in *Ed. Pr.* 1.403B *(PL* 113.476B*);* Aug., *Contra Faust.* in *CSEL* 25.6.1, 301.

7 Sequitur de secundo principali, scilicet scire qui sunt vere diligentes Deum et sermonem eius. Notandum autem, quod isti sunt qui servant eum. Unde in evangelio hesterno dictum est: *Si diligitis me sermonem meum servate.*[37] Glossa: "ut faciatis,"[38] non supple, scribatis vel aures apponatis ad audiendum solum. Notandum autem, quod quinque sunt modi servandi sermonem Domini.

8 Primus est ut ponas eum ad opus vel in opus. Unde in dicto evangelio convenienter dicitur: *Qui habet mandata mea et servat ea, ille diligit me.*[39] Glossa: "qui habet sciendo et servat custodiendo."[40] In Eccli.: *Si servaveris mandata mea, servabunt te.*[41] In Matt.: *Si vis ingredi ad vitam serva mandata.*[42]

9 Secundus modus servandi sermonem Domini, est sic praedicare, quod non vendat eum. Unde qui vendit rem, eam sibi non retinet, sed tradit ementi; et etiam qui vendit sermonem Domini se damnat nec sibi proficit. Notandum autem, quod ille vendit sermonem Domini, qui praedicat, ut laudetur. Augustinus super illud ad Col.: *sive per occasionem*[43] etc. "Pseudo ex occasione evangelizant, ut quaerentes commoda sua;"[44] et potest cognosci de facili, qui sunt tales. Apostolus: *Qui gloriatur, in Domino glorietur.*[45] Augustinus in Glossa: "Ille gloriam suam quaerit, qui praedicat non vocatus a Deo."[46] Et quis sit vocatus a Deo docet Apostolus ad Heb.: *Nec quisquam accipiat sibi potestatem, sed qui vocatus est a Deo tamquam Aaron.*[47] Augustinus in Glossa: "Ille vocatur a Deo, qui ab ecclesia electus est."[48] Et isti sunt solum praelati et archdiaconi, qui gerunt vicem praelatorum, sacerdotes curati electi ab ecclesia, quia isti obtinent locum duodecim apostolorum et alii discipulorum Domini.[49] Item, secundo modo potest cognosci talis quaerens

[37] Ioan. 14:15.

[38] *int.* in Ioan. 14:15 in *Ed. pr.* 4.259a.

[39] Ioan. 14:21.

[40] *ord.* in Ioan. 14:21 in *Ed. pr.* 4.258B (*PL* 114.409A); Aug., *Tract. in Ioan.* in *CCSL* 36.517.

[41] Eccli. 15:16.

[42] Matt. 19:17.

[43] Phil. 1:18; *QDM,* n. 115; *DP,* 60*;* *QAP,* n. 30; *Dephar.,* n. 10.

[44] *ord.* in Phil 1:18 in *Ed. pr.* 4.381A; Aug., *Serm. 137* in *PL* 38.757; *DP,* 60-1; *QAP,* n. 30; *Dephar.,* n. 9.

[45] I Cor. 1:31; II Cor. 10:17; *DP,* 61; *QAP,* n. 17; *Dephar.,* n. 10.

[46] *int.* in II Cor. 10:17 in *Ed. pr.* 4.350b (*PL* 114.521C); Aug., *Enarr. in Ps.* in *CCSL* 39.840-1; *DP,* 61; *QAP,* n. 17; *Dephar.,* n. 10.

[47] Heb. 5:4; *DP,* 24, 61; *Dephar.,* n. 8.

[48] *int.* in Heb. 5:4 in *Ed. pr.* 4.430a; Aug., *Contra Faust.* in *CSEL* 25.4.1, 769; *DP,* 24, 61; *Dephar.,* n. 8.

[49] *ord.* in Luc. 10:1 in *Ed. pr.* 4.177A (*PL* 114.284A); Beda, *Expo. in Luc.* in *CCSL* 120.213-4; *DP,* 24; *QAP,* n. 17.

gloriam suam. Apostolus: *Nos in immensam non gloriamur, sed secundum mensuram quam dedit nobis Deus.*[50] Qui ergo praedicat populo, cuius curam non habet, pseudo est, nec vocatus nec rogatus. Unde talis, licet auditoribus proficiat in praedicando, tamen sibi nocet, quia se damnat. Sed sic non in confitendo, quia qui confitetur alii quam qui habet curam animae suae sine licentia illius qui habet curam animae suae, non potest absolvi.[51] Unde si sic confessus moriatur, vadit in infernum ex contemptu sui pastoris, simul confessus cum confessore. Sed modernis temporibus trahuntur paulatim quidam in infernum, quia primo confitentur aliquibus fratribus, qui dicunt quod redeant ad ipsos, et sic toto tempore vitae suae suo proprio sacerdoti non confitentur, et in morte fit totaliter testamentum eius per tales fratres, nihil sciente sacerdote, qui totum debet scire, et sic mittitur in infernum ille confessus per consilium istorum fratrum. Unde quilibet tenetur confiteri semel in anno ad minus suo proprio sacerdoti de omnibus peccatis suis,[52] nisi de aliquibus, si sint tangentia personam sacerdotis ratione affinitatis, quam habeat ad aliquos, qui sunt causa quodamodo illius peccati.

Tertius modus servandi sermonem Domini est eum praedicare propter 10
beatitudinem habendam solum. Unde[53] ille vendit sermonem Domini, qui praedicat, ut aliquod mundanum acquirat vel sibi, vel domui suae, vel religioni suae; et sunt aliqui, licet de se non accipiant, tamen per medium

5 sine ... suae] *add. in cap.* E^C

[50] II Cor. 10:13; *DP*, 25.

[51] *Extra.* V, t. 38, c. 12 *Omnis*: "Si quis autem alieno sacerdoti voluerit iusta de causa sua confiteri peccata, licentiam prius postulet et obtineat a proprio sacerdote, quum aliter ipse illum non possit absolvere vel ligare."

[52] *Extra.* V, t. 38, c. 12 *Omnis*: "Omnis utriusque sexus fidelis, postquam ad annos discretionis pervenerit, omnia sua solus peccata saltem semel in anno fideliter confiteatur proprio sacerdoti, et iniunctam sibi poenitentiam propriis viribus studeat adimplere, suscipiens reverenter ad minus in Pascha eucharistiae sacramentum, nisi forte de proprii sacerdotis consilio ob aliquam rationabilem causam ad tempus ab huiusmodi perceptione duxerit abstinendum; alioquin et vivens ab ingressu ecclesiae arceatur, et moriens Christiana careat sepultura."

[53] *Cf. Resp.*: pp. 350-1: "Item, dixit in sermone Pentecostes quod ille qui praedicat et petit aliquid per se vel per alium, vel etiam si recipit pro se petitum, quamvis non fuerit petitum ad eius suggestionem, gratiam praedicationis vendit, et est simoniacus." "Respondeo: Dixi quod, si praedicator, non missus, post suam praedicationem petat vel peti faciat ab illis aliquid quibus praedicavit, sperans eos libentius daturos propter suam praedicationem, simoniam videtur committere vendendo gratiam praedicationis, ad instar Giezi, qui petiit vestes a Naaman Syro, sperans se ab ipso habiturum, eo quod dominus eius, scilicet Eliseus, dederat ipsi Naaman gratiam sanitatis et pro tanto dixit Gregorius Nazianzenus quod Giezi vendidit Naaman Syro gratiam sanitatis, licet vestes illas pertierit Eliseo nolente."

accipiunt. Et isti odibiles sunt Deo. Unde in libro Regum habetur, quod rex quidam Naaman, qui infectus erat lepra venit ad Eliseum prophetam, virum Domini sanctum, ut per eum curaretur a lepra, et ipse fuit curatus.[54] Tunc obtulit Eliseo magna munera auri et argenti, et ipse nullo modo voluit accipere, et tunc recessit ille rex ab Eliseo. Dum distaret autem parum a domo Elisei, adhuc assecutus est eum quidam servus Elisei, et assecutus illum regem sic allocutus est eum <dicens>: "Domine, modo venerunt ad dominum meum tres pueri nobiles et ipse est pauper. Non habet quid det eis. Mittite ei de divitiis vestris, quas det eis." Hoc audiens rex laetus fuit multum et tradidit ei magna munera et pondera auri et argenti. Serviens reversus ad dominum suum, non fecit mentionem de hoc, tamen ipse Eliseus, cui Deus totum revelaverat, dicit ei: "Hoc fecisti, talem poenam portabis; propter hoc et incurres illam egritudinem quam ille rex habebat." Iste servus Giezi nuncupabatur et commisit primo simoniam. Et de hoc fecit Gregorius quoddam decretum, quod est 1 q. 1, *Giezi Naaman gratiam sanitatis vendidit*[55] etc. Sic vendere verbum Dei est periculum et praedicare propter mundana acquirenda. Unde notandum quod in recipiendo etiam sine rogatione et petitione est periculum multipliciter.

11 Primum periculum est, quod qui accipit, in accipiendo procurat excaecationem suam. In Ex.: *Munera excaecant oculos sapientium et pervertunt visum illorum.*[56]

12 Secundum periculum est, quod in hoc quod accipit, potest scire se placere istis a quibus accipit, et mundo placere malum est. Apostolus ad Gal.: *Si mundo placerem, servus Dei non essem.*[57] Glossa: "placerem, id est placere vellem."[58]

13 Tertium periculum est, quia omnis accipiens procurat negotia mundanorum. Unde sunt aliqui, qui copulant matrimonia et sunt mediatores, et ad hoc laborant, ut gratiam utriusque partis acquirant vel saltem partis alterius. Iac.: *Quicumque amicus mundi efficitur, inimicus Dei constituitur.*[59]

17 etiam] *add. sup. lin.* E^{C}

[54] IV Reg. 5; *DVM*, 340.
[55] *sub nomine Gregorii apud Grat.* C.1 q.1 c.11 *Qui studet; DVM*, 340; *QDM*, n. 17; *DP*, 64.
[56] Ex. 23:8.
[57] Gal. 1:10; *DP*, 66.
[58] *int.* in Gal. 1:10 in *Ed. pr.* 4.356a; *DP*, 66.
[59] Iac. 4:4; *DP*, 71.

14 Quartum periculum est, quod omnis accipiens, in hoc quod accipit, facit se servum. Salomon: *Qui accipit mutuo, servus est foenerantis.*[60] Multo magis qui accipit munera gratis.

15 Quintum periculum est, quod omnes accipiens perdit cor suum. Salomon: *Qui dat munera, aufert corda recipientium.*[61] Talis, qui cor amisit, non potest facere bonam dietam, nec placere Deo.

16 Tertius vel alius modus servandi sermonem Dei est verbo utendo, scilicet in ordinando verbum Dei ad salutem animae, non ad damnationem, sicut quidam, qui dicunt hominibus: "Confitere mihi, non sacerdoti tuo." Ipse ribaldus est et nihil scit, et ducit eum paulatim in infernum, quia nullus potest ipsum absolvere, nisi suus sacerdos proprius.[62] Apostolus: *Hii sunt, qui penetrant domos et captivas ducunt mulierculas.*[63] *Domos*, id est, conscientias audiendo confessiones, et dicuntur *penetrare* quia non *intrant* in *ovile per ostium*,[64] scilicet per licentiam sui praelati et sui sacerdotis; sacerdos enim est ostium conscientiae sui subditi. Talis damnat animas male consulendo eis cum debeat eas salvare, et ideo male utitur verbo Dei.

17 Quartus modus servandi sermonem Dei attenditur in sustinendo scripturam sacram et defendendo. Unde qui reprobat scripturam per scripturam aliam et per scriptas rationes, ille male servat verbum Dei. Apostolus: *Operemini manibus vestris, unde vivatis.*[65] Item, Apostolus: *Qui non laborat, non manducet.*[66] Augustinus super dictum Apostoli in Glossa sic dicit: "Vult Apostolus Christi ministros corporaliter operari, ne compellantur egestate petere aliena,"[67] et contra istud praeceptum praecipit, ne aliquis insurgat. Unde tales, qui sic reprobant praeceptum Apostoli, frangunt <silentium> sibi iniunctum ab Apostolo. Unde Augustinus in Glossa ibi dicit: "Isti qui disputant contra scripturam Apostoli tam manifeste frangunt silentium, quod eis imponit Apostolus dicens: *Cum silentio comedant panem suum.*"[68] Tamen isti debent tenere praeceptum Domini, quia dicebat totum a Spiritu Sancto. Unde ipse Apostolus: *An experimentum quaeritis eius, qui*

7 vel alius] *add. sup. lin.* E^C 20 Apostolus] Augustinus *E*

60 Pr. 22:7.
61 Pr. 22:9.
62 *Extra.* V, t. 38, c. 12 *Omnis.*
63 II Tim. 3:6; *DP*, 20, 22, 32-3, 46; *QAP*, n. 19.
64 *cf.* Ioan. 10:1; *DP*, 23, 33, 35; *QAP*, n. 19.
65 I Thess. 4:11; *DQE*, 328; *DVM*, 337; *QDM*, n. 8; *DP*, 52.
66 II Thess. 3:10; *DQE*, 329; *DVM*, 336; *QDM*, n. 6.
67 *ord.* in II Thess. 3:10 in *Ed. pr.* 4.403B (*PL* 114.624B); Aug., *De op. mon.* in *CSEL* 41.5.3, 535; *DVM*, 336; *QDM*, n. 6.
68 *int.* in II Thess. 3:10 in *Ed. pr.* 4.403b; Aug., *De op. mon.* in *CSEL* 41.5.3, 537; II Thess. 3:12.

loquitur in me Christus.[69] Et Dominus in evangelio: *Non vos estis, qui loquimini, sed Spiritus Patris vestri, qui loquitur in vobis.*[70]

18 Quinto modo non servatur sermo Domini ab illo, qui totaliter legem Dei destruit et annihilat, sicut destruitur per illum maledictum librum Ioachim, in quo faciendo multi laboraverunt.[71] Unde quinquaginta quinque anni elapsi sunt quod inceptus fuit. Et non solum peccant qui fecerunt, sed et omnes qui sciunt impugnare illum et possunt, et non impugnant, tam magistri theologiae quam sacerdotes curati et reges et principes. Et causa huius est, quia vident Dominum suum exheredari et patiuntur hoc. Et ideo merito tales exheredandi sunt. Unde Dominus vocat se regem dicens: *Rex regum et Dominus dominantium.*[72] Psalmus: *Et regni eius non erit finis.*[73] Et in Prov.: *Per me reges regnant et legislatores iudicia discernunt.*[74] Et reges patiuntur, quod Dominus noster spolietur regno suo per illum librum, quia ibi dicitur, quod regnum Dei adhuc non durabit nisi usque ad quinque annos,[75] et tunc Ordo quidam regnabit, qui ibunt nudipedes,[76] de quo exponitur ibi quod scriptum est: *Et dominabitur a mari usque ad mare, et a flumine usque ad terminos orbis terrarum.*[77] Nos tamen dicimus quod est adimpletum in Christo, quando descendit in terram. Item, per illum librum spoliatur Dominus noster suo sacerdotio,[78] quia dicitur ibi, quod deficient sacramenta ecclesiae infra quinquennium,[79] cum tamen dicat Psalmus: *Tu es sacerdos in aeternum secundum ordinem Melchisedech.*[80] Item, dicit maledictus liber ille quod evangelium Christi deficiet infra quinquennium,[81] et ita Dominus noster

69 II Cor. 13:3.

70 Matt. 10:20; *QAP*, n. 12.

71 *Cf. DP*, 38.

72 Apoc. 19:16.

73 Luc. 1:33.

74 Prov. 8:15.

75 "Quartus quod novum testamentum non durabit in virtute sua nisi per sex annos proximos futuros, videlicet ad annum dominice incarnationis MCCLX." Benz, "Exzerptsätze,"417; "...ibi enim numeratur regnum Ecclesiae, scilicet Evangelium Christi, et concluditur in 1260 annis ab Incarnatione." *DP*, 39.

76 "Septimus quod nullus simpliciter idoneus est ad instruendum homines de spiritualibus aeternis nisi illi qui nudis pedibus procedunt." Benz, "Exzerptsätze," 417.

77 Ps. 71:8.

78 "Sextus quod evangelio Christi aliud evangelium succedet et ita pro sacerdotio Christi aliud sacerdotium succedet." Benz, "Exzerptsätze," 417.

79 "Item in eodem libro in tractatu de historia de Iudith invenitur, quod sacramenta novae legis non durabunt amodo nisi per sex annos a tempore libri conditi conputandos, videlicet usque ad annum dominice Incarnationis." Benz, "Exzerptsätze," 425-6.

80 Ps. 109:4.

81 Benz, "Exzerptsätze," 416-17; *DP*, 38-9.

spoliabitur suo magisterio qui dicit: *Vos vocatis me Magister et Domine et bene dicitis; sum etenim.*[82] Tales non diliguntur a Domino, qui haec patiuntur. Sapientia: *Ego diligentes me diligo et qui mane vigilaverint ad me, invenient me.*[83]

Sequitur de tertio membro principali, scilicet quis sit fructus, qui 19
acquiritur ex observantia verbi Dei. Iste erit, quia Dominus manebit apud eum. Unde talis erit penitus sine peccato et ita erit in gaudio. Nullus qui est in peccato potest esse in gaudio perfecto. Unde tali dabit Dominus cognitionem trinitatis perfectam, quam non potest habere in hac vita mortali. *Et ad ipsum veniemus*;[84] Glossa: "Pater et Filius et Spiritus Sanctus."[85] Augustinus, in libro *De spiritu et anima* dicit, "quod homo habet duos sensus: interiorem et exteriorem; interior reficietur deitate et exterior humanitate."[86] Ita quod quando ingredietur et egredietur pascua inveniet. Et in hac vita erit immunis a peccato et in futuro habebit cognitionem trinitatis ad plenum et humanitatis assumptae in Beata Virgine.[87] Quod nobis concedat Deus. Amen

1 spoliabitur] spoliabibitus *E* 15 Amen] *add.* Finitur sermo ille *E*

[82] Ioan. 13:13.
[83] Prov. 8:17.
[84] Ioan. 14:23.
[85] *int.* in Ioan. 14:23 in *Ed. pr.* 4.259a.
[86] Pseudo-Aug., *De spiritu et anima* in *PL* 40.785.
[87] "Primus [error fratris Stephani] quod divina essentia in se nec ab homine nec ab angelo videbitur. Hunc errorem reprobamus et assertores et defensores auctoritate Wilhermi episcopi excommunicamus. Firmiter autem credimus et asserimus, quod Deus in sua essentia vel substantia videbitur ab angelis et omnibus sanctis et videtur ab animabus glorificatis." *Chart.* I, No. 128, 170-1; *Cf. Chart.* I, No. 285, 328.

<DE PHARISAEO ET PUBLICANO>

Deus gratias tibi ago, quia non sum sicut ceteri hominum: raptores, iniusti, velut 1
etiam hic Publicanus:[1] Luc. 18.

In hodierno evangelio proponit nobis Dominus in parabola duas 2
personas, quasi duo specula vel exempla; unum superbiae, videlicet Pharisaeum, et alterum humilitatis, videlicet Publicanum. In qua parabola possumus ad praesens considerare quattuor ad nostram instructionem. Primo, quid significatur per Pharisaeum et quid per Publicanum ibi: *Duo homines ascenderunt*.[2] Secundo, comparationem Pharisaei ad Publicanum et eorum dissimilitudinem ibi: *Pharisaeus autem*[3] etc. Tertio, Domini sententiam super meritis amborum ibi: *Amen dico vobis*[4] etc. Quarto, fructum parabolae sive ad quid indicatur ibi: *Quia qui se exaltat*,[5] etc.

Circa primum, notandum quod Pharisaei erant quidam religiosi apud 3
Iudaeos, sicut sunt apud nos regulares, quorum quidam extra in habitu, in austeritate vitae, in observantiis spiritualibus et traditionibus suis, praetendebant *sanctitatis speciem*,[6] quam non habebant in corde. Et isti erant hypocritae. In habitu praetendebant sanctitatem, quia membranculas, in quibus scriptus erat Decalogus, gestabant in frontibus, quasi semper

2 *Deus*] Sermo Magistri Guillelmi *praem. W* | *tibi ago*] ago tibi *transp. P* 3 18] 19 *W* 4 proponit] ponit *P* 8 significatur] signetur *A:* significentur *P:* signatur *W* 9 *ascenderunt*] considerandi *P* 10 ibi *om. P* 11 *ibi om. P* 12 ibi *om. P* | indicatur] inducatur *P: add.* parabola *P* 13 notandum *add.* est *P* 14 extra *om. P* 16 praetendebant] detendebant *W* 17 quia *add.* in *W*

[1] Luc. 18:11.
[2] Luc. 18:10.
[3] Luc. 18:11.
[4] Luc. 18:14.
[5] Luc. 18:14.
[6] *Cf.* II Tim. 3:5; *DP*, 28, 54-5; *QAP*, n. 9.

meditantes legem Dei.[7] Et etiam gestabant eas in manibus, quasi semper operantes secundum legem.[8]

4 Item, habebant quadrata pallia, in quibus fimbriae dependebant. Austeritatem vitae praetendebant in hoc, quoniam in fimbriis illis ligabant spinas acutas, quibus sive ambulando sive sedendo, pungerentur, quasi sic commoniti retraherentur ad servitium Dei.[9] Ex quo apparet quod ambulabant discalceati; aliter enim ambulando non pungerentur a spinis. Hoc dicit Glossa Matt. 23 super illud: *Dilatant phylacteria*[10] etc. "Isti autem, ut per hoc humanum gloriam assequerentur; non in claustris, non in solitudinibus habitare volebant, sed coetus et turbas hominum frequentabant."[11] Unde Matt. 23: *Amant primos recubitus in coenis, et primas cathedras in synagogis, salutationes in foro*[12] etc., quod videtur contrarium religioni. "Sicut enim piscis sine aqua vita caret, ita sine monasterio monachus," ut dicit Eugenius papa 16 q. 1 *Placuit.*[13] Unde Hieronymus ad Paulinum monachum: "Si cupis esse quod diceris monachus, id est solus, quid facis in urbibus, quae solorum non sunt habitacula, sed multorum?"[14] Isti etiam, ut maiorem gloriam apud homines obtinerent, praeferebant traditiones suas legi divinae. Unde dicit Dominus Matt. 15: *Quare transgredimini mandata Dei, propter traditiones vestras?*[15] Et ideo Pharisaei, "id

1 semper *om. W* 2 secundum] huiusmodi *W* 5 ambulando ... sedendo] ambularent ... sederent *W* 6 commoniti] commoti *P*

[7] Rutebeuf, *De regles*, ll. 33-6: "Mais il croient ces ypocrites; Qui ont les enseignes escrites; Einz vizages d'estre preudoume; Et il sont teil com je les noume."

[8] *Cf. ord.* in Matt. 23:5 in *Ed. pr.* 4.71A: "...datis mandatis per Moysen intulit dominus ligabis ea in manu tua et erunt immota ante oculos tuos, id est sunt tibi in opere et meditatione. Et Pharisaei male interpretantes scribebant decalogum in membranuculas et ligabant in fronte per quod religiosi viderentur populis." Hier., *Comm. in Matt.* in *CCSL* 77.211.

[9] *Cf. ord.* in Matt. 23:5 in *Ed. pr.* 4.71A: "Iusserat etiam Moyses ut in quattuor angulis palliorum facerent fimbrias ut per hoc essent discreti israelitici populi. Illi vero faciebant grandes fimbrias et in eis ligabant acutas spinas ut eundo et sedendo interdum pungerentur quasi sic commoniti retraherentur ad officia Dei." Hier., *Comm. in Matt.* in *CCSL* 77.211-2.

[10] Matt. 23:5.

[11] *int.* in Matt. 23:5 in *Ed. pr.* 4.71a.

[12] Matt. 23:6-7.

[13] C.16 q.1 c.8 *Placuit.*

[14] Hier., *Epist. 63* in *CSEL* 54.1, 533; C.16 q.1 c.5 *Si cupis.*

[15] Matt. 15:3.

est, divisi a populo dicebantur."[16] Unde dicit Glossa Matt. 3 super illud: *Videns Ioannes multos Pharisaeorum venientes ad baptismum,*[17] scilicet propter gloriam etiam maiorem humanam, faciebant quidam eorum se scribas, id est legis doctores, ut in maiori reverentia haberentur tamquam magistri.[18] Unde Matt. 23: *Amant ab hominibus vocari Rabbi,*[19] "id est magistri,"[20] dicitur de Pharisaeis. Unde ibidem supra: *Super cathedram Moysi sederunt Scribae et Pharisaei, quae dicunt, facite.*[21] Patet ergo quod aliqui Pharisaei erant simul et scribae, quia non sedebant in cathedris, nisi scribae, id est legis doctores, et isti peiores erant aliis Pharisaeis.[22] Unde in uno eodemque sermone gravius invehitur Dominus contra eos, comminans eis et praedicans mortem aeternam, dicens octies Matt. 23: *Vae vobis Scribae et Pharisaei hypocritae.*[23] Isti Pharisaei hypocritae praecipue procuraverunt mortem Salvatoris, exhibentes etiam ministros Iudae proditori ad capiendum Dominum, Ioan. 18: *Iudas cum accepisset cohortem, et a Pontificibus et Pharisaeis ministros, venit illuc cum laternis, et facibus, et armis.*[24]

Per praedictum Pharisaeum qui erat hypocrita, ut ostendetur inferius, 5
significantur hypocritae nostri temporis, et praecipue illi qui in habitu et gestu exteriori et ostentatione vitae austerioris et spiritualibus observantiis per suas traditiones inventis, *speciem sanctitatis* et religionis praetendunt, ut ab hominibus laudentur et honorentur, videlicet falsi religiosi, quod ex eorum operibus cognosci potest, Matt. 7: *A fructibus eorum cognoscetis eos.*[25] Non dico ab illis operibus quae ipsi ostentant ut sanctiores videantur; illa

2 scilicet *om. P* 5 *vocari ante ab P* 6 ibidem supra] dicit evangelium *A:* supra evangelium *W* 7 Patet ergo] Ex quo patet *P* | erant simul] simul (similter *A*) erant *transp. AW* | et] etiam *W* 10 praedicans] comminans *P* 17 significantur] signantur *W* 18 spiritualibus] *P:* specialibus *W* 20 ex *om. W* 21 cognosci] *P:* coniicitur *A:* concuri *W* | 7] 17 *W*

[16] *ord.* in Matt. 3:7 in *Ed. pr.* 4.11B (*PL* 114.80B); Hrab. Maur., *Comm. in Matt.* in *PL* 107.770B; *SQD*, n. 5.

[17] Matt. 3:7.

[18] *Cf.* Luc. 7:30.

[19] Matt. 23:6-7.

[20] *int.*in Matt. 23:7 in *Ed. pr.* 4.71a.

[21] Matt. 23:2-3.

[22] *int.*in Matt. 7:29 in *Ed. pr.* 4.31b.

[23] Matt. 23:13-29.

[24] Ioan. 18:3.

[25] Matt. 7:16; *DP*, 29, 36.

enim bona esse apparent hominibus. Unde Glossa ibidem: "In conspectu hominum similes sunt ministris iustitiae, dum ieiunant, orant, eleemosynas dant; sed non sunt eorum fructus, quia pro vitio eis reputantur,"[26] videlicet propter vanam gloriam ad quam tendunt. Sed ab illis operibus cognoscuntur, quae ipsi non ostentant; sed tamen ea faciunt ut mundi gloriam vel delicias assequantur. Sunt enim quidam illorum *voluptatum amatores magis quam Dei,*[27] ut dicit Apostolus II Tim. 3.

6 Ad cognoscendum autem Pharisaeos et scribas hypocritas per ipsorum opera quae sub *pietatis specie*[28] machinantur, ponit Deus quattuor signa infallibilia, quoniam mentiri non potest, dicens Matt. 23: *Amant primos recubitus in coenis, primas cathedras in synagogis, salutationes in foro, et vocari ab hominibus Rabbi.*[29]

7 Circa primum signum notandum, quod *illi primos recubitus in coenis* videntur *amare,* qui coenas publicas regum et principum et praelatorum sectantur, sedentes in capitibus mensarum, ut ab hominibus honorentur et delicate pascantur. Quod in viris regularibus, et praecipue in praedicatoribus, non bene sedet. Unde super illud Matt. 12: *Qui mollibus vestiuntur in domibus regum sunt.*[30] Dicit Glossa: "Rigida vita et praedicatio," id est regulares et praedicatores, "declinare debent mollium palatia quae frequentant, mollibus indutis adulantes."[31] Nisi enim adulatores essent, non diutius amarentur in curiis, cum sint manibus otiosi, ut dicit Glossa super illud II Thess. 3: *Non quasi non habuerimus potestatem,*[32] etc. Glossa: "Qui ad alienam mensam frequenter convenit otio deditus, aduletur necesse est pascenti se; cum tamen religio nostra ad libertatem homines advocet, videlicet ut libere dicant veritatem et non adulentur."[33] Ideo Apostolus, licet potestatem haberet vivendi de evangelio, tamquam missus a Domino, ut

1 conspectu] despectu *W* 4 ad quam tendunt] quam praetendunt *W* 6 *voluptatum*] voluptatis *P* 11 *recubitus*] accubitus *P* 13 notandum] *add.* est *P* 15 honorentur] honorifice *P* 17 praedicatoribus] viris *praem. W* | 12] 11 *W* 20 indutis] induti *P* 25 Apostolus licet] l. A. *transp. P*

[26] *ord.* in Matt. 7:15 in *Ed. pr.* 4.30B (*PL* 114.110C); Aug., *De serm. Dom.* in *CCSL* 35.179; *DP*, 29, 36-7, *QAP*, n. 12.

[27] II Tim. 3:4; *DP*, 22.

[28] II Tim. 3:5.

[29] Matt. 23:6-7.

[30] Matt. 11:8.

[31] *ord.* in Matt. 11:8 in *Ed. pr.* 4.41A (*PL* 114.120C); Hier., *Comm. in Matt.* in *CCSL* 77.79.

[32] II Thess. 3:9; *DQE*, 327; *DVM*, 339; *DP*, 49, 69.

[33] *ord.* in II Thess. 3:9 in *Ed. pr.* 4.403B (*PL* 114.624B); Amb., *Comm. in Epist. ad Thess.* in *PL* 17.485C; *DQE*, 327; *DVM*, 339; *QDM*, n. 7; *DP*, 49, 69.

ipse probat I Cor. 9 dicens: *Non sum liber? Non sum Apostolus?*[34] etc., volebat tamen potius vivere de labore manuum suarum, "ne cuiquam onerosus esset vel adulari necesse haberet."[35] Illi ergo qui potestatem apostolicam non habent, utpote qui non praesunt regimini animarum, non de evangelio debent vivere, sed potius de labore manuum suarum. II Thess. 3: *Neque enim gratis manducavimus panem ab aliquo, sed in labore et fatigatione.*[36] Glossa: "Id est in labore fatigante, scilicet labore manuum, nocte et die laborantes."[37] Glossa: "Tunc isti pseudo, magis vivere debent de labore, quoniam non habent potestatem hanc quam nos habemus, videlicet potestatem apostolicam."[38] Hanc enim habent soli episcopi et alii rectores ecclesiarum vel eorum vicarii,[39] ut dicit Glossa super illud Psalmi: *Pro patribus tuis nati sunt tibi filii*[40] et 68 D. *Quorum vices.*[41] Heb. 5: *Nec enim quisquam sibi assumit honorem, sed qui vocatur a Deo tamquam Aaron.*[42] Glossa: "A Deo vocatur, qui ab ecclesia recte eligitur."[43]

Item, illi videntur *amare primos recubitus in coenis,* qui ut splendide 8
pascantur in domibus divitum et potentum, curiosi existunt de negotiis eorum, et propter illa tradenda discurrunt contra quos Apostolus II Thess. 3: *Ipsi enim scitis, quoniam non inquieti fuimus inter vos.*[44] Glossa: "Id est curiosi, ut illi qui aliena negotia curant, vagantes hac et illac."[45] Et infra: *Audivimus enim quosdam inter vos ambulare inquiete, nihil operantes, sed curiose agentes.*[46] Glossa: "De negotiis alienis, et hoc modo pasci merentur; quod factum

2 ne ... suarum *om. AW* 7 Glossa *om. P* 8 Tunc ... magis] Id est multo magis isti pseudo *P* | vivere debent] d. v. *transp. P* 9 quoniam] qui *W* 12 68 D.] habetur D. 68 *P* 17 tradenda] tractanda *P*: *add.* huc et illuc *P* 18 Glossa *om. W* 20 *quosdam inter vos*] i. vos q. *W*

[34] I Cor. 9:1.

[35] *Cf. ord.* in I Cor. 9:1 in *Ed. pr.* 4.320A; Amb., *Comm. in Epist. ad Cor.* in *PL* 17.241B.

[36] II Thess. 3:8; *DQE*, 328; *DP*, 60.

[37] *int.*in II Thess. 3:8 in *Ed. pr.* 4.403b.

[38] *int.*in II Thess. 3:8 in *Ed. pr.* 4.403b; *DP*, 60.

[39] *int.*in Ps. 44:17 in *Ed. pr.* 2.509b; Aug., *Enarr. in Ps.* in *CCSL* 38.516.

[40] Ps. 44:17.

[41] D.68 c.6 *Quorum vices.*

[42] Heb. 5:4; *DP*, 24, 61; *SQD*, n. 9.

[43] *int.*in Heb. 5:4 in *Ed. pr.* 4.430b; Aug., *Contra Faust.* in *CSEL* 25.4.1, 769; *DP*, 24, 61; *SQD*, n. 9.

[44] II Thess. 3:7; *DP*, 48.

[45] *ord.* in II Thess. 3:7 in *Ed. pr.* 4.403B; *cf.* Aug., *De op. mon.* in *CSEL* 41.5.3, 585-6; *DP*, 48.

[46] II Thess. 3:11; *QDM*, n. 107; *DP*, 48.

abhorret disciplina dominica. *Quorum enim Deus venter est,*[47] qui hac foeda cura necessaria sibi provident,"[48] videlicet procurando negotia aliena.

9 Secundum signum datum a Domino ad cognoscendum scribas et Pharisaeos hypocritas est, quoniam *amant primas cathedras in synagogis.*[49] *Primas cathedras amare* videntur *in synagogis,* qui in congregationibus, quae fiunt in ecclesiis propter aliquas solemnitates, procurant, ut vocentur ad cathedram praedicantis, plerumque a principe saeculari qui potestatem ad hoc vocandi non habet; non deferentes in hac parte episcopis et aliis praelatis, nec expectant quod ab eis vocentur, sed per tales vocationes minus canonicas se ingerunt ad praedicandum plebibus alienis contra illud Apostoli Rom.10: *Quomodo praedicabunt, nisi mittantur?*[50] Nec enim episcopus praedicare potest publice plebi alterius episcopi 9 q. 2[51] *Episcopum,* nisi ab eo vel plebano illius plebis ad hoc invitatus 7 q. 1 *Episcopi vel Presbyteri.*[52] Qui enim ingerit se ad praedicandum populo, super quem non habet a Domino potestatem, non Dei gloriam, sed suam quaerit. II Cor. 10: *Qui gloriatur, in Domino glorietur.*[53] Glossa: "Quod non potest ille qui non habet a Domino potestatem; talis enim, si praedicet, gloriam suam quaerit."[54] Phil. 2 super illud: *Sive per occasionem, sive per veritatem Christus annuntietur*[55] etc. Glossa: "Pseudo ex occasione evangelizant, quaerentes commoda sua, vel pecuniaria, vel honorum vel laudis humanae."[56] Tales praedicatores volunt plus in sua praedicatione commendari sapientiam aut eloquentiam suam quam ipsam rem praedictam, sicut faciebant pseudo. I Thess. 2 dicit Apostolus: *Neque quaerentes ab hominibus gloriam.*[57] Glossa: "Tangit pseudo,

3 Secundum] Sed tamen *W* 9 praelatis] *add.* qui praesentes existunt *P* 11 10] 11 *W* 12 9] 60 *W* 14 ingerit se] se i. *transp. P* 15 suam] *add.* propriam *P* 20 volunt] *post* plus *P* 21 sapientiam] sapientia *P* | eloquentiam suam] eloquentia sua *P* 22 I] 2 *W* 23 Glossa] Unde *praem. P*

[47] Phil. 3:19; Rom. 16:18; *DVM,* 342; *DP,* 48, 68.

[48] *ord.* in II Thess. 3:11 in *Ed. pr.* 4.403B; Amb., *Comm. in Epist. ad Thess.* in *PL* 17.406B; *DP,* 48.

[49] Matt. 23:6.

[50] Rom. 10:15; *DP,* 24, 36, 58; *QAP,* n. 17.

[51] C.9 q.2 c.7 *Episcopum non debere.*

[52] C.7 q.1 c.38 *Episcopi vel Presbyteri.*

[53] I Cor. 1:31; II Cor. 10:17 *DP,* 61; *QAP,* n. 17; *SQD,* n. 9.

[54] *int.*in II Cor. 10:17 in *Ed. pr.* 4.350b (*PL* 114.521C); Aug., *Enarr. in Ps.* in *CCSL* 39.840-1; *DP,* 61; *QAP,* n. 17; *SQD,* n. 9.

[55] Phil. 1:18; *QDM,* n. 115; *DP,* 60; *QAP,* n. 30; *SQD,* n. 9.

[56] *ord.* in Phil 1:18 in *Ed. pr.* 4.381A; Aug., *Sermo 137* in *PL* 38.757; *DP,* 60-1; *QAP,* n. 30; *SQD,* n. 9.

[57] I Thess. 2:6; *DP,* 60; *QAP,* n. 17.

qui se potius quam Dei doctrinam commendari volebant; Apostolus autem, qui non ad praesens sed in futuro gloriam quaerebat, se humilem faciebat ut Dei praedicatio exaltaretur."[58] Unde I Cor. 1: *Non in sapientia verbi*[59] etc. Glossa: "Qui Christi doctrinam verbis exornare vult, obscurat illam splendore verborum, ut non illa, sed ipse laudetur."[60]

Sed quare ita ostentant sapientiam et eloquentiam suam? Hoc ideo, ut 10
eorum doctrina praeferatur doctrinae saecularium et simplicium praelatorum, sicut et faciebant pseudo. II Cor. 11 super illud: *Nam si imperitus sermone.*[61] Glossa: "Corinthii praeferabant pseudo veris Apostolis, causa accurati sermonis."[62] Et quod sola ostentatione sapientiae et eloquentiae hoc faciant, et ut libentius audiantur, ex hoc patet, quoniam non aliud praedicant quam praelati, licet magis ornate, sicut dicit Glossa super illud II Cor. 11: *Existimo me nihil eiusmodi fecisse a magnis Apostolis.*[63] Glossa: "Quidam favebant pseudo a quibus compositis verbis eadem audiebant, quae ab Apostolo incompositis."[64] Non enim erant Apostoli eloquentes, sed pseudo componebant verba, ut dicit Glossa in eodem capitulo super illud: *Nam si imperitum sermone,*[65] "tales autem, quia periculosi sunt, iubet Dominus evitari."[66] Luc. 20: *Attendite a scribis, qui amant primas cathedras in synagogis.*[67] Glossa: "Duplici ratione iubemur attendere a vanae gloriae cupidine, ne vel eorum simulatione decipiamur vel eorum exemplo ad amorem temporalis gloriae inflammemur."[68]

2 quaerebat] querit *W* 3 Cor.] Rom. *W* 8 super illud *om. P* 9 *sermone*] *P*: servire *A*: servirem *W* 11 ex hoc patet] ex eo apparet *P* 14 pseudo] Pseudoapostolos *A*: Pseudoapostolis *P* 18 evitari] vitari *W* 20 cupidine] cupidis *P* | ne *om. W*

[58] *ord.* in I Thess. 2:5 in *Ed. pr.* 4.395B (*PL* 114.616D); Amb., *Comm. in Epist. ad Thess.* in *PL* 17.469C; *DP*, 60; *QAP*, n. 17.

[59] I Cor. 1:17.

[60] *ord.* in I Cor. 1:17 in *Ed. pr.* 4.308A; Amb., *Comm. in Epist. ad Cor.* in *PL* 17.198B.

[61] II Cor. 11:6; *DP*, 34, 61; *QAP*, n 17.

[62] *ord.* in II Cor. 11:6 in *Ed. pr.* 4.351A (*PL* 114.556D); Amb., *Comm. in Epist. ad Cor.* in *PL* 17.339C; *DP*, 34, 61; *QAP*, n. 17.

[63] II Cor. 11:5; *QAP*, n. 17.

[64] *ord.* in II Cor. 11:5 in *Ed. pr.* 4.351A (*PL* 114.566D); Amb., *Comm. in Epist. ad Cor.* in *PL* 17.339B; *QAP*, n. 17.

[65] II Cor. 11:6; *DP*, 34, 61.

[66] *ord.* in II Cor. 11:6 in *Ed. pr.* 4.351A; *DP*, 34, 61.

[67] Luc. 20:46.

[68] *ord.* in Luc. 20:46 in *Ed. pr.* 4.210A (*PL* 114.333D); Beda, *Expo. in Luc.* in *CCSL* 120.361.

11 Tertium signum datum a Domino ad cognoscendum scribas et Pharisacos hypocritas est, quoniam *amant salutationes in foro.*[69] "Forum," ut dicit Isidorus, "est exercendarum litium locus."[70] Illi ergo Pharisaei, id est regulares, qui procurant et amant ut vocentur ad consistoria principium et praelatorum et eadem frequentant, sedentes ibi pro tribunali ad iudicandum vel assessores existentes, ut eis litigantes reverentiam iudicialem exhibeant, et salutent eos capite inclinato, *salutationes in foro amare* videntur, cum secundum Apostolum hoc eis non liceat. II Tim. 2: *Nemo militans Deo implicat se saecularibus negotiis, ut ei placeat cui se probavit.*[71] De antiquis et veris sanctis cantat ecclesia, contemnentes aulas regias pervenerunt ad regna coelestia. Igitur ab oppositis, amantes aulas regias pervenient ad ignominiam infernalem, unde dolendum.

12 Quartum signum est, quoniam *amant ab hominibus vocari Rabbi.* Hoc signum videtur esse in illis Pharisaeis sive regularibus, qui cum sint in statu perfectionis, et eis dictum sit a Domino: *Nolite vocari Rabbi,*[72] Matt. 23. Et paulo post: *Nec vocemini Magistri.*[73] In quorum primo prohibetur eis nominis magistri desiderium;[74] in secundo vero, ipsum magistri vocabulum. Ipsi tamen nihilominus per multorum excommunicationem et per alia scandala procurant ut magistri vocentur.

13 Sed dicet quis: "Non appetunt magisterii nomen propter ipsum nomen, sed propter animarum utilitatem, videlicet quia plus creditur de salute animarum magistris quam non magistris." Sed quaero, quare est hoc? Respondebis: "Quia praesumitur in eis maior sapientia, et melius et discretius sciunt praedicare et docere." Sed vide quam sit hoc longe a veritate! Magisterium enim et profunditas litterarum indifferens est ad bonum et malum. Magni magistri enim fuerunt Arius et Sabellius, Eutyches et Nestorius in divinis litteris, et tamen haeresiarchae fuerunt.

1 cognoscendum] cognoscendos *P* 2 Forum] Forus *P et Isidorus* 7 salutent] salutant *W* 8 Tim.] Thess.: *om. W* 13 signum] *add.* Scribarum et Pharisaeorum hypocritarum *P* | *vocari ante ab P* 18 nihilominus *om. P* 20 Non] Sicut *W* 22 quare est] cur *P* 23 Respondebis] Respondebunt *P* | Quia] Quod *P* 24 discretius] disertius *P* | sit hoc] hoc sit *transp. P* 26 magistri enim] e. m. *transp. P*

69 Matt. 23:7.

70 Isid., *Etymol.* XVIII.15.1 p. 402: "Forus est exercendarum litium locus..."

71 II Tim. 2:4; *DP*, 48.

72 Matt. 23:8.

73 Matt. 23:10.

74 *int.* in Matt. 23:10 in *Ed. pr.* 4.71a.

Item, cum Apostolus sciret quid esset utile animabus, si scivisset 14
eminentiam sapientiae et eloquentiae, quae in magisterio attenditur, utilem esse profectui animarum, eis utique in praedicando usus fuisset, cuius contrarium dicit I Cor. 2: *Et ego, cum venissem ad vos, fratres, veni non in sublimitate sermonis aut sapientiae, annuntians testimonium Iesu Christi;*[75] *nihil enim me iudicavi scire inter vos, nisi Iesum Christum, et hunc crucifixum.*[76] *Non enim in sermone est regnum Dei, sed in virtute,*[77] I Cor. 4. Sed vide qualiter Apostolus confirmabat praedicationem suam: non utique per magisterium, non per ostentationem sapientiae aut eloquentiae, sed per humilitatem patientiae, per miracula, per opera virtutum. II Cor. 12: *Signa Apostolatus mei facta sunt super vos in omni patientia, in signis, et prodigiis, et virtutibus.*[78] Glossa: "Castitate et ceteris operibus virtutum."[79] Miracula tamen hodie suspecta essent, cum iam simis *in novissimis diebus*[80] aut prope novissimos dies, de quibus dicitur Matt. 24: *Surgent Pseudoprophetae, et seducent multos.*[81] Et Marc. 13: *Exurgent Pseudoprophetae, et dabunt signa et prodigia ad seducendum, si fieri potest, etiam electos.*[82]

Item, si non sufficit tibi exemplum Apostoli ad ostendendum quod 15
praedicator propter magisterium suum non plus proficit animabus quam alius, do tibi exemplum Christi, qui cum inter discipulos suos haberet quosdam magistros bonos et sanctos, videlicet Nathanaelem, de quo dixit Ioan. 1: *Ecce vere Israelita, in quo dolus non est*[83] et Nicodemum, cui dixit Ioan. 3: *Tu es magister in Israel*[84] etc. Neutrum tamen legitur misisse ad praedicandum; sed alios discipulos simplices et imperitos misit, et ex discipulis, Apostolos sive missos fecit. Matt. 10: *Ecce ego mitto vos.*[85] Glossa: "De discipulis missos vos facio."[86] Sic ergo habemus quattuor signa praedicta, per

1 si scivisset] et sciret *W* 3 utilem] utile *W* | usus] necesse *W* 4 dicit] dicitur *W* 12 virtutum *om. P* 18 quam alius *ante* proficit *P* 19 suos *om. P*

[75] Cor. 2:1; *DP*, 71.

[76] I Cor. 2:2.

[77] I Cor. 4:20.

[78] II Cor. 12:12; *DP*, 58.

[79] *int.* in II Cor. 12:12 in *Ed. pr.* 4.353b; *DP*, 58.

[80] II Tim. 3:1.

[81] Matt. 24:11; *DP*, 40, 59; *QAP*, n. 12.

[82] Marc. 13:22.

[83] Ioan. 1:47.

[84] Ioan. 3:10.

[85] Matt. 10:16; *DP*, 65; *QAP*, n. 35.

[86] *int.* in Matt. 10:16 in *Ed. pr.* 4.39a.

quae cognosci possunt scribae et Pharisaei hypocritae, id est, falso simulantes religionem exterius, quam non habent in corde.

16 Nunc restat videre, cuiusmodi homines significantur per Publicanum. Publicani uno modo dicebantur "publica vectigalia exigentes,"[87] alio modo "sua mercimonia publicantes";[88] alio modo, homines communi modo viventes, non se a communi vita hominum distinguentes. Per Publicanum significantur homines saeculares, qui etsi sint pecccatores, tamen sanctitatem non simulant, sed se peccatores cognoscunt. Deinde tam apud Deum quam apud homines humiliantur, et sibi ipsis indignantur, quod eis prodest. Is. 63: *Indignatio mea auxiliata est mihi.*[89] Nec erubescunt confiteri peccata sua,[90] iuxta illud Eccli. 4: *Non confundaris confiteri peccata.*[91] Et ideo tales de facili veniam assequuntur. Psalm. 31: *Dixi confitebor adversum me.*[92]

17 Viso cuiusmodi homines significentur per Pharisaeum et cuiusmodi per Publicanum, quod erat prima pars sermonis nostri; secundo videndum est comparatione utriusque. Et primo videamus superbiam Pharisaei, deinde humilitatem Publicani. Pharisaeus superbus, ostentans se iustum, primo iactat se de prima parte, quae est declinare a malo, dicens se immunem esse a peccatis tam spiritualibus quam carnalibus. Inter spiritualia, causa exempli, asserit se immunem ab iniusta rerum alienarum ablatione seu detentione cum dicit: *Non sum sicut ceteri hominum: raptores.*[93] Deinde asserit se immunem ab avara rerum suarum retentione, cum dicit: *iniusti.*[94] Iniusti enim sunt, qui res proprias avare retinent, quae debent pauperibus communicare. Eccli. 4: *Declina aurem pauperi sine tristitia, et redde ei debitum tuum.*[95] Postea asserit se immunem a peccatis carnalibus, et gratia exempli,

3 significantur] *A*: significentur *P*: signantur *W* 4 alio ... publicantes *om. P* 7 significantur] signantur *AW* 8 cognoscunt] agnoscunt *P* | Deinde] Et exinde *P* 11 *peccata*] *add.* tua *P* 12 31] *om. W* | *me*] *add.* iniustitiam meam Domino et tu remisisti impietatem peccati mei *P* 15 comparatione] *add.* sive controversia *AW* | deinde] secundo *P* 17 esse *om. P* 18 tam] *ante* a *P*: *add.* a *W* | quam *add.* a *W* | Inter ... exempli] Primo quidem a peccatis spiritualibus quia *P* 20 asserit se immunem *om. P* 24 asserit se immunem] vero *P* | et ... exempli] quia *P*

[87] *int.* in Matt. 5:46 in *Ed. pr.* 4.23b.

[88] *int.* in Matt. 5:46 in *Ed. pr.* 4.23b.

[89] Is. 63:5.

[90] *Cf.* Luc. 18:13.

[91] Eccli. 4:31.

[92] Ps. 31:5.

[93] Luc. 18:11.

[94] Luc. 18:11.

[95] Eccli. 4:8.

ponit adulterium cum dicit: *adulteri.*[96] Consequenter iactat se habere secundam partem iustitiae, quae est facere bonum. Primo asserit corpus suum sacrificare Deo per abstinentiam, cum dicit: *Ieiuno bis in Sabbato;*[97] deinde iactat se bona sua dedicare Deo cum dicit: *Decimas do omnium quae possideo.*[98]

Circa superbiam et iactantiam Pharisaei nota quinque.

Primo nota, cum deberet missam suam incipere a *Confiteor*, id est, 18
orationem suam ab accusatione sui, Prov. 18: *Iustus prior est accusator sui,*[99] missam suam reversat, incipiens a Deo gratias, dicens in principio orationis suae: *Deus, gratias tibi ago, quia non sum sicut ceteri hominum.*[100]

Secundo nota quod, cum de aliis peccatis se iactet immunem, non 19
tamen de hypocrisi, quoniam forsan non cognoscebat se esse hypocritam. Talis enim est natura huius morbi, quod cum fuerit radicatus, ignorat eum morbosus, quia credit se sanctum apud Deum, sicut apud homines sanctus reputatur. Unde Moralium lib. 15 super illud Iob 20: *Velut somnium avolans non invenitur,*[101] dicit Gregorius: "Hypocritae, dum ab hominibus immoderate laudantur, tales se apud Deum existimant, quales se gaudent hominibus innotuisse. Unde fit ut de humanis favoribus hic exultant, in futuro se habituros requiem omnino non dubitent."[102]

Tertio nota quod, cum ipse Publicanum de nullo peccato arguat, hoc 20
solum reputat eum peccatorem, quoniam est Publicanus et non Pharisaeus, sicut ipse dicens: *velut etiam hic Publicanus.*[103] Hic est enim mos hypocritarum, quod omnes illos, qui non sunt hypocritae, reputant peccatores; unde et alios ad imitationem invitant. Unde Moralium 8 super illud Iob 8: *Si absorbuerit de loco suo*[104] etc., dicit Gregorius: "Utinam hypocritis

1 Consequenter] Secundo *P* 10 *tibi ago*] ago tibi *transp. P* 12 forsan] forte *P* | cognoscebat] agnoscebat *P* 13 natura huius] naturalis *W* | quod] cui *A* | radicatus] dedicatus *W* 14 morbosus] morbus *W* | quia credit] eorum est *W* 15 reputatur] deputatur *W* 17 gaudent *add.* ut *W* 21 solum] solo *P* 22 Hic] Hoc *W* 24 imitationem] simulationem *P*

[96] Luc. 18:11.

[97] Luc. 18:12.

[98] Luc. 18:12.

[99] Prov. 18:17.

[100] *Cf. supra*, n. 1.

[101] Iob 20:8.

[102] Greg., *Mor.* in *CCSL* 143A.753.

[103] Luc. 18:11.

[104] Iob 8:18.

perditio sua sola sufficeret, et nequaquam alios ad vi[t]am duplicitatis instigarent. Hoc namque uniuscuiusque proprium esse solet, ut qualis ipse fuerit, tales sibi coniungi et alios velit, simplicitatem vitae defugiat, atque hoc imitandum imprimat quod amat. Unde apud hypocritarum sensum, simplicitas omnis in crimine est. Apertas quippe mentes diiudicant et puritatem cordis hebetudinem appellant."[105]

21 Quarto nota, quod in omnibus de quibus se iactat iste Pharisaeus, mentitur. Primo mentitur in hoc, quod se asserit *non raptorem*;[106] immo certe raptor est, usurpando sibi titulum bonitatis qui soli Deo convenit. Mar. 10: *Nemo bonus, nisi solus Deus.*[107] Secundo mentitur, asserens se non esse iniustum;[108] immo certe iniustus est proximum, scilicet Publicanum, temere iudicando. Rom.14: *Tu quis es, qui iudicas servum alienum? Domino suo stat, aut cadit.*[109] Tertio mentitur, dicens se non esse adulterum; immo *adulter*[110] est propriam sponsam Domini sui, quam sibi soli retinuit, sibi usurpando, scilicet gloriam, quae soli Deo debetur. Is. 42: *Gloriam meam alteri non dabo.*[111] Quarto mentitur, dicens *ieiuno*;[112] immo certe solvit ieiunium suum vilissimo pane, videlicet pane serpentis infernalis, scilicet pane vanae gloriae de quo legitur: *Serpenti pulvis panis eius.*[113] Quinto mentitur, dicens *decimas do*;[114] immo certe non dat, sed reddit tamquam tributum suum ad quod tenetur, quia "decimae tributa sunt egentium animarum"[115] ut dicit Augustinus 16 q. 1 *Decimae.* Mal. 3: *Inferte omnem decimam in horrea mea, ut sit cibus in domo mea.*[116] Mentiuntur ergo illi, qui dicunt decimas esse ceremoniales et non deberi modo nisi secundum consuetudinem religionis, cum dicit

1 perditio sua] sua praedictio *P* 3 velit] vere ut *W* | defugiat] refugiat *P* 7 nota] notatur *W* 12 *Domino suo*] suo D. *transp.* *W* 13 esse *om.* *W* 18 legitur] Is. 65 *P* 21 *decimam*] *Vulgata:* decimationem *APW* 23 religionis] regiminis *W*

[105] Greg., *Mor.* in *CCSL* 143.449.
[106] Luc. 18:11.
[107] Marc. 10:18.
[108] Luc. 18:11.
[109] Rom. 14:4; *DP*, 23, 33.
[110] Luc. 18:11.
[111] Is. 42:8.
[112] Luc. 18:12.
[113] Is. 65:25.
[114] Luc. 18:12.
[115] C.16 q.1 c.66 *Decimae.*
[116] Mal. 3:10.

Augustinus: "Qui sibi aut praemium comparare, aut peccatorum desiderat indulgentiam promereri, reddat decimam; et de novem partibus studeat facere eleemosynam pauperibus."[117] 16 q. 1 *Decimae.* Et Ambrosius dicit: "Quid est fideliter decimam dare, nisi ut nec minus nec peius decima parte offerat de grano aut de vino aut de fructibus arborum, aut de pecoribus,aut de horto, aut de negotio, aut de propria venatione sua?"[118] Sic ergo apparet Pharisaeum culpabilem esse de omnibus, de quorum contrariis se iactabat. Et ita apparet superbia et hypocrisis Pharisaei.

Nunc videamus e contrario humilitatem Publicani, quae apparet in 22
quattuor. Primo, quia reputans se indignum et despicians seipsum, reveretur accedere ad sacra. Unde dicitur: *Publicanus stans a longe,*[119] quod est contra illos qui irreverenter approprinquant altari dum missa celebratur. Non sic centurio Matt. 8: *Domine, non sum dignus, ut intres sub tectum meum.*[120] Non sic Petrus Luc. 5: *Exi a me, Domine quia homo peccator sum.*[121]

Secundo in hoc, quia *oculos non audet ad coelum levare*[122] quasi iudicans se 23
reum apud Dominum coeli. Rei enim est faciem non levare II Reg. 2. Dicit Abner ad Asael: *Noli me sequi, ne compellar confoedere te in terram, et non potero levare faciem meam ad fratrem tuum Ioab,*[123] quod est contra illos qui scientes se esse in peccato mortali, irreverenter aspiciunt corpus Christi. Cum tamen Oza Levita, quia pollutus tetigit arcam Domini, volens etiam iuvare ne caderet bobus recalcitrantibus, morte perpessus est. II Reg. 6.[124]

Tertio, quia *percutiendo pectus,*[125] sub quo est cor, detestabatur peccata sua, 24
quae ex corde procedunt,[126] Matt. 20.

5 offerat] offeratur *P* 11 reveretur] veretur *P* 14 Non] Et *W* 16 Secundo] *add.* apparet humilitas Publicani *P* | quia] quod *P* 17 Dominum coeli] c. D. *transp. P* 18 *confoedere*] foedere *W*: confoedere W^c

[117] C.16 q.1 c.66 *Decimae.*

[118] C.16 q.7 c.4 *Quiscumque recognoverit.*

[119] Luc. 18:13.

[120] Matt. 8:8.

[121] Luc. 5:8.

[122] Luc. 18:13.

[123] II Reg. 2:22.

[124] *Cf.* II Reg. 6:6-7.

[125] Luc. 18:13.

[126] Matt. 15:18

25 Quarto, quia non erubescit confiteri peccata sua et ponere ante oculos misericordiae Domini, dicens: *Domine, propitius esto mihi peccatori*[127] iuxta consilium Eccli. 4: *Pro anima tua non confundaris dicere verum, est enim confusion adducens gloriam.*[128] I Ioan. 1: *Si confiteamur peccata nostra, fidelis est Deus et iustus, ut dimittat nobis peccata nostra.*[129] Vere iustum est hoc, propter verecundiam et erubescentiam quae est in confitendo.[130] Unde Moralium 22 super illud Iob 31: *Si abscondi peccatum meum,*[131] dicit Gregorius: "Mirentur in Iob alii integritatem iustitiae, mirentur viscera pietatis; ego in eo non minus admiror confessionem humillimam peccatorum, quam tot sublima gesta virtutum. Scio enim quod propter infirmitatis verecundiam plerumque gravioris est certaminis peccata commissa prodere, quam admissa vitare."[132]

26 Habita collatione Pharisaei et Publicani, sequitur sententia Domini super meritis utriusque dicentis: *Amen dico vobis descendit hic iustificatus in domum suam ab illo,*[133] id est ad comparationem illius gratiae. Ezech. 16, ubi dicit Dominus ad Ierusalem: *Iustificasti sorores tuas in omnibus abominationibus tuis,*[134] id est, "quasi comparatione abominationum tuarum."[135] Ex hac humilitate Publicani et superbia Pharisaei, potest argui quod melior est peccator humilis quam iustus superbus, id est, qui se reputat iustum. Augustinus, *De civitate Dei*: "Audeo dicere, superbis utile esse cadere in aliquod apertum manifestumque peccatum, unde sibi displiceat, qui iam interius sibi placendo ceciderat. Salubrius enim sibi Petrus displicuit, quando flevit; quam sibi placuit, quando praesumpsit."[136]

4 *gloriam*] peccatum *A*: *add.* et *P* 5 Vere ... hoc] Hoc enim iustum est *P* 10 quod] quia *P* 17 quasi *om. P* 21 displiceat] displiceant *P* 22 ceciderat] ceciderant *P* | sibi Petrus] P. s. *transp. P*

[127] Luc. 18:13.

[128] Eccli. 4:24.

[129] I Ioan. 1:9.

[130] "...verum etiam erubsecentia quae est magna pars poenitentiae tollitur..." in *Etsi animarum* in *Chart.* I, No. 240, 269.

[131] Iob 31:33.

[132] Greg., *Mor.* in *CCSL* 143A.1116.

[133] Luc. 18:14.

[134] Ez. 16:51.

[135] *int.* in Ez. 16:51 in *Ed. pr.* 3.252b.

[136] Aug., *De civ. Dei* in *CCSL* 48.436.

Ultimo ad quid indicatur parabola, ostenditur, cum dicitur: *Quia omnis qui se exaltat, humiliabitur.*[137] Exaltationem in praesenti sequitur humiliatio, id est vilificatio in futuro. Is. 14: *Ascendam super altitudinem nubium et similis ero altissimo.*[138] Et sequitur: *verumtamen ad infernum detraheris in profundum laci.*[139] Sequitur: *et qui se humiliat,* in praesenti, *exaltabitur,*[140] scilicet in futuro. Iob 22: *Qui humiliatus fuerit erit in gloria;*[141] supple aeterna, ad quam nos perducat etc. 27

1 indicatur] inducatur *APW* 5 scilicet *om. P* 7 etc. *add. sed va-cat:* (*va-*) Ex hac humilitate Publicani et superbia Pharisaei, potest argui quod melior est peccator humilis quam iustus superbus, id est qui se reputat iustum. Augustinus, De civitate Dei: Audeo dicere, superbis utile esse cadere in aliquod apertum manifestumque peccatum, unde sibi displiceat, qui iam interius sibi placendo ceciderat. Salubrius enim sibi Petrus displicuit, quando flevit; quoniam sibi placuit (*-cat*). Qui humiliatus fuerit erit in gloria, supple aeterna, ad quam nos perducat *W*

[137] Luc. 18:14.
[138] Is. 14:14.
[139] Is. 14:15.
[140] Luc. 18:14.
[141] Iob 22:29.

BIBLIOGRAPHY

Primary Sources and Collections of Documents

Angelo of Clareno. *Historia septem tribulationum.* Ed. Franz Ehrle. *ALKG* 2 (1886):106-336.

Antilogia papae, hoc est de corrupto ecclesiae statu et totius cleri papistici perversitate, scripta aliquot veterum auctorum, ante annos plus minus CCC et interea: nunc primum in lucem eruta et ab interitu vindicata cum praefatione D. Wolfgangi Wissenburgii Theologi Basiliensis. Ed. Flaccius Illyricus. Basel, 1555.

Appendix ad fasciculus rerum expetendarum et fugiendarum. Ed. E. Brown. 2 voll. London, 1690.

Bede. *De tempore ratione.* In *CCSL* 123B, Ed. Ch. W. Jones. Turnhout: Brepols, 1977, 263-460.

Bonaventure. *Opera omnia.* 10 voll. Quaracchi: Collegium S. Bonaventurae, 1882-1902.

Chronica Normanniae. In *Recueil* 23, Paris: Imprimerie nationale, 1876, 212-22.

Conciliorum oecumenicorum decreta. Edd. J. Alberigo et al. 3rd ed. Bologna: Istituto per le scienze religiose, 1973.

Corpus iuris canonici. Ed. Aemilius Friedberg. 2 voll. Leipzig: B. Tauchnitz, 1879-81. [rpt. Graz: Akademische Druck-U. Verlagsanstalt, 1955]. v.1 = *Decretum magistri Gratiani.* v.2 = *Decretalium collectiones.*

Denifle, Heinrich. O.P. "Das Evangelium aeternum und die Commission zu Anagni," *Archiv für Litteratur- und Kirchengeschichte des Mittelalters* 1 (1885):49-142.

Documenta antiqua franciscana. Ed. Fr. L. Lemmens. Quaracchi: Collegium S. Bonaventurae, 1901.

Du Boulay, César Égasse. *Historia universitatis parisiensis.* 6 voll. Paris, 1665-73 [rpt. Frankfurt am Main: Minerva, 1966].

Expositio Regulae fratrum minorum. Ed. P.L. Oliger. Quaracchi: Collegium S. Bonaventurae, 1912.

Francis of Assisi. *Opuscula Sancti Francisci assisiensis.* In *Bibliotheca franciscana ascetica medii aevi* 12. Ed. C. Esser O.F.M. Quaracchi: Collegium S. Bonaventurae, 1978.

Geoffrey of Beaulieu. *Vita Ludovici noni.* In *Recueil* 20, Paris: Imprimerie royale, 1840, 3-27.

Les Grandes chroniques de France, selon que elles sont conservées en l'église de Saint-Denis en France. 6 voll. Paris: Techener, 1836.

Guillaume de Lorris et Jean de Meun. *Roman de la Rose.* Ed. Ernest Langlois. 5 voll. Paris: Honoré Champion, 1921.

Guillaume de Nangis. *Chronicon.* Ed. H. Géraud. 2 voll. Paris,1843.

Humbert of Romans. *Opera de vita regulari.* Ed. Fr. Joachim Joseph Berthier. 2 voll. Rome,1888-9. [rpt. Turin: Marietti, 1956].

Joachim of Fiore. *Expositio in Apocalypsim.* Venice, 1527. [rpt. Frankfurt: Minerva, 1964].

La legenda antiqua S. Francisci: texte du ms. 1046 (M.69) de Pérousse. Ed. P. F.-M. Delorme. Paris: Éditions de la France Franciscaine, 1926.

Legenda trium sociorum: édition critique. Ed. T. Desbonnets O.F.M. in *AFH* 67 (1974): 38-144.

Martène, Edmond O.S.B. et Ursinus Durand. *Brevis historia ordinis fratrum praedicatorum.* In *Veterum scriptorum et monumentorum historicum, dogmaticorum, moralium amplissima collectio.* Vol. 6, Paris, 1731, 331-396.

Pseudo-Dionysius. *The Complete Works.* Trans. Colm Luibheid. Mahwah, NJ: Paulist Press, 1987.

Pseudo-Isidore. *Decretales.* Ed. Paul Hinschius. Leipzig, 1863 (*PL* 130:1-1178).

Scripta Leonis, Rufini et Angeli sociorum S. Francisci. Ed. and Trans. Rosalind B. Brooke. Oxford: Clarendon Press, 1970.

Speculum perfectionis ou Mémoires de Frère Léon. Ed. Paul Sabatier. 2nd ed. British Society of Franciscan Studies vol. 13. Manchester: University Press, 1928.

Thomas Aquinas. *Contra impugnantes.* In *Opera omnia* 41A. Ed. H.F. Dondaine. Rome: S. Sabina, 1970.

William of Auxerre. *Summa aurea.* Ed. Jean Riballier. 4 voll. Paris: C.N.R.S., 1986.

William of Saint-Amour. *Liber de antichristo.* In *Veterum scriptorum et monumentorum historicum dogmaticorum moralium amplissima collectio...* Edd. E. Martène and U. Durand. Paris, 1724-33 [rpt. New York, 1968], IX:1271-1446.

____________________. *Opera omnia quae reperiri poterunt.* Ed. Alithophilius. Constance [Paris], 1632.

Secondary sources

Bazàn, B.C. "Les questions disputées, principalement dans les facultés de théologie," *Les questions disputées et les questions quodlibétiques dans les facultés de théologie, de droit et de médecine.* Turnhout: Brepols, 1985, 21-149.

Bierbaum, Max. *Bettelorden und Weltgeistlichkeit an der Universität Paris.* Münster: Aschendorffsche Verlagsbuchhandlung, 1920.

Bloomfield, Morton W. and Marjorie E. Reeves. "The Penetration of Joachism into Northern Europe," *Speculum* 29 (1954):772-93.

Bougerol, Jacques G. O.F.M. *Introduction à l'étude de Saint Bonaventure.* Tournai: Desclée et Cie, 1961.

________. "De la *reportatio* à la *redactio*," *Les genres littéraires dans les sources théologiques et philosophiques médiévales: définition, critique et exploitation.* Louvain: Institut d'études médiévales, 1982, 52-65.

________. "Saint Bonaventure et le roi Louis," *S. Bonaventura: 1274-1974.* Grottaferrata: Collegium S. Bonaventurae, 1973, II:489-93.

Boyle, L. "Notes on the Education of the *Fratres* communes in the Dominican Order in the Thirteenth Centry," *Xenia medii aevi historiam illustrantia oblata Thomae Kaeppeli O.P.* Rome: Edizione di storia e letteratura, 1978, I:232-56.

Brady, Ignatius O.F.M. "The Edition of the *Opera omnia* of Saint Bonaventure (1882-1902)," *AFH* 70 (1977):352-76.

Burr, David. "Mendicant Readings of the Apocalypse," *The Apocalypse in the Middle Ages.* Edd. Richard K. Emmerson and Bernard McGinn. Ithaca, NY: Cornell University Press, 1992, 89-102.

_________. *Olivi's Peaceable Kingdom: A Reading of the Apocalypse Commentary.* Philadelphia: University of Pennsylvania Press, 1993.

Clasen, P. Sophronius O.F.M. "Die Kampfpredigten des Wilhelms von Saint-Amour gegen die Mendikanten Orden," *Kirchengeschichtliche Studien* (1941):80-95.

Clasen, S. *Legenda antiqua des Heiligen Franziskus.* Leiden: Brill, 1967.

Congar, Yves M.-J. O.P. "Aspects ecclésiologiques de la querelle entre mendiants et séculiers dans la seconde moitié du XIIIe siècle et le début du XIV," *AHDL* 28 (1961):35-151.

Coulton, George Gordon. *From Saint Francis to Dante.* 2nd ed. Philadelphia: University of Pennsylvania Press, 1972.

D'Avray, D.L. *The Preaching of the Friars: Sermons Diffused from Paris before 1300.* Oxford: Clarendon Press, 1985.

Dawson, James Doyne. "William of Saint-Amour and the Apostolic Tradition," *Mediaeval Studies* 40 (1978):223-238.

Douie, Decima L. *The Conflict between the Seculars and Mendicants at the University of Paris in the Thirteenth Century.* Aquinas Paper 23. London: Blackfriars, 1954.

______."Saint Bonaventure's Part in the Conflict between Seculars and Mendicants at Paris," *S. Bonaventura: 1274-1974.* Grottaferrata: Collegium S. Bonaventurae, 1973, II:585-612.

Dufeil, Michael-Marie. "Correction au «Répertoire des maîtres en théologie de Paris au XIIIe siècle» de P. Glorieux," *Bulletin de la Société internationale pour l'étude de la philosophie médiévale* 4 (1962):135.

__________________. *Guillaume de Saint-Amour et la polémique universitaire parisienne.* Paris: A. Picard, 1972.

__________________. "Gulielmus de Sancto Amore, opera omnia 1252-1270," *Miscellanea Mediaevalia* 10 *Die Auseinandersetzungen an der Pariser Universität im XIII. Jahrhundert.* (1976):213-8. [rpt. *Saint Thomas et l'histoire.* Aix-en-Provence: Publications du CUER MA, 1991, 495-504].

__________________. "Le roi Louis dans la querelle des mendiants et des séculiers," *Septième centenaire de la mort de Saint Louis.* Paris: Les Belles Lettres, 1976, 281-90.

Emmerson, R. K. *Antichrist in the Middle Ages.* Seattle: University of Washington Press, 1981.

Féret, Pierre. *La Faculté de théologie de Paris et ses docteurs les plus célèbres. Moyen Age.* 4 voll. Paris: A. Picard, 1894.

Glorieux, Palémon. "Le Conflit de 1252-1257 à la lumière du mémoire de Guillaume de Saint-Amour," *RTAM* 24 (1957):364-72.

________________."Le «*Contra impugnantes*» de S. Thomas: ses sources-son plan," *Mélanges Mandonnet.* Paris: Librairie philosophique J. Vrin, 1930, I:51-81.

________________. "L'Enseignement au moyen âge: Techniques et méthodes en usage à la Faculté de Théologie de Paris au XIIIe siècle," *AHDL* 35 (1968):65-186.

________________. *Répertoire des maîtres en théologie de Paris au XIIIe siècle.* 2 voll. Paris: Librarie philosophique J. Vrin, 1933-4.

Hinnebusch, William A. O.P. *History of the Dominican Order.* 2 voll. New York: Alba, 1965.

Jordan, William Chester. *Louis IX and the Challenge of the Crusade: A Study in Rulership.* Princeton, NJ: University Press, 1979.

Lambertino, Roberto. *Apologia e crescita dell'identità francescana (1255-1279).* Rome: Palazzo Borromini, 1990.

________________. "La scelta francescana del'università di Parigi. Il *Bettelordenstreit* fino allo *Exiit qui seminat,*" *Gli studi francescani.* Ed. Francesco Santi. Spoleto: Centro italiano di studi sull'alto medioevo, 1993, 143-172.

Landini, Lawrence C. O.F.M. *The Causes of the Clericalization of the Orders of Friars Minor.* Chicago: Pontificia universitas Gregoriana, 1968.

Lawrence, C.H. *The Friars: The Impact of the Early Mendicant Movement on Western Society.* London: Longman, 1994.

Leff, Gordon. *Paris and Oxford Universities in the Thirteenth and Fourteenth Centuries.* New York: John Wiley and Sons, 1968.

Lerner, R. "Refreshment of the Saints: The Time after Antichrist as a Station for Earthly Progress in Medieval Thought," *Traditio* 32 (1976):97-144.

Little, Lester K. "Saint Louis' Involvement with the Friars," *Church History* 23 (1964):125-148.

Maierù, Alphonse. *University Training in Medieval Europe.* Ed. and Trans. D.N. Pryds. Leiden: Brill, 1994.

Mäkinen, Virpi. *Property Rights in the Medieval Discussion on Franciscan Poverty.* Helsinki: Limes ry, 1998.

Marrone, John Thomas. "The Ecclesiology of the Parisian Secular Masters, 1250-1320," unpublished Ph.D. dissertation, Cornell University, 1972.

McKeon, Peter R. "The Status of the University of Paris as *Parens Scientiarum*: An Episode in the Development of its Autonomy," *Speculum* 39 (1964):651-675.

Michaud-Quantin, Pierre. "Le droit universitaire au XIIIe siècle," *Septième centenaire de la mort de Saint Louis.* Paris: Les Belles Lettres, 1976, 303-14.

______________________. "Le droit universitaire dans le conflit parisien de 1252-1257," *Studia Gratiana* 8 (1962):577-599.

Moorman, John. *A History of the Franciscan Order.* Oxford: Clarendon Press, 1968.

Mulchahey, M. Michèle. "*First the Bow is Bent in Study*": *Dominican Education before 1350.* Studies and Texts 132. Toronto: Pontifical Institute of Mediaeval Studies, 1998.

Peuchmard, M. O.P. "Mission canonique et prédication: Le prêtre ministre de la parole dans la querelle entre mendiants et séculiers au XIII e siècle," *RTAM* 30 (1963):122-144, 252-76.

Pugh, C.M. "*Le Roman de la rose*: The *Contraire* Allegory of Jean de Meung" unpublished Ph.D. dissertation, Louisiana State University, 1999.

Quinn, John F. C.S.B. "Chronology of St. Bonaventure," *Franciscan Studies* 32 (1972):168-86.

______________. "Chronology of St. Bonaventure's Sermons," *AFH* 67 (1974):145-53.

Richard, Jean. *Saint Louis.* Trans. Jean Birrell. Cambridge: University Press, 1983.

Robson, Michael O.F.M.Conv. *St. Francis of Assisi: The Legend and the Life.* London: Geoffrey Chapman, 1997.

Roest, Bert. *A History of Franciscan Education (c. 1210-1517).* Leiden: Brill, 2000.

__________. *Reading the Book of History: Intellectual Contexts and Educational Functions of Franciscan Historiography 1226-ca. 1350.* Groningen: Regenboog, 1996.

Schleyer, Kurt. *Anfänge des Gallikanismus im 13. Jahrhundert: der Widerstand des französischen Klerus gegen die Privilegierung der Bettelorden.* Historische Studien Hft. 314. Berlin: Verlag Dr. Emil Ebering, 1937. [rpt. Vaduz: Karus, 1965].

Serper, Arié. "L'influence de Guillaume de Saint-Amour sur Rutebeuf," *Romance Philology* 17 (1963-4):391-402.

Szittya, Penn. *The Origins of the Antifraternal Tradition in Medieval Literature.* Princeton, NJ: University Press, 1986.

Thouzellier, Christine. "La Place du *De periculis* de Guillaume de Saint-Amour dans les polémiques universitaires du XIIIe siècle," *Revue historique* 46 (1927):69-83.

Tierney, Brian. *The Origins of Papal Infallibility: 1150-1350.* Leiden: Brill, 1972.

Töpfer, B. "Eine Handschrifte des Evangelium aeternum des Gerardino von Borgo San Donnino," *Zeitschrift für Geschichtwissenschaft* 7 (1960):156-63.

Traver, Andrew G. "The *Liber de Antichristo* and the Failure of Joachite Expectations," *Florensia* 14 (2000):1-12.

_______________."The *Reportatio* of St. Bonaventure's Disputed Question *De mendicitate,*" *AFH* 92 (1999): 287-98.

_______________. "Rewriting History? The Parisian Secular Masters' *Apologia* of 1254," *History of Universities* (1997-9): 9-45.

_______________. "William of Saint-Amour's Two Disputed Questions *De quantitate eleemosynae* and *De valido mendicante,*" *AHDL* 62 (1995): 295-342.

Verger, Jacques. "*Nova et vetera* dans le vocabulaire des premiers statuts et privilèges universitaires français," *Vocabulaire des écoles et des méthodes d'enseignement au Moyen Age.* Ed. Olga Weijers. Turnhout: Brepols, 1992, 191-205.

_____________. "Patterns," *A History of the University in Europe.* Ed. Hilde de Ridder-Symoens. Cambridge: University Press, 1992, I:35-74.

INDEX OF NAMES

Italicized numerals indicate that the referent is located in a footnote.

TOPICAL INDEX